Constitutionalism in Africa

Creating opportunities, Facing challenges

Editor

J. Oloka-Onyango

Fountain Publishers

Fountain Publishers
P.O. Box 488
Kampala
E-mail: fountain@starcom.co.ug
Website: www.fountainpublishers.com

Distribution in Europe, North America and Australia by African Books
Collective (ABC), The Jam Factory, 27 Park End St., Oxford OXI 1HU,
United Kingom.+44(0) 1865-72686 (tel), 1865-793298 (fax)

© Fountain Publishers 2001
First published 2001

All rights reserved. No part of this publication may be reproduced, stored in a
retrieval system or transmitted in any form or by any means electronic,
mechanical, photocopying, recording or otherwise without the prior written
permission of the publisher.

ISBN 9970 02 2717

04 03 02 01 4 3 2 1

Cataloguing-in-publication Data

Constitutionalism in Africa: Creating opportunities, facing challenges/edited
by J. Oloka-Onyango – Kampala. Fountain Publishers, 2001.
  p.cm
  Includes bibliographical references and index
  ISBN 9970 02 271 7.
  1. Constitutionalism in Africa 2. Constitution and Law in Africa
  I. Oloka-Onyango, J.

342.6–dc 21

Contents

Contributors

Tajudeen Abdul Raheem has been the General Secretary of the Pan-African Congress (PAC), based in Kampala, Uganda since 1992. He is a Rhodes Scholar with degrees from Bayero and Oxford universities, and has taught as visiting lecturer at several universities around the world.

Ola Abou Zeid is Professor of Political Thought at Cairo University, Egypt and holds a PhD from the University of Toronto, Canada. She is the author of numerous articles on Islamic Political Thought, and her interests include Women's Studies, especially within the context of Islam and religion.

Aminata Diaw is a Professor of Political Science at the Chiek Anta Diop University in Daka, Senegal.

Bibiane Gahamanyi-Mbaye is the *Administrateur* of the Union for African Population Studies (UAPS) – a Pan-African NGO based in Dakar, Senegal devoted to the promotion of interdisciplinary research in relation to African population developments. She has worked with several civil society groups around African population developments. She has worked with several civil society groups around Africa, and written several articles.

Anthonia Kalu is Professor of African American and African Literature at the University of Northern Carolina in Greeley Colorado, USA where she has been based since 1989. Her publications and research interests address issues of Multiculturalism, Women in the African Diaspora, African and African American literary theory and construction and African development issues. Dr Kalu is an Igbo from eastern Nigeria.

Jean-Marie Kamatali has a doctorate of law as from the Karl-Franzens University, Graz, Austria. He is currently the Dean of the Faculty of Law at the National University of Rwanda, where he also teaches Introduction to Rwandan Law, International Humanitarian Law, International Law of Development and International Relations.

Kivutha Kibwana is the Executive Director of the Centre for Law and Research International (CLARION) based in Nairobi, Kenya. He has served as the Dean of the Faculty of Law at the University of Nairobi and is an Associate Professor teaching several subjects in the area of Public and International Law. He is a founder of the National Convention Assembly (NCA) and the National Convention Executive Committee (NCEC).

Ali A. Mazrui is the Albert Schweitzer Professor in the Humanities and Director of the Institute of Global Studies at Binghamton University, State University of New York (SUNY), USA. He has taught at universities all over the world, and is a renowned scholar on politics and the humanities, as well as being a much-consulted expert on international affairs.

Willy Mutunga is the Executive Director of the Kenya Human Rights Commission (KHRC), and has variously served as a lecturer at the University of Nairobi and with a number of civil society organisations in Kenya. He holds a doctorate of the science of law (JSD) from York University and is the author of *Constitution-Making from the Middle: Civil Society and Transition Politics in Kenya, 1992 – 1997* (1999).

B. J. Odoki is the Chief Justice of Uganda. He was chair of the Uganda Constitutional Commission from 1989 to 1992. Justice Odoki has been the Director of the Law Development Centre (LDC) in Kampala, and is the author of numerous articles and books on diverse subjects.

J. Oloka-Onyanyo is the Dean of Law at Makerere University and the author of numerous works on constitutionalism.

Charmaine Percira is an independent researcher based in Abuja, Nigeria. She has taught in universities in the United Kingdom and at Ahmadu Bello University, Nigeria. She has also been active in a number of women's organisations addressing gender justice and women's human rights, and is currently the National Coordinator of the Network for Women's Studies in Nigeria (NWSN). Her writing covers work on women organising, feminism and institutional change. Other research interests include the politics of religion and cultural practice.

Bereket Selassie is Professor of Law and of African and African American Studies, at the University of North Carolina, Chapel Hill, USA, and was the chair of the Eritrean Constitutional Commission from its inception in 1993, until it concluded its activities in 1997. He is the author of numerous works on constitutionalism.

Sylvia Tamale is a Senior Lecturer at the Faculty of Law, Makerere University and a prominent activist in Uganda's Women's movement. She is the author of *When Hen's Begin to Crow: Gender and Parliamentary Politics in Uganda* (1999), and of several other works on the issue of women's human rights, globalisation and constitutionalism.

G. P. Tumwine-Mukubwa is a Professor of Law at Makerere University, and has taught in a number of universities around Africa. He has been Dean of Law at Makerere University and has published on constitutionalism and human rights in numerous journals and books.

Makau wa Mutua is Professor of Law and Director of the Human Rights Centre at the State University of New York (SUNY), where he teaches international human rights, international business transactions, and international law. He has been visiting professor at Harvard Law School and the University of Puerto Rico, and has written numerous articles exploring topical subjects in international law, human rights and religion.

Peter Walubiri is a Senior Lecturer at the Faculty of Law, Makerere University and an Advocate of the Supreme Court of Uganda, who has litigated many of the most important constitutional cases in the recent Ugandan jurisprudence. He is the author of *Constitutionalism at the crossroads* (1999).

Acronyms

AAWORD	Association of African Women for Research and Development
ABAKO	*Alliances des Bakongo*
AHI	Action Health Incorporated
ANC	African National Congress
APROSOMA	Association for the Social Progress of the Masses
BAOBAB	Women's Human Rights Organisation, Nigeria
CA	Constituent Assembly
CCE	Constitutional Commission of Eritrea
CEDAW	Convention on the Elimination of All forms of Discrimination against Women
CGE	Commission for Gender Equality
CLO	Civil Liberties Organisation
CLP	Community Life Project
COSATU	Confederation of South African Trade Unions
CP	Conservative Party
CRP	Constitutional Rights Project
DAWN	Development Alternatives with Women for a New Era
DP	Democratic Party
DRC	Democratic Republic of Congo
ECOMOG	ECOWAS Military Observer Group
ECOWAS	Economic Community of West African States
EOC	Equal Opportunities Commission
EPLF	Eritrean People's Liberation Front
FAR	Armed Forces of Rwanda
FIDA-Kenya	International Federation of Women Lawyers-Kenya
GADA	Gender and Action Development
GPI	Girls Power Initiative
HIV/AIDS	Human Immuno Deficiency Virus/Acquired Immunity Deficiency Syndrome
NGO	Non-governmental Organisation
IAC	Inter-African Committee
ICCPR	International Covenant on Civil and Political Rights
ICESCR	International Covenant on Economic, Social and Cultural Rights
ICT	Information and Communication Technologies
IFI	International Financial Institutions
IMF	International Monetary Fund

IPPG	Inter-Parties Parliamentary Group
KADU	Kenya African Democratic Union
KANU	Kenya African National Union
KWPC	Kenya Women's Political Caucus
LC	Local Council
LRRDC	Legal Research and Resource Development Centre
MFDC	Movement of the Democratic Forces of Casamance
MNC	*Mouvement National Congolais*
MRND	*Mouvement Revolutionaire National pour le Developpement*
MYWO	*Maendeleo ya Wanawake* Organisation
NAWOJ	Lagos State Council of the Nigerian Association of Women Journalists
NCA	National Convention Assembly
NCA	National Constitutional Assembly
NCC	National Conventional Council
NCEC	National Convention Executive Committee
NCEC	National Convention Executive Council
NCSW	National Committee on the Status of Women
NCWK	National Council of Women of Kenya
NECON	Nigerian Electoral Commission
NRA	National Resistance Army
NRM	National Resistance Movement
OAU	Organisation of African Unity
OIC	Organisation of the Islamic Conference
PARMEHUTU	Party for the Emancipation of the Hutu People
PCD	Dahomeén Communist Party
RADER	Democratic Reassembling for the Republic
RFP	Rwandese Patriotic Front
RPA	Rwanda Patriotic Army
SADC	Southern African Development Community
SAP	Structural Adjustment Programme
SDP	Social Democratic Party
SERAC	Social and Economic Rights Action Centre
SRI	Shelter Rights Initiative
UDHR	Universal Declaration of Human Rights
UDHRI	Universal Declaration of Human Rights in Islam
UN	United Nations
UNAR	National Rwandese Union
UNESCO	United Nations Educational, Scientific and Cultural Organisation

UNIFEM	United Nations Development Programme for Women
UNITA	*Uniao Nacionale para a Independencia Total de Angola* (National Union for the Total Liberation of Angola)
UNLF	Uganda National Liberation Front
UPC	Uganda Peoples Congress
UPM	Uganda Patriotic Movement
US	United States
USA	United States of America
WEM	Women Empowerment Movement
WHON	Women's Health Organisation of Nigeria
WIN	Women in Nigeria
WHP	Women Health Programme
WJP	Women Justice Programme
WLDCN	Women, Law & Development Centre of Nigeria
WLUML	Women Living Under Muslim Laws
WTO	World Trade Organisation
ZANU-PF	Zimbabwe African National Union-Patriotic Front
ZAPU	Zimbabwe African Patriotic Union

Acknowledgements

The completion of any work of scholarship or art is always a collective endeavour, particularly if the work is an anthology such as the present one. The gestation of *Constitutionalism in Africa* was a conference organised by the Faculty of Law at Makerere University that was held in Kampala, Uganda in October 1999. Bringing together over one hundred distinguished scholars, activist and researchers, the Kampala conference was a lively inter-change of theory and *praxis*, as well as a critical inspection of the condition of African constitutionalism at the turn of the twentieth century. Delegates were concerned about both the grand issues of constitutional change, as well as the minuscule questions of daily economic and social struggle that were confronting the African situation. The papers collected in this book give some flavour of the diversity of viewpoints and experiences that were covered at the conference. Although as editor I brought the pieces together, the individual authors who contributed chapters represent the intellectual thread by which the work is bound. They graciously put up with my knit picking, and gave immeasurably of their time and energy in making this book possible. Beatrice Ngonzi and Barbara Munube of the Faculty of Law proved an invaluable and indefatigable team in liasing with the authors, tying up the loose ends, researching footnotes and references and copy-editing the final texts.

Support for the conference and for this book was provided by the Ford Foundation. In its New York Programme Officer–Julius Ihonvebere – the Faculty of Law found an ardent proponent of dynamic constitutional change and of the need to have African voices articulating the various dimensions of the issue. Tade Aina and Joseph Gitari of the Nairobi office ensured that the local logistical issues were dealt with without a hitch. The Local Organising Committee for the conference was made up of Harold Acemah, Maria Nassali, Norah Matovu Winyi, Harriet Busingye, Joanna Kayaga and Christine Ssali. In them, I found a team that was not only committed to the subject-matter of the conference, but also a great resource for all the logistical and other issues involved in the organisation of an international conference of such a nature.

Behind every book there is of course a publisher. In Fountain Publishers, we were fortunate to work with Justus Mugaju who took the book through its final paces. The book is dedicated to all African peoples engaged in the struggle for progressive constitutionalism on the continent.

Editor

1

Introduction
Constitutionalism in Africa: Yesterday, Today and Tomorrow

J. Oloka-Onyango

New winds are definitely blowing across the African continent. From Dakar to Dar es Salaam, from the Cape to Cairo, a resurgence of both popular and elite concern with issues revolving around governance, statecraft and constitutionalism is clearly discernible. Recent reverberations of constitutional discourse, engineering and contestation in countries as disparate and diverse as Côte d'Ivoire, Zimbabwe, Senegal, Egypt and Benin, speak loudly to the fact that at the commencement of the twenty-first century, issues of constitutionalism in Africa have gained considerable prominence. It is a prominence that has not been witnessed on the continent since the heady early days of independence. Indeed, with only slight trepidation, we could describe the present developments as constituting a new epoch in African history—the epoch of the rebirth of constitutionalism.

At the same time, both the velocity and the direction of these winds remain unclear: is Africa heading for a new political *nirvana*, or will the forces of regression, dictatorship and autocracy reclaim the day? Has the spirit and culture of constitutionalism found a renaissance, or are we bearing witness to a painful and excruciating stillbirth? Are the efforts to address persistent questions of marginalisation, discrimination and exclusion genuinely motivated, or are they simply the latest ruse in the quest for the reconfiguration of state structures to assure political hegemony amongst a leadership primarily concerned with self-preservation? Are all these experiments in constitutional engineering built upon sustainable foundations, or will they wither away with the departure of the political and legal architects who designed them? To paraphrase MacMillan, are these 'winds of change,' or simply a change in the wind?

The authors brought together in this anthology engage the issue of constitutionalism in a bid to provide critical and well-considered responses to these and the numerous other questions that confront contemporary Africa in its most recent political evolution. They are also concerned with the various struggles for progressive constitutionalism that are taking place on the continent as we start a new era in human history. The issues examined here go to the core of the many critical phenomena that the peoples of the African continent confront at this historical juncture. They demand that we review the point from which we have come, the contemporary realities by which we are faced, and the prospects for the future—both those which may appear difficult and daunting and those that are benevolent and enabling. Such a review must take us back to the point at which debate on these issues commenced in order to inform our comprehension of contemporary realities, as well as the numerous opportunities and challenges presented by the future. In other words, what was the state of African constitutionalism yesterday; how is it faring today, and in which possible directions will it evolve tomorrow?

Some points of clarification

For many scholars, politicians and activists, the notion of constitutionalism is one that produces numerous and oftentimes conflicting responses. For some— especially the more positivist or legally inclined—constitutionalism simply represents a concern with the instrumentalities of governance.[1] These range from the constitution itself and the other legally constructed documents that have been created to support it, to the structures and institutions that are established under their framework. They outline, in other words, the 'power map' of the particular state and the formal relationship between the governed and those who govern them. Others adopt a more nuanced and embracing view, considering constitutionalism within the much broader context of the social, economic, political, gendered and cultural milieu wherein those instrumentalities operate.[2] A nicely worded or eloquently phrased document means nothing if the context in which it is supposed to operate is harsh and hostile—a context in which you may have a 'constitution without constitutionalism.'[3]

Yet others ascribe to constitutionalism a certain degree of postmodernism, where it is considered impossible to find '… a coherent, unitary self, text or set of moral principles'[4] by which the process of constitutionalism is guided. In other words, constitutionalism and the processes and structures it engenders are basically indeterminate; one may even venture to say that they are incoherent and manifestly contradictory.[5] Particularly susceptible to the attack of postmodernist analysis is the concept of separation of powers. Although regarded by many as a sacrosanct element of progressive constitutionalism, it is a concept which can be easily dismissed as a malleable notion that suits whosoever seeks to invoke its reasoning against another arm of the state. Moreover, in this day and age, is it really correct to assert that the executive does not perform a legislative and even a judicial function? With the majority of African states pursuing a Westminster (quasi-parliamentary) style of government in which cabinet members are drawn principally from the legislature, how can claims of separation be really taken as gospel? What of the perennial law student's examination question: 'do judges make law?' Finally, in a situation where executive power is regarded as sacrosanct and unassailable in the mode of the 'imperial presidency' does it really make sense to speak of a separation of power? In short, constitutionalism is concerned about all the various dimensions of statecraft and governance—from the seemingly miniscule and mundane, to the great and vexing issues of political and economic management in a world that has increasingly become smaller.

Needless to say, despite the many varying voices that have spoken out on the issue, the basic interests of virtually all whom concern themselves with the phenomenon of constitutionalism remain fairly uniform and consistent. How should state structures in contemporary Africa be arranged and governed? What are the main values and issues of social, economic, cultural and political concern that a country wishes to preserve and enshrine within its basic organisational framework? How do you ensure not simply that the structures operate effectively within the context of existing realities, but also that they are transmitted to posterity without excessive damage or distortion? What can be done to cater for the numerous and diverse interests that have been brought together within the framework of a nation-state, whether these are expressed in terms of class, gender, religion, ethnicity or political interest and affiliation?

What about notions of accountability and inclusion, and the ever-present concerns with the creation of transparent mechanisms of governance and effective oversight? In a nutshell, the critical question is how we can move away from merely theorising about constitutionalism to a practical institutionalisation of its basic tenets.[6] Furthermore, as Ali Mazrui points out in the opening essay in this collection, it is not as if there is a lack of models from which we can make consultations. But it is not simply enough to look to models of building effective institutions and following the paths to constitutionalism that have been trodden elsewhere, especially in the West— the region of the world most often looked to in the search for constitutional 'models.' Such attitudes reinforce one of the pervasive critiques of the phenomenon of constitutionalism in Africa, namely that it is too closely dictated by forces external to the continent. In the words of Samuel Adelman: 'Whatever their apparent diversity, African constitutions are increasingly mere variations on a Western theme and as such, appear to encourage pluralism while producing its exact opposite.'[7]

Given such a context, it is necessary, first and foremost, to turn inwards and to examine Africa's own rich and extremely diverse heritage. Then we must critically review the cultural dimensions also: how much is the process of constitution-making and implementation not only a political or economic project, but also a profoundly cultural one? Mazrui argues that constitutionalism will in fact not take root in Africa in the absence of a 'massive consultation' with traditional culture, customs and legal precedents. Such consultation could lead to greater acceptance of the diversity that is so much a component part of the African mosaic. To better appreciate this point, it is necessary to revisit some of the salient features of the main issues of contention in the constitutionalism debate especially as they relate to the antecedents that we have inherited from the colonial past.

Constitutionalism yesterday: A historical reprise

Africa's experience with the phenomenon of constitutionalism has not been an easy or uncomplicated one. Within the colonial empires constructed under European imperialism, the idea that governance of the 'natives' should be mediated by norms and practices that constrained state power, fostered individual autonomy and promoted equality were obviously considered anathema. Consequently, while colonial systems of state management possessed the formal attributes of constitutional government through ostensibly separated and functioning executive, legislative and judicial bodies, at so many points of their operation, these powers were in fact fused. This was particularly the situation at local levels of government—the levels at which state power was most acutely experienced by the vast majority of the populace in the colonised territories. For an African peasant therefore, it mattered little that on the face of it there was a governor or commissioner exercising executive power, a legislative assembly ostensibly to make laws for the 'good governance' of the 'natives' and a judiciary designed to mediate and determine disputes. The clear fact was that these powers often encountered them as a consolidated, fused and manifestly obtrusive entity. The analogy to a 'clenched fist' most appropriately captures the manner in which the powers of the state confronted the indigenous populace at every turn of their social and economic existence. Mention does not even need to be made of the political which was the area most effectively cordoned off from popular participation and democratic involvement.[8]

It goes without saying that the colonial experience had a marked influence on both notions of constitutionalism that the post-colonial leaders of the continent expressed, as well as in their desire to move away from that inheritance. This paradox—which we can describe as the legacy of colonial non-constitutionalism—is a running theme in all of the early struggles by African countries to find their footing within the global community of states. The inheritance of Africa's postcolonial leaders was thus particularly complicated—not simply by the absence of a constitutional instrument from which they could learn and adapt, but also by the absence of the substantive elements of constitutionalism as we know them today. One could not speak of the 'rule of law,' an 'independent' judiciary, or any of the other notions of constitutionalism taken for granted without running into serious difficulties. Furthermore, inherited instruments of the state such as the army had to be reformed and reconstructed. And yet, Julius Nyerere's fanciful idea that the army could be abolished—as Mazrui points out in his poignant opening example of post-independence Tanzania—was rudely rebuked by concrete realities on the ground.

Put another way, the leaders of the newly independent African states inherited both a form of state governance and its substance that were largely inimical to the progressive realisation of the democratic rights and interests of their people. Some addressed this paradox by seeking to reconstruct the colonial inheritance to make it more responsive to the needs and demands of the populace. Notions of negritude, authenticité, and African Socialism were animated by the search for a genuinely African form of governance mediated by existent African reality—described as the quest for 'autochthony.' In contrast, others such as Hastings Kamuzu Banda in Malawi viewed that inheritance as a sacrosanct indication of their country's incorporation into the 'community of nations.' No deviations from the 'appropriate' line were acceptable in the quest to create a modern state that was the mirror image of the metropolis.

But clearly, whatever the direction that was eventually pursued, there was one critical ingredient that was lacking. In an anthology on constitutionalism in Africa written at the beginning of the 1990s, Tanzanian Professor Issa Shivji[9] argued that the issue of constitutionalism could not be divorced from the wider phenomenon of democracy:

> Constitutional documents have neither been the outcome of a clash of principles nor are they seen as embodying a political commitment to a global societal vision. Their utility lies in serving the 'constitutional moment' (i.e. transfer of power).... They do not even have much of a 'constitutional function,' i.e. ordering of the state apparatus; division and allocation of power etc.) and much less ... ideological legitimacy.[10]

Thus, the early constitutional instruments in Africa had very little to do either with creating democratic space or in promoting notions of enhanced participation and inclusion on the ground. Instead of developing the idea of constitutional supremacy, most such instruments instead paid homage to an executive supremacy.[11] All power came from and returned to the executive; the other arms of government merely functioned as props to the often-megalomanic desires and interests of the autocratic and domineering leader. Autonomous agencies outside the state such as the media, worker's organisations and civil society groups were brought under the rubric and stifling control of the single-party state or simply abolished. The long road to deterioration that culminated in so many African countries with the establishment of military dictatorships and the collapse of their economies is a tale that has been recounted on numerous occasions, and need not be retold here.

It is thus fairly clear that African states were handicapped by the absence of an instrument that clearly demarcated the contours of state power. Those instruments also failed to chart out the relationship between the ruled and their rulers. Conversely and paradoxically, they were also handicapped by an inheritance that was much more concrete and defined: the inheritance of language. As Anthonia Kalu points out in her essay on language and constitutionalism, serious limitations were entailed by the fact that as each African nation commenced the process of constitution making upon the attainment of independence or before, they did so largely through the medium of the coloniser's language. Whether the language was French, Portuguese, English or Spanish,[12] the fact that it only resonated with a small portion of the populace of the former colony already portended a crisis of legitimacy. In other words, many of the processes lacked the authentic African imprint, i.e. the imprint of an African language. By implication, they lacked an authentic African voice to give expression to the fundamental interests and desires of the African peoples. Of what effect are principles and policies that are not only 'top-down' in origin, but also 'foreign' in the medium in which they are being communicated? In other words, how can you speak about constitutionalism through a medium that is both alien and alienating? Or to use Kalu's words, the problem of language in African constitutions is in the 'attitudes conveyed and the values they do not uphold.'

Kalu's rich tapestry analysing the work of a number of African writers cogently illustrates how their choice of words and language convey much more than the story about which they are writing. Rather, the stories of the African fiction writer express the values, the hidden meanings, and the social as well as the political frameworks within which the stories were being written. But African writers such as Ngugi wa Thiong'o and Chinua Achebe have had a long and torturous battle with the fact that African writers are forced to convey their stories in the language of the coloniser.[13] From this analysis, we are compelled to view not simply the formal instrument that we consider to be the constitution, but also the 'traditional codes' of a nation's various language groups. To be authentic, Kalu urges, constitutionalism in Africa must be given an African voice.

The point of alienation is one also pursued by Tajudeen Abdul Raheem, who approaches the subject with a focus on the telling issue of Pan-African identity and citizenship in the post-Cold War situation. Raheem asks the poignant question: what does the notion of constitutionalism offer to Pan-Africanist struggles for unity within a context that is highly diversified? Can we look to the Organisation of African Unity (OAU) as a possible framework within which so many of the transnational and supra-constitutional issues of conflict resolution, regional cooperation and the movement of peoples (especially refugees) be resolved? Are there creative ways in which the negative inheritance of Africa's borders can be converted into a positive and liberating benefit for all Africa's citizenry? Raheem argues that it is not enough to consider the contemporary African state as our point of reference, especially given the obvious disjuncture between African states and their peoples. But while emphasising and extolling the need for popular participation by African peoples in fostering the culture of constitutionalism, he also warns of the dangers presented by continuing armed conflict, growing impunity and economic globalisation. The latter has especially brought with it numerous new questions that directly impinge on the condition of the state in contemporary Africa. In a nutshell, to build a constitutionalism that transcends the confining boundaries of the African state, it is essential that we also reform the internal operations of those states.

Identity, ethnicity and the role of civil society

Few other issues of contemporary concern to the debate over constitutionalism are as vexed as the phenomenon of ethnicity and citizenship. Several of the authors express a concern with issues relating to identity, culture and citizenship—issues that extend to the fundamental question that the process of constitutionalism is supposed to address. Common to the essays of both Bibiane Gahamanyi-Mbaye and Jean-Marie Kamatali in this anthology is a concern with the manner in which ethnicity and identity have been played out within the context of post-independence struggles over constitutionalism. Mbaye does this through a comparative examination of Rwanda and Senegal, and Kamatali with an extended focus on the situation in Rwanda. For Mbaye, the understanding of ethnicity and its consequences must be rooted in the notion of culture and the manner in which it has evolved in individual countries. Needless to say, factors such as globalisation, underdevelopment, and the manipulation of citizenship rights also have a role to play in the process of dealing with the issue of ethnicity.

The Senegalese and Rwandan examples may appear rather incongruous comparative case studies. Nevertheless, the two offer both stark contrasts as well as striking similarities in the debate about citizenship and ethnicity in contemporary Africa. Whereas Rwanda is marked by the 1994 genocide that rocked the world, Senegal's conflict in the southern Casamance region of the country has received little international attention, despite having festered for at least two decades. Factors such as economic marginalisation, poverty, social discrimination and religious tension are common to both countries, with a variance only in terms of degree. The colonial heritage also left its mark, and, as Kamatali illustrates in the case of Rwanda, that influence continues to be manifest right up to the present day. The Senegalese election in 2000 portended some hope that the roots of democracy may have taken hold in that country. However, unless the Casamance question is dealt with in a non-conflictual and amicable fashion, it will certainly resurface and cause numerous problems for Senegal's new leaders. Consequently, as Mbaye argues, there is a serious role for constitutional mechanisms of conflict resolution and mediation to be deployed in a context that still remains latent. Constitutionalism in Rwanda in the aftermath of the genocide is considerably more complicated. As Kamatali points out, although considerable efforts have been made at the restoration of democratic rule, the wounds are still raw; genuine reconciliation may be hard to achieve. Moreover, within a context of serious threats to law and order, the premium placed by the government on security issues has led to even more tension.

Against such a background, to what extent can new frameworks of civil society operation, citizenship participation and popular enfranchisement operate as effective barriers to their most negative repercussions? This is an issue taken up by both Peter Walubiri and Willy Mutunga. Walubiri is mainly concerned with the disjuncture between the hallowed statements of inclusion and empowerment that are spliced throughout the constitutions of virtually all African countries, and the reality on the ground. Lofty references to 'the people' and 'popular sovereignty' have failed to create the necessary conditions of genuine participation on the part of African civil society; where does the failing lie? Walubiri connects constitutionalism to the broader phenomenon of human development, and argues that to be relevant we must nurture our constitutions in order to 'embrace new values and aspirations' in the struggle against underdevelopment. He concludes his chapter with a call for a radicalisation of African civil society, which process would entail new practical strategies for confronting the issues of human development, engaging the media, utilising the legislature and actively litigating constitutional and human rights cases in the courts.

But are there no limitations to the power of civil society? In which instances can we look beyond the concept of civil society in order to create a framework for operation that effectively challenges the abuse of state power? Willy Mutunga provides some indication with a discourse on what can only be described as the 'right to rebel.' Mutunga argues that where peaceful and non-conflictual means for checking the abuse of power have failed, recourse must be had to methods that are directly insurrectionary. He contends that civil society actors should not be shy to assume overtly political positions in a situation where traditional civil society action has reached a stalemate. Invoking the theories of the German philosopher Hans Kelsen on the legitimacy of radical political action to overthrow oppressive state apparati, Mutunga sites numerous examples of alliances between civil society and political actors in the quest to establish a new democratic order. Such action is not only warranted in the African context where dictators abound, but it is also legitimated by numerous examples of popular action around the world. Civil society also has a much broader agenda that goes beyond the mere capture of state power—the primary objective of traditional political parties.

Of course, civil society has never been insulated from the choppy and turbulent waters of political action. Nevertheless, serious questions of theory and praxis are presented by any analysis of the political character of civil society. In the first instance, because of the lack of homogeneity that Mutunga points to, can you really speak about civil society action under a single all-embracing framework? How insulated from the 'narrow political interests' of traditional political actors is civil society? Finally, can't civil society reproduce the same or similar attributes of dictatorship, oppression and marginalisation that are apparent in the very state that it seeks to overthrow? What about the position of civil society vis à vis the situation of women—an issue that was of concern in several of the essays in this anthology.

The question of gender equality

Described as the 'missing agenda' by Ali Mazrui, the subject of gender and equality within the context of constitutionalism is taken up by several authors. With concrete examples drawn from several countries, the numerous conceptual and practical issues relating to the struggle for gender equity within the context of progressive constitutionalism are fundamentally explored. What should states do to comprehensively address the phenomenon of discrimination against women? How effective are the programmes of emancipation designed by civil society actors? What is the place and role of constitutionalism in mediating the many tensions that abound in the struggle to ensure that women have a fair share of the bounties of political governance? What about the highly controversial issue of homosexuality and gay and lesbian rights—an issue that Mazrui discusses in a context of outright attacks against the gay community by African leaders such as Robert Mugabe of Zimbabwe, Daniel arap Moi in Kenya and Uganda's Yoweri Museveni?

Charmaine Pereira commences her analysis of gender struggles in a Nigeria that is not only just emerging from decades of military rule, but is also confronting different and diverse forms of social, political and economic restructuring. She situates the phenomenon of gender equity within the patriarchal structures of culture, 'tradition,' and religion. The nexus between these three overlapping institutions has mutated over time, and is directly linked to the relationships of power in any society. Justifications for gender discrimination can thus often be retraced to the dominant control over the structures of power (both political and personal) that men have traditionally exercised. Under the scrutiny of international human rights law, and evolving norms of domestic constitutional restructuring however, changes are beginning to be registered. Unfortunately, as Pereira points out, Nigerian women still lack many of the 'enabling conditions' that would foster gender equity—a problem that is shared by women in many of the other states around the continent.

Pereira's focus on women's organisations, enriched by the personal observations of those who run them, enables us to move away from the arena of esoteric theoretical analysis to a consideration of concrete conditions on the ground. For the activists in groups like Women, Law & Development Centre of Nigeria (WLDCN), Baobab, and the Women Empowerment Movement (WEM), the formal recognition of rights in a constitutional instrument can only be the commencement-point of the struggle; the notion that women also require empowerment—social, economic and political—is one that comes through in all the testimonies Pereira provides to illuminate her point. Thus, constitutional reform *per se* is clearly insufficient and must be accompanied by consciousness raising and the transformation of culture. Neither process is free of obstacle or struggle. However, as Pereira argues, without directly confronting these twin issues of practical action, the situation of women will remain a problematic one.

In turning the spotlight on the issue of discrimination within the context of Muslim Africa, Ola Abou Zeid raises another structural construct that greatly impinges on the realization of women's human rights within the framework of constitutionalism—the phenomenon of religion. Abou Zeid offers a broad-based analysis of the manner in which several constitutional and human rights instruments developed within the Muslim community approach the issue of gender and equality. Unlike most of the other essays in the collection, Abou Zeid's is concerned primarily with three constitutional instruments and with their impact over a whole collection of countries that can be described as Muslim Africa. A discussion of constitutionalism in this context brings starkly to the fore the issue of cross-cultural tensions. With respect to Islam, the question becomes more poignant not only on account of the religious aspects, but also because Islam and the instruments Abou Zeid discusses, have had a 'deep influence' on the social and political ordering of many of these societies.

Equality and non-discrimination are issues of concern to all societies irrespective of socio-cultural heritage or political leaning. For Abou Zeid, under the constitutional instruments she examines, there is a problem of 'ambiguity and inconsistency.' In other words, although the notion of equity may be found acceptable in principle, the practice and the application of the notion is riddled with ambivalence. Consequently, the language of these instruments appears to confer equality with one statement, while seriously undermining it, or taking it away with another. Nowhere is this problem more apparent than with the situation of women. This is true whether one looks at the regime of marriage, religious rights, employment, property-ownership and freedom of movement, to mention only a handful of the various categories examined in the chapter. Moreover, the attitude of many such governments is confirmed in the considerable number of reservations they have made to the Convention on the Elimination of All forms of Discrimination against Women (CEDAW)—outstripping their reservations to any other international human rights instrument. Despite her criticisms of the Islamic constitutional texts, Abou Zeid nevertheless highlights a counter-trend in Islamic philosophy and scholarship that takes the religious edicts and arrives at manifestly different conclusions. With respect to the situation of women, such scholars argue that it is the distortion of the texts which has led to their subordination. According to this argument, a more liberal reading thereof would produce manifestly different results. That struggle is an on-going one, and the results thereof are still to be realised.

The politics of gender struggles is thus key to the attainment of equality in societies where the subordination and oppression of women has been taken for granted. This is a question taken up by both Kivutha Kibwana in his study of the Kenyan situation and by Sylvia Tamale on Uganda. The Kenyan situation is one in which the struggle for gender equality has been long and hard, but in which the results and gains have remained rather elusive. Although there is a strong women's movement in the country that dates back to the colonial period, it is a movement afflicted by 'change without substantial change' to borrow Kibwana's characterisation. Kibwana also offers a criticism that is often made of the movement, namely, the disjuncture between its elite and grassroots components and the need for bottom-up consultations on strategies and agendas. This is particularly important in a context where discrimination sanctioned by personal or customary law is not prohibited by the constitution. A twofold struggle is thus brought into play, one against the structural and legal frameworks that inhibit gender equality, and the other in reinvigorating the movement to confront state ambivalence about support for this issue.

A context in which the struggle for gender equality appears to have made some progress is presented by the Ugandan example. Sylvia Tamale explores this issue in her essay on affirmative action. The case of Uganda has been one in which the issue of women's human rights within the constitutional framework has been on the table since the mid-1980s, and has registered several constitutional reforms that contrast with the stagnation that prevail for the first quarter century of independence. Tamale takes the provisions in the 1995 constitution and places them alongside the actual progress that has been made by women in the spheres of politics and education. Does affirmative action actually deliver on the realisation of equality, or is it simply a smokescreen for the continuation of inequalities in a more subtle form? The Ugandan case study cogently demonstrates the necessity for constitutional reform, and the possibilities that are attainable with it. This does not mean that the struggle is thus concluded. Reading the Ugandan constitutional instrument, the far-reaching implications of such reform are manifestly clear. However, this is only a first (albeit necessary) step. There is still a need to ensure that affirmative action reforms (which tend to be narrowly focused and directed) are married to the wider context of social, political and economic struggle, as well as to a frontal attack on the pervasive structures of patriarchy.

Constitutionalism tomorrow: The travails of constitution-making and implementation

At the end of the day, constitutionalism in Africa will depend on the manner in which the issue of constitutional reform and implementation is concretely addressed. The method or process by which this is done is as important as the eventual outcome. In other words, the biggest challenge confronting those involved in the struggles for constitutional reform around the continent is how to strike a balance. The balance in question is that between ensuring that the path toward such reform is a participatory and inclusive one, and that it comprehensively addresses both the large and the small issues of social, political and economic concern. Several essays in the concluding part of the book take up this issue with a particular focus on the issue of legitimacy, a point made by both Bereket Selassie and Justice Benjamin Odoki on the Eritrean and Ugandan experiences respectively. Both countries came to the constitution-making process against the backdrop of serious civil strife, and in this regard were seeking to literally open a new phase in the historiographies of their countries. The Eritrean and Ugandan examples illustrate the need for processes of constitutional reform that address the particular context of each situation. In other words, there is no blueprint or template for constitutional reform. Issues that are important and complex in one situation may be fairly simple and straightforward in another. While there is much to learn from these experiences by those seeking to introduce constitutional reform in their own countries, the necessary cautions must be borne in mind.

But there are other ways in which new constitutional devices can be designed. Aminata Diaw looks broadly at the phenomenon of national conferences that swept across several countries in Francophone Africa, many producing new governments on the back of popular dissatisfaction and revolt against *ancien regimes*. Grace Tumwine Mukubwa and Makau Mutua are concerned less with the processual dimensions of constitutionalism than with the conceptual and the substantive. In particular, how do we deal with the 'relics' of doctrines, influences and practices that continue to plague the African body politick? What radical measures need to be taken in order to ensure that constitutionalism becomes not only a lived reality for all the peoples of the continent, but that it is also sustained for the benefit of posterity? How do we—to borrow from Mutua (via Lenin?)—literally smash the postcolonial state and substitute it with a new instrument of governance that effectively accommodates the diversity of the African lived reality?

As all the essays in Part IV of this anthology make clear, the influences that have to be confronted by those committed to constitutional reform are numerous and diverse. There are the contemporary issues and problems, and of course there is the legacy of Africa's chequered past. Among the most pervasive is the impact of colonialism, which extended well beyond the immediate post-independence period. In Francophone Africa—snapshots of which are contained in Aminata Diaw's essay on national conferences—the looming presence of the ex-colonial power (France in this case) served to determine at least some of the deliberations on constitutional futures that rocked the Francophone African states throughout the late 1980s and the 1990s. But it was compounded by the inheritance of postcolonial militarism and autocracy that were the legacy of Africa's single party and military dictatorships, encapsulated in regimes like those of Matthieu Kerekou in Benin, and Gnassinbge Eyadema in the Togo republic. Thus, in the euphoria of constitution-making of which the national conferences were the exemplar, issues such as the culture of autocracy, militarism and ethnic exclusion, as well as plain legal chicanery, often found their way into the process—negatively influencing the eventual constitutional outcome.[14] Diaw's short point is that for all the high-sounding postulations and the legal niceties that may accompany it, constitution making is a profoundly political process.[15] While the framework within which we seek to pursue constitutional reform is important, it is necessary to be attuned to the interplay of social and political forces within that framework. Comprehending this basic fact is fundamental to an appreciation of both the limits and the possibilities of achieving positive constitutional reform and progressive constitutionalism in any African country.

Looming over the African horizon one can envisage numerous different scenarios in so far as the phenomenon of constitutionalism is concerned, and its possible impact on society. Perhaps the most prominent among them is the phenomenon described as globalisation.[16] Although a catchall phrase currently in vogue to mean virtually anything, some of the salient features of globalisation (the increased use of information technology, the 'shrinking' of time and space, and the privatisation and marketisation of the economy) have several implications for constitutionalism in Africa.[17] In the first instance, globalisation seriously affects and even undermines national sovereignty. Thus, the degree of discretion and options that are available to governments have been seriously diminished. Constitutional principles of social inclusion, gender equality, and transparent and democratic governance may also be undermined by globalisation. The international mobility of capital weakens the ability of governments to pursue independent monetary and fiscal policies, and thereby delimits so many of the social objectives that have become key demands for reform in African countries. So many of our countries are so dependent on international financial institutions (IFIs) that to speak of autonomous action is anachronous. Against such a background, we must come back to the original question: is constitutionalism the panacea for all Africa's problems? The essays in this anthology suggest that the answer is a complex and multifaceted one.

Notes

1. See Ojwang.
2. See, for example, Baxi (2000), at 1183.
3. This phrase is borrowed from a much-quoted essay by Kenyan Prof. H.W.O. Okoth Ogendo.
4. Boyle (2000).
5. For an analysis of the concept within American jurisprudence, see Balkin, (1992), 1966.
6. cf. Ndulo, (1998-99).
7. Adelman.
8. Mamdani, (1996).
9. Shivji, (1990).
10. Ibid., at p.254.
11. See, Prempeh, (1999).
12. Although a little-known fact, Equatorial Guinea is the only former Spanish colony on the African continent.
13. See Ngugi, (1986), and p'Bitek (1973).
14. See also Oko (2000).
15. Cf. Sinjela, (1998).
16. For a good analysis, see van de Walle (1999).
17. See, for example, Steytler (1999).

References

Adelman, Samuel 'Constitutionalism, Pluralism and Democracy in Africa,' *Journal of Legal Pluralism and Unofficial Law* Vol.

Balkin, J.M. (1992) 'What is Postmodern Constitutionalism?' Vol.90 *Michigan Law Review.*

Baxi, Upendra (2000), 'Universal Rights and Cultural Pluralism: Consumerism as a Site of State Formative Practices,' *Cardozo Law Review,* Vol.21.

Boyle, James (2000) 'Anachronism of the Moral Sentiments? Integrity, Postmodernism and Justice,' (accessed on 12 September 2000 at: http://www.law.duke.edu/boylesite/pomo.htm).

Mamdani, Mahmood, (1996) *Citizen and Subject: Contemporary Africa and the Legacy of Late Colonialism,* Princeton, N.J.: Princeton University Press.

Ndulo, Muna (1998-99) 'The Democratic State in Africa: The Challenges of Institution Building,' *National Black Law Journal.*

Ojwang, J.B. 'Constitutionalism—in Classical Terms and in African Nationhood,' *Lesotho Law Journal.*

Oko, Okechukwu (2000) 'Consolidating Democracy on a Troubled Continent: A Challenge for Lawyers in Africa,' *Vanderbilt Journal of Transnational Law,* Vol.33, no.3.

Okot p'Bitek (1973) *Africa's Cultural Revolution,* Nairobi: Macmillan.

Okoth Ogendo, H.W.O. (1991) 'Constitutions Without Constitutionalism,' Issa Shivji (ed.), *State and Constitutionalism in Africa,* Harare: SAPES Publications.

Shivji, Issa (1991) 'Contradictory Class Perspectives in the Debate on Democracy,' in Shivji, Ibid.

Prempeh, H. Kwasi (1999) 'A New Jurisprudence for Africa,' *Journal of Democracy,* Vol.10, No.3.

Sinjela, Mpazi (1998) 'Constitutionalism in Africa: Emerging Trends' *The Review,* No.60 (June).

Steytler, Nico (1999), 'Global Governance and National Sovereignty: The World Trade Organization and South Africa's New Constitutional Framework,' *Law, Democracy & Development,* Vol.3, No.1.

Van de Walle, Nocolas, (1999), 'Globalisation and African Democracy', in Richard Joseph (Ed.) *State, Conflict and Democratization in Africa,* Boulder/London: Lynne Rienner.

Wa Thiong'o, Ngugi (1986) *Decolonising the Mind: The Politics of Language in Literature,* Nairobi: Heinemann.

PART I

CONSTITUTIONALISM IN AFRICA: NEW CHALLENGES, NEW OPPORTUNITIES

2

Constitutional Change and Cultural Engineering: Africa's Search for New Directions

Ali A. Mazrui

Long before the idea of a no-party state was considered in East Africa, the idea of a no-army state was given some thought. While Uganda has led the way in exploring the concept of a no-party state in the 1990s, Tanzania led the way in floating the scenario of a no-army state in the 1960s. Both concepts were designed to help stabilise society and reduce risks of internal conflicts. Mainland Tanzania was still called 'Tanganyika' in 1960. The mutiny of the *Force Publique* in neighbouring Congo Leopoldville (now Kinshasa) from June 1960 onwards was a disturbing occurrence to Tanganyika at the time. Hence it made some sense to agonise on whether to build much of an army. Julius Nyerere's brother, Joseph, was particularly articulate in expressing his reservations. 'To arm or not to arm! That is the question.' In the end those in Tanganyika who regarded an army as a necessary symbol of sovereignty prevailed. The country became independent with a military force that was not under United Nations command as Joseph Nyerere had recommended. Tanganyika chose to have a sovereign national army.

By the close of 1961 Julius Nyerere had been converted to the side of these who believed that Tanganyika was fundamentally different from Congo-Leopoldville, and could therefore risk having an army. The idea of the no-army state was thereby debunked. A few years later, Nyerere was proved partially wrong. Like the Congolese army in 1960, the Tanganyikan army mutinied in 1964 and Nyerere was forced into hiding. Even more humiliating was being forced to invite the troops of the former imperial power, Britain, to come back and disarm Nyerere's own soldiers. These events constituted the most humiliating experience in Nyerere's entire political career.

Nyerere asked Nigeria to send in troops to replace the British troops as soon as possible. Nineteen sixty four was another opportunity for Tanganyika to establish a no-army state built on the Costa Rican model. The British had disarmed Nyerere's old troops, and the whole Tanganyikan army was disbanded. Should Nyerere now do without an army—or create a new one based on new principles? Julius Nyerere decided that Tanganyika was not

Costa Rica. A new army was created, based on new principles of accountability. When in the same year Tanganyika united with revolutionary Zanzibar to form Tanzania, the new Tanganyikan army acquired additional justification. It was needed to defend the new union and to help maintain order and peace in Zanzibar that had now become part of the new state.

In the same year, both Uganda and Kenya experienced their own army mutinies. They too were forced to invite British soldiers to come and disarm their mutinous troops. But in the case of Uganda and Kenya, the concept of a no-army state was never a serious consideration. Thus, the year 1964 was allowed to slip by. British troops came and went. They could have helped to create at least one no-army state. This did not happen. The dream of a no-army state in East Africa slipped off into oblivion.

Thirty or so years later, Yoweri Museveni has shifted the debate from whether to have an army or not, to whether to have political parties. Once again, the issue of stability was at the heart of Museveni's dilemma. Just as some Tanganyikans had been alarmed in 1960-61 by the mutinous behaviour of armed forces in Congo, so too did some Ugandans draw similar lessons from the destabilising consequences of multiparty politics in Congo, Sudan, Nigeria and indeed even in Uganda. It has been argued that multiparty politics in most of Africa has tended to activate inter-ethnic rivalries. On the other hand, the one-party state in Africa has tended to encourage dictatorship and the personality cult.

Kings, cultures and constitutions

Neither a standing army nor a political party are part of African culture. What were part of African culture in southern Uganda were monarchs and kings. While Museveni's Uganda has initiated a debate on the no-party state, Milton Obote's Uganda of the 1960s embarked on a campaign for the no-monarchy or the no-king state. Museveni has regarded political parties as destabilising; Milton Obote regarded monarchies as destabilising. Obote believed Uganda needed a special kind of cultural engineering. In 1966, Obote succeeded in chasing Kabaka Mutesa II out of the country; Obote had not yet abolished the monarchy. On one occasion in 1966, I was part of a panel on Uganda television interviewing President Obote. Obote was making the case that Kabaka Mutesa had turned himself into a commoner when he accepted a knighthood from the British crown ('Sir' Edward Mutesa). Obote was preparing the country for the dethronement of Mutesa if not the abolition of the Kabakaship. A knighthood in British protocol was a title for a commoner.

I decided to rebut President Obote. I knew he was a great admirer of Kwame Nkrumah, the founder president of Ghana. I said that both Mutesa and Nkrumah had been subjects of a British monarch and felt they had to accept British royal favours. Just as Mutesa had accepted a British knighthood, Nkrumah had accepted to be a member of Her Majesty's Privy Council, and had also been flattered when he was the first non-British person to be confidentially informed when Her Majesty was pregnant.

President Obote's anger at my rebuttal was in his eyes. I could tell that I had seriously offended him. But he remained in control on television, and instead shifted the discussion by eulogising the greatness of Kwame Nkrumah and attempting to belittle Sir Edward Mutesa. I decided not to offend the president any further. Not long afterwards, President Obote abolished the monarchies of Uganda and thereby created a no-royalty state.

A quarter of a century later, another president decided that kings were less dangerous to the stability of Uganda than political parties. Yoweri Museveni ended the era of the no-monarchy state in Uganda, and initiated an equally fundamental debate about the no-party state. Museveni was increasingly convinced that while kings should be depoliticised and become mere cultural symbols of their ethnic groups, political parties were by definition impossible to depoliticise. Indeed they could become dangerous rallying points of ethnic loyalties. Monarchies lend themselves to ceremony; in a country like Uganda political parties may lend themselves to conflict. Clearly Milton Obote and Yoweri Museveni had different ways of using constitutional change as an instrument of cultural engineering.

Particularly important within African monarchies are the lessons we might learn from them for both cultural and constitutional engineering in Africa. There has been a tendency for the drafters of African constitutions to ask themselves questions such as:

- How do the Swiss deal with this issue?
- What does the US constitution have to say about this process?
- How does the Federal Republic of German handle this federal puzzle?
- What are the implications for the Westminster model?

Almost never do the drafters of African constitutions ask themselves the following alternative or additional questions:

- What kind of processes of conflict-resolution did the Banyoro have before colonialism?
- How did precolonial Ashanti (Asante) treat the issue of differences of religion?
- In Ankole how were property rights affecting cattle handled?
- Were land rights in Buganda originally colonial or pre-colonial?
- In traditional Africa what were the roles and rights of women?

Constitutionalism in Africa can never take root if there is no massive consultation with traditional culture, custom and legal precedents. One consequence of giving greater recognition to African cultures may be a greater acceptance of federalism as an institutionalisation of the diversity of African countries. In the second half of the twentieth century, federation has been a dirty word in most of Africa outside Nigeria. And, even in Nigeria, federalism has most of the time been negated by militarism. The question for the twenty-first century is whether many more African countries should not examine federalism as a possible solution to some of their own ethnic and regional problems. Federalism would be a recognition of cultural diversity.

One particularly controversial area would be asymmetrical federalism. The 1962 constitution of Uganda left Buganda with more autonomy than any other kingdom or district in Uganda. Buganda was treated as a distinct society. Quebec in Canada has been similarly caught up in a debate as to whether it should be treated as a distinct society. Canada is already a federation, but should Quebec be treated as even more 'non-federal?' Should it be granted more autonomy?

In Ethiopia before the 1990s, there was the question of whether Eritrea should be treated as a distinct society. Neither Emperor Haile Selassie nor the military ruler Mengistu Haile Mariam were prepared to concede special autonomy to Eritrea. The result was a thirty-year war, which finally culminated in Eritrea's secession into a separate independent state. In Uganda, the question remains whether Buganda should be demarcated and treated as a distinct society. The Baganda have been the largest and politically most central ethnic community, lying astride the capital city Kampala. They have shown astonishing capacity for synthesising tradition with modernity, indigenous allegiances with western ways.

If Uganda moves in the direction of federalism, there are two major options. One is symmetrical federalism within which all provinces or constituent districts are treated as equals. This would be an adaptation of the US model that gives every state two members on the Senate regardless of size, and accords every state the same constitutional rights. On the other hand, Uganda might decide to return to the 1962 model of asymmetrical federalism under which Buganda was indeed treated as a distinct society, and accorded more autonomy than any other part of the country. The other monarchies in Uganda were given special status rather than special autonomy.

Although asymmetrical constitutional arrangements are rare, they are best illustrated by Uganda's former imperial power, the United Kingdom. Scotland and Wales have only just acquired regional assemblies. However, the assemblies have different powers. Northern Ireland had a regional assembly long before the civil conflict, and the assembly is now in the process of being resurrected. England has no regional assembly at all, and must rely on the national parliament of the United Kingdom. Scotland has its own currency, though the currency of the United Kingdom is legal tender and widely used. Scotland also has its own law, which differs in important respects from English law. Northern Ireland and Wales have no currencies of their own, neither do they have distinct legal systems. On the other hand, the Welsh language is alive and well, though understood only by a minority. In recent decades Welsh has had more recognition in schools, broadcasting, publishing and other media. On the other hand, the old Gaelic and Celtic languages of Northern Ireland and Scotland have not survived as well, in spite of periodic efforts to revive them. It is also worth noting that Scotland has a distinct educational system of its own, in some respects superior to that of the rest of the United Kingdom.

What all this means is that the United Kingdom's political, constitutional and cultural order is predicated on a lack of symmetry. The British are masters of the science of muddling through. In spite of their asymmetrical constitutional order, the country has been one of the most stable in the world for more than three hundred years. For Uganda we cannot even claim that it has been one of the most stable in East Africa. Is one of the reasons for the instability an inadequate constitutional recognition of the ethnic diversity of the country? Would symmetrical federalism go some way towards defusing ethnic rivalries? Or will Uganda dare to 'go British' and create an asymmetrical constitutional order—with Buganda treated as a distinct society? Only the people of Uganda as a whole can resolve such dilemmas.

But the problem of good governance in Africa is not simply a matter of what kind of constitutions we devise. Sometimes what is required is simple obedience to the criminal law of the land. Good governance is more than putting constitutional limits to the powers of the government. It also requires putting legal limits to the economic and commercial behaviour of the elite. The new Africa of the twenty-first century should consider having a special *Ombudsman* system on corruption—control, both at the national level and in each district. Complaints about bribery, nepotism and other forms of corruption would be lodged with the Ombudsman who would be equipped with resources and staff to investigate, warn, and where necessary sue. Corruption can be a deadly cancer on both the economy and the political system, and deserves considerable investment of resources. The Ombudsman system may need the support of a corruption investigative police. There will need to be a different Ombudsman for human rights and civil liberties. In a bid to increase mediation and reduce litigation, complaints about violations of civil liberties at either the national or the provincial level would initially be lodged within the Ombudsman system.

Government: Referee or intruder?

The relationship between governance and economic development is deeply affected by the following inter-related factors:

- Size: how big the government is;
- Role: how much the government does;
- Effectiveness: how well the government does it;
- Legitimacy: how representative the government is;

The first consideration of 'bigness' includes the size of not only the civil service proper but also the parastatals. The second consideration relates to the role of the state in the economy and the nature of government's functions therein. The third consideration is about behaviour. The fourth conditioning factor is about constitutionalism and representativeness—or the lack of them.

It is important to remember that in Africa representativeness is sometimes measured ethnically rather than electorally. Ethnic arithmetic helps to reassure different groups whether or not they are truly part of the machinery and are among the beneficiaries. A government is deemed to be more or less representative to the extent to which it reflects the ethnic composition of the wider society. In Nigeria, this principle of representativeness is often referred to as 'the federal character' of the nation. In Zimbabwe the united front ideal was originally designed to make it possible for Ndebele (ZAPU) to share power with Shona (ZANU-PF). President Robert Mugabe succeeded in enlisting Joshua Nkomo's Ndebele after all, with the late Joshua Nkomo becoming vice-president. However, opposition among fellow Shona emerged.

The dynamic of ethnic representativeness has a propensity to enlarge governmental and bureaucratic institutions. The civil service and parastatals can become 'bloated' in response to the delicate balance of ethnic arithmetic. Both ethnic arithmetic and ethnic nepotism may give an African country a more bloated bureaucracy. On the other hand, insensitivity to the need for ethnic balance can sometimes be destabilising. The absence of ethnic representativeness in a country like Nigeria or Uganda is often a bigger political risk than the absence of electoral representativeness at the ballot box. Ethnic arithmetic is often a more compelling imperative than the ballot in the liberal sense.

As for the criterion of performance of the government, one central dilemma in Africa concerns the relationship between economic liberalisation and political liberalisation. There are certain countries in Africa where political pluralism has tended to be economically destabilising. Nigeria in the second republic (1979-1983) was politically open and competitive. It reached its highest point in freedom. But economically the country was sheer economic anarchy. Ghana under Hilla Limann (1979-81) and Sudan under Sadiq el

Mahdi (1986-89) were also politically open but economically devastated societies.

In such African countries there is a genuine moral dilemma. Political pluralism carries a higher risk of economic decay. Africa must avoid being put in a situation where it is a choice between either political freedom or economic development - but not together. There was a time when institutions like the World Bank and the IMF would actually prefer military regimes like that of pre-democratic Jerry Rawlings in Ghana to democratically elected regimes like those of Shehu Shagari in Nigeria. Jerry Rawlings has been effective both as military ruler and as elected president. Is there still a risk that external bodies would encourage economic liberalisation while discouraging political liberalisation? Could the latter *de facto* encouragement of military regimes occur implicitly – sometimes almost unconsciously?

As for the role of corruption in governance, this sometimes takes the form of privatisation of the state itself. Ethnic privatisation occurs when ethnic representativeness is abandoned - and one particular ethnic group monopolises or disproportionately controls the state. Examples include the Nubian control of Uganda in the 1970s. Dynastic privatisation occurs when the resources and symbols of the state are monopolised by an individual and his or her more immediate family. Jean Bedel Bokassa in the Central African Republic literally attempted to create a dynasty. Anarchic privatisation occurs when the wealth and power of the state are dissipated in a free-for-all scramble for advantage. Nigeria under Shehu Shagari became a case of anarchic privatisation, especially from 1981 until Shagari was overthrown at the end of 1983.

In the political domain, Africa's worst evils are the danger of tyranny on one-side and the risk of anarchy on the other. Tyranny is too much government; anarchy is too little. The tyrannical tendency is frequently a centralisation of violence. Anarchy is decentralised violence—often neighbour against neighbour. Ethiopia, Angola, Mozambique and Liberia have experienced both centralised and anarchic violence. In the economic domain, Africa's worst evils are the risk of economic dependency, on one side, and the peril of economic decay, on the other. Dependency is a truncated capacity for self-reliance. Decay is a truncated capacity for development.

The crisis of governance in Africa concerns the relationship between the political evils of tyranny and anarchy on one side and the economic evils of dependency and anarchy on the other. What is the way out? Part of the answer may indeed lie once again in the role of central planning within political engineering. Even democratisation may need to be planned. In Africa the choice sometimes is between planning for democracy and plunging into democracy. There is also the need to plan for reducing gross inequalities between states, regions and ethnic groups. I regard those ethnic and geographical inequalities as much more dangerous to Africa than social class inequalities in a Marxian or neo-Marxian sense. There has been no militarised class war in Africa; but there have been all too many militarised ethnic conflicts.

What the Ogoni people endured in the Niger Delta was a kind of internal colonialism in post-independence Nigeria. Internal colonialism occurs when the resources of a particular part of the country are exploited for the benefit of others with little benefit going to the people where the resources are located. In the case of the Ogoni people, while their oil served the rest of Nigeria and foreign enterprise (i.e. Shell Oil), the Ogoni themselves and their environment were badly damaged. The coast of Kenya is a major tourist resource for Kenya—with spectacular beaches and the best historical monuments in the country. But, for most of the period since independence, the tourist industry at the coast has been overwhelmingly controlled by non-coastal people, owning the best hotels, and managing the best tours. That is also internal colonialism.

In Uganda, the North has not been exploited but it has been cruelly neglected even when Northerners have been in power. In the 1990s, Uganda has been beset by inter-ethnic tensions and upheavals involving other groups as well. Uganda would need not only to iron out the differences and mitigate the inequalities, but also to strengthen underprivileged regions with greater resources. A more fundamental solution to the tensions of society is to reduce the inequalities between the groups.

Matters can get rather difficult if one ethnic group in a dual or plural society is economically or professionally much more successful than the other. Malaysia is, in some respects, a dual society with Muslim Malays consisting of nearly half the population and ethnic Chinese nearly a third. Until the 1970s, the ethnic Chinese were far more entrepreneurial and more economically successful than their Malayan brethren. The skill differential led to differences in income. Grievances exploded in the anti-Chinese communal riots of 1969. Since then the Malay-led government has pursued affirmative action policies in favour of the economically disadvantaged but more numerous Malays. For more than a quarter of a century Malaysia has contained and controlled the explosiveness of ethnic dualism by these affirmative action policies—and by a division of power in which Malays are politically pre-eminent while Chinese continue to be economically triumphant. Applying a similar principle, whites were allowed to keep the jewels if they would hand over the crown to the blacks in South Africa.

The troubles between the Hutu and the Tutsi in both Rwanda and Burundi may or may not have originated in skill-differences. However, inequalities in privileges definitely developed, with the Tutsi as the upper stratum for most of their mutual history. In the past, when the Tutsi were on top they never tried to even out the playing field. When the Hutu prevailed, they discriminated against the Tutsi. The worst lesson in this tit-for-tat masochism was the 1994 genocide in Rwanda.

Differences in skills between ethnic groups are not, of course, peculiar to neat dual societies like Rwanda. Malaysia's neighbour—Indonesia—has elements of both a plural society and a dual one. But once again ethnic Chinese have out-classed indigenous Malays in entrepreneurial skills. The stresses have had even more catastrophic consequences than in Malaysia. In 1965, the ethnic Chinese were accused of two contradictory charges: first, that they were plotting to stage a communist revolution; and secondly, that they were the vanguard of exploitative capitalism in Indonesia. In the riots and repression which followed, hundreds of thousands of ethnic Chinese perished. In the 1990s Malays have repeatedly rioted against the disproportionate prosperity of ethnic Chinese. Indonesia has to find a more effective affirmative action policy in favour of Malays if future inter-ethnic outbursts are to be contained.

In the past, anti-Buganda sentiment in Uganda was partly due to the marked material success of the Baganda and their perceived arrogance towards non-Baganda. Such inequalities need to be addressed and defused. The cruel neglect of northern communities also has to be speedily ended as part of the peace process in Uganda.

Between party systems and the barracks

Every African political system has continued to walk the tight rope between too much government and too little. At some stage an excess of government becomes tyranny; at another, too little government becomes anarchy. Either trend can lead to the failed state. Anarchy produces more displacement and more refugees than tyranny. Yet it is easier to get political asylum if one is a victim of tyranny than if one is a victim of anarchy.

A basic dilemma concerning too much government versus too little hinges on the party system. Nigeria has never experimented with the one-party state, but there is little doubt that one-party states tend towards too much government. This has been the case in most of Africa, though Mwalimu Nyerere's party *Chama cha Mapinduzi* was relatively benign. On the other hand, multiparty systems in Africa have often degenerated into ethnic or sectarian rivalries resulting in too little control. This tendency was illustrated by Ghana under Hilla Limann, Nigeria in the first and second rrepublics and the Sudan under Sadiq El-Mahdi in the 1980s. The state was losing control in all those cases.

Since the Movement option has been confirmed by the referendum in 2000, Uganda is feeling its way towards one solution to the dilemma—a no-party state. Concerned that a multiparty system would only lead to a reactivation of Uganda's ethnic and sectarian rivalries, President Yoweri Museveni lent the weight of his name, office and prestige to this principle of a Uganda without political parties for at least another five years.

There are other possible solutions to the dilemma between multiparty anarchy and one-party tyranny. One possibility is a no-party presidency and a multiparty parliament. This could give a country a strong executive with extensive constitutional powers, but one who is elected in a contest between individuals and not between party-candidates. Parliament or the legislature, on the other hand, could remain multiparty. The president would not be allowed to belong to any political party, though he (or she) cannot but belong to an ethnic group. A system of a presidency without a political party may indeed give undue advantage to Africa's millionaires—the black Ross Perots or other M.K.O. Abiolas. That may be the price to pay for a no-party presidency in a multiparty society.

Both Uganda and Ethiopia may be drifting away from a strict unitary state. Federalism—which used to be a dirty word in most of Africa outside Nigeria—is discovering a new legitimacy. Nigeria has a lot to teach Africa about federalism—both good and bad. But Nigeria itself has to make federalism more real and meaningful. Federalism with militarism is a contradiction in terms.

Another major unresolved dilemma lies in the arena of civil-military relations. Perhaps in everybody's experience military rule leads to too much government— almost by definition. On the other hand, civilian rule in countries like Nigeria and Sudan has sometimes meant too little government, with politicians squabbling among themselves and sometimes plundering the nation's resources. If military regimes have too much power, and civilian regimes have too little control, coup-prone countries like Nigeria and Sudan have to find solutions for the future. Otherwise destruction and displacement loom threateningly.

Dr Nnamdi Azikiwe, the first president of Nigeria after independence, once proposed a constitutional sharing of power between the military and civilians—it was called *diarchy*, a kind of dual sovereignty. At the time Dr Azikiwe proposed the dual sovereignty idea (part military, part civilian) in 1972, he was roundly denounced, especially by intellectuals and academics who were against military rule. But the dilemma has persisted in Dr Azikiwe's own country, Nigeria, and elsewhere in Africa: how to bridge the gap between the ethic of civilian representative government and the power of the military? The prospect of military coups casts its shadow on the future of Uganda as well.

Has Egypt itself since the revolution of 1952 evolved an unofficial internal diarchy—a system of government of dual sovereignty between civilians and soldiers? Has Azikiwe's dream found fulfilment in Egypt—however imperfectly? Or is the Egyptian system still in the process of becoming a diarchy but one that has not yet arrived? Starting as a military-led system in 1952, Egypt has certainly become increasingly civilianised—yet still falling short of full power-sharing.

An alternative method in coup-prone countries, like Nigeria, Burkina Faso, Uganda, Democratic Republic of Congo and Ghana, is the actual institutionalisation of the dual sovereign. Different constitutional arrangements are feasible. One possible constitutional outline could encompass a powerful French-style executive president who is a civilian, but combined with a French-style semi-powerful prime minister, who in this case would be a soldier elected by members of the armed forces.

Alternately, a whole new concept of a tricameral legislature could come into being—the House of Representatives and Senate consisting of civilian legislators democratically elected and the House of National Defence consisting of representatives of the security services (army, navy, air force and police and prisons). No bill concerning national security or constitutional change would become law unless it was initially passed by all three houses. These houses would therefore need to establish committees of negotiations on such special legislation to reach compromises acceptable to both the civilian legislators and the security services. In the United States, the House of Representatives and the Senate have special 'conferences' to hammer out compromises on legislation. A similar process would be needed in Africa between the two civilian houses and the National Defence House.

With regard to the presidency, it is in fact conceivable to have a system whereby the running mate of every civilian candidate is in fact a military man or woman. A vice-president could be an alternative to a prime minister. The vice-presidency could always be reserved for a member of the security forces. Such arrangements would be for those African countries which would otherwise be coup-prone. From 1994 to 2000 such a system—a civilian president and a much stronger military vice-president was tried in Rwanda. The balance of power between president and vice-president is not systemically ideal, and indeed the latter may decide—as Major General Paul Kagame has done —to assume the higher position.

In an election, every civilian presidential candidate would have to negotiate with a credible military running mate. Channels of communication would have to be worked out between aspiring politicians and aspiring members of the security forces. In our scheme, the president would have to be more powerful than the vice-president. The presidential candidate in an election should indeed always be drawn from the ranks of the civilians. This would be the edge of civilian advantage which the system of the dual sovereign would have. The executive branch would have a civilian bias, but the legislative branch would be equal. If the civilian president died in office, would his or her military vice-president automatically become president? This issue of succession may have to vary from country to country. It would not be wise to encourage assassinations of civilian presidents to facilitate succession by their military deputies.

The other edge of civilian advantage would be in the judiciary. All the justices of the Supreme Court would be civilians. But the court would also be advised by three military assessors on every case before it. The justices would take into account the views of the three assessors, but not be bound by them. The tradition of 'assessors' has a long record in British colonial judicial practice, and is still in use in many countries around the continent.

I had suggested that in coup-prone countries a system of the dual sovereign should be tried out in the first twenty to forty years of the twenty-first century. This would be part of political planning. After the first two to four decades of the dual sovereign, steps should be taken towards the establishment of a more thorough-going and pure civilian democracy. The ultimate goal should always be undiluted civilian supremacy in a viable democratic system. But we must also constantly bear in mind that our soldiers need a sense of purpose, a *raison d'être*, a professional mission. If Nigeria has no external enemies, we must find our soldiers an alternative sense of national purpose. Museveni has given his soldiers a temporary region-wide mission in the Great Lakes area.

Armies differ greatly in their national contexts and regional predicaments. At one extreme is Israel which regards every one of its neighbours as a potential military enemy, and has therefore evolved a culture of siege and militarised national mission. The Israeli army does not suffer from a sense of anomie or lack of purpose. It is in constant military preparedness—though it has sometimes been taken by surprise. If Israel is on one extreme of military purposefulness, the majority of African armies are at the other extreme of military purposelessness. Most African countries have no external enemies to fight, nor do they expect any. The only wars they are likely to have are skirmishes on the border with this or the other neighbour. Boredom in the barracks poses a serious risk to political stability. If soldiers do not have military goals to achieve, will they seek political or economic goals instead? That is why it is of utmost importance that Africa as a whole finds long-term solutions to its civil-military relations.

The immediate end of military rule can lead to weeks of democratic euphoria and civilian celebration. But the problem of civil-military relations has not gone away in Nigeria or Sierra Leone. Once the euphoria is over, we must once again explore how best to give our soldiers a sense of national purpose. A number of inquiries can inform this quest: Should the army slowly be retrained to become a militia of development rather than a force for defense? Should new recruits be taught skills of making the desert bloom—rather than skills of destruction and war? Should the Ugandan army become a wider regional force like ECOMOG in West Africa? Is there a need for *pax nilhana*—a regional peace which is kept and enforced from the source of the Nile? The third kind of sense of mission for the military in Africa could be a system of power-sharing with civilians - but in conditions in which civilians are the senior partners, rather than subordinates. Under this third heading falls the institutional arrangements I suggested in which a civilian is president and a soldier is a vice-president or prime minister; or there is a tricameral legislature, with elected soldiers occupying the House of National Defence.

Gender: The missing agenda

Whatever one may think of Ibrahim Babangida's precise measures for reforming Nigeria (1984-1993), his grand design showed a certain sensitivity to the following divisions in Nigerian society:

* the ethnic divide;
* the religious divide;
* regional distinctions;
* the divide between political generations (old politicians versus new); and
* the class divide (as affected by structural adjustment, for better or worse).

The divide that was still missing in the grand design was the gender factor. Throughout Africa there is inadequate planning for the empowerment of women in the political process. The Babangida administration in Nigeria was no different.

It has been more by default than by design that post-colonial Africa has started using women in senior diplomatic positions more readily than in almost any other major public service. Uganda has had a woman foreign minister and a woman vice-president sooner than the United States had a woman secretary of state, and while the US has still not had a woman vice-president. Uganda has also had a number of senior female ambassadors since independence—at posts which have ranged from Accra to Paris, Copenhagen to Washington, and Paris to Ottawa. Paris itself has had a diverse number of African women ambassadors - representing a range of political regimes from Ghana to Tanzania, and from the African National Congress to Uganda. The ANC envoy—Ms Dulcie September—was indeed assassinated in Paris in 1988, probably by agents of the apartheid regime.

The most famous African woman of the 1970s was Elizabeth Bagaya, princess of Toro. Dictator Idi Amin made her ambassador and then foreign minister of Uganda. He then tried to humiliate this proud African woman with allegations of sexual misconduct at a French airport. The lies proved much more of a disgrace to Idi Amin than to the princess.

The most famous African woman of the 1980s was Winnie Mandela. Again this was not through planned political design. In a sense, Winnie Mandela's ascent to political prominence was in the same tradition as Corazon Aquino of the Philippines (in the wake of a martyred husband), Benazir Bhutto in Pakistan (in the wake of a martyred father) and Sirimavo Bandaranaike in Ceylon (now Sri Lanka—in the wake of a martyred husband). Winnie—like the other women—was another illustration of female succession to male martyrdom. Moreover, the 1990s were a mixed bag for her. Her husband was released but he divorced her. She had ambivalent standing within the African National Congress and also faced serious legal charges.

Will Winnie Madikizela Mandela one day become the foreign minister of the new black-ruled South Africa? Although thoroughly controversial in South Africa itself, Winnie Mandela would stand a chance for a ministerial position in post-apartheid South Africa—though she does indeed combine diverse critics at home with fervent admirers abroad. However, for the time being, the African National Congress is a little more equipped with an agenda for the empowerment of women than any other liberation movement has been.

South Africa—like Zimbabwe before it—did experiment, under black-rule, with a system of disguised racial reservation of seats for whites at least for a while. But should not planned governance in Africa as a whole include the gender reservation of seats? Uganda under Yoweri Museveni has made an impressive start with women parliamentarians, but a schedule of empowerment is still needed.

One possible design would be to have the following three phases of gender representation:

Phase 1: Reserved seats for women in the legislature elected by women only—without prejudice to the rights of women as voters or candidates on the common electoral roll as well.

Phase II: Reserved seats for women in the legislature, elected by a franchise consisting of both men and women.

Phase III: Abolition of special seats for women when the evidence shows a commensurate and more balanced representation of men and women through a common electoral roll without the need for reserved seats.

Where is this kind of gender-planning most likely to happen? Apart from places like Uganda, the most likely laboratories of gender planning in Africa may turn out to be Muslim countries. For one thing, Muslim societies are more used to gender separation in other areas of social life. Secondly, Muslim countries like Pakistan and Egypt have already experimented with special seats for women. Thirdly, Muslim African countries like Somalia and Libya have experimented with gender-regiments in the armed forces—in a continent where soldiers remain among the major actors in politics. Fourthly, it is a Muslim country—Algeria—which seems to have led the way in using women in the air force. And the air force is often a major influence on political strategies in Africa. Indeed, the attempted coup in Kenya in 1982 was led by the air force.

The sex code and the constitutional order

Constitutionalism is not only about relations between families and genders, perennial and vital as these are; nor is constitutionalism only about political participation and ethnic accommodation, crucial as these dimensions may be. Constitutionalism is also about the limits of state power in the lives of private individuals. They say 'an Englishman's home is his castle,' ready to be defended by him even against all unwarranted officialdom. Under what circumstances is 'an African's home his kraal,' ready to be defended by him even against state intrusion? Constitutionalism is therefore also about the curbing of state power from intruding too far into the private life of the individual.

John Stuart Mill (1806-1873) drew a distinction between self-regarding actions, which have consequences only for the person doing them, and other-regarding actions, which have consequences for other people. According to Mill's view of liberty in his 1859 book, *On Liberty*, a democratic government does not interfere in the self-regarding actions of an individual, even if the government or the society disapproves of them. Thus, if a man and a woman decide to live in sin and never get married, a democratic government and a free society should not interfere, even if they disapprove of the sinful lifestyle.

What if a man and a man lived in sin as homosexuals, or a woman lived with another woman in sin as lesbians? John Stuart Mill himself would still have said that self-regarding immorality between consenting adults may be a matter for the church, but not for the state. The Almighty may judge in the hereafter, but not the government in the here and now! What is immoral need not be illegal. However, John Stuart Mill was ahead of his own Western society. During his own time the state and society vigorously interfered in the private behaviour of individuals. Indeed, even a generation after John Stuart Mill, the Anglo-Irish writer Oscar Wilde (1854-1900) was imprisoned (1895-1897) in Britain for homosexual behaviour.

What has happened in the West since then? Here we must distinguish between individual offences against the economic order (such as stealing and bribery and corruption) and individual offences against the sexual code of conduct of the society. John Stuart Mill lived during Victorian times. At the elite level, this period was characterised by high tolerance of economic deviance (e.g. corruption) and low tolerance of sexual deviation (adultery, fornication and homosexuality). In high English society of the time, it was a bigger scandal to be discovered as being homosexual than to be discovered as economically corrupt. Sexual deviation was regarded with greater disapproval than economic deviance–although corruption was more 'other-regarding' than homosexuality. Since John Stuart Mill and the imprisonment of Oscar Wilde there has been a reversal of priorities in the West. There are more and more laws against individual economic deviance (such as kickbacks and bribery) and fewer and fewer regulations to moderate individual sexual deviation. When I was a student in England there were laws against male homosexuality (but not against lesbianism). Since then both forms of homosexuality in Britain have become legal. Within the European Union, discrimination against homosexuals can be taken to the European Court of Human Rights.

In the United States' armed forces it is no longer permitted for the army to ask new recruits if they are homosexuals, 'Don't ask, don't tell!' is the rule. On the other hand, there are much tougher restrictions in American public life against bribery, nepotism, kickbacks and other forms of corruption. In 1961, John F. Kennedy was able to appoint his own brother, Robert, as attorney-general of the United States. Today a nepotistic appointment at such a high federal level would be impossible. The rules against nepotism in the US system have become much tighter. It is all part of this dialectic in the West's liberal order. Sins of economic and political corruption are less and less tolerated—while sins of the flesh and of sex are more tolerated. John Stuart Mill would have approved. Private sex is self-regarding and should not be any business of the state; corruption is more harmful to society and is therefore other-regarding. The state should try to stamp out corruption.

In most of Africa, is the order of priority closer to the days of Oscar Wilde in Britain than to the days of 'Don't ask, Don't tell' in the United States today? Apart from South Africa (where homosexuality is legalised), are most African governments more targeted against sexual 'deviation' than against economic deviance? The governments of Robert Mugabe, Daniel arap Moi and Yoweri Museveni have recently shown greater indignation against homosexuality than against economic corruption, relatively speaking.

President Museveni played host to President Bill Clinton of the United States in 1998. President Clinton had a sex scandal in 1998; did he use war to divert attention from it? President Museveni had a war scandal in 1999, did Museveni use sex to divert attention from it? Clinton's war-games in 1998 ranged from bombing Afghanistan and Sudan to new confrontations with Iraq; his sex scandal was of course primarily the Monica Lewinsky affair. President Museveni's war scandal in 1999 was the degree of his army's involvement in the conflict of the Democratic Republic of the Congo. His sex-diversion in 1999 was the intemperate attack on the gay community in Uganda, and giving the green light to the police to engage in massive harassment of homosexuals.

In the United States the self-regarding actions of the most powerful man in the country were exploited by his political enemies in 1998. But American public opinion insisted that private adultery was self-regarding and irrelevant for Clinton's public office. The Senate of the United States refused to convict Clinton of 'high crimes and misdemeanours.' In Uganda, the most powerful man in the land was not cast in the role of the accused but in the role of accuser. And the real accused were a vulnerable sexual minority (homosexuals) who even in the West continue to be exposed to intolerance and violent bigotry. In much of the Western world recently, the state has been trying to protect homosexuals from the bigotry of heterosexual extremists. In Zimbabwe, Uganda and Kenya the state seems to be eager to join the heterosexual extremists in their bigotry. The West has learnt that private sinners should be left to the efforts of religious and moral institutions. In Museveni's Uganda and Mugabe's Zimbabwe homosexual sinners may be victimised by the state—while corrupt officials, politicians and soldiers often get away with most of their loot. In most of Africa, other-regarding corruption often enjoys more *de facto* licence than self-regarding sexual deviation. The constitutional order can defend either set of values provided it is implemented with proper procedure and according to due process. While it is true that excessive sexual deviation hurts society, is it not equally true that excessive sexual deviation hurts the family?

The West is better than Africa in defending the economic order. But is the West better than Africa in defending the family? Economic achievements are among the glories of the West; but the disintegration of the family are among its abject failures. So Africa needs to find a better balance, a new equilibrium, a new kind of constitutionalism. The fact is that we can defend the African family without using our gay brothers and sisters as scapegoats. They are also part of the African family. The African family is threatened by many other forces—by HIV and AIDS among heterosexuals, by rapidly loosening family ties, by labour migration and urbanisation, and by the wider forces of Westernisation and globalisation. Constitutionalism in the broader society is supposed to be one of the anchors of stability—helping to define the rules of the game, helping to check the excesses of power, seeking to extend democratic rights and due process even to those who might stray to economic deviance and even to those who might manifest sexual deviation.

Conclusion

While written constitutions in Africa are a feature of the twentieth century, constitutionalism in Africa is a much older phenomenon. Constitutionalism is a process of political rules and obligations which bind both governors and the governed, both kings and ordinary citizens. There is no constitutionalism under absolute monarchs or absolute presidents. Constitutionalism is of necessity a version of limited government. Many societies in Africa before colonialism endeavoured to limit the powers of their rulers. In Uganda, pre-colonial constitutionalism was best realised in northern Uganda. The northern societies might have been stateless but they certainly were not constitution-less. Some groups were 'tribes without rulers' –but they were not 'tribes without rules.' On the other hand, monarchies in the south were often absolutist. They had *de facto* constitutions giving, say, the Kabaka all powers. But having a constitution is not the same thing as having constitutionalism. Where the powers of the rulers were almost unlimited, constitutionalism atrophied.

Written constitutions arrived in Africa as colonialism was coming to an end. Major dilemmas confronted African countries. Tanganyika (later Tanzania) agonised on whether having an army was a good option at all. Uganda under Milton Obote agonised about whether having monarchies was sensible. Later, Uganda under Yoweri Museveni debated whether having political parties was not a dangerous idea. Issues of order, stability and freedom have always been at stake in these fundamental reappraisals. But governance is also about economics and about wider cultural issues. While central economic planning (the old five-year planning) has declined in Africa, political planning is on the rise. South Africa is looking for ways to plan the next phase of empowering Black people in the face of White economic dominance. The new Nigeria under President Olusegun Obasanjo is planning ways of reducing the powers of the military and the violence-proneness of the Delta region. And President Yoweri Museveni of Uganda has been feeling his way towards planning for democracy instead of plunging into democracy. Political planning is becoming respectable in Africa of the new millennium. But Africa also needs to defend individual privacy against state intrusion.

Gender planning is perhaps the most serious of all the omissions in Africa's political and economic reforms. We are indeed witnessing a general shift in popular participation in Africa. We have noted the declining faith among Africans in 'heroes and hero-worship'. We have witnessed in select African examples the emergence of a new optimism about political engineering and planned governance. We need to add gender planning if Africa's grand design for the twenty-first century is to become comprehensive and fundamental enough to tilt the balance in favour of genuine societal transformation. *Afrostroika* is the re-structuring of Africa. Afrostroika needs to be androgynised if it is to avoid some of the pitfalls of perestroika elsewhere in the world. *Perestroika* and *glasnost* led to the collapse of the Soviet Union. Afrostroika can yield better results. The silences have ended; the struggle has resumed for a new constitutional order in the Africa of the new century.

3

Language and Politics: Towards a new Lexicon of African Constitutionalism

Anthonia Kalu

In his essay, *The Privatization of Public Discourse,* Alan Brinkley asserts the necessity of public forums to the development of a healthy American political life.[1] Using significant examples from early United States political life, he shows how politicians were able to maintain and nurture the democratic ideal. While acknowledging the limitations of democratic practice on a number of different levels, he explores the contemporary situation and asserts that,

> The sudden rise of new vehicles of communication—and possibly the possibility that they may transform the way in which Americans conduct their politics—raises a major question for public life.[2]

For Africa and Africans, the 'sudden rise of new vehicles of communication' became a significant issue since the colonial era when Western interference established Western-style classrooms, churches and written documents in African life. To the extent that these brought about changes to indigenous socio-political, religious and educational practices, that period jeopardised African public life. Brinkley and his colleagues examine the impact of new communication vehicles such as the Internet on democratic practice, the individual and community. Although, the new communication vehicles Brinkley explores are internal inventions, citizens still take them seriously and are acting promptly in favor of the nation and its citizens. For Africa and Africans therefore, the colonisers' languages, which impact on the way different African groups conduct their politics as well as indigenous languages need consistent exploration and unified action. Since language and other communication vehicles enable the transmission of values and norms, the African situation raises unique concerns about constitutionalism.

This chapter focuses on language and constitution-making in Africa. Because a constitution authorises a group, society or nation, its power as a communication vehicle cannot be overestimated. A constitution provides the most viable limits of a society's norms and values by encapsulating its basic ideals and values. By calling attention to the framework of a society's tradition and culture a constitution reformulates and authorises citizens' participation by placing limits on governance systems such that all members become liable to the practical maintenance of society's ideals, values and goals. This means that constitutions humanise societal ideals; they are the foundation for viable legal systems. By making a society's ideals accessible to all, constitutions provide viable routes to nationhood and therefore citizenship. For the purposes of this chapter, constitutionalism is defined as the carefully crafted relationship between recognisable national ideals and the day to day practice of citizenship. It is the work of responsible and accountable leadership.

Colonialism and the dilemma of liberty

Constitutionalism deals with the match between the language of the constitution and that of citizens. To understand what this means, we will consider the example of a multi cultural, multi-language African State. In the above discussion of the constitution and its capacity for group authorisation, we can infer that before colonisation, African societies had developed recognisable ways of limiting governance. Since most contemporary African societies (not states!) remain predominantly oral, this means that before colonialism, indigenous ideals were very well embedded within the oral tradition and culture. Consequently, socio-political practices were normalised within the oral tradition. For example, when political power resided in a recognised leadership structure as was the case in ancient Ghana, Mali and other empires and kingdoms, the oral tradition and norms of vassal communities were not jeopardised. Rather, the maintenance of power and authority depended on the ability to maintain harmony within the various parts. I want to submit here that such harmony and order were the result of the functional ideals of those societies, i.e., constitutions based on oral traditions and cultures.

The effectiveness and coherence of political practices and their impact on public life can be inferred from the uniqueness of African ethnic groups. In many post-independence African communities, members still function on the embedded knowledge of indigenous society's ideals, norms and values controlled by relevant practical implications on individual and communal behaviour. Serious exploration of the current dilemma of African politics and public life must consider the fact that colonisation brought different language groups together into contemporary African states. Regarding the notion of indigenous traditions and limited governance; it becomes possible to see that although the colonial state was made up of different language groups, citizens' ideals and aspirations were not different or divergent. This can be inferred from early resistance movements and the push for independence and self-rule throughout the continent. However, changes in governance using the colonisers' languages, which ignored and/or discredited existing indigenous efforts resulted in a new competitiveness between groups. What this means is that the acquisition of language is concurrent with the concept of freedom. Liberty cannot exist without language; for, it is language that expresses the substance and scope of the practice of liberty.

Colonial states were problematic because they gave the semblance of a forward-looking freedom through the imposition of languages foreign to the colonised. It is significant to note here that foreignness was not a problem for Africans because inter-group trade and intermarriage epitomised relationships between groups. No matter how different the language groups are from each other, such relationships are based on essential indigenous expectations and norms. Colonial languages were often used to present cultures that were incompatible with indigenous ideals and socio-political practices. This element of negation in the colonisers' interaction with colonial states maintained incoherence with indigenous methods of governance. The refusal to acknowledge the existence of indigenous ideas of liberty, justice and peace denied indigenous languages their rights as contenders for truth. This made it difficult for the speakers of those languages to participate meaningfully in politics and government. Consequently, it was not until Africans began to discuss liberty and justice using the colonisers' languages that political independence became a reality. This situation informs the current constitutional dilemma in contemporary African states. The result is that rather than function as power maps designed to direct and limit government, most contemporary African constitutions are tools for internal domination and neo-colonisation.

Ultimately, the problem of language in African constitutions is in the attitudes they convey and the values they do not uphold. Of concern here is the fact that as written documents, they claim a totalitarian viewpoint that leaves no room for public discourse. For example, to the extent that the Abdulsalami Abubakar draft constitution was not open to public debate or discourse, the 1999 Nigerian constitution could easily be titled 'the autocratic military constitution' for Nigerians. This attitude is incompatible with the persistence of orality in most African traditions and customs. Like other predominantly oral cultures, African traditions and cultures embed permanence without leaving behind visible relics or monuments. Consequently, people in predominantly oral cultures perceive the spoken message as a more plausible agent for ensuring knowledge transmission and skills. Also, although writing is valued in technologically advanced societies, citizens place a high value on individuals and groups with strong verbal communication skills. This is why the forum is the most effective tool for the enactment of democracy. Groups of people that share a common written or oral text make textual contents relevant with effective discussion.

Africans began to participate in the colonisers' political-economic projects when they became convinced of the permanence of the colonisers' message of progress. This has not been the case with African leaders. Most Africans still do not understand the meaning of independence because the contemporary African version seems to applaud disunity, chaos and distrust. Even the colonisers' were able to convince the colonised of indigenous shortcomings for political practice through their own ability to extend and therefore unify those indigenous norms and values that coincided with theirs. By encouraging all indigenes to send their children to western-style classrooms, for example, colonists appeared to be buying into African ideals for socialisation and upward mobility. Although the major problem of colonisation was in its misrepresentation of change, its success depended on the consistency of its projects. While Africans became educated and upwardly mobile, both were achieved outside coherent indigenous norms. For the most part, contemporary African leadership lacks even this ability for consistency in its efforts at disunity. The number of military takeovers, for example, suggests that the only consistent element is individual hunger for power. In other words, we cannot even expect our leadership to excel at incompetence because existing communication vehicles at the national level are not fully developed.

Constitutionalism and the centrality of language in democratic practice

Unanimous projects are products of compatible goals and objectives. On the surface it appears that contemporary Africans' capacity for learning the coloniser's languages should facilitate relationships between national constitutions and citizens. However, given the experiences of colonial domination, most framers in Africa have tended to produce constitutions that are incommensurable with citizens' goals, objectives or aspirations. A logical question here is: how does one measure citizens' goals? Deductively, to the extent that the masses remain impoverished, intellectual flight abroad continues, we can expect that the goals of citizens are not being met. Citizens' goals are not being met as long as suffocation and fragmentation of civil society remain tools for the abrogation of their basic rights as humans. To the extent that freedom of expression remains mediated and/or abrogated across the continent, we can deduce that African political leaders have largely operated in a context that is incompatible with the goals of their citizens. Furthermore, if the framers of constitutions work within the limits placed on the nation by such leaders, then their goals will also conflict with those of citizens.

A cursory look at contemporary African literature's efforts to address the language question will illustrate the depth of this problem for the contemporary

African state. In 1952 African writers met at Makerere, Uganda to discuss African literature and the language question.[3] Since then, dominant questions have revolved around what languages African writers should write in, which *lingua franca* and/or official languages they should promote. In the case of written constitutions, the works of significant writers address the general expectation that framers will produce maps of the power structures of post-colonial states, giving directives for the extent and limits of government and leadership.[4] A closer look at African literary projects reveals that citizens mostly proceed as though such documents are transparent and fully accessible. In practice, most constitutions of contemporary African states do not speak the language of indigenous peoples because the post-colonial state has yet to acknowledge the entrenched oral power maps of different indigenous language groups. This does not mean that contemporary constitutions are not written in indigenous languages.

The point here is that the language of these new power maps is incommensurate with indigenous attitudes and expectations about peace, progress, justice and dignity. For congruity to prevail, the new constitutions must fully explore basic questions such as: do the Kikuyu of Kenya want liberty more than the Akan of Ghana? Does the need for good schools and roads among the Hausa of Nigeria exceed that of the Wolof in Senegal? If our responses to these questions are in the affirmative, then we have no further need for discussion about national constitutions and constitutionalism. But, if we find that the Kikuyu as Kikuyu have a culture with deeply embedded ideas of liberty, peace and justice, then it is possible to work toward a better understanding of the ways in which Kikuyu governance maps are congruent with those of the Luo, the Masai and other groups within post-independence Kenya. An example of embedded indigenous processes for liberty, justice and the common good is appropriate at this point.

As an Igbo from Nigeria, I grew up seeing people breaking and eating kola. Most Igbo children do not like the taste of the kola nut but they learn to respect kola's ritual import in their communities. Chinua Achebe popularised both the ritual and its significance in *Things Fall Apart*.[5] Among the Igbo, the kola breaking ritual is important to private and public forums. For example, it is used to welcome casual and formal houseguests and to begin naming, marriage and funeral ceremonies.[6] Whenever kola is broken, an Igbo expects at least cordial conversation, at best a fulfilling economic or social transaction. In *Things Fall Apart*, Achebe also uses this ritual as a literary device to introduce important beginnings and endings within the plot structure. It becomes a major narrative technique. The first time we encounter the kola breaking ritual is in Chapter One when Okoye goes to collect a debt from Unoka, Okonkwo's father.

Unoka went into the inner room and soon returned with a small wooden disc containing kola nut, some alligator pepper and a lump of white chalk.

> "I have kola," he announced when he sat down, and passed the disc over to his guest.
> "Thank you. He who brings kola brings life.... But I think you ought to break it," replied Okoye, passing back the disc.
> "No, it is for you, I think," and they argued like this for a few moments before Unoka accepted the honor of breaking the kola....
> As he broke the kola, Unoka prayed to their ancestors for life and health, and for protection against their enemies. When they had eaten, they talked about many things.... [Okoye] cleared his throat and began:
> "Thank you for the kola. You may have heard of the title I intend to take shortly."[7]

As a narrative, *Things Fall Apart* is convincing because Achebe articulates Igbo ways clearly in the new language. With each new presentation of the kola ritual, we learn more about Igbo socio-political thought and practice. Whether we see the kola ritual in a narrative setting or in real life, we begin to expect that among the Igbo, "He who brings kola brings life," and we pay attention and respect. More importantly, we begin to act as if it is true because we expect that kola, among the Igbo, is coterminous with life. In our minds, we begin to expect the characters to treat each other respectfully when kola is mentioned not because kola merits respect but because of how the characters, beginning with Unoka and Okoye, behave in its presence.

In the scene where Okoye goes to collect his debt, the most important element is not his errand but how it is conducted. Achebe makes this clear by focusing on Unoka's failures and the fact that he does not pay his debt to Okoye. Although both men know the rules of the kola ritual, custom and tradition insist that they engage each other on the rules and order of kola breaking. This allows them to reassess each other for the imminent conversation. If Okoye had accepted the dubious honour of breaking Unoka's kola in Unoka's house there would be no conversation. Although Unoka refuses to fulfil his obligations to Okoye, both men are bound by the fact of having shared kola to respect each other. They must part peacefully regardless of the outcome of the conversation. This makes it possible for Okoye to think about alternative approaches to collecting his money while Unoka, a failure socially and economically, retains his dignity.

Further, according to the codes of this tradition, if Okoye were to initiate a binding contract with Unoka, he would have to take at least a pot of palm wine to Unoka. We see this later when Okonkwo goes to ask Nwakibie for some seed yams and when Obierika's in-laws visit. Depending on the seriousness of the contract, part of the wine is used to pour libation. Always, the wine and the kola are consumed. In any case, the owner of the house brings the kola before conversations begin. Clearly, presenting kola to one's guests assures them of their safety and health for the duration of their visit. Within Igbo custom and tradition, the promise of kola as that which brings life is the carrier of socio-political potential. Thus, between individuals and/ or groups, the contract is not transferable from one transaction to the next except minimally among family members and close friends. In those situations kola breaking assumes a ceremonial role unless there is a breach of confidence. In all situations, if kola is expected but unavailable, the host/ess must state the absence of kola and provide a substitute.[8] No well-raised Igbo ignores the kola ritual or the implications and stipulations of its codes. And, all elders are held responsible for the transmission of its embedded norms and rules. Individuals who ignore the rules of the kola ritual do so at their own risk. Sometimes, that risk involves the loss of one's liberty and/or life. Anchored through gestures of hospitality, the kola text of reciprocity, health and peace is embedded in all aspects of Igbo life.[9] In *Things Fall Apart,* Okonkwo's suicide illustrates the implications of the inability (or indifference) to understand the relationship of the kola text to other aspects of Igbo socio-political thought.

Essential to Igbo codification, the kola text precedes other Igbo rules and laws, but especially Igbo elders' behaviour as citizens and leaders. This is why Okonkwo's story makes sense to most Africans. His rise to prominence among his people was predicated on his ability to show signs of leadership. But the group that recognises his potential in the first place limits his leadership roles and functions. Igbo expectations about life, justice and peace do not allow Okonkwo to change Igbo law on his own or in consultation with other members of the group of elders. Such changes require discussion in public forums. This is why the *egwugwu* is called forth when Uzowulu, Okonkwo's parallel, decides to change the law about his wife, Mgbafo's rights as a woman of the clan. When Uzowulu abrogates Mgbafo's rights, his in-laws remove her from her home of marriage and Uzowulu demands a public hearing. At the hearing, Evil Forest (the Speaker of the House?) tells him, 'Go to your in-laws with a pot of wine and beg your wife to return to you. It is not bravery when a man fights with a woman.' He also tells Uzowulu's in-laws, 'If your in-law brings wine to you, let your sister go with him....'[10] The in-laws' response is therefore conditioned by Uzowulu's line of action after Umuofia revisits its constitution about gender equity in the context of domestic violence. As male citizens of Umuofia, Mgbafo's brothers and her husband are only allowed to act in certain ways by the constitution once Mgbafo's rights are jeopardised. Representing the authority of Umuofia's oral tradition, Evil Forest protects Mgbafo while guaranteeing her rights and restoring her dignity. If and when she returns to Uzowulu (Achebe does not tell the rest of the story), Uzowulu will not easily abuse her again. Significant to the successful end of this episode is the fact that Evil Forest remains respectful toward all involved.

Mediated structures: Literary frameworks and constitutional language in Africa

In the contemporary state, rather than convene a forum and uphold the local constitution, the leadership (Evil Forest and the other *egwugwu*) would have asked Uzowulu to forgive them for giving him a bad wife and told the in-laws to support Uzowulu's 'manly' acts. Also, the forum where Uzowulu's case is adjudicated is different from the one where Okonkwo kills the court messenger. In the latter forum, the absence of the *egwugwu* indicates the falling apart of things for Umuofia. Here, Okonkwo misunderstands procedures and takes matters into his own hands and violence rules.

The gradual removal of the *egwugwu* and other stabilisers of Igbo (African) codification become evident in *No Longer at Ease*.[11] In this story, Obi Okonkwo, Okonkwo's western educated grandson also misunderstands the norms and rules. Like his grandfather, Obi speaks the language but does not understand the culture that structures and directs its meanings. Although he earns a degree in English (classics) in England, he does not understand English/colonial norms and rules. Caught in the new cult of the 'big man,' where the kola ritual, which is anchored to Igbo hospitality, is misinterpreted and exploited, Obi accepts a bribe and is arrested.

No Longer at Ease is a flashback, an exploration of why the Obi Okonkwo's--Africa's new leaders--fail. In *No Longer at Ease*, Chinua Achebe brings the question of language and rupture in social interactions to the attention of African intellectuals in burgeoning postcolonial Nigeria. For example, on his way home from Lagos after a long sojourn in England, Obi boards a mammy-wagon called 'God's Case, No Appeal.' He pays for the first-class seat in front with the driver and a woman with her baby. Later, when the driver stops as a result of drowsiness, Obi wakes up from his own sleep and decides to stay awake. Concerned, the traders offer the driver anti-sleep remedies like the kola nut. The driver refuses, insisting that he ate kola all day and that sleep deprivation is not a deterrent to his driving abilities. After the journey resumes, the traders in the mammy-wagon begin to sing a song whose refrain catches Obi Okonkwo's attention:

> *An in-law went to see an in-law*
> *Oyiemu—o*
> *His in-law seized him and killed him*

Oyiemu—o
Bring a canoe, bring a paddle
Oyiemu—o
The paddle speaks English
Oyiemu—o

Early recognition of the impact of the new vernacular languages was addressed in terms of education and the individual rather than as group or national ideas of progress in the new dispensation. Like Obi Okonkwo, those who learned the new language were assigned positions of high status. A significant number of those jobs were in the civil service or related positions. Most of the jobs were away from the individual's hometown or village. In other words, the building of a new socio-political system that remains largely incompatible with the existing order marks the post-colonial state. This means that the educated elite had little or no opportunity for learning from indigenous elders. That denial of opportunities for comparison entrenched the new leaders in the new socio-political system. For all practical purposes, this new system is the postcolonial state. It is incongruent with the physical national territory whose boundaries were demarcated by the colonists. This state is the location of the new constitution with expansionist claims that continue to maim citizens.

In light of the foregoing, it is obvious that any given African nation has more than one constitution—that of the postcolonial state and the embedded traditional codes of the nation's various language groups. For countries like the United States, whose early politics and political debates were not structured around predominantly oral traditions and codes, constitution-making involved a combination of written arguments, debates and public discussions.[12] In Eastern Europe, when early written constitutions became unpopular, constitutional reform has taken the form of rejection of untenable aspects of the old.[13] The African situation is different from those of the United States and East Europe in that Africa has yet to acknowledge the existence of ancestral constitutions.

The formulation of viable constitutions in Africa has to consider some difficult questions. Some of them include: Are existing constitutions congruent with familiar African socio-political instruments? As instruments of governance, are they compatible with African codes of conduct and laws? How do current constitutions relate to those codes and rules that the majority of citizens are familiar with? Who are the framers of the existing constitutions? Are they 'big men' like the driver of the mammy-wagon above whose individual goal of reaching his destination at all costs jeopardises the safety of other citizens? Or, are they 'big men' like Obi Okonkwo who look askance at indigenous practices except when they can exploit them? How should we read Obi Okonkwo's position in the first class compartment where he is involved in a do-nothing fault-finding cogitation of the evolving system delineated by the mammy-wagon trip from Lagos to his hometown? How is Obi Okonkwo's 'big man' posture similar to or different from the driver's? How are the postures of both men related (or similar) to those of the framers and/or reformers of existing constitutions? Are these leaders aware of the depth and breadth of indigenous African laws and customs? When Obi Okonkwo, the newly made 'big man' wakes up after the mammy-wagon stops, why is it more important for him to 'turn [the logic of the traders' song] round and round in his mind...'[14] rather than encourage the driver to do something positive to ensure their safety in his vehicle?

A possible contemporary response to the last question would be, 'But the vehicle reached its destination.' Anyone who has travelled Nigeria's roads knows that this is not always the case. Besides, as illustrated above, the promise of kola cannot be transferred to subsequent transactions. More importantly, for the purposes of the narrative which illustrates some of the failures of the new leadership, it would be fatal to crash the vehicle.

Representing the new elite, Obi makes some obvious mistakes. But, unlike his grandfather's, his mistakes are not his alone. Although Umuofia communities in Lagos and his hometown applaud his success in the new dispensation, they do not hold him responsible for the careful acquisition of the skills of the new position; a demand that marked his grandfather's career and life. And, although his family opposes his decision to marry an *osu*, they cannot convince him because his lack of education in indigenous norms and rules makes him defensive of his views and vulnerable to the caprices of both cultures. Ultimately, his formal Western education does not serve him in a situation that has the potential to link new ideas to old. In the end, his fiancée, Clara, also loses as Obi fumbles his way across the delicately balanced cultural terrain of the new dispensation, which is laden, with un-reconciled expectations of a nation in conflict and transition.

As with the woman in the mammy-wagon, Obi's response to Clara is focused on her ability to satisfy his sexual fantasies and needs. Neither woman's safety nor socio-political existence makes sense to his unbridled journey toward self-destruction and negation of his community's efforts to support his demonstrated potential for leadership. After Obi loses the case, the Umuofia community in Lagos can only repeat the question their ancestors had asked about Obi's grandfather, 'Why did he do it?'[15] The only difference is that in Umuofia the people understood where Okonkwo, a member of the group of elders, had gone wrong. They had reprimanded him several times before for crimes against the Earth Goddess when he beat his wife during the Week of Peace and exiled him when he committed manslaughter. So, when he killed the court messenger, they were at a loss for words. Their question was not about their ignorance but about Okonkwo's inability (or refusal) to pay attention to the limited powers of those responsible for others' well being. The Umuofia Progressive Union's approach to solving Obi Okonkwo's wilfulness demonstrates the powerlessness of the new leadership. Away from home, the Union tries to protect Obi from a system they do not understand. In the face of the British legal system, the Union is as powerless as Ngugi wa Thiong'o's Rich Old Man, Mr Gitahi when Wariinga, whose life he had almost destroyed, decides to kill him[16]. Like Obi Okonkwo, Mr Gitahi cannot believe that the woman who had given him her youth would kill him. Both men betray the trust of the people. In each case a young woman's future is involved. And, when women's futures are jeopardised, national progress is also at risk.

Popular participation and progressive constitutionalism

The leadership dilemma of the African state implicates the safety, dignity and liberty of all citizens. When contemporary Africans develop values and systems that demonstrate a level of integrity comparable to those of the elders who could collectively invoke ancestral dictums to protect one woman's rights as in the case between Uzowulu and Umuofia, then the African state will have no choice but to move forward. The problem is: How can such a unified viewpoint be achieved?

Previous experience suggests that borrowing or reworking the constitutions of other nations will produce many more decades of arrested development and incoherent constitutions. African states have to develop a consistent process for rebuilding citizens' respect and pride in the state. Lawyers should be trained with the capacity to do research in the ex-colonial[17] and indigenous legal systems. When the Lagos branch of the Umuofia Progressive Union gave Obi Okonkwo the scholarship, they wanted him to study law. He changed his mind and studied English.

But we now know that law is not independent of language and that the need for dedicated constitutional lawyers is considerable. What is indicated here is a continent-wide call for effective utilisation of available resources. Most African states have adequate numbers of efficient lawyers and other professionals. However, for the most part, many highly skilled individuals are either misemployed or under-employed. In this example of how to establish a viable constitutionalism, I want to use lawyers as the focus of an accepted national programme. Finding and defining a focus, a base that works for a particular nation is the key to successfully embedding constitutionalism. In this example, the state should employ, listen to and use the counsel of skilled and efficient constitutional lawyers, as well as intellectuals in other disciplines with the commitment to furthering citizens' goals. This category of lawyers and scholars should also be used as workshop facilitators for groups identified as framers/reformers of the national constitution. Their work should include interpreting a viable constitution into indigenous languages as well as the interpretation and analysis of the constitution itself. Starting with this base means that the training of more lawyers will necessitate the maintenance of an efficient and effective educational system nationwide.

Because a strong educational system supports, ideally, citizens' as well as the national interest, all schools must be involved in the maintenance of basic goals and rights. To the extent that the lawyers who work to sustain the nation's (and citizens') interest in the extent and limits of government, to such extent will the nation commit to teaching the youth about national goals and ideals. It is significant to state here that since we are exploring possibilities for nations that have been in transition and conflict, all adults should become involved in continuing re-education programmes on national goals. Such programmes are good starting points for debates on the constitution.

Since, by training, lawyers are not teachers, some of the workshops referred to above will be used to provide hands-on experience for a significant number of lawyers to learn how to interpret the constitution and consequent laws to non-professionals. This will facilitate public engagement of debates about the constitution in local, regional and national newspapers. Eventually, this means that the constitution referred to here is a draft constitution that will take a few (limited) years to ratify.

A basic assumption of the suggestions made here is that those who embark on the programme with a focus will remain honest and committed to that focus. If, for example, the focus here deviates from the use of skilled lawyers to effect the training of better lawyers who will facilitate a national project to one of producing only lawyers, the goal will never be reached. Such a deviation will amount to a loss of integrity at the base. One of Africa's major dilemmas is tied to the fact of misrepresentation of and mis-education on the theme of upward mobility during colonialism. European scramble for Africa's resources is only surpassed by the African scramble for European positions after independence. It is a well-known secret that the latter scramble is more disabling for national and continental progress. At some point in the rush for political and administrative positions vacated by the colonisers, the yearning to regain control of power and rights resulted in Africans forgetting that

> ..... in a great man's household there must be people who follow all kinds of strange ways. There must be good people and bad people, honest workers and thieves, peace-makers and destroyers; that is the mark of a great *obi*. In such a place, whatever music you beat on your drum there is somebody who can dance to it.[18]

Although individual skills and accomplishments are significant, the focus must remain on maintaining the greatness of the homestead, the nation. This means that individual skills and interests should be encouraged at all levels. Such an approach nurtures creativity and maintains productivity at close to optimum levels. Productive citizens who achieve their goals are more likely to support and participate in a local or national government whose ideals are seen as being aligned in such a way as to sustain those goals.

A constitution that commits to the maintenance of greatness at the national level invariably supports greatness of individual citizens, groups and organisations. This does not always mean perfect agreement as to the ways and means of sustaining the framework of a constitutional style of governance. Rather, it means that the constitution in all its clauses is committed to maintaining and respecting each citizen and their rights and privileges. In most post-independence African situations, the rush for government and administrative positions is at the root of the flight of capital to urban areas. The movement to urban centres must be reversed. A good starting point is to ensure that lawyers, for instance, can make as good a living representing farmers as they would if they represent city dwellers.

In the above example of the driver of the mammy-wagon, such jobs should have built-in benefits that make it possible for them not to want to work all night. The national constitution should include a clause that makes work shifts respectable by freeing lawyers to represent them without either group losing their right to speak freely. Discussions about such issues should involve Africa's Motor Park workers—a group that lacks representation despite its responsibility for maintaining the continent's transportation workforce. This critical workforce for example needs to develop a better relationship with law enforcement officials. The incessant exploitation of Africa's transportation workers should be addressed by the constitution because they make up a significant portion of the population that maintains the communication systems in our predominantly oral societies. For the most part, these minimally educated workers are unaware of their rights as citizens and/or as individuals and are therefore unable to help either themselves or their clients in situations involving law enforcement officers on the highways. Because these groups of workers move large numbers of citizens daily, protection of their individual rights will encourage them to participate in the discussion of road safety and related issues. Heightening awareness in this manner will help to reduce incidents of bribery that negate citizens' freedom of movement.

An issue related to road transportation systems, as a significant part of Africa's communication vehicles is the rights and dignity of women. As the major participants of the African local marketplace, women should receive visible attention in the constitution. Framers should make the language of the constitution gender sensitive enough to create a living awareness in citizens regarding the linkages between women and the market, transportation, education and other relevant areas.

No discussion about constitutions and constitutionalism would be complete without addressing voting and voting rights. In order to make these issues clear from a traditional African language viewpoint; it is necessary to look at how women participate in decision making in indigenous settings. One of the most familiar scenes in African life is the marketplace. Because more women than men are involved in agriculture across the continent, they have a significant impact on local economies. Their significant control of subsistent farming also means that they control, to a large extent, the local staples. Income from local and inter-ethnic marketplaces enables women who are single parents in the rural areas and women in polygamous households to maintain economic control of their lives and those of their children. Recognition of these functions by women will facilitate consideration of their impact on intra-ethnic and intra-continental trade. This focus will also reduce dependence on 'traditional' cash crops.

Finally, those who believe that traditionally African women did not vote should look again at marriage traditions and customs. It is virtually impossible for a woman to get married in most ethnic groups without the consent of the women on both sides. Although, on the surface, the men formalise in-law relations in most cultures, women do a great deal of the legwork before and after marriage alliances are formed. Framers of contemporary constitutions would do well to study the ways in which African women conduct the campaigns necessary to maintain local marketplaces and in-law relationships. The apparently informal dynamics of these familiar institutions have a great deal to offer as Africans consider again the possibilities of reopening access to discussion about public life in which all may participate without fear of losing life or limb. Success in this project for gaining an African independence, that will bring about a dignifying liberty, will involve commitment and collaboration of those who are knowledgeable about Africa's potential for greatness in this millennium—its citizens.

Notes

1. Brinkley *et al* (1997): 139-150.
2. Ibid: 139.
3. Achebe (1975): 55.
4. See for instance: Achebe (1966); wa Thiong'o (1982); Soyinka (1965); el Saadawi (1987), and Dangarembga (1988).
5. Achebe (1959).
6. See for instance: Ogbalu (1979) and Uchendu (1965).
7. Achebe (1959): 9-10.
8. Ogbalu (1979): 55.
9. Uchendu (1965): 74-75, and Ogbalu (1979): 54-56.
10. Achebe (1959): 89.
11. Achebe (1960).
12. See for instance: Rossiter (1961).

13. Gross (1994).
14. Achebe (1960): 42.
15. Achebe (1959): 188.
16. Ngugi wa Thiong'o (1982): 253.
17. The term 'ex-colonial' here indicates not just the post-colonial environment but a new space of action which involves the African's awareness and practice of a new and different research strategy that takes cognizance of the need for Africans to purposefully operate in a non-colonial environment. Having spent so many years within post-colonial frameworks, this approach needs to be developed carefully and objectively.
18. Achebe (1964): 51.

References

Achebe, Chinua (1959) *Things Fall Apart,* New York: Fawcett Crest.

_____. (1960) *No Longer At Ease,* London: Heinemann.

_____. (1969) *Arrow of God,* New York: Doubleday & Company, Inc.

_____. (1975) *Morning Yet on Creation Day: Essays,* London: Heinemann.

Brinkley, Alan, and others (1997) *New Federalist Papers: Essays in Defense of the Constitution,* New York: W. W. Norton & Company.

Grudziska-Gross, Irena, (ed.) (1994) *Constitutionalism in Eastern Europe: Discussions in Warsaw, Budapest, Prague, Bratislava,* Bratislava: Czecho-Slovak Committee of the European Cultural Foundation.

Ihonvbere, Julius O. "The 1999 Constitution of Nigeria: The Limitations of Undemocratic Constitution Making." (Paper presented at the Center for Democracy and Development, Abuja, Nigeria, 1999)

_____. (1999) 'Between Imposed and Process-Led Constitutionalism in Africa.' (Unpublished Paper).

Okpewho, Isidore (1992) *African Oral Literature: Background, Character, and Continuity.* Bloomington: Indiana University press.

Rossiter, Clinton, (ed.) (1961) *The Federalist Papers: Hamilton, Madison, Jay.* New York: Penguin Books.

Wa Thiong'o, Ngugi (1982) *Devil on the Cross,* Oxford: Heinemann Educational Books.

4

Pan-Africanism and Constitutionalism

Tajudeen Abdul Raheem

It may sound obscene to state that these are very interesting times in Africa, given the humanitarianism-driven media focus and crisismania that characterise the bulk of academic, NGO and international discourses on Africa. By no means are the usual suspects such as imperialism, or the Afro-pessimists, alone in this. Many African experts, NGOs, political leaders, consultants, academics and politicians are so addicted to bad news from Africa they seem unable to look beyond their crisis lenses. It is almost as if they will have no jobs or careers if there is no crisis on the continent. Yet the most interesting aspect of the current transitional processes in Africa is the resilience of Africans, their innovation and creativity in confronting the various challenges faced by the continent in its struggle for social progress, democracy and peace. In this respect therefore, the general theme of this book—*Challenges and Opportunities*—is a welcome departure from the crisis focus. One may be too focused and fixated on crisis to realise the small gains and entry points—slow but deliberate shifts in the confluence of ideas whose culminative effect may lead to fundamental change.

The last decade of the twentieth century has seen changes in the relations between peoples, states and individuals, some for the better and others in the opposite direction. The end of the cold war released pro-democracy movements in Africa and other parts of the Third World from the stultifying exigencies of the past. No longer was it possible for every struggle for democratic rights to be viewed as communist-inspired. Dictators could no longer blame every demand for accountability and transparency on the handiwork of 'dangerous radicals in the pay of some foreign power' to destabilise moderate pro-Western or Eastern regimes.

However, the release from cold war strait-jackets did not mean that Africa became an island able to redesign its institutions of governance, or reform its state structures and systems without let or hindrance. Indeed, one can clearly discern a new drive for hegemony in this era of globalisation where Western powers are pushing certain ideas as universal and insisting that every country must follow that path or face retribution. The struggle for democracy, good governance and human rights in Africa is caught up in this complex matrix of donor push-and-pull and the genuine struggle for democracy.

Lest I am misunderstood; I am not arguing that democracy is Western or that Africa is not ready for democracy. What I am saying is that issues such as democracy, human rights, good governance, accountability, transparency and constitutionalism to mention a few, are not neutral. They are political and are being pushed by different people for different interests. That they have become buzzwords, donor-friendly and propagated by everybody does not and should not depoliticise them.

As Africa begins to sober up from the heady mix of optimism and the limited gains of the pro democracy movements of the early 1990s, these issues have been given their baptism of fire. We are thus forced to return to the drawing board. There was a bland belief in democracy, pluralism and multi-partyism in the face of totalitarian regimes, one-party dictatorships and military autocracies such that not enough attention was paid to the conditions, processes and details of the transition forced on the *ancien* ruling cliques. After initial resistance, they displayed a remarkable capacity to adapt to the new conditions to the extent that many of them were able to snatch victory from the proverbial jaws of defeat. Consequently, in some countries you see change without a difference. In others, the challenges of the new dispensation make some people look back at the certainties of the bad old days with some nostalgia. Amidst all these there are some remarkable success stories that appear to be meeting the challenges of democratic transition with deliberate perseverance. But there is a collective lesson about democracy being a process with unpredictable zigs and zags.

From a theological belief in democracy and elections as the litmus test of legitimacy, attention is now shifting to the full infrastructure of democracy. For, no matter how elegant the football pitch and wonderful the players, if the referee is bent the outcome will not be fair. The interest in constitutional development and the fostering of a culture of constitutionalism in Africa is part of a continuing attempt to deepen the democratic struggle and anchor it on our specific experience. In this contribution I take the view that while the particularity of each country is important, it is fundamentally necessary to consider and analyse the broader Pan-African connections. Failure to do so risks limiting the gains that can be made locally. In other words, there are Pan-African possibilities and constraints and opportunities as well as obstacles. A relevant point of commencement of this debate is the issue of citizenship.

Citizenship today

It is certain that any talk of Pan-Africanist constitutionalism must begin with the very sensitive issue of citizenship. Any constitution be it for a private club, a professional association, an NGO, community groups, international organisations or states, must have a definition of its constituency or membership. In addition, it must also contain specific provisions on who can join, how to join and also how membership can be withdrawn both voluntarily or compulsorily. A Pan-African constitution therefore has to define who an African is. On the face of it this should not be difficult. Any citizen of any of the 54 states and Western Sahara that constitute the Organisation of African Unity (OAU) would qualify. Such a constitution will also give full citizenship rights to all persons of African origin in the diaspora. Mahmood Mamdani's seminal book, *Citizen and Subject,* gives a refreshing account and analysis of the contradictory processes of citizenship that has made it such a political time-bomb on the landscape of African politics. The duality of citizenship and subject under one flag has meant that Africans are not equal before the law. 'Citizens' are by and large city people while 'subjects' are confined to the rural area. One is governed by law and has access to due process, while the other is governed by invented custom and constructed tradition that concentrates power in the hands of the local headmen of autocratic central governments. Mamdani's solution is to reform political institutions and power relations so that the rural masses become citizens and can then have reasonable expectation of the rule of law.

A Pan-Africanist constitution must go beyond simply making us Ghanaian, Sudanese, Cameroonian, or Mozambican. It must reaffirm our Africaness with full citizenship rights anywhere we may reside between Cape Town and Cairo, Madagascar and Marrakesh. This is the only way in which we can stop the shame of a Kenneth Kaunda being declared a non-citizen after leading the nationalist movement that gained independence for Zambia and ruleing the country for 25 years. A similar point can be made relating to the attempt by former Cote d'Ivoire President Henri Conan Bedie to declare his rival Alassane Ouattara, former prime minister, a foreigner simply because he dared to aspire to become president. The Christmas eve coup d'etat at the end of 1999 could be said to have partly resulted from this stand-off.

The Kaunda and Ouattara cases received justifiable media attention and political focus because of their class status and political profiles. However, millions of ordinary Africans, who are often descendants of many generations of migrants or long term settlers or residents continue to suffer discrimination and the denial of basic political rights. Such a situation persists because citizenship is still very much tied to indegeneity and 'tribe' when it comes to African populations. That is why most constitutions on this continent go to great lengths to identify 'the tribes' that constitute the country. In some cases, new tribes were even invented in order to justify indegeneity. For example, the 1995 Constitution of Uganda recognised 'Bafumbira' as a Ugandan nationality in order to distinguish Ugandan ethnic Banyarwanda from other Rwandese. Yet there is no history of a people called Bafumbira. However, by popular perception and political practice all Banyarwanda can only have full citizenship rights in Rwanda. Therefore their cousins on the other side of the Bufumbira mountain ranges (Kisoro) that colonial arbitrariness put in Uganda, may feel safer being named after a group of mountains than to be identified with their Banyarwanda kith and kin.

The only group of ethnic or racial minorities that are accommodated in most African post-colonial constitutions as citizens are often non blacks such as Asians, Lebanese or Whites. They can easily be citizens. However, if you have African origins, your citizenship is on the whole prisoner of your assumed ethnic origin. Even these privileged citizens have occasionally suffered from the whimsical denial of their citizenship either as individuals or groups, as was the case with the Asians in Idi Amin's Uganda.

At the level of gender, the citizenship laws in many countries are extremely discriminatory against women for marrying someone from a different country. Even marrying a man from the same country but one from a different ethnic group could invite political victimisation in terms of property rights or, the right to stand for elective office among others. And yet, all of these constitutions have standard provisions about acquiring citizenship such as registration, naturalisation, marriage, etc. Only a minority of the elite are able to take advantage of such provisions while the majority of African populations caught on different sides of borders, Pan-Africanist entrepreneurs (derogatorily referred to as 'smugglers'), long term residents or descendants of migrants from other African countries are regarded as 'aliens' or 'foreigners'. They are often subjected to harassment and extortion by immigration and security officials.

If states cannot award citizenship to all Africans living in their countries a practical thing that can be done would be to remove the obnoxious visa requirements for Africans. Also, the procedure for acquiring citizenship for African residents must be made easier. And finally, the insistence that to be a citizen of one country you must renounce your citizenship of another is a bad law that diminishes the stature of law itself and therefore should be abrogated. In any case, such laws are not really enforceable at a practical level.

Human and people's rights

Such excesses as those recounted above go on without much attention because even the so-called indigenous populations face enormous difficulties in exercising their full citizenship rights. There is no one to look out for the 'aliens.' The business of indigeneity is extremely comical considering the history of migration, settlement, conquest and state formation on the continent.

Who is an indigenous Nigerian, Congolese, Togolese or Ghanaian? When did these countries become indigenous to Africa? What were these peoples before they became Kenyans, Nigerian or Gambians? Are Ewes indigenous to Togo or Ghana? Are Tswana-speaking peoples indigenous to Botswana or South Africa? We can go on *ad infinitum* because these borders are arbitrary. The micro-nationalist focus of the work of our human rights organisations coupled with the country-focus of donor funds combine to militate against sustainable advocacy on behalf of these groups.

The African Charter on Human and People's Rights ratified by a majority of African states in 1981 and acceded to by almost all others since then, offers protection to these groups as both individuals and groups. The charter is unique as a regional instrument because of its treatment of individuals and groups and also its insistence on the equality of all rights whether of the so called first generation (civil and political), the second generation (economic, social and cultural) or solidarity rights (peace, environment and development).

While the issues of individual liberty, civil and political rights have become part and parcel of our daily discourse and focus of work, a lot more needs to be done in the area of group rights. The hegemony of individual libertarianism in the human rights community is part of the Western hegemony at the level of ideas and funding. There is also a disturbing tendency for our NGOs to respond more readily to so-called universal values and the system of rights and institutions like the United Nations, the European Union, and the Commonwealth at the expense of African institutions and charters.

The failure is not just a lack of funds but also a lack of political will. In a Pan Africanist framework, the African Charter on Human and People's Rights would become part of the constitutions of all countries. Rights and protections granted under the charter could be creatively used to change bad laws and local oppressive practices and traditions across the continent. For instance, under the charter it is not possible to deport people *en masse*. You have to specify the crime of each individual. Therefore, the shameful mass expulsions by both the Eritreans and Ethiopians that took place during the bloody war between the two countries would be deemed patently illegal under the charter. African activists, NGOs and civil society must show courage, perseverance and determination to force the hand of governments on these issues. The Pan-African movement along with a number of NGOs from both Ethiopia and Eritrea have lodged formal complaints with the African Commission so that it can pronounce itself on these expulsions.

There are many cases being handled by the commission thanks to the effort of human rights NGOs around the continent. However, the work of the commission and the participation of African NGOs and civil society need to receive more focus. Concerted effort needs to be brought to bear on the commission to improve the quality of its work and also to bolster its courage to engage the critical human rights issues of the day. Finally, the commission needs to transform itself into a court of last resort. It has great potential as a source of legal and constitutional reform.

Putting Africans at the centre

It may sound pedantic to state that an African constitution should guarantee the sanctity of African life. All constitutions contain words to that effect. In practice however, what are our lives worth? It is not enough to guarantee life but the right to the means of sustaining that life must also be protected. The unjust wars on this continent that are daily claiming thousands of lives and the equally unjust economic and political policies that are wrecking lives contradict the affirmation of the right to live. Therefore we have to seek constitutional remedies. The African charter guarantees the right to peace and also the right to development. These rights are usually made non-justiciable in national constitutions yet without these rights there may not be many Africans for the constitution to protect.

If people have a right to peace how do we make this right operational in a bid to stop all the unjust wars on the continent? The right to development must mean people being able to decide the priorities of public spending and to bring sanctions against non-cooperative governments. For instance, how can the people stop the war in the Democratic Republic of Congo (DRC) and the consequent loss of lives? If we don't like the wars what are our options for ending them? It is instructive that none of the countries militarily involved in the DRC sought parliamentary approval for their actions. Furthermore, in a majority of them public discussion about the war is either avoided or denied. Yet national security and regional commitments are the main reasons given for the war. There is something grotesque about governments which cry out to foreigners when it comes to development projects and yet are ever ready to mobilise for and wage wars even with the miniscule reasons they have.

Regional cooperation

As individual states lose their significance, African states are turning to regional cooperation as a means of gaining new relevance. There are two basic problems with this new enthusiasm. In the first instance, they are narrowly focused on economic cooperation despite the fact that these economies are historically competitive rather than cooperative. Secondly, to the extent that they summon the political will to act together, it is primarily on the basis of self-interested security issues. Even the security concerns are narrowly defined as regime security. Poverty or the alienation of the bulk of the people from the political processes which should be considered as the greatest threat to people's security are of no consequence in the leaders' concerns. That is why we have the Monitoring Observer Group (ECOMOG) superimposing itself over the Economic Community of West African States (ECOWAS) and the Political and Security Organ taking precedence over the wider economic and development issues in the Southern African Development Community (SADC). Organisations of this kind are seeking regional cooperation without involving the people. Consequently, military pacts within regional economic groupings tend to receive greater attention from the leaders.

There is thus a great need to democratise regional cooperation by involving all stake holders including elected bodies such as Parliament, political parties, Professional groups, the business community, civil society, NGOs, youth, students, workers and women. Regional cooperation and integration cannot be successful without regional consensus on broad political issues. The limited progress made in the new East African Cooperation Treaty is one step in the right direction. Civil society and other non-governmental forces are being involved. The efficacy of some of the supranational bodies like parliament and a regional court may be questioned, but a start has been made. Civil society must seize the opportunity to go beyond the limited space provided to extend the frontiers of cooperation. Is it not contradictory that many Africans can vote and be voted for in the countries of their former colonial masters and yet have no right of full political participation in an African country no matter how long they may have lived there? If national democratic institutions do not have control over national security how can regional institutions control regional security matters?

Globalisation

There are new threats to state and people's sovereignty by the fundamental changes taking place in the global political economy. The revolution in information technology demonstrated by the onset of electronic mail and the Internet has great democratic potential in terms of access and general communications. However, the economics of globalisation pose a grave threat to the possibilities of democratisation. States as we have traditionally known them are disappearing, and increasingly losing control over major economic decisions as large corporations and dominant countries assert their hegemony over what we eat, drink, the way we live and how we reproduce. For instance, if a country, for whatever reason, decides that it does not want Coca-Cola or McDonald's on its territory the decision cannot hold anymore. Coca-Cola can haul such a country before the World Trade Organisation (WTO) which can compel the offending country to open up or impose sanctions if it remains belligerent.

Already in most of Africa the International Monetary Fund (IMF) and the World Bank are in control of major economic decisions with elected parliaments having little or no influence over national budgets and the allocation of resources. How can democratic (constitutional) control be exercised over institutions and corporations that are so influential in our lives yet are unelected and unaccountable? Most African states are not viable and therefore cannot stand in the way of this globalising roller coaster, but as bigger units regionally and continentally they may be able to manoeuvre politically. The battle between the European Union and the USA government over Caribbean bananas is instructive of future wars over trade and resources. The challenge is to look beyond our borders and link up with other democratic forces that are seeking democratic control of these new threats.

Creating an enduring culture of constitutionalism

The outbreak of processes of constitutional review and the writing of new constitutions across Africa in the last few years may cause one to be cynical about their viability and sustainability. Were there no similar processes in the late colonial period? What happened to most of the independence constitutions? Were they not overthrown, abandoned or manipulated by the ruling elite to deny democracy and institutionalise one party regimes and all kinds of personal rule and life presidencies?

Yes and No. There are no guarantees that the new constitutions will not be manipulated or even overthrown. But we are living in changed and changing circumstances. In the first place, the current constitutional engineering is no longer taking place in Lancaster House, Paris or Lisbon. They are the direct result of political struggles. They signify a political give and take, or in some cases, take it or leave it, among Africans. Optimistically, the constitutions that will emerge will reflect the reality of concrete conditions. One is not unmindful of the manipulation, intimidation and gerrymandering by the powers that be in these circumstances. Many of these constitutions are not the result of any input by different social forces, but rather are made on terms of surrender by retreating discredited military regimes. Such is the case with Nigeria's constitution of 1998. Others, like that of the Gambia, were written to facilitate the mutation of military rule into civilian autocracy. But as they say, 'imitation is the most sincere form of flattery.' It is a triumph for constitutionalism that those rulers are no longer able to rule as they wish and have to seek some form of constitutional cloak in order to legitimise their claims to power.

Secondly, there are determined political groups, civil society organisations and other stakeholders who have placed constitutional change firmly on the agenda. For instance, state repression and political opportunism have not suppressed the efforts of Kenyans for constitutional reform. Even in states like Uganda and Ghana, where the constitutional reform processes were relatively more inclusive, sustained political agitation is continuing to change some fundamental aspects of the constitution in order to guarantee a level playing field.

Africa's present rulers do not have it as easy as the earlier nationalists most of whom enjoyed the complete confidence of the masses. They trusted them to bring Uhuru from their negotiations with the colonialists. Even in the more radical nationalist states and in those that got independence through armed struggle, people trusted the liberation movement as the 'sole representative.' Today's leaders are not that lucky. But this is good news for the nascent movement for constitutionalism in Africa. The distrust and suspicion people have for political leaders means that there is a more active interest in these matters.

There is a growing confidence and resilience of civil society and NGOs in prising open debate and creating opportunities for a more inclusive and participatory constitutional development. As with every opportunity there is also opportunism and danger. One area is the current confusion between civil society and NGOs. The other is the unequal power relationship between donor-friendly NGOs and civil society groups on the one hand, and also the unequal power relations between local NGOs and their donors and international NGOs on the other. There is also the donor-driven impulse that may turn constitutionalism (as with previous issues) into a mere fad, another fanciful project that is fundable but could be dumped in another 3 year funding cycle. Finally, there is the question of the accountability of the groups advocating change. Who do they represent? Who are they accountable to? What is their social responsibility?

These issues cannot be wished away because as the space for democracy opens and the state is forced to make concessions and more victories are recorded, civil society groups and activists also have to raise their democratic quotient. They have to demonstrate in theory and practice the same respect for the rule of law, due process and constitutionalism that they are demanding from the state. In the same way that we cannot build democracy without democrats, it is impossible to establish constitutional regimes if we do not have respect for whatever constitutions we voluntarily enter into. How many pro democracy parties and groups are themselves democratic? How many obey their own constitutions? The widespread practice among NGOs where they are more accountable to their foreign funders than the people they serve, if ever, has to be discouraged. Often their well written project reports, field assessments and annual reports are available locally but regularly sent to funders against the next funding cycle. Running political parties, professional associations, or NGOs like little corner shops is not the best recipe for sustainable constitutionalism. Some of these organisations proclaim their independence so much that one cannot help feeling that they believe and operate as if they are also independent of the people they claim to serve and of the reality of their existence! There are so many uncivil threats to constitutionalism in civil society that have to be checked.

Finally, there is the danger of NGOs and civil society groups operating as if they are themselves governments. In other words, they are intolerant of other stakeholders' claims. They have a legitimate role in governance but they are not the government. Some of them become so anti-government that they exaggerate their capacity to block particular courses of action and end up on the sidelines when some of the changes they have been advocating actually begin to take place.

Armed conflict and constitutionalism in Africa

As 1999 came to a close, Corporal Foday Sankoh, the Revolutionary United Front (RUF) rebel leader in Sierra-Leone, and Major Johnny Paul Koroma former leader of the military junta that had overthrown the elected government of President Ahmed Tejan Kabbah, returned to Freetown. This was the result of a peace deal signed in July and brokered by the regional grouping, ECOWAS/ECOMOG. As part of the deal, Sankoh became vice-president and chairman of the country's Mineral Commission. But, as in the old parable of the leopard and its spots, Sankoh continued to support the atrocities of his insurgents and once again tried his hand at overthrowing the civilian government.

Four years before the Sierra-Leonean deal, a similar arrangement had been reached in Angola with UNITA and Jonas Savimbi whose party had been defeated in popular elections. In order to persuade him to stop the 25 years of carnage in the country, a combination of regional and international pressure by war-fatigued neighbours and Savimbi's international backers forced a deal on the Angolan government to create a second vice-presidency for him. There was even the unprecedented step of gazetting, by a special law, Savimbi's position, status and privileges! To date, Savimbi remains in the bush bent on marching into Luanda.

What is the message from these deals? That whatever the wishes of the electorate, all that a determined and power-hungry militarist has to do is remain long enough in the bush, destroy enough of the country, and be rewarded with a peace deal that will give him (and so far it is only he) a big political post as a reward. Where is the incentive to use constitutional means to obtain legitimate political power? The challenge here is how to achieve a peaceful resolution of armed conflict without appearing to reward impunity and unconstitutional practice.

Participation of the people

It is not a matter for dispute that the widest possible cross section of the people for whom the constitution is meant should participate fully in its drafting and adoption. It is also widely acknowledged that continuing public education through avenues like schools, universities, colleges, newspapers, television, radio, political activities and civic education, is necessary after the adoption of the constitution. Constitutions are no longer the exclusive preserve of lawyers and politicians. However, this democratic aspiration is comprised by the fact that our constitutions are written and operated in foreign languages that are quite inaccessible to a majority of the people. Some states such as Tanzania have made qualitative changes by translating their constitutions into local languages and even using local languages in their parliaments. In a few countries, African languages are used as the official language of government. However, the majority of our states are still trapped in the colonial mindset of believing that foreign languages are more 'convenient' even if inaccessible to the vast majority of the populace.

It is a political challenge to our linguists and cultural activists to advance the cause of popular constitutionalism by translating these documents into local languages. Related to this is the common practice in many of our constitutions of stipulating minimum educational qualifications for elections into specific public offices. Is it not an act of discrimination and denial of democratic rights to say I am not qualified to be voted for yet I can vote for others? Does a state that does not provide universal education to its citizens have a right to demand minimum educational qualifications for elective office? Put differently, shouldn't the requirement for minimum educational standards become a ground for making 'the right to education' justiciable.

The OAU as a source of advancing constitutionalism

The OAU is much maligned as an organisation. And yet, it remains the singlemost important diplomatic and political institution on the African continent. It is currently seeking relevance and renewal. Instead of simply bashing and lashing out against it, it is important for civil society, NGO activists and scholars, to examine what opportunities there are or can be grabbed from its current restructuring and reform process. To the surprise of many Africans at the ordinary summit in Algiers, the OAU adopted a resolution saying 'no' to military coups. The meeting agreed that no leader(s) who have assumed office by military coup will be welcomed at subsequent summits. Many critics consider this a small step but I do not think it is too late. A start must be made somewhere. The challenge is to see how to compel the organisation to measure up to this new standard.

The other significant development was the extraordinary summit of the OAU in Sirte, Libya, that was held from 9 to 11 September 1999. The Sirte Declaration established a framework for OAU reform and the acceleration of the process of African unity. It is not enough to simply snigger at these efforts but to stake our claims and broaden the participation and scope of the reviews. There are a number of issues that African NGOs and civil society can mobilise around and put firmly on the review agenda of the OAU and its agencies; full participation in the proposed African parliament; and also making the proposed African Court on Human Rights very effective. In addition, there must be a review of the OAU Charter that takes into account the possibilities of establishing an African parliament and an African constitutional court, and also takes up the issue of Pan-African citizenship.

In concluding this essay, it is important to note the many challenges ahead in building, consolidating and sustaining constitutionalism in Africa. However, there are also tremendous opportunities. What is necessary for all those who believe they have a stake in the struggle for constitutionalism is to recognise the legitimate claim of all African peoples to be involved in this struggle, and to provide the necessary support to achieve this object.

PART II

ETHNICITY, IDENTITY AND THE ROLE OF CIVIL SOCIETY

5

Culture, Ethnicity and Citizenship: Reflections on Senegal and Rwanda

Bibiane Gahamanyi-Mbaye

In the context of the apparent triumph of ideologies espousing the liberalisation of the economy and globalisation, and a world that has entered its post-industrial phase, Africa seems to be continuing its economic and political regression. Indeed, it appears to be even more at the mercy of ethnic conflict, economic bankruptcy and other forms of deconstruction. Parallel to this state of affairs, we are participating in a revival of political awareness at the internal level and increasing goodwill from African states to play a role in solving African crises, such as those in Sierra Leone.

The reasons for this regression which have been analysed so many times have been attributed to several factors, including the cultural specificity of Africa, ethnicity, the historical context of the creation of African states, and external factors to mention a few. From these (inexhaustive) observations we notice the importance of analysing the notions of culture, ethnicity, citizenship and their interrelation, with the hope of proposing steps for the necessary re-organisation or re-configuration of African politics.

This chapter commences by asking the following questions: is it ethnicity or 'cultural factors' that are a major cause of the civil wars that are affecting African states with increasing frequency? Or is it, on the contrary, a consequence of the construction of the modern post-colonial state, whose decomposition we are today witnessing? In other words, what is the role played by culture and ethnicity in the construction of the state? What of the role of the state in constructing ethnicity? Is globalisation and the promotion of a single model regulated by the market as the only means of development compatible with the plurality of cultures? Does globalisation play a role in stimulating ethnic conflict by frustrating identity demands? Finally, does the decomposition of the post-colonial state lead towards chaos or rather towards a discernible or identifiable reestablishment of African systems and peoples?

The last question presents a link between the cultural, the political and the economic. While this essay cannot pretend to offer comprehensive answers to all these questions, it attempts to explore the mechanisms that link the notions of culture, ethnicity and citizenship in order to explain a tension that is common to a good number of African countries. The radically different itineraries of contemporary Senegal and Rwanda will help us to clarify on the manifestations of these ethnic and citizenship identities at the level of cause and implications.

The chapter commences with a very sketchy resume of the two countries being examined. I give a brief overview of some of the extremely complex concepts that are involved in an examination of culture, citizenship and ethnicity. Thereafter, the essay examines the two countries in more detail paying particular attention to the phenomena of ethnicity and citizenship based partly on the hypothesis that the present situation in Africa proceeds less from cultural particularities than from the phenomenon of negotiating political space.[1] Such renegotiation will eventually lead to the decomposition and recomposition of state systems on the continent.

Comparing Senegal and Rwanda

The two countries are good case studies for an analysis of the process of the construction or deconstruction of the nation state. Rwanda—a former German territory then latterly a Belgian protectorate in East/Central Africa—is made up in the main of adherents of the Catholic religion and witnessed the evolution of an autocratic Hutu State which lasted more than 30 years. In 1994 this culminated in genocide. At the present time, we are witnessing a 'transition' that is trying to establish a pluriethnic state. As one would expect, the economic and socio-political situation in the country is still under the trauma of 1994 and remains precarious. Before colonisation, Rwanda, had already ensured that there was cultural homogeneity within its different ethnic groups (same language, same religious and traditional practices, same social organisations and the same customs relating to marriage, death and birth) because of several factors described below; Rwanda witnessed the reclamation of ethnic identities, a separate and different history for each ethnic group, and supremacy of one of the ethnic groups above the others in turns. All these were coupled with the execution of racist theories and the elimination of one of the ethnic groups by the denial of its national identity and by genocide and finally the on-going attempt to reconstruct the nation and the 'munyarwanda' identity.

By contrast Senegal, an ex-French colony in West Africa, with a populace that ascribes to the mainly Islamic religion, has always been pluriethnic. Ethnicity demands in Senegal have been largely non-violent. Ethnic conflicts are almost non-existent with the noticeable exception of the province of Casamance where the separatist Movement of the Democratic Forces of Casamance (MFDC) (which is predominantly of Diola origin) has been fighting for 18 years. Senegal was also formed around different political realities. The independent state wanted—following the European model—

to homogenise the different cultures and create a single national culture and identity. To do this, it based itself on the Islamic faith and the Wolof language and identity. Judging from the near absence of ethnic problems, from the political stability and the time-tested openness to multipartyism (as long ago as 1974), Senegal could be largely said to have succeeded. At the same time, however, one notes that Senegal's mode of state management has failed to integrate certain ethnic groups, especially those situated outside the groundnut growing area. As a result, some ethnic groups and peripheral territories including Casamance have been marginalised. This is how the Joola protest emerged, culminating in the demand for independence by Casamance, and a problem that has plagued Senegal for 18 years.   .

In many respects however, the situation in Senegal reminds one of several other African countries. Although the country has enjoyed considerable political stability since independence, it still has numerous problems. State institutions have been increasingly 'privatised', the economic situation is extremely precarious and social tensions ending in violence are endemic. We return to a further examination of the two countries following some general conceptual observations on the questions of culture, ethnicity and citizenship.

Culture: Its porousness and plurality

There are several ways in which people understand the notion of culture. In the popular perception that it is most often used, culture is reduced to the artistic expressions of peoples, e.g. dance, music, art...etc. For others, it connotes knowledge rather than anything else. Thus, when we say that a person is 'cultured' or has a lot of culture, it means that he or she has a substantial level of knowledge in all areas of the mind. A cultivated mind is one that has studied and acquired knowledge beyond the common level. Culture, for some people simply corresponds to the notion of ideology that was a cherished concept by Marxists.[2] As a matter of fact, the content differs according to the context, and the concept appears like a 'hold all'[3] such that one could evoke the Marxist culture, the culture of outskirt zones, a musical culture, a Jewish culture, etc. Studying and conceptualising culture has brought out its multidimensional and pluridisciplinary aspects. In essence, it encompasses, the normative as well as the cognitive.

The different conceptualisations of culture have been respectively: the elitist, the holistic, the hegemonic and the pluralistic. The elitist conceptualisation presented culture as an affair of the superior minority, an 'aristocracy.' The majority, the common man or woman, had no culture. This notion presents a code of conduct which can be acquired by studying or by belonging to the appropriate social context.[4] The proponents of the holistic approach believe on the other hand that culture is an entity within which a given society is evolving. The hegemonic theory argues that there is only one culture, that is the one of the dominating group which imposes itself on others. On its part, the pluralists' conception recognises the existence of several cultures or sub-cultures within the same society. It even recognises the existence of 'counter' cultures. The counter culture is the one that emerges in reaction to the 'official' or 'dominant' culture. This notion of the counter-culture ably demonstrates the dynamism and potential of manipulating identities.

The debate about the cultural dimension in Africa can be reviewed through several phases. Towards the end of the colonial period and through to the 1970s, there was an attempt at the rehabilitation and re-ownership of 'African cultures.' These varied from theories such as 'negritude' to the triumph of culturalism, *via* 'Third World' theories. Thereafter, an era of 'developmentalism' followed during which the phenomenon of culture was re-examined in close relationship with its contribution to or role in development. Today, these two theories seem to have lost their importance mainly due to the emergence of the theory of human rights, the advancement of information communication technologies (ICT) and the phenomenon of globalisation.

Cultural relativism or culturalism

Cultural relativism or culturalism is a well-known thesis of anti-universalism in the field of human rights. According to this theory, since every value or norm is related to its culture of origin, it cannot be applied to the whole of humanity. This theory comes directly from decolonisation as it affirms plurality and differences in equality. It is this relativism which gave birth to the phenomenon of 'third worldism'.

Having started off from a premise which refuted the hegemony of a model culture and its supremacy or superiority, culturalism however produced some monstrosities. This is why, for example, during the Stockholm conference[5], African women adamantly defended sexual mutilation as practised on small girls in the name of cultural relativism. The people who rose against these practices were regarded as imperialists and colonialists. Using the same argument, African dictators have justified single parties and their authoritarianism.

The era of human rights and the principle of the right to interfere have pushed back culturalism by 'levelling norms.' It has also institutionalised humanity as the guardian of the norms which henceforth have become universal. Finally, the triumph of the market economy and communication technologies has widened even more this opening on the sovereignty of states.

Culture, development and globalisation

The process of linking culture and development emerged as a result of studies on the failure of the development theories that were applied to Africa. For some people, this simply meant justification of this failure through 'cultural behaviour' (nepotism, ethnicity etc.). Others view such cultural behaviour and development or non-development, as a relationship of reciprocal causality. The eternal question of links between governance and development, for example, finds their place here. Although there seems to be a consensus on the necessity to adopt a holistic approach to development problems, with a fitting place to be accorded to cultural identities, challenges linked to 'how' this will be done will start emerging.

Globalisation and the marked advancement of communication technologies have broken down state frontiers and sovereignties. Multilateral institutions and large multinational companies increasingly intervene in the formulation of national economic policies. Nothing can stop the advance of ideas and images. The cultural model of the West is penetrating every household. In addition, with the younger generations who never experienced colonisation and decolonisation, and thus do not suffer any complexes we are witnessing in the words of Suleiman Bachir Diagne; 'a true renewal of the feeling of excellence since the end of the 70s of culture and the democratic values of the West, as well as the will to recenter culture on oneself.'[6] This message has been widely circulated, causing diverse and contradictory reactions.

Ethnicity and citizenship

The meaning and explanation of ethnicity cannot be understood out of context. In fact, certain aspects of ethnicity are inherited while others are continually re-invented; in order to respond to new needs.[7] Nevertheless, the five approaches proposed by J. Lonsdale summarise the different theories that have been formulated on the issue of ethnicity: -

- The 'modernists' (non-Marxists) explain ethnicity as an African cultural factor, bound to disappear with the modernisation of African countries and increasing cultural assimilation.
- Ethnicity or tribalism is simply a reaction to the exploitation and oppression of state power, and is in fact a product of modernity.
- Ethnicity can also be the result of the creation of states and the introduction of policies of divide and rule by the colonialists. Contrary to the preceeding theory where ethnicity was a defensive reaction, this theory contends that ethnicity is invented and used for accessing power.
- According to Marxist theorists, ethnicity stems from a 'false consciousness'

of people caused by the ideological manipulation of the African bourgeoisie who lead the state and its enterprises. These ideological manipulations make these leaders appear to be 'representatives' of their ethnic groups or tribes instead of what they really are, i.e. exploiters.

Ethnic groups are culturally distinct groups within a state. These groups retain their cultural identity even when they accept and operate within the institutional framework of the state.[8] What process leads this 'natural' phenomenon to become a source of conflict? What are the causes of the resurgence of ethnicity (ethnic revival) that almost all the regions of Africa are currently experiencing? By what means can we maintain a positive ethnicity (or what J. Lonsdale calls 'moral ethnicity'), that is compatible and complementary to full citizenship?

In order to explain the creation and consolidation of ethnic identities that question citizenship by resorting to belonging to a native soil—a phenomenon D. Horowitz termed 'struggles over belonging'—I will briefly trace the evolution of the situation in Senegal and Rwanda, from the colonial period until the present.

The creation of modern Rwanda: Reviewing the ethnic and cultural invention of the Bahutu and Batutsi.

It must be recalled that the Banyarwanda,[9] namely the Bahutu, Batwa[10] and Batutsi all speak the same language—Kinyarwanda and live in the same territory: some parts of the country however, could have more inhabitants of one group than the other. This aspect, together with some form of organisation fascinated the Europeans who wanted to have nation-states that are culturally homogenous.

Before colonisation, Rwanda did not have its present socio-political set-up. Power was not centralised and certain regions were traditionally refractory to the *mwami* (king) of Rwanda. Certain parts of the north and the northwest *(Bushiru, Bugoyi, Busozo)* were administered by Hutu *bahinza* and *bakande*, in an autonomous manner and they kept a symbolic allegiance to the mwami of Rwanda. The south and centre, known as Nduga, were directly under the administration of the mwami. For the Rwandese from the north (the majority being Hutu) the Rwandese from the South, both Hutus and Tutsi, were called the *Banyanduga,* or the *Tutsi* or even *Banyiginya* (royal clan). The majority of those who were called moderate Hutu turned out to be from the centre or the South. The people from the north were the *Bakiga*, who were 'crude' mountain dwellers (both Hutu and Tutsi). By the time of colonisation, the bami of Rwanda had not yet concretised the political integration of these regions into central Rwanda.

Between 1925 and 1930, the Belgian authorities attached the administration of the Hutu peripheral principalities to central Rwanda. The *Bahinza* were deprived of their powers and the administration entrusted to Tutsi who came from the south. The colonial power installed all over Rwanda a Tutsi hegemony and deposed all the Hutu *Batware*, so as to replace them with Tutsi ones. The 'bami' considered dangerous were eliminated.[11] The traditional structures of governance and social organisation—guarantors of social cohesion—were destroyed.strictly hierarchical responsibilities for the 'chief' and 'sub-chief', structured according to the European style, with territorial demarcations, were institutionalised and allocated to Tutsi only. All the politico-administrative functions within the region, the chieftaincy and the sub-chieftaincy were also made hereditary. The Hutu thus found themselves cut off from the reins of power and a Tutsi monopoly was institutionalised.[12] The Tutsi chiefs, closely controlled by the Belgian colonial administration and with no real powers of decision making, were only instruments of oppression serving the coloniser who had the power to depose them at will.

It should be noted in this connection that the Belgian colonial administration, even though it was termed indirect, was one of the most direct systems of colonial control. Forced labour—*uburetwa*—was institutionalised; Tutsi chiefs and sub-chiefs were responsible for supplying humanpower. An ethnic division marked by the mode of attributing power to only Tutsi and the 'aristocratisation' of the same was born. The Rwandese, in particular the educated elite, were fed with 'biblical and racist anthropological'[13] theories, quickly assimilated them and identified themselves with them, thus creating new Tutsi and Hutu identities. The Hutu were to be the real indigenous people and the Tutsi became 'foreign invaders.' In this context at the end of the 1950s, the elite Hutu, educated by Catholic missions and with the help of missionaries, formed PARMEHUTU (Party for the Emancipation of the Hutu People). The Tutsi chiefs who wanted to keep their power and liberate themselves from the colonialists created UNAR (National Rwandese Union) which tried to mobilise the Hutu and Tutsi around the independence of Rwanda and under the authority of the mwami and the Tutsi chiefs.

The two eternal allies, the colonial power and the church, made a complete turn around by supporting PARMEHUTU in their struggle and fighting the Tutsi who by this time had attracted their enmity by demanding for independence and linking up with other nationalistic African movements.[14] The Tutsi chiefs were retired and Hutu chiefs replaced them. Hatred against the Tutsi culminated in the pogroms of 1959. Under this climate of violence, the United Nations organised a referendum (*Kamarampaka*) for or against the abolition of the monarchy, at the same time as legislative elections, which in any case were boycotted by UNAR. The 'social revolution' of the Hutu kept the Tutsi and the king away from power. The latter, labelled oppressors were chased away, dispossessed of their goods and/or exterminated. They left the country by the hundreds of thousands, while tens of thousands were massacred. Those who stayed in the country and survived were considered second class citizens, continually victims of pogroms and discrimination of all types. The written history of Rwanda, taught in schools up to the 1980s, was modelled to give license to the racist theories implanted by the colonialists.[15] The regional element was also dominant, as we saw that the northern and southern regions did not have the same political history and were even in conflict.

The first president of independent Rwanda was Gregoire Kayibanda, Secretary of the Archbishop of Rwanda Mgr. Perraudin. This first president was not elected, despite the provisions of the constitution. The constitution of 24 November 1962 underscored the power of the people through the parliamentary regime, the president of the republic was subjected to the control and sanction of a national assembly which could use the censureship motion against him. The first amendment to this constitution saved the president from the test of the ballot.

The second revision to the constitution was enacted under the law of May 18, 1973. It installed the system of 'democratic socialism' and modified executive powers by substantially strengthening the functions of the president. From that point onwards, the term of office of the president was prolonged from 4 to 5 years; the limitation of successive terms of offices fixed at 3, and the limit at 60 years for candidates to presidential elections were both abolished.[16]

The above amendment reflected the desire of the ruling clique to cling to power. In particular, it reflected the wish of the first president of the Rwandese republic after 11 years in power to convert his tenure into a life presidency. Multipartyism was replaced by the single party,[17] namely PARMEHUTU— which, as its name clearly states, represented only the Hutu). The other parties of the time, UNAR, RADER (Democratic Reassembling for the Republic) and APROSOMA (Association for the Social Progress of the Masses) were dismantled and their leaders, either massacred, imprisoned or exiled.[18] Politics in Rwanda became increasingly ethnicised. In addition, the people from the central and southern regions—the birth region of the president—were favoured. The frustration of those from the north forced some of them, to support the *coup d'etat* of then Major Juvenal Habyalimana, the chief of the 'Etat Major' of the Rwandese army, who came from the north. The first president and the dignitaries of the regime, all from the southern region, were assassinated shortly after.[19] Following the coup of 5 July 1973, a new constitution was enacted, and a new party, the Movement for the National Revolution and Development (MRND) was formed. Every Rwandese individual was entitled to be a member of the party. Nevertheless, the fact was that the party remained effectively closed to non-Hutu. F. Reytjens, a Belgian lawyer who at the time was very close to President Habyalimana, has written: 'the second republic and its constitution, is Juvenal Habyalimana.'[20]

The manifesto of the founding chairman and the Status of the Movement were more important than the constitution and the laws. This is how the system of regional and ethnic quotas, imperatively applied to all sectors was not in any legal text but rather in one of the manifestos of the founding president and in the statutory documents of the MRND.[21] Not only did the rules issued by the executive contradict the constitution but none of the constitutional provisions guaranteeing public freedoms was respected.

Right from the beginning of the second Republic, every 'ethnic group' and region was given a quota that was meant to represent their respective numbers within the total population. In reality however, the system was aimed at ensuring and sustaining the supremacy of the Hutu from the North in all areas of life. These quotas were introduced in the fields of education, employment, and the private sector. In some areas, however, they were far from respected. For example, in the army[22] or in the area of local government, one could hardly find any Tutsi. The injustice that Rwanda experienced during the colonial period was not corrected by the 'social revolution' which simply reversed and aggravated the situation by institutionalising 'state racism.' Inspired by the colonial model, the first two republics which lasted from 1962 up to 1994 were based on racism and exclusion.

The first republic (1962-1973), with all the good conscience of support by strong anthologies, confiscated the identity of the state. Rwanda became Hutu country. The Hutu, also called *rubanda nya mwishi* (the majority of the people) by the authorities became synonymous with legitimacy. To be Tutsi became a disadvantage, an original sin—a sin that must be expatiated. Accompanying all these processes was the invention of the Hutu culture which, in fact, was a counter culture in that it took the opposite of all that closely or slightly resembled the norms, practices and attitudes in use at the *ibwami* (the royal court) or in the big Tutsi families. The second republic (1972-1994) did not question this process. However, the systematic massacre of Tutsi ended and was instead channelled into systematic political discrimination in all areas of socio-economic life. At the same time, the right to return to their country was denied to the 'oldest refugees of Africa,' under the pretext that there was not enough space in Rwanda. The founder myth of the 2 republics was 'Hutuism' or power to the Hutu (which later became 'Hutu power') a phenomenon on which the 1959 social revolution was based, and which led to the massacre and genocide of the Tutsi and moderate Hutu in 1994. Collectively, the two republics lasted from 1962-1994 a period of more than three decades. If one counts the colonial period it makes a total of 75 years of practising a policy with either strong pro-Tutsi or pro-Hutu racist connotations. What has happened since 1994?

The role of the RPF

In 1990, the Rwanda Patriotic Front (RPF) made a serious disruption of the Rwandese political scene with the declaration of a liberation war. The population that was under the influence of racist ideologies, that had been gradually inculcated, did not believe the rallying speeches of the RPF that made reference to the whole of the nation and not to ethnic belonging. On the whole, the factor of ethnic solidarity did play a part. The major factor however, remains close supervision and maintenance of a political machine that was well organised and determined to execute a well-planned programme. The genocide was executed by the militia of the ruling party together with the military and the misled people. The RPF triumphed and put an end to the genocide in July 1994. Since 1994, and for the first time since independence, the state of Rwanda has become pluriethnic, although the army, the Rwanda Patriotic Army (RPA) the main element of the new power, is in the majority made up of Tutsi. This aspect stems from the non-application of the Arusha Accord which envisaged the creation of a national army through the combination of the two warring armies. Due to the role played by the Armed Forces of Rwanda (FAR) in the genocide, the integration of the FAR elements will not take place according to the modalities provided for by the Protocol of the Accord on the integration of the armed forces from the two sides. It will be done by selecting the 'sane individuals, who had not personally been compromised by reprehensible acts.'[23] Nonetheless, what is essential and new to note is the possibility for any Rwandese who feels like it, to enrol in the RPA.

The period of transition that was originally envisaged to last 5 years has been prolonged by an additional four years, and will end in 2003. This time must be used to give root to the rule of law. In spite of the difficulties which are almost insurmountable, some crucial phases have been covered. The choice in favour of a State of Law has been clearly indicated and the legal institutions are slowly settling in: exceptional jurisdictions have been repealed, the supreme court has been reinstalled, the High Council of the Magistrature, elected by peer members has been created. In the same vein, a bar and a National Commission of Human Rights have been created for the first time since independence. Finally, a Constitutional Commission has also been put in place as envisaged by the Fundamental Law. The commission will be responsible for making consultations with the people and formulating the constitution which will be used after the transition.

Senegal and the promotion of 'the Islam-Wolof'

Senegal was constructed during the colonial period from several kingdoms and ethnic groups in the area. The country of the Wolof where the groundnut trade was to be developed played a central role. France used the direct mode of administration passing through 'traditional' chiefs who were chosen by its agents. The legitimacy of these chiefs varied according to each case. But one could generally note that the area placed under their jurisdiction was bigger than the territories formerly under their control.[24] Coming from a system of direct administration, these chiefs had no power and were simply intermediaries 'solely serving to transmit orders' from the district commissioner,[25] the only state authority. This same period brought to light several Muslim brotherhood and Muslim chiefs (called *Marabout*); mainly due to their capacity to produce ground nuts. The *Marabout* were also used by France as intermediaries and whole 'communes' were put under their control.[26]

Another significant aspect of French colonial administration was the policy of assimilation and the attribution of different statuses to the indigenous people. These were French citizens or subjects respectively, according to whether they were natives of the urban centres of Saint Louis, Dakar, Rufisque or Gorée or the rural area of Senegal. These 4 communes, (all in Wolof country) were the only ones with 'full rights,' i.e. administratively and politically governed according to the norms of the metropole.

Aware of the advantages that one could gain from political assimilation, the Senegalese did not oppose the system and used it to secure the status of French citizenship for all. In turn however, they resisted cultural assimilation and used Islam to this end.[27] The struggle of the Senegalese was centred on how to obtain French citizenship without being subjected to the civil code. Before independence, there was a bill that accorded autonomy to the colonies. The period of independence was not an interruption. As Mamadou Diouf explains, the elected political leaders have never questioned the institutional model of the metropolitan state.[28] All that they opposed was the dichotomy between the theory and governmental practice of metropolitan France and those in progress in the colonies. These were based on an autocratic theory of administration and not one of participatory government.

Independence did not result in a fundamental breaking away from the colonial system. Rather, it was characterised by continuity in the political process, dominated by the alliance of the neo-traditional authorities, the *marabouts*, and the newly elected political leaders. The latter were elected thanks to the support of the former. The heads of religious groupings were the principal supporters of state power in the rural areas. In return, the state ensured that they maintained and consolidated their privileges and granted them favours. The structures and resources of the state were utilised for constituting, strengthening and expanding the network of its customership.

The Senegalese constitution of 1962 adopted a double tier parliamentary system with Mamadou Dia and Leopold Sedar Senghor becoming *Président du Consiel de Ministers* and prime minister respectively. Very quickly, a mis-understanding stemming from different economic choices provoked a crisis, following which a strong presidential system with Senghor at its head was adopted. During this period, African Socialism[29] also became the official state ideology, and President Senghor its chief theoretician. In the absence of a class of local businesspeople, the state was going to be on the one hand an instrument of national development and promote the grooming of a local bourgeoisie, and on the other used to 'establish and consolidate the material base of power.'[30] The philosophy of 'negritude' and African Socialism were serving as the theoretical reference-points for the construction of Senegalese national identity.

Following the economic crisis of 1968, another political crisis broke out in 1970 where the discomfort of peasants was manifest under Prime Minister Abdoul Ahad Mbacke, the Khalife of the Mourides groupings.[31] In response, the post of one of the most influential religious 'ministers' was created and a change at the level of political elites brought some 'technocrats' to power and a multipartyism limited to 3 years and then to 4 years was institutionalised. However, the regime was still presidential and the role of the prime minister was counterbalanced by French cooperation agents, advisors to the president, mainly in the economic field.

The work of consolidating the state in Senegal came to its climax during the first 2 decades of independence. The particularity of this system was the great mastery and capacity to manoeuvre that the political leaders exhibited in manipulating the political machine. The exercise of power was based on a subtle mixture of 'negotiation and buying of allegiance' plus strict repression.[32] Under the instigation of donors and following a serious economic and social crisis that erupted at the end of the 1970s, the 'entrepreneur' state began to disinvest itself. Senghor resigned from his presidential functions at the beginning of the 1980s. To ensure succession in favour of Abdou Diouf who was then prime minister, Senghor appropriately modified the constitution. Abdou Diouf thus managed to succeed to the presidency without major problems except for some disgruntlement within the ruling party.

The Abdou Diouf period has been characterised as one of continuity within change. Although several economic and political innovations (unlimited multipartyism) new agricultural economic and educational policies came to light, the political management did not question the system of 'sharing tasks and negotiation,' nor the use of repression, or 'mercenary support,'[33] as the pillars of Senegalese stability. On the eve of presidential elections in early

2000, the political situation came to a head. Discontent about the persisting economic crisis was apparent, in spite of official speeches touting the 'recovery.' The social cost of structural adjustment programmes (SAPs), the endemic unemployment and the unpunished politico-financial scandals of the political elite, all provoked real discontent. Like Togolese President Eyadema, Abdou Diouf announced that if his term of office was extended, he would subsequently retire and not present himself as a presidential candidate anymore. For the first time in Senegal's history, however, a run-off presidential election in March 2000 resulted in the defeat of the Socialist Party (PS) and its candidate Abdou Diouf, and the triumph of his archrival Abdoulaye Wade.

The question of Casamance

In 1981, the Movement of the Democratic Forces of Casamance (MFDC) and its armed wing, ATIKA, commenced an armed struggle for the independence of the southern region of Casamance. The immediate cause of the conflict, unlike in Rwanda, was not the leaders but the masses. The underlying factors as we saw above were structural, economic, political and cultural. The structural causes were linked to the nature of the state in Senegal, first of all from the geographic point of view. Casamance is partially separated by Gambia from the rest of Senegal. Gambia cuts across Senegal, a fact that accentuates the territorial isolation of Casamance. In addition, the theory of negritude preached by the regime of Senghor was based on the affirmation of Negro-African values and the opening to the West. This policy officially overshadowed the cultural and ethnic realities of the region while using them for political games instead of developing them into an integrationist policy. Finally, this region has never been integrated into the economic and administrative networks which link the regions to the centre. Consequently, Casamance has been economically marginalised by policies practised throughout the last three decades of independence.

The political authorities either did not know how to or did not want to integrate Casamance economically. Since colonial times, the economy of Senegal has been based on the groundnut trade and the policies of Senghor and his successor respected the interests of the colonial powers. The region has not been integrated into the network of national economic activities and the problem of the salinisation of the soil by sea water has reduced the productivity of the rice fields and thereby undermined the self sufficiency of the people of Casamance.[34] All these problems have not been dealt with by the Senegalese state. This has provoked a feeling of injustice more so due to the fact that the inhabitants of Casamance are conscious of the real potential of their region.

The cultural question here is linked to the 'invasion' by the Northerners, to cultural particularities and to the religion of the Joola. The immigrants who came from the northern regions arrived with their own dynamism, language, religion and customs. To employ the theories of the extreme right-wing parties, one could say that the ethnic and linguistic balance was upset by the arrival of the Saloum-Saloum, the Wolof, and other Toucouleurs. The feeling of invasion was aggravated by the distribution of land in urban centres like Ziguinchor to the new comers and by the subsequent expropriation of some locals who were given land outside the urban centres.[35]

To compount the problem, the administration was headed by Northerners. This in itself would be a sufficient cause of conflict in a society with traditional horizontal organisational structures, especially if it is imposed by 'foreigners'. In effect, the Joola society is not hierarchical and does not have a caste system like the Wolofs or the Toucouleurs or the other stratified societies in the country. The term 'Casamancian problem' hides a problem which is specifically Joola, one of the ethnic groups of the lower Casamance. The Joola resort to their land to express themselves and use a version of the history of their region which is somehow manipulated in order to demand independence. In addition, reference to the republic of Joola is exclusive and accords rights, on this part of Casamance, only to Joola. It is instructive that despite a lull in the fighting over the period of the presidential election and a short honeymoon thereafter, hostilities resumed. Quite clearly the Casamance question will remain a major issue within the context of Senegal's continuing struggle for democracy,

Conclusion

The situations which we have just seen are fundamentally different; war in Rwanda and the genocide were provoked by the leaders whereas the conflict in Casamance was provoked by the masses. However, the causes that determine the construction of conflicting ethnic identities in essence are similar. They stem from the nature of the state and its institutional weaknesses, economic crises, discriminatory policies, or those perceived factually as such and culturally exclusive identities of the states. At the beginning of the colonial state, the 'collusion' between African social structures and the European system provoked the politicisation of ethnicity in order to negotiate new political space. In the same manner, with the manifest failure of the colonial and post-colonial state in the construction of the nation-state (and in certain cases like Rwanda, its fall)[36], we are witnessing a repositioning of negotiation spaces within the new systems that are still being created.

According to Brown, the politicisation of ethnicity and its manipulation by the elite in order to seize power seems to have been the biggest immediate cause of ethnic violence. The biggest problem was, according to him, 'the bad leaders.'[37] However, it is obvious that this reason cannot suffice to explain the many problems in independent Rwanda. Brown, therefore, poses the following question: 'why do the leaders lead and why do the followers follow?' In addition to the immediate causes, there are underlying ones, including the structural, economic, political and cultural. In Rwanda's case, they are linked to the historical process of state formation to the economic crisis, and to the political, economic and social discrimination to which the Tutsi were subjected. It is also linked to external reasons such as the role of Belgium, France and the United Nations. Understanding these processes is central to the solution of ethnicity in this century.

Notes

1. Mbembe (1999).
2. See Worsley (1984).
3. Diagne and Ossebi (1996): 5.
4. Worsley, op. cit.: 44.
5. See Diagne & Ossebi op. cit.: 8.
6. *Ibid*: 12.
7. *Ibid*.
8. Clay (1998).
9. In some areas of the Great Lakes region, such as Congo, 'Banyarwanda' is assimilated to an ethnic group, in reference to the indigenous people who speak Kinyarwanda, both Hutu and Tutsi combined. One can thus be Munyarwanda without being of Rwandese nationality.
10. The Batwa who were characterised as Pygmoids by colonial anthropology, constitute one of the 3 components of the Rwandese people. Unfortunately, they are very few in number and the bloody conflicts between the Hutu the Tutsi have largely overshadowed their situation.
11. The Mwami Yuhi Misinga who was in power up to the moment when the Belgians replaced the Germans, was deposed and sent into exile in the Belgian Congo. His son, Mutara Charles Rudahigwa was enthroned in his place upon his death. He managed with time to convince the Rwandese about his legitimacy and began some social reforms (one of which was the abolition of the buhaka client list system based on the ownership of cows); and the demand for independence. His death in 1959—following an infection administered by a European doctor—has never been clarified. The post mortem report was rejected for political reasons. Since that time, heavy suspicion has weighed on the Belgians who have never explained this death.
12. See Twagiramutara (1992).
13. See, Chretien (1997), and Prunier (1995).
14. Leaders like Lumumba and Nasser were much appreciated by the UNAR, with the latter even extending some financial support to the organisation.
15. For an analysis of the falsification of the history of Rwanda, see Chretien *op.cit.*
16. Reyntjens (1982): 24.
17. For more details see Mubashankwaya (1971): 322.
18. For an historical analysis of political parties in independent Rwanda, see Tabara *op. cit.*
19. President George Kayibanda and another fifty highly placed individuals in his regime mysteriously died in detention.
20. See, Reyntjens *op.cit.*: 24.
21. A collection of these speeches exist and is the process of being published.
22. See Twagiramutara *op. cit.*

23. Declaration du FPR du 17/07/1994 Relative a la Mise en Place des Institutions.
24. Diouf (1993): 228.
25. *Sovernor Vanvolen hoven*, quoted by Douf, *idem*.
26. *Ibid.*
27. Lambert (1993).
28. M. Diouf *op. cit.*
29. For more details on African socialism, see L.S. Senghor (1961).
30. See Diop et Diouf (1990), op.cit: 1.
31. It must be mentioned that Moslem religious leaders were the principal supporters of Senghor in the rural areas. This aspect was fundamental in determining his success in the 4 communes, for example against Lamine Gueye of Saint Louis.
32. Diop et Diouf *op. cit.*, 11.
33. For a description of this system, see Diop and Diouf *op.cit.*
34. *Idem.*
35. *Idem.*
36. Mazrui (1995).

References

Baylis, J. and Steve Smith (Eds.) (1997) *The Globalisation of World Politics*, Oxford University Press.

Brown, Michel E. (1996) 'The Causes and Regional Dimensions of Internal Conflict,' in Michel E. Brown, (ed.) *The International Dimensions of Internal Conflict*, Studies in International Security, 575.

Clay, J. W (1998) 'The Ethnic Future of Nations in World Politics,' *Third World Quarterly*, vol. 11 (4), October.

Chretien, J. P. (1997) *Le defi l'ethnisme au Rwanda et au Burundi 1990-1996*, Khartala.

Diagne, Sulieman Bachir et Henri Ossebi (1996), *La question culturelle en Afrique: contextes, enjeux et perspectives de recherche*. CODESRIA, Document de travail 1.

Diop, M.C. (ed.) *Senegal: Essays in Statecraft*, Dakar: CODESRIA.

_____ et M. Diouf (1990) *Le Sengal sous Abdou Diouf: Etat et Societe*, Khartala.

Horowitz, D.L. (1993) 'The Challenge of Ethnic Conflict: Democracy in Divided Societies' in *Journal of Democracy*, vol.4 (4), Oct.

Kaarsholm P. and J. Hultin, (1994) 'Inventions and Boundaries: Historical and Anthropological Approaches to the Study of Ethnicity and Nationalism,' Occasional Paper no. 11. International Development Studies, Roskilde University.

Lambert M.C (1993) 'From Citizenship to Negritude: Making a Difference in Elite Ideologies of Colonized Francophone West Africa' in *Comparative Studies in Society and History, An Alternative Quarterly* (35) 2.

Logiest, G. (1998) *Mission au Rwanda*, Bruxelles, Didier-Hatier.

Mazrui, Ali A. (1995) 'Social Engineering and Political Bridge-Building For the 21ˢᵗ Century: An African Agenda' in *African Development Review.*

Mafeje, Archie (——) 'African Socio-cultural Formation in the 21ˢᵗ Century,' in *Revue Africaine de Development.*

Mbembe, A. (1999) 'Du gouvernment prive indirect' *Serie etat de la literature* CODESRIA, 1-

Mubashankwaya, M. (1971) *Le Rwanda depius 1959. Evolution politique, economique et sociale. Aix, Universite de provence* (these de 3eme cycle).

Prunier G. (1995) *The Rwanda Crisis: 1959-1994 History of a Genocide.*

Noli, Okwudiba (ed.) (1998) *Ethnic Conflicts in Africa,* CODESRIA.

Raporo y'Inama y'Abaperezida yongeye gusuzumu umushinga w'itegeko rogenga imitunganyirize y'ikurukirana ry'ibyanha bigize icyaha cy'itsembatsemba n'itsembabwoko cyangwa ibyaha byibasiye inyoko mintu. Inteko ishinga amategeko, N 112/Ano. /1996.

Reyntjens, F. (1989) *Rwanda; Constitutions Africae,* 1ˢᵗ Semestre.

Shivji, I.G. 'A New Democratic Perspective,' in I.G. Shivji (ed.) *African Debate on Democracy*

Sindjoun, L. 'Les nouvelles constitutions africanes et la politique internationale: contribution a une economie internationale des biens politico-constitutionels,' in *Afrique 2000* no. 22.

Tabara, P. (1992) Afrique: *La face cachee,* La Pensee Universelle, Paris.

Twagiramutara P. (1992) *Conflits ethniques en Afrique: le cas du Rwanda,* CODESRIA, seminaire de Nairobi, 16-18 Nov.

——, *Etat multipartisan, pluralisme ethnique, populisme et democratie,* Departement des Sciences Sociales, Universite Nationale du Rwanda (Butare).

Worsley P. (1984) *The Three Worlds: Culture and World Development,* London, Weidenfield & Nicolson.

6

Liberating African Civil Society: Towards a New Context of Citizen Participation and Progressive Constitutionalism

Peter Mukidi Walubiri

Numerous constitutions in Africa—present and past—open with the lofty expression 'we the people....'[1] The preamble to the Constitution of the Peoples Republic of Mozambique 1975 is even more captivating. It begins with the expression 'Mozambicans' and ends with the phrase 'Mozambicans, Women and Men, this is the first state in which power belongs to us....'

The literal meaning of these expressions is that the constitution and the process leading up to its promulgation, future implementation and development belong to the people of the African nation concerned. Ultimately, the message conveyed is that the constitution is derived from the people. For example, in Sierra Leone a new constitution was adopted in 1978.[2] It had a very long preamble parts of which stated,

> AND WHEREAS the British during the period of their colonisation of this country governed Sierra Leone under an authoritarian system which did not tolerate any political opposition but nevertheless they required us to adopt a multi-party system (with an inbuilt opposition element) as a sine qua non to the granting of independence, all of which tantamounted to our adopting a political system completely at variance with the system which the British had practiced with us.

The preamble then went on to highlight how the multiparty experiment instituted at independence had failed in Sierra Leone and had instead bred disharmony, political instability, unrest and economic problems. It ended with a solution: - 'THEREFORE we the people of Sierra Leone proclaim this *one-party* Republican Constitution....' (emphasis added)

By this deed 'the people' of Sierra Leone were getting rid of the imported multiparty system and through a home grown constitution adopted a one party republican constitution as a solution to their national problems. We now have the hindsight of history to appreciate that the 'peoples' solution of 1978 did not work in Sierra Leone. The history of many African states with their constant change of constitutions has not been much brighter.

Beyond such preambles that exalt the role of the people in constitutionalism, the substantive articles in the constitutions of many African states proclaim that sovereignty resides in the people. For example the 1980 Constitution of the Republic of Togo proclaimed as follows, 'sovereignty shall be vested in the Togolese people who shall exercise it by their representatives or in a referendum.'[3] In Guinea-Bissau, the constitution proclaimed that national sovereignty of the Republic of Guinea-Bissau lay with the people.[4]

In almost similar terms the 1995 Constitution of the Republic of Uganda provides that all power belongs to the people who shall exercise their sovereignty in accordance with the constitution:[5] 'All authority in the state emanates from the people and the people shall be governed through their will and consent.'[6] Seen in this context constitutionalism is a process of actualising the sovereignty of the people. It is about empowering the people to more fully participate in the nation's body politic at all levels. However, this begets several questions. Who are the people? Have they in the past and are they at present actually involved in the constitutional processes in their countries? If not, how can they be empowered to fully participate in the processes of constitutional government?

In an attempt to grapple with these questions, this chapter in the first instance discusses the concept of constitutionalism before analysing how the people in different African contexts have through civil society and other means attempted to exercise their sovereignty. The obstacles that have enfeebled the effective role of civil society in constitutionalism will then be discussed before focusing on the challenge of liberating African civil society to enable it play a more meaningful role in contemporary constitutional developments shaping the African continent.

Revisiting the concept of constitutionalism

Up to the eighteenth century most scholars viewed constitutionalism in terms of the general system of government as laid out in the written or unwritten constitution. They saw this constitution as a set of fixed principles of reason. In 1733, Bolingbroke stated as follows:

> By constitution, we mean whenever we speak with propriety and exactness that assemblage of laws, institutions and customs, derived from certain fixed principles of reason...that compose the general system according to which society hath agreed to be governed.[7]

Later in the same century constitutionalism came to be identified with the written constitution. Thomas Paine stressed that a constitution is not an act of government but of a people constituting government, and government without a constitution is power without a right.[8] The concern here was that government should derive its powers from the constitution. The limit and content of that power was not an issue at this stage nor was it seriously contended that power should be derived from the people themselves and not from the constitution.

However, in this century the concern shifted to the desire to democratise government by controlling the extent of governmental powers. The demand shifted to limited government.[9] In this vein, Professor Vile argued that western institutional theorists have concerned themselves with problems of ensuring that the exercise of governmental powers which is essential to the realisation of the values of their societies should be controlled in order that it should not itself be destructive of the values it was intended to promote.[10]

The concept of constitutionalism has now developed to become a critical ingredient of the broader process of human development. Human development is the process of enlarging people's choices. The choices are created by expanding human capabilities and functions—what people can and cannot do with their lives.[11] These capabilities are to lead to long and healthy lives, to be knowledgeable and to have access to the resources needed for a decent standard of living. But many additional choices are valued by people. These include political, social, economic and cultural freedom, a sense of community, opportunities for being creative, promoting self-respect and protecting human rights. Yet, human development is more than just achieving these capabilities; it is also the process of pursuing them in a way that is equitable, participatory, productive and sustainable.[12]

The pursuit of human development in an equitable, participatory, productive and sustainable manner necessarily entails following a constitutional path. In this sense then, constitutionalism is a process of constantly enlarging people's choices by freeing them from those forces— including a repressive state—that inhibit human development. It encompasses the embracing of new values that reflect the people's new choices. The process is not simply about writing constitutions, but most importantly, it is about nurturing those constitutions to embrace new values and aspirations as society responds to the challenges of development.

Taken in this perspective then, constitutionalism entails that the constitution is taken as a living instrument which must be construed in light of present day conditions.[13] The constitution that is normally drafted in broad terms must be interpreted by the courts as a living instrument to enable it to grow and embrace new values and aspirations that emerge with the changing times. In the words of Justice Aguda in the famous Botswana case of *Unity Dow* v. *Attorney General*,[14]

> The constitution is the supreme law of the land and it is meant to serve not only this generation but also generations yet unborn. It cannot be allowed to be a lifeless museum piece; on the other hand the courts must

continue to breath life into it from time to time as the occasion may arise ... I conceive it that the primary duty of the judges is to make the Constitutions grow and develop in order to meet the just demands of an ever developing society which is part of the wider and large human society governed by some acceptable concepts of human dignity.

Constitutionalism consequently entails that the constitution be used as the anchor to the pursuit of human development. It should be conceived 'as an organic instrument meant to serve not only the present generation, but also several generations yet unborn.'[15] There should be living principles in the constitution that authorise and limit the powers of government. In terms of human rights, true constitutionalism demands that there should be scope for further development and the recognition of human rights and freedoms beyond those that are codified in the constitution itself.[16]

This approach to constitutionalism recognises that behind the letter of the constitution, lies its spirit.[17] The language used in the constitution must be construed in order to ensure that the constitution remains a living organism capable of growth and development just as the body politic of a country itself is capable of change and progress. The spirit of the constitution consists of those basic values and principles that underlie the written letter. An account must be taken of those values and principles to bring their import to bear on the written law in order to make the law conform to the needs of the time. This is necessary because while the language of the constitution does not change, the changing circumstances of a progressive society for which it was designed may give rise to new and fuller import to its meaning.[18]

Taken in this perspective, then, all organs of state, namely the executive, judiciary and legislature must constantly watch their practices to ensure that they conform to the ever-changing realities of the constitutional dispensation. By participating in state organs the citizens would be part of this change, but perhaps more important is the participation of citizens outside the state organs. It is these citizens that constitute civil society whose role it is to put pressure on the state to respond to the ever-changing socio-economic and politico-cultural values. Without this initiative by civil society the complacent state cannot let the living constitution flourish. It is only through eternal vigilance by civil society that a culture of constitutionalism can become rooted in society.

The role of civil society

Civil society has sometimes been narrowly defined to refer to civil society organisations. For example, de Tocqueville defines civil society as 'the stratum of private associations that schools citizens in the civic virtue,' while another scholar described civil society as 'independent groups and associations at various levels pushing for particularistic interests which form the totality of the concerns of society.' The definition by Alfred Stephen is a little broader. He describes civil society as 'an arena where manifold social movements and civic organisations from all classes attempt to constitute themselves into an ensemble of arrangements so that they can express themselves and advance their interests.'[19]

I prefer an even broader definition of civil society that encompasses both formal and informal civil society organisations and the wider public who act or work either collectively or solely in a public sphere to express their interests, passions, ideas, exchange information, make demands on the state and hold the state and civic authority and its officials accountable for its actions. Taken in this context, civil society would include professional associations, trade unions, the media—both print and electronic—religious organisations and cooperative societies. It would also include all kinds of political parties or associations, ethnic societies, and non-governmental organisations working in a variety of fields such as the environment, rural development, women's empowerment, refugees, HIV/AIDS and several others.[20] Civil society also encompasses the general public which is not formally organised in any civic organisation but which forms the recruiting pool for these organisations. Whatever the definition adopted, civil society is supposed to be separate from the state although state officials in their individual capacities can participate in civil society albeit with restrictions of both a formal and an informal nature.

Under the authoritarian principle, whether under a monarchical set up or a one-party/movement dictatorship or open military autocracy, it is falsely assumed that the public interest lies beyond all party/political or social pluralism. Furthermore, there is the belief that the power and authority of the state should be left undivided and free from the influence of social movements.[21] According to this principle, the state and civil society are separate. Politics falls in the sphere of the state and outside the realm of civil society. Under this authoritarian structure there is no room for the expression of social pluralism nor can civic organisations and groups such as political parties be given a chance to perform the function of mediating between the multiplicity of social ideas and interests and the activities of state, because the state lays claim to a position above society and above parties.[22] This is what Professor Yash Ghai calls patrimonialism or personal rule and is a situation in which the ruler and his officials are above the law and outside of the rule of law.[23] Society in this setting is not in control of its destiny.

The history of the world in general, and that of Africa in particular, illustrates that this authoritarian principle is based on wrong premises and the political struggles witnessed in Africa over the last century have been geared towards throwing out authoritarian rule in favour of democratic governance. Under a democratic constitutional order, there has to be room for civil society.

This is premised on the argument that the state however democratic it may be or pretend to be, is not the best or the sole guardian of the public interest. In any democratic constitutional regime it is an accepted principle that there is social pluralism and the legitimacy of expressing it. Secondly, it goes without saying that society has a right to a say in the decisions of the state.[24]

Civil society has been very active in different African political contexts. During the colonial period, civil society organisations were formed to campaign for increased economic and political space within the colonial set up. In Uganda, for example, several groups were set up to protest the monopoly over trade exercised by Asians especially in coffee processing and cotton ginning.[25] The rationale for their formation at this time was to seek political space to ensure effective participation in the process of governance and in the distribution of resources. These groups later gave way to extremely vocal cooperative societies and trade unions whose aims were explicitly more political. Trade unions played a vital role in the political agitation for independence, and in South Africa the Confederation of South African Trade Unions (COSATU) actively participated in the struggle against apartheid.[26]

From the late 1940s through the 1960s numerous political parties were set up in several African countries to champion better working conditions for Africans, for Africanisation and, finally, for independence. Through their demonstrations, strikes, trade boycotts and campaigns, sometimes supplemented by armed resistance, these political parties finally won independence.[27] The larger of the parties took over the reigns of government, while the rest took to the opposition in the belief that they would continue to be part of the nation's polity.

The period after independence has been the most traumatic for civil society in Africa. It was hoped that the citizens of African countries would take the destiny of their countries into their own hands. The hope was that there would be room for civil society to work hand in hand with the state to build up the independent African states. After all, with the departure of colonial rule even civil society organisations like churches, professional associations, cooperative unions, trade unions, the media, and at a later stage non-governmental organisations, would firmly come into the hands of the citizens. This Africanised civil society it was hoped, would play a leading role in constitutional developments after independence. Unfortunately, in many African counties this dream has not been realised because of the many constraints that have dogged the African polity. It is to an analysis of those constraints that we can now turn.

Constraints on the operation of African civil society

Before citizens can actively and effectively participate in the constitutional process, they must be free from the shackles of fear, persecution, suppression, ignorance, poverty and disease. A people who live in want, fear, ignorance and persecution cannot meaningfully participate in the constitutional processes of their respective countries. Unfortunately, the economic and social statistics reveal an extremely depressing picture of Africa. In its 1999 *Human Development Report,*[28] the United Nations Development Programme ranks 45 countries as having a high human development index; 84 as having a medium human development index and 34 as having a low human development index.[29] None of the African countries have a high human development index while only 18 have medium human development indices. The majority of African states have a low human development index. The life expectancy at birth for the majority of African countries is less than 60 years and is as low as 37.2 years for Sierra Leone and 39.6 years for Uganda.[30] The adult literacy rate for most African countries is below 50 per cent and is as low as 14.3 per cent for Niger and 20.7 per cent for Burkina Faso.[31] The detailed statistics for health and survival,[32] education,[33] and information flows[34] make depressing reading. The new millennium has not heralded a fundamental change in the situation on the continent, and it remains dire.

With the downsizing of the civil service and the privatisation of state enterprises under the auspices of IMF structural adjustment programmes (SAPs) millions of Africans have been left without work and without a means of livelihood. There is however a silver lining to this retrenchment and divestiture exercise. When the retrenched workers eventually settle down and acquire alternative means of livelihood, they are finally freed from state control and patronage. They can now act more independently in the struggle for their private and public interests. Because of the pressing economic needs these ex-public workers would, at least for selfish reasons, be more active in struggles for more economic and political space. In my view, this promotes constitutionalism.

The numerous military dictatorships and the one-party/movement governments that have reigned over most African countries[35] have traumatised the citizens, denying them the chance to organise and the ability to speak out. The bloody and increasing civil wars that have been fought on the African continent to reign in those dictatorships or to overthrow democratically elected governments have left their psychological and economic scars. This has led to a process of the miltarisation of politics and apathy towards peaceful attempts to resolve conflicts. As a consequence, the role of free civil society actors beyond the militarised corridors of state politics has been severely diminished.

In these circumstances, the average individual citizen is too isolated to effectively participate in matters of a political nature. The average citizen is struggling to survive. Matters political are out of his or her purview. The African citizen is a pathetic lot. These pathetic conditions were decried by Justice Lugakingira of the High Court of Tanzania in the case of *Mtikila* v *Attorney General*, in which he stated,

> The relevance of public interest litigation in Tanzania cannot be over emphasized. Having regard to our socio-economic conditions, this development promises more hope to our people than any other strategy currently in place. First of all, illiteracy is still rampant. We were recently told that Tanzania is second in Africa in wiping out illiteracy but that is statistics juggling which is not reflected on the ground. If we were that literate it would have been unnecessary for Hanang District Council to pass bye-laws for compulsory adult education which were recently published as Government Notice No.191 of 1994. By reason of this illiteracy a greater part of the population is unaware of their rights, let alone how the same can be realised. Secondly, Tanzanians are massively poor. Our ranking in the world on the basis of per capita income has persistently been the source of embarrassment.[36]

Individual citizens in these pathetic conditions are unable to meaningfully participate in the political process. The emergence of public-spirited individuals with guts and initiative is the only way to fill the gap. Such public-spirited individuals can act alone but they are more effective under the rubric of organised groups. This configuration provides the only mechanism to engage the citizens in the quest for constitutionalism.

Authoritarian regimes in Africa have been alive to the potential of organised groups to wrest power from the state and have, over time, devised all sorts of means, including legal ones, to ensure that they ban or limit the role of organised civil society in politics. Such laws normally set difficult conditions that have to be satisfied before an organisation is registered by the state.[37] Normally, the organisation will have to be cleared and monitored by the intelligence agencies and will also be restricted from participating in political debate or in elections. The slightest deviation into the political field will lead to the arrest of its leaders or the cancellation of its licence. Such devices have had the effect of stifling the freedoms of association, assembly and speech. Particularly targeted have been political parties and yet these play a crucial role in constitutionalism. Political parties influence public opinion, collaborate in political education, motivate citizens to participate in politics, train political leaders, recruit candidates and influence parliament and governments. They also introduce political objectives into the formation of the will of the state and assure a permanent and active connection between the people and the organs of state.[38]

In Uganda, for example, the Movement/military regime imposed a ban on political party activities between 1986 and 1996 during which period a new constitution was debated and promulgated.[39] The resulting constitution continued this ban[40] and subjected the return of multiparty politics and therefore the enjoyment of the freedom of association and assembly, to the vote of majorities. This was totally oblivious to the fact that while majorities may vote governments into office, those majorities have no constitutional right to vote away the inherent rights of minorities. Justice Jackson in the American case of *West Virginia State Board of Education v. Barnette* stressed this point when he stated,

> One's right to life, liberty, and property to free speech, a free press, freedom of worship and assembly and other fundamental rights may not be submitted to vote, they depend on the out come of no elections.[41]

In similar terms, Justice Arthur Chaskalson—president of the South African Constitutional Court—was of the view that the constitutionality of fundamental rights,

> cannot be referred to a referendum in which a majority view would prevail over the wishes of the minority. The very reason for establishing a [new] constitutional order, and for vesting the power of judicial review of all legislation in the court was to protect the rights of minorities and others who cannot protect their rights adequately through the democratic process. Those who are entitled to claim this protection include the social out casts and marginalised people of [our] society.[42]

Instead of allowing free political organisation, the new Ugandan constitution regimented people according to sex, age, and occupation. There are provisions for women members of parliament, youth representatives, military representatives and workers.[43] These sectoral representatives are not elected on the basis of autonomous women, youth or military organisations but at the organisational initiative of the state. The youth and women councils were constituted under state tutelage. The right to self-organisation was denied and instead hijacked by the state and in this way the movement transformed itself into a hegomonic force thereby denying all other sectors of society the right to freely organise.[44]

In other countries like Nigeria, the military perfected the art (or science) of approving and registering political parties.[45] All political parties not approved by the state, would not be allowed to function. The military would then proceed to write the nations' constitution and hand it down to the new civilian administration. Evidently this Nigerian brand of constitutionalism has been a dismal failure. In many African countries, there are restrictive electoral laws that bar civic organisations and groups from freely canvassing political support, addressing gatherings and rallies or even holding meetings of more than a specified number of people without state permission. In Uganda, all candidates at parliamentary and local elections are not allowed to hold independent campaigns, and are instead supposed to address a single platform described as the 'candidates meeting.'[46] Sometimes even voter education is state-controlled.[47]

All authoritarian regimes justify the denial of the freedoms of expression, assembly and association on grounds of maintaining public order. This justification does not take into account the fact that in a democratic society the rights to freedom of expression, assembly and association are important to the maintenance of public order.

This important factor is well captured in the words of Justice Brandeis of the United States Supreme Court:

> Those who won our independence...recognised the risks to which all human institutions are subject. But they knew that order cannot be secured merely through the fear of punishment for its infraction; that it is hazardous to discourage thought, hope and imagination; that fear breeds repression; that repression breeds hate; that hate menaces stable government; that the path of safety lies in the opportunity to discuss freely supposed grievances and proposed remedies.... Recognising the occasional tyrannies of governing majorities, they amended the Constitution so that free speech and assembly should be guaranteed.[48]

The right to free expression, which includes the right to freely assemble and the uninhibited expression of ones views, should be regarded as an important pressure valve for an excluded political minority in a democratic society where total exclusion may be prejudicial to public order and safety.[49] Stifling the peaceful expression of legitimate dissent can only result in a catastrophic explosion of violence.[50] In every African state where these freedoms have been suppressed the oppressed people have sought recourse in violence.

The challenge of liberating African civil society

Although a healthy pastime, lamentations about the pathetic condition of the African citizen are not a solution to that condition. What is instead needed are practical strategies to liberate the oppressed and impoverished citizens of this continent from the shackles of poverty, disease, ignorance, fear and oppression. This will allow individual citizens to have the confidence, knowledge and means to express themselves and to actively participate in the political dispensation. This challenge is a tall order. From the outset it has to be emphasised that the African citizen will not be freed by the state.[51] It is the citizens themselves that have to break loose from the bondage of oppression, poverty and ignorance. In other words, the challenge is for civil society to free itself. In this regard it should be pointed out that the task of liberating civil society should not be left to politically oriented civic organisations alone. All organisations such as churches and charities should realise that they cannot freely operate in an atmosphere of terror.

Furthermore, they should realise that most of the social and economic calamities that their organisations strive to deal with such as famine, disease, street children, orphans, environmental degradation, displaced persons and refugees are both the direct and indirect result of policies and practices of authoritarian governments that misuse public funds and sometimes wage war on their own people.[52] It is thus necessary to devise new strategies that may be used to liberate civil society.

Civil society acting through the media

Freedom of expression is recognised as 'an essential foundation of a democratic society.'[53] The freedom of expression is seen as the foundation of the government of a free people. The purpose of such a guarantee is to prevent public authorities from assuming the guardianship of the public mind.[54] The independent media should encourage a robust discussion of public issues. This was emphasised by the High Court of Nigeria when Chief Justice Araka stated,

> Freedom of speech is, no doubt, the very foundation of every democratic society, for without free discussion, particularly on political issues, no public education or enlightenment, so essential for the proper functioning and execution of the processes of responsible government, is possible.[55]

Robust public discussion is necessary because there can be no claim to a monopoly of the truth. Most African constitutions allude to the right to freedom of expression. Indeed most African states are signatories to the Universal Declaration of Human Rights and the International Covenant on Civil and Political Rights both of which protect the freedoms of expression, assembly and association. However, there are ancient and sometimes new laws on the statute books that inhibit the exercise of these freedoms. These laws create draconian offences such as sedition, the publication of false news, incitement to violence, wrongfully inducing a boycott, and defamation of foreign princes.[56]

The challenge to the independent media is threefold. First of all, they must strive to ensure that they give room to all diverging opinions so that the citizens are broadly informed about the competing opinions on public matters especially those relating to economic and political affairs. The media should not be party to the suppression of rival opinions or to the manipulation of facts, events or statistics. If competing views are not forthcoming from the public, it is the duty of the media to initiate and sustain debate. The independent media should be prepared to counter propaganda in the official media by exposing the falsity of such propaganda and misinformation. Since the circulation of the print media in most African countries is small, the growing electronic media in form of private television and radio stations should do more to promote the culture of constitutionalism. The easiest way to do so would be to host panel discussions on topical issues. Such programmes can be made more interactive by allowing the public to phone in and air their views. The public can also be encouraged to send written opinions that can be discussed by the panel.

The second challenge to the independent media is to ensure that opinions are expressed in terms that do not fall foul of the law of sedition, the publication of false news and such other similar draconian laws. There should be deliberate care to ensure that the presentation is in substance a peaceful articulation of opinion and not an incitement to violence or the deployment of illegal methods of protest. Of course this is not easy to achieve especially where the state is determined to frustrate the media. Accordingly, the fear of prosecution should not lead the media to practice self-censorship. Media practitioners should always bear in mind the risk at hand and be prepared for the inconveniences of prosecution. They should take comfort in the fact that not all prosecution will be successful.

The third challenge for the independent media is to take the lead in confronting unconstitutional laws and state practices that inhibit the exercise of freedom of expression. The media can do this by exposing the unconstitutionality of those laws and by lobbying for their repeal. Secondly, the media should challenge those laws and practices in the courts at least in those countries where the courts have constitutional powers to declare the statutes and practices of the state as unconstitutional. There are already many such challenges that have been handled by the courts throughout Africa.[57] Even when court challenges fail, the independent media should give great publicity to those judgments touching upon the matter in order to keep alive public debate on the subject of freedom of expression and assembly.

Civil society acting through the legislature

Legislative bodies are normally vested with powers to control the executive arm of government. Parliament can investigate the conduct of a particular ministry or department and adopt specific resolutions calling upon government to take a particular course of action. Parliament also controls the executive through the budgetary process and can pass into law private members bills on top of those submitted by government. In most cases, the government has a majority in parliament and uses this majority to pass through unpopular legislation or policies. The voices of the opposition or of moderates in parliament are always shut down. This may be frustrating for those few members of parliament who may wish to pass through progressive legislation or who may wish to block unpopular legislation as was the case with the referendum law in Uganda.[58] Parliament in this sense ceases to be an instrument of democracy and turns into a bastion of dictatorship.

Can civil society ever penetrate this bastion and make good use of it? The answer is yes. It must be realised that the human mind and condition is not static especially in the face of changing economic and political circumstances. What civil society has to do, especially those groups which are organised, is to constantly engage parliament. This engagement can assume several different forms. The most innocent and least suspicious is through education. Many legislators act on the basis of ignorance. They may not be aware of the consequences of their actions. They may even be unaware of their rights and powers. All effort has to be put in to expose the honourable members of Parliament to the conditions in which their people live, and to their rights and aspirations. Seminars targeting these legislators are a worthwhile vehicle for a start but other more subtle methods to reach the minds of legislators have to be innovated.

Clearly, general exposure to constitutionalism is not enough. Particular groups of members of parliament should be targeted to be used as the spokespeople of civil society. For example, a number of parliamentarians can be targeted by an NGO working on prisoners' rights and given detailed information on pathetic prison conditions. Visits to prisons can be arranged for these targeted members so that they can see for themselves the conditions obtaining. They can then be exposed to literature on how the problem has been tackled in other countries. After such intense exposure these legislators can then be guided on how they can formally and informally raise the issue in parliament. Not all of them will be as responsive but the few who do respond may be bridging the gap between parliament and civil society. Leaders of civic organisations should make more appearances at parliamentary committee hearings. They should go armed with empirical data. Civil society organisations should learn to work like missionary groups painstakingly penetrating an unsuspecting society.

The other way of engaging parliament and other civic fora such as district councils and other local government units is for civil society to prepare private members bills and bye-laws and to interest private members of parliament to table such bills in the House. In many instances, such a bill will not be passed. However, the mere act of presentation in parliament will spur further debate on the subject. Such debate may eventually force a reluctant executive to introduce its own bill albeit not of such far reaching import or coverage.[59]

Acting through the court system

Even in the most authoritarian regimes in Africa[60], a semblance of a court system survives. Initially, the system needs a Judge to swear in the dictator and courts to 'lawfully' jail or even kill opponents of the regime who are demonised and dubbed counter-revolutionaries, traitors, imperialist agents or simply backward forces. However, this same court system can entertain suits to seek compensation for property confiscated by the state—claims arising out of assault, torture, unlawful imprisonment and malicious prosecution by state officials. Such suits will not threaten the regime's survival and yet they will keep alive the belief in and the practice of human rights and constitutionalism.

In the more sophisticated or enlightened dictatorships, the regime will even allow the existence of a constitutional court.[61] Not that the regime will necessarily want the court to function effectively, but it will point to its existence as evidence of institutional democracy. When a serious case comes before the court, the regime may try to interfere but it will not do so in the open. Here then is space for civil society to exploit. Public spirited individuals and civil organisations and interest groups should take courage and submit to the courts well documented and investigated human rights and constitutional cases. Sometimes the victims of human rights abuse are disadvantaged individuals—disadvantaged by fear, poverty, ignorance, or disease. These need to be protected through public interest litigation.[62] Many constitutions in Africa now provide *locus standi* for persons to bring suits on account of the violation of other peoples' rights or the breach of the constitution without the necessity for a personal cause of action.[63] Such provisions have freed civil organisations and groups from the necessity of going through the rigours of representative actions. Such representative actions were in the past used as a mechanism of denying organised groups of civil society access to the courts.[64]

The importance of public interest litigation does not largely lie in the outcome of individual cases since at least in the short run many of them will be dismissed. Rather, these cases will serve a number of important functions. In the first instance, the parties and lawyers involved in these cases will in the course of preparing these cases take lessons in constitutional jurisprudence with the result that an informed and activist citizenry and bar will emerge. Over time the quality of preparation and presentation of constitutional and human rights cases will be enhanced. Secondly, the largely conservative bench will be exposed to new jurisprudence. Initially, the bench will not accept new radical jurisprudence but over time the jurisprudence will gradually sink into the judicial mind. A few judges will embrace the new jurisprudence with zeal and their initial dissenting opinions will one day be embraced by the majority of the court especially after the court is subjected to intense public criticism. Thirdly, and perhaps most importantly, the wide publicity given to these constitutional cases will activate further public debate on the constitutional issues raised.

There are additional benefits. Other actors such as politicians will then take the debate to further heights.[65] The result will be a more informed citizenry, ready to challenge outdated doctrines, laws and practices. In Uganda the unsuccessful attempts to challenge the constitutionality of the Constituent Assembly election regulations[66] and the 1996 presidential and parliamentary elections[67] have had a considerable impact on constitutional jurisprudence. The legal profession is becoming more activist and some judges are warmly embracing progressive constitutional jurisprudence.[68]

Strengthening political parties and organisations

We have already outlined the important functions of political parties in enhancing a culture of constitutionalism. But before these parties can play their part in the constitutional dispensation, they need to be strengthened in terms of their internal democratic organisation and functioning. The biggest obstacle to be overcome is the curtailment of open political party activities in countries like Uganda, Libya and Rwanda. In such countries, the political parties have a tall order to survive in closed political systems. And yet, survive they must. In these countries, the political parties should challenge the constitutionality of the restrictions imposed on them in courts of law. Whether they succeed or not does not matter because the publicity of the court hearings will keep their cause alive. However, it has to be pointed out that this litigation may be expensive. Even getting a brave lawyer to take the bull by the horns may be a difficult task.

Political parties should also build an underground network of branches and cells in villages, work places and schools. This is a risky venture but with determination it can be achieved. The political parties can also survive and spread their message through a network of other civil society organisations which the law may allow to function. They have to devise strategies to network with other groups and organisations while always being aware of the presence of criminal prosecutors and crackdowns by state agents. Public and private functions like marriage festivals can be useful fora to be exploited to make contact between the party leaders and their branches.

The other aspect that political parties in Africa need to attend to is the need to improve their research capacities. As long as parties base their policies on mere assumptions, they will never be taken seriously. Political parties need to develop an in-house capacity to research and come up with comprehensive reports based on actual data. These reports can then be used in any engagement with other civic organisations, the state and the international community. When presented with such hard facts the public is more likely to react positively. However, it must be pointed out that there are restrictions on access to official information and permission to conduct public research may be refused by national research councils or agencies.

There is no doubt that the political parties also need to democratise internally. This will be the surest way to prove to society that they practice what they preach and that they can therefore be entrusted with the management of public affairs. However, as long as parties do not put in place democratic structures that ensure the smooth transfer of power, they will be seen in the same light as the autocratic state. Of course the state may intentionally frustrate the parties efforts at democratisation by denying them the right to convene assemblies at which they can elect their leaders.[69]

Impacting on the military

No other single institution in Africa has been more responsible for the retrogression of constitutionalism than the military. It has been the bedrock on which all authoritarian regimes, be they military dictatorships, one-party or movement regimes have been built. The most horrendous of human rights abuses have been committed by the army, intelligence services, the police, para military forces, and armed state cadres and vigilantes. The troubling reality is that the military as an institution cannot be wished away. It is a reality that we have to live with. The challenge is how to tame the military and/or bring it under the control of civil society. One strategy would be to use all available legal means to expose the excesses of the military. This may involve suing individual members of the security forces for the abuses they commit and sometimes joining government in such suits where the abuses form part of systemic government policy. The abuses of the security services can also be subjected to intense media publicity so that public opinion is galvanised to protest the abuses. This strategy can only succeed where the state does not condone the abuses. Where the state deliberately uses security forces to suppress the people, any attempt to rein in errant officers will be met with forceful resistance and retribution.

In the long run civil society can impact on the security forces by adopting a strategy of constitutional mass mobilisation. Civil society organisations can recruit and train their own cadres in constitutionalism and then release them into the public domain. This may take the form of constitutional and human rights education not only in law schools but also in all institutions of secondary education and higher learning, para legal training, street law projects and legal cadre development. Some of these cadres can then be absorbed into the security forces and other government departments where they may bring their influence to bear upon the policies and practices of their respective departments.

This strategy would, in the long run, aim at building a core body of officials within the departments of government including the security forces that is alive to the challenges of constitutionalism. It then gradually becomes more difficult for the state to employ such an enlightened body of officials to suppress the people. This will be the surest safeguard for the institutionalisation and development of an enduring culture of constitutionalism.

Conclusion

Civil society is not an homogenous entity. It is a complex web of individuals and groups all operating in the public domain to advance their interests. Some of those interests may be conflicting. And yet beyond this pluralistic and sometimes antagonistic existence there are common interests and values that tie them together and which civil society should champion. The values of respect for human dignity and the aspiration for human development are common to all persons. And yet, the realisation of these values, which is the essence of constitutionalism, remains a far cry because the citizens are enfeebled by poverty and ignorance and afflicted by disease, while they are also continuously subjected to terror. They need to free themselves. The process has to be ignited by the most enlightened and public-spirited citizens acting through the media, the legislature, the courts, political parties, and inevitably the hitherto repressive security services. One area that has to be focused on as a prerequisite to enhancing the culture of constitutionalism is the need to reform or indeed repeal those laws that restrict the formation and operation of civic organisations. There must be utmost freedom to form and operate civic organisations. The process of liberating African civil society is agonising just as it is time consuming. However, the effort is worthwhile. It is an unending and ongoing process and the catchword for the citizen remains 'eternal vigilance'.

Notes

1. See for example the preamble to the *Constitution of the Republic of Namibia*, 1990 and that of the *Constitution of the Republic of Uganda*, 1995.
2. The *Constitution of Sierra Leone*, 1978.
3. *Constitution of Togo*, 1980, Article 2.
4. The *Constitution of The Republic of Guinea-Bissau*, 1984, Article 2(1). See also *Constitution of Ghana*, Article 1.
5. Article 1(1).
6. Article 1(2) & (3).
7. Quoted in Wade & Bradley (1993): 4.
8. See, Paine, (1969): 93 and 207.
9. Wheare (1966) 7.

10. Vile (1967): 1.
11. See Streeten (1999): 16.
12. *Ibid.*
13. *Muhozya v Attorney General*, Civil Case No.206 of 1993, High Court of Tanzania, unreported: 2.
14. [1992] LRC (Const.)623
15. *Nafiu Rabiu v. The State* (1981) 2 NCLR 293.
16. Article 33(3) of the *Constitution of Republic of Ghana*, 1992 and article 45 of the *Constitution of the Republic of Uganda*, 1995 explicitly embrace this principle.
17. *Tuffuor v Attorney General* [1980] GLR at 647 (Sonah J.S.C.)
18. *Tinyefuza v Attorney General*, Constitutional Petition No.1 of 1997, Constitutional Court of Uganda (Manyindo D.C.J. at 16)
19. Sewanyana (1997): 1.
20. *Ibid*: 1-2.
21. See Oberreuter (1995): 26.
22. *Ibid.*
23. Ghai (1996) in Steiner at 717-719.
24. Oberreuter *op.cit*: 26.
25. Sewanyana op.cit.
26. COSATU working hand in hand with the banned and underground ANC engaged in boycotts and demonstrations to sustain the anti-apartheid struggle.
27. There were armed struggles in many African countries including Kenya, Algeria, Angola, Mozambique, Namibia and Zimbabwe.
28. UNDP (1999).
29. *Ibid.*, see table: at 47, 49, 134.
30. *Ibid.* table at 137
31. *Ibid.*
32. *Ibid*: 172-175
33. *Ibid*: 176-179.
34. *Ibid*: 54-56.
35. Algeria, Angola, Benin, Code d'Ivoire, Egypt, Ethiopia, Gabon, Chad, Lesotho, Liberia, Malawi, Madagascar, Mali, Mauritania, Morocco, Mozambique, Niger, Somalia, Zambia, Uganda, Sudan, Nigeria, Rwanda, Burundi, Sierra Leon, Libya, Zaire/Congo Kinshasha, Ghana, Kenya, Tanzania and Togo have all experienced either one party/movement rule or military dictatorship. South Africa suffered under the yoke of apartheid. Zimbabwe has had to live with the consequences of a bitter civil war and the voter turn out in the last general elections in 1999 was about 25%.
36. Civil Case No. 5 of 1993, 11 & 12.
37. See for example the *Non Governmental Organisation Statute* No. 5 of 1989 (Uganda)
38. See Oberreuter, *op cit*, 39-42.
39. Rule 11 of the *Constituent Assembly Election Rules*, which appear as schedule 3 to the *Constituent Assembly Statute* No. 6 of 1993 specifically prohibited candidates aspiring to be delegates to the Constituent Assembly to use a political party platform in their campaigns because political parties were labelled sectarian.
40. See Article 269 which prohibits political party activities.
41. [1943] 319 US 624: 638.
42.. *State v Makwanyane* [1995], LRC (Const): 311
43. Art. 78(1) (b) (e)
44. See Mamdani (1989).
45. Before his surprise death, Sani Abacha had been chosen by all the political parties registered by his own government as their presidential candidate!
46. *Parliamentary Elections (Interim Provisions) Statute*, 1996, S.48; *Local Government Act*

No. 4 of 1997; S. 123.
47. In Uganda S. 12(g) of the *Electoral Commission Act* No. 3 of 1997 vests in the Electoral Commission power to 'promote and regulate through appropriate means civic education of citizens.'
48. *Whitney v. California* 274 US 357 at 375. [Emphasis added].
49. Article 19 (1997), 64.
50. *Amarantunga v. Sirimal & Ors*, Judgment of the Supreme Court of Sri Lanka. [1993] 1 Sr. L.R. 264 at 270-1. See also *Free Press of Namibia Pty Ltd v. Cabinet for the Interim government of South West Africa* Supreme Court of Namibia, 1987(1) SA 312, 614: 624.
51. Article 6 of the Transitional Constitution of the Republic of Sudan, 1985 ironically stated that the state shall endeavour to establish and entrench the foundation of democracy in the country and shall strive to secure the citizens participation in public affairs through its democratic institutions!
52. Amartya Sen—the 1998 Nobel Laureate in Economics—has argued that no substantial famine has ever occurred in a country with a democratic form of government and a relatively free press, see Sen (1998): 10.
53. See for example *Re Munhumeso & Ors*, Judgment of the Supreme Court of Zimbabwe (1995) (2) BCLR 125(25) at 130B, *Mulundika & Ors v The People* judgment of the Supreme Court of Zambia, 10 January, 1996 Appeal No 95 of 1995 1995: 13-14.
54. *Banda v. Attorney General*, High Court of Zambia, Case no. 92/HD/1005, at p.14 (Chitoshi J.)
55. *State v Ivory Trumpet Publishing* [1984]5 NCLR 736 at 747.[Emphasis added]
56. For example see section 49A, 50, 50A, 51 of the *Penal Code Act*, Cap. 106 (Uganda).
57. See for example, *Imanyara v Attorney General*, Civil suit No.1208 of 1994, High Court of Kenya; *Seif Sharrif Hamad v The Regional Commission of North Region,* Unguju Civil Appeal No.32 of 1994, High Court of Zanzibar; *New Patriotic Party v. The Inspector General of Police,* writ No.4 of 1993, Supreme Court of Ghana; *Mulundika & Ors v. The People,* Appeal No.95 of 1995, Supreme Court of Zambia; *Nabulyato & Ors v. Post News Paper Ltd*, High Court of Zambia; *Uganda Journalist Safety Committee of Kanabi v Attorney General,* Constitutional Petition No. 6 1997, Uganda; *Uganda Journalist Safety Committee & 2 Ors v. Attorney General,* Constitutional Petition No.7 of 1997, Uganda; *Woods & Others v Minister of Justice, Legal & Parliamentary Affairs & Ors* [1996] 1 CHRD 53 Supreme Court, Zimbabwe; *Kanesa v Minister of Home Affairs & Ors* [1996]2 CHRLD 209, Supreme Court, Namibia; *Concord Press of Nigeria Ltd v. Attorney General & Ors* [1996]1 CHRD 47, High Court, Lagos; *Santa v. Post Newspaper Ltd & Anor* (No.2) [1996] 2 CHRLD 212 High Court, Zambia.
58. Act No.2 of 1999. It is noteworthy that Parliament passed this law without quorum. This was admitted by Rosette Alleluya Ikote, Member of Parliament (Women) for Pallisa District and Vicechair of the Movement Caucus in Parliament in an article *'NRM Must Take on Multipartyists in a Fair Fight,'* The East African No.248, August 2-8, 1999: 12. The Act has been challenged in Constitutional Petitions No.3 and 4 of 1999.
59. Art. 50(4) of the Uganda Constitution *in a ripe* candidate for a private members bill.
60. Like in Idi Amin's Uganda (1971-1979) the court system survived even with the killing of Chief Justice Benedicto Kiwanuka and other law officers.
61 See for example article 137 of the *Constitution of the Republic of Uganda*, 1995.
62. On public interest litigation see: Grace Tumwine Mukubwa (1999) 'Public Interest Litigation and Public interest Law: The role of the Judiciary,' in Peter Mukiidi Walubiri op.cit, .99.
63. E.g., Uganda [Art.50 (2) and 137(3)]; Namibia (Art.25); Tanzania [Art. 6(2)] and Botswana [Art.18 (1)].
64. Inspite of the presence of article 50(2) in the Ugandan Constitution the Constitutional Court

in *Rwanyarare & Anor v. Attorney General* Constitutional Petition No. 11 of 1997 struck out a Petition by one of the Petitioners on behalf of a group on grounds that he had not first obtained a representative order.

65. The unsuccessful court challenges to President Moi's failure to appoint a Vice President could have partially influenced his decision to appoint or re-appoint Prof. George Saitoti as vice-p resident.

66. *Dr James Rwanyarare & 2 ors v. Attorney General*, Miscellaneous Application No. 85 of 1993, High Court.

67. *Dr James Rwanyarare & Anor v. Attorney General*, Constitutional Petition No. 11 of 1997, Constitutional Court.

68. See for example the majority decision in *Attorney General v. Abuki* Constitutional Appeal No.1 of 1998, Supreme Court and the dissenting opinions of Justices Oder, Tsekooko and Mulenga in *Ismail Serugo v. Kampala City Council & Attorney General*, Constitutional Appeal No. 2 of 1998, Supreme Court.

69. In Uganda for example Art.269 of the Constitution prohibits political parties from holding delegates conferences.

References

Article 19 (1997) *The Interpretation of Fundamental Rights Provisions*, London.

Ghai, Yash (1996) 'The Theory of the state in the Third World and the problematic of Constitutionalism,' in H.J. Steiner (ed.) *International Human Rights in Context*, Oxford: Clarendon Press.

Mamdani, Mahmood (1989) *Social Movements and Constitutionalism in the African Context*, CBR Working Paper No. 2.

Oberreuter, Heinrich (1995) 'Political Parties: Their Position and functions within the Constitutional System of the Federal Republic of Germany,' in Joseph Thesing and Wilhelm Hofmeister (ed.) *Political Parties in Democracy*, Bonn: Konrad Adenauer Stiftung.

Paine, Thomas (1969) *Rights of Man*, New York: Collins.

Sen, Amartya (1998) 'Democracy and a Frese Press are Good Economics,' *The EastAfrican*, 19-25 October.

Streeten, Paul (1999) 'Ten Years of Human Development,' in UNDP *Human Development Report*, New York: Oxford: Oxford University Press.

UNDP (1999) *Human Development Report*, New York: Oxford; Oxford University Press.

Tumwine Mukubwa, Grace (1999) 'Public Interest Litigation and Public interest Law: The role of the Judiciary,' in Peter Mukiidi Walubiri.

Vile, M.J.C (1967) *Constitutionalism and Separation of Powers*.

Wade A.C. & Bradley (1993*)* *Constitutional and Administrative Law,* (11th ED.), London and New York: Longman.

Walubiri, Peter Mukiidi, (1998) *Constitutionalism at the Crossroads*, Kampala: Uganda Law Watch.

Wheare, K.C. (1966) *Modern Constitutions,* London: Oxford University Press.

7

Ethnicity and Constitutionalism in Post-Genocide Rwanda

Jean Marie Kamatali

The Rwandese genocide has baffled a number of researchers and humanity as a whole. Close to one million innocent people were barbarously butchered, countless women were raped and property was looted and destroyed. These base acts of humankind were willingly and publicly perpetrated by other Rwandans sharing the same country, the same language and the same history with their victims. Faced by this reality, one may wonder how this could happen on the eve of the twenty-first century, in a country combining all features of a state and claiming to be governed by the rule of law and endowed with effective government. How was it possible that human beings, possessed with all the rights that have come to be globally accepted could be deprived of their inherent rights to life and dignity? How was it that such people could be transformed overnight into human prey to the extent that they feared to seek protection from state institutions and authorities or even to seek shelter and protection in governmental and administrative buildings?

At the time of the genocide, in 1994, Rwanda was ruled according to the 1991 constitution. The third since independence in 1962, it was no different from other well-written and soundly conceptualised constitutions. It solemnly recognised not only that Rwanda was a democratic republic with executive, legislative and judicial powers, but it also ensured that there was separation of these powers between the different organs of government. More significantly, however, it faithfully repeated the high-sounding words of the Universal Declaration of Human Rights and its two covenants. Thus, Article 12 of the constitution stressed that 'the human person is sacred' and went on to guarantee 'the liberty of the human person.'[1] Despite the perfection of this constitution which prescribed the structure and principles of limited government and which also established a state governed by the rule of law, it did not prevent the genocide. Even more disturbing is the fact that the genocide was meticulously planned and mathematically executed without any obstacles. Indeed, the genocide took place as if there was no law, no government and absolutely no human sense.

This was so notwithstanding the fact that Rwanda ratified the Convention on the Prevention of Genocide in 1975. The events of 1994 must be understood as the result of a long and complex socio-economic and political history of Rwanda, but ultimately they are the expression of a drastic failure of law and order in general, and of the constitution in particular. This makes one wonder if indeed in 1994, Rwanda had a 'comprehensive constitution' or *Gesamtverfassung*, or in other words, a constitutional order that has an authoritative legal force and reflects the normalised conduct of its society. If it did not, then this situation constitutes the most serious challenge to constitutionalism in post genocide Rwanda.

As Heller has put it, the state's constitution includes a normative constitution which is the formally regulated and legally organised component on the one hand, and the non-formally regulated yet normalised behaviour which on the other hand constitutes the 'social substratum' component of the constitution.[2] Usually the 'normalized behavior,' which is the emanation and expression of a commonly experienced history and culture, precedes the normative constitution. According to the same author, in a 'comprehensive constitution' the 'normalized behavior' must be reinforced and supplemented by normativity.[3] Constitutional law should therefore be an expression of constitutional reality. Once adopted, such constitution should provide the guidelines to regulate future behaviour.

Constitutionalism in pre-colonial Rwanda

Prior to the advent of colonialism, Rwanda was a strong kingdom with a hierarchical society characterised by a constitutional order with highly centralised powers. Orders, binding by themselves, were transmitted from the top and, through a series of chiefs, were passed on to every citizen[4]. At the top of the political structure was the King, who was the supreme leader exercising all powers over the whole territory and population. The King was supported by administrative and military institutions organised in a deconcentrated manner and was assisted by his advisors including the queen mother.[5] The institutions of the kingdom were also strengthened like that of ubuhake.

The king in pre-colonial Rwanda was extremely powerful. He incarnated the supreme legislator, the supreme administrative chief and the supreme judge. The king was the sole authority to declare war, appoint and dismiss chiefs—military or administrative—as well as their deputies. He distributed land and cattle to anyone as it pleased him and set up political and administrative units in his kingdom.[6] Underpinning the king's authority was his believed connection to the supernatural. These divine powers were most important because the king received them directly from God. The king was the only lord and sovereign and was only accountable to God. He was not simply another human being; he was a superman, a mwami. The king had no ethnic attributes; he was neither Tutsi nor Hutu or a Twa, he was above any ethnic group. Ostensibly, the king resembled a human being by his body; but not by his heart and mind.[7] The power he exercised came directly from God and that is why his authority could not be challenged.

The religious atmosphere surrounding the personality of the king contributed to the veneration, loyalty and confidence of the people towards him. People believed that in exercising his powers, the king was incapable of doing anything wrong. Whenever there was anything wrong it was not done by the king but rather by his advisers and emissaries.[8] This is what is known in the Kinyarwanda language as *'umwami ntiyica hica rubanda':* the king does not kill; only those under him kill.

Insofar as legislative power was concerned, the king exercised it alone through the mechanism of laws and decrees.[9] The law or *'itegeko'* was a solemn act by which the king introduced a new custom or abrogated an old one. This activity was organised in a solemn and special ceremony: The people were called to a public place *ku karubanda* and the king, surrounded by chiefs, declared publicly the decision he wanted to become a law. This decision was accompanied by the special rhythms of a special drum known as *Ruca-bugome*, meaning literally anti-rebellion. The chiefs in turn, using local authorities, had to forward this decision to everyone. The decree applied in the area where the law did not intervene and could be permanent or temporary. This difference was specified at the time of its adoption. A permanent decree was introduced with a special formula stating that it shall be observed *ingoma ibihumbi*, literally meaning thousands of reins, or now and forever. A temporary decree was a provisional measure taken by the king to appease or pacify the people following a threat of disease, famine or war.[10]

Only the king exercised legislative power. Anybody else who attempted to assume the same power could be condemned to death. Moreover, whoever acted contrary to the king's laws and decrees, which in Kinyarwanda meant: *guca mu iteka ly'umwami*, could be condemned to death. In certain cases, such punishment could even be extended to members of his whole family.

As the supreme chief of the whole of Rwanda, the king also exercised executive power.[11] He exercised this authority in all parts of the country and could delegate it to the army commanders in provinces at risk of foreign invasion. In the latter case, the king had to set the guidelines within which the exercise of this delegated power had to be carried out.[12] The king appointed and removed the chiefs of land and the chiefs of pasture. These appointments were made at his sole discretion; the appointments or removals did not require any consultation or any other formalities.

Judicial power was also in the hands of the king who was the supreme judge in the country. Rendering justice was one of the important responsibilities of the king. Every morning before any other activities, the king rendered justice to his people. It was only after this ceremony that chiefs and other members of the royal court were allowed to talk to him.[13] He ensured the right to property of any member of the family and restored the rights of any victim of injustice from a powerful neighbour.[14] The king was available to listen to the grievances of every citizen.[15] However, to secure his justice the citizen was required to be under the protection of an army commander who acted as the lawyer of the victim, except when the former was involved in the case[16]. This arose from the principle that the authority of the king did not apply to rebellious or insubordinate citizens.[17]

The king's entourage and the queen mother

As with many other African situations, the king did not rule alone. The queen mother, the *abiru* and the chiefs were the most influential personalities surrounding the king in pre-colonial Rwandan society. The first and most important member of the king's court was the queen mother. The king had to have a queen mother. When his own mother was dead, it was necessary to find a replacement who acted as queen mother. She had to carry the name the king was conferred with at the time of his enthronement. For example, if the king was called *Kigeli*, the queen mother was called *Nyirakigeli;* if he was named *Mibambwe,* the queen mother would be called *Nyiramibambwe.*

Although she had no known official function, the queen mother was the most influential personality in the king's entourage.[18] She shared power with her son. When the king was enthroned at a very young age, the queen mother was the one who exercised the regency. She was the first adviser to the king. Whoever sought favours from the king had to pass through her. However, some authors have argued that her powers should not be overestimated.[19] Her role resulted from the fact that she represented one of the most influential groups in the country.[20] In any case, her influence depended much more on her personality and on that of her son because the latter could easily abrogate any of her decisions.[21]

Among the political institutions of pre-colonial Rwanda, the 'esoteric code' was of great significance as it was like the fundamental law of the dynasty.[22] This code was in the custody of the *abiru* and contained all the secrets about different rituals and traditions on how the king was chosen, enthroned and exercised his powers. The code even stipulated how the king could be removed. Usually three in number, the *abiru* were the depositories of the big secrets of the dynasty.

The function of *abiru* was hereditary and before assuming this office they had to take a special oath. This oath was followed by the swallowing of a special mixture known as *igihango*. The brew was believed to be a strong and efficient guarantee against any indiscretion. Indiscretions—even those committed inadvertently known as *gutatira igihango*—automatically triggered the sentence contained in the sibylline formula pronounced during the swallowing of the *igihango*.[23]   It is under this oath that secrets of the kingdom were kept. The fact that the *abiru* detained the secrets unknown to anybody else including the king himself and the queen mother, ensured them an extremely influential role and place in the entourage of the king and in the royal institutions.[24]

The *abiru*, who have been compared by one author to the Egyptian priests during the time of pharaohs,[25] were the source of reference on the organisation of the royal powers and of the succession to the throne. They ensured the legitimacy of the new king. Their powers were so strong to the extent that a king designated by them in conformity with the esoteric code, could not be contested.   One author argues that the institutions of pre-colonial Rwanda were functioning perfectly because of the wisdom and knowledge of the *abiru*.[26]

It is worth underlining the fact that although there were three *abiru* in total, each held a different chapter of the esoteric code. And yet, no one of the three knew the whole code. Furthermore, each was bound by the secret of the chapter of which he had custody. Thus, for example, one detained the secret on the order of succession of queen mothers and the ethnic groups they should come from. The second held the secrets concerning the ceremonials of enthronement, while the third kept the secret on how to decorate the royal drum.

As far as territorial administration of the pre-colonial kingdom was concerned, Rwanda was divided into provinces and districts. A province was composed of a number of districts and was run by the paramount chief who was known as the *umutware w'intebe*. In provinces located on borders and which were thereby exposed to external attack, this chief also performed the function of army chief. As *umutware w'intebe* such a chief could claim a cow from each of his cattle-owning subjects as a sign of recognition of his authority. When this chief was also promoted to be chief of army, he was entitled to another cow from each of his subjects. Furthermore, whenever one of his subjects was in need of a favour, the former had to give a cow known as *ituro*. The paramount chiefs usually resided at the royal court, which allowed them to remain close to the king so that they could retain his sympathy and stay vigilant to confront any intrigue likely to make them lose the king's favour.

Each district was governed by two independent chiefs, respectively known as the chief of land *umutware w'ubutaka*, and the chief of cattle or pasture, *umutware w'umukenke*. The former was in charge of collecting taxes on agricultural products while the latter distributed pastures and collected the taxes attached to them. Both chiefs were endowed with administrative and judicial authority.[27]

Every district in the kingdom was divided into hills. Each hill was governed by a chief of the hill *umutware w'umusozi*, appointed by the paramount chief *umutware w'intebe* but under direct authority of both chiefs of land and pasture. The chief of the hill, being on the lowest level of administration was the last stage of executive authority in the kingdom. He was aided by a civil servant (*umukoresha* or *ikirongozi*) who was mainly in charge of collecting taxes and supervising drudgery. In the execution of his duties, the civil servant could only reach taxpayers or those called for drudgery by the intermediary of the chiefs of families (*abakuru b'imilyango*).[28]

The above discussion allows us to extract some particularities of pre-colonial Rwanda that require highlighting for their relevance to the contemporary situation. First of all, although there was no written constitution pre-colonial Rwanda was well organised with well known and established institutions: On the one hand there were rules governing the organisation and succession to the throne, kept in an esoteric code and entrusted to the *abiru*. Furthermore, the administrative institutions were well organised and ensured an efficient mechanism through which laws and orders were conveyed to the people.

Another important characteristic of pre-colonial Rwanda is the role of individuals who incarnated power. In the eyes of the people, it was from this authority that the law (*itegeko*) came from, and who was in charge of its execution. In a society of oral tradition this seems to be justified. As in most traditional societies, the law is known subsequent to its application to a specific case: prior knowledge of the law is unprofitable, as it does not guarantee the citizen its use against the authority because the latter can change it in any way he or she pleases. For the ordinary citizen, what mattered was the chief's intention because it is from the chief that both rewards and punishment emanated. The consequences of this organisation were mostly the creation of a submissive but calculated attitude among the Rwandan people. This is an attitude which was reinforced by the practice of *ubuhake*—the act by which the weaker in the society worked for and tried to please his stronger patron so as to win material favours and protection.

The features of this well organised society of oral tradition evolved over centuries and become well accepted by the whole population.[29] This situation affected the mentality, attitude and behaviour of the rulers and those of their subjects. It is this 'real constitution' which survived the colonial constitutional order and which continued to characterise informal relations between the political authorities and the citizens throughout the development of the Rwandan constitution. However, the intervention of colonial rule certainly left its mark on all these structures and institutions. It is thus essential to turn to an examination of this period before considering the contemporary context.

The institution of *Ubuhake*

Alexis Kagame defines *ubuhake* as a pastoral serfdom contract by which a person called *umugaragu* (servant) offers his services to another person of a higher social rank called *shebuja* (master).[30] In this contract the *umugaragu* wants to obtain cattle. Maquet adds that the *umugaragu* offers his services and asks for protection in exchange.[31] A broader definition is, however, provided by Murego who attaches three meanings to *ubuhake*: the first one generally considers the *ubuhake* as the act of making oneself a subject, the second meaning is derived from the popular language and sees *guhakwa* as an act of paying a visit to an authority or to pay court to him. The third meaning considers this practice as an art of pleasing a superior to win his favours, or an act of subservience.[32]

In the practice of *guhakwa* the reward of the *umugaragu* was not a right which could be claimed in exchange for his services. All depended on how he would satisfy his master. The *umugaragu* had the duty to do all the jobs required by his master (cultivate, night watch, accompany and protect the master, etc) and pay court to his master by pleasing him and assuring him of his faithfulness. In turn, the *shebuja* had the duty to protect his client. If satisfied with the job, the *umugaragu* would receive one or several cows as payment.

The practice of *ubuhake*—although not exercised throughout the whole country, has been considered by some authors as a political institution in traditional Rwanda.[33] More significant however, is the manner in which this institution has affected the mentality of Rwandans in their relation to the authorities. Clientelism as the most important element of *ubuhake* has continued to characterise all the political regimes in Rwanda and has been considered the ideal way to gain advantage and to secure the favours of the political or economic master. Although the institution of *ubuhake* in its traditional sense was abolished before Rwanda's independence, the term *guhakwa* (the verb deriving from *ubuhake*) did not disappear in the popular vocabulary of Rwandans. Today it means mostly paying court to an authority and offering him presents in order to gain economic favors and to secure political positions.

The colonial period

With the beginning of colonisation, a new era of constitutional development was initiated in Rwanda. Fundamental laws were introduced by Germany and later Belgium with little attention to the local needs and the 'real constitution.' The ultimate objective of both imperial powers was to reinforce European domination.[34] We can basically divide the colonial period into the German and Belgian stages of colonisation.

German colonisation

In the system of protectorates or *Schutzgebiete* adopted by the German Empire during its colonisation of East Africa, the fundamental law of the colonies and other principal laws were adopted by the empire itself. According to the fundamental laws of the German colonies, at the apex of each colony was the governor appointed by the emperor. The governor was assisted by a number of civil servants among whom was a *Kanzler,* a high judge or *Oberrichter* as well as a civil servant in charge of finance, also appointed by the Emperor.[35] Larger colonies such as that of the East African German Protectorate (Tanganyika) were divided into several administrative districts or *Bezirksaemter* run by the administrators of the district or *Bezirksamtmaenner.* Those administrators were appointed either by the chancellor or the governor, depending on their rank.[36] The general administrative organisation was completed by indigenous chiefs who, due to their power over the population, acted as auxiliaries of the administration.[37]

From this analysis it appears clear that in maintaining the indigenous organisation intact and in basing their system on traditional authorities, the German Empire grounded its system of colonisation on the policy of indirect rule. As a consequence, there was a gap between the ordinary people and the colonial authorities.[38] For an ordinary Rwandan the institutions of the kingdom remained the source of authority and protection. As is well known, following the defeat of Germany in the First World War, all of its colonies were parcelled out to its victors. The Germans were driven out of Rwanda and other territories under their protectorate.[39] Those territories were subsequently distributed among the allies victorious in the War. In 1923, Belgium received from the League of Nations the mandate on Rwanda-Urundi.[40] This mandate was transformed by the United Nations into a trusteeship in 1945.[41]

The phenomenon of Belgian domination

Belgian domination marked the beginning and the reinforcement of a constitutionalism based on the separation between the 'real' and 'formal' constitution. On the one hand, there was a colonial administration comprising the white rulers from the colonial power. On the other, there were the indigenous authorities. In many respects the two operated in essentially distinct spheres.

The very first written law to be introduced in Rwanda was the *arrêté royale* of 22 November 1916 which appointed the *commissaire royale* in charge of the administration of East African German territories occupied by Belgian troops after the Germans were driven out of those territories.[42] Article 1 of this *arrêté* provided that the *commissaire royale* should exercise all powers delegated to the general governor (*gouverneur*) and the general prosecutor (*procureur général*) by the colonial law. The same article provided that this power was to be exercised only vis-à-vis military troops and civilian and judicial personnel of the occupation corps.

The Belgian military occupation ended in 1919 and a civilian administration was established to replace it. It was, however, six years later that the law of 21 August 1925 defined the political organisation of Rwanda.[43] This law declared the union of administration between Rwanda and Burundi. Article 1 of the law automatically rendered applicable to Rwanda all laws in application in the Belgian Congo, that were not incompatible with the goal of the mandate. These laws were adopted by the Belgian parliament and sanctioned as well as promulgated by the king of the Belgians. The most important of them was the law of 18 October 1908 known as the 'Colonial Charter'—considered by some as the constitution of the Belgian colonies.[44]

During Belgian trusteeship the constitutional powers (legislative, executive and judicial) were in the hands of the king of the Belgians and the colonial administration.[45] While ordinary legislative power was in the hands of the king of the Belgians,[46] exceptional legislative power was given to the general governor and governors of the provinces.[47] In the exercise of his executive power, the king of the Belgians was assisted by the minister of colonies and in some cases by the minister of foreign affairs. This power was delegated in general matters to the general governor and to the vice-general governor as well as to the governor of Rwanda-Urundi.[48] Judicial power was also exercised by the colonial administration.[49]

Indigenous authorities

Article 4 of the *Ordonnance—Loi* No. 2/5 of 6 April 1917—provided that the sultans should continue to exercise (under the supervision of the Resident Governor) their political and judicial powers according to indigenous customs and the instructions of the *Commissaire Royale*.[50] The decree of 14 July 1952 which replaced the above ordon nance-loi determined the power of indigenous authorities. They included the king of Rwanda, the chiefs of provinces or *chefferie* and the *sous-chefs* who ran districts or *sous-chefferies*.

The decree organised the councils on each administrative level and the High Council of the country at the national level. The members of the lowest level were appointed by the people. Those appointed had to choose from among themselves those who were to sit on the high administrative council. The high administrative council elected the High Council of the country from among themselves.[51]

As far as judicial organisation was concerned, the regulation of the resident as contained in his letter No 96/O.R.G. of 5 November 1926 provided that a roving tribunal had to be created at the *chef-lieu* of each province. This tribunal was composed of one judge, five assessors and the registrar. The resident, his deputy and the administrator of the province were automatically judges of this tribunal which was competent for all cases that arose between Banyarwanda or between the latter and the indigenous people of neighbouring territories. Later in 1929 and 1936, judicial organisation in the territory was restructured. The king could sit on the bench of any indigenous tribunal and revise any sentence rendered by these tribunals.[52]

The above description of the hierarchical character of executive and other powers in Rwanda illustrate that due to the gap between the colonial authority and the ordinary people, the traditional authority was required to serve as a bridge between the former and the latter. This had the consequence of maintaining the well-organised and efficient traditional authorities, and in particular of securing their direct political power over the population. The local population was thereby forced to learn how to serve both the European and the traditional authorities at the same time. Sometimes these authorities followed rather contradictory political goals. Under such circumstances it is obvious that only the orders and regulations compatible with the goal of the traditional authorities were likely to reach the population. This practice contributed significantly to the creation—in the minds of the Rwandan people—of two different attitudes towards the law. One attitude regarded the law as a norm by itself. The second regarded the law as understood by the enforcing authority. It is argued for example, that whenever an unwanted decision by the court was taken by the colonial administration, the court and its notables twisted it by postponing its execution or by modifying it whenever the colonial administration was not present to oversee its application.[53] An example of such a situation can be illustrated by the attitude following the interdiction in 1917 by the colonial authority of King Musinga with regard to the death penalty.[54] The interdiction was accepted in theory, but simply ignored in practice as citizens continued to be subjected to the penalty for a long period of time.[55]

To sum up, one may say that in the eyes of the citizens the law was not obligatory and enforceable by itself. Rather, it depended on the attitude of the authority who not only brought it to the people but also enforced it. Here again—as was the case during the pre-colonial period—the people had to consider not the content of the law as they knew it but rather how it was perceived and interpreted by the colonial authority. Still, in this period the traditional authority, while pursuing his own political goals, could allow himself to blame the legislator and clear himself of all responsibility in the eyes of the people whenever the law was disadvantageous to the latter.

Towards a construct on ethnicity in Rwanda

Many writers have tried to define the term 'ethnicity' and to distinguish it from other terms such as race, caste and the like.[56] While Eriksen defines the term 'ethnicity' as groups whose members consider themselves distinctive,[57] Breton goes further to distinguish ten constitutive elements of an ethnic group namely: language, race, demography, territory, economy, social class, culture, urban network, the metropolis, and political institutions.[58] More interestingly, however, is the manner in which he divides these elements into three groups. The first, which he calls 'pre-structure', consists of basic elements generating ethnicity: physical anthropology, demography, language and territory.[59] The second is called 'structure' and includes such elements as economy, social classes, culture and the consciousness of belonging to a given ethnic group; the third and last category is the 'post-structure' which includes elements such as political and urban organisation.[60] This last category is identified as the crystallisation of an ethnic group. [61]

Breton, Kombanda and Mountali define ethnic groups as composed of four elements: the first one is the community of memories that includes for example a common historical tradition and myths.[62] The second is the community of values which concerns a minimum common culture of a group or certain concepts, symbols or codes which are common and distinctive for this group.[63] The third and fourth elements are the common name and aspirations or the consciousness of the member of a group to belong to the same group and to live together.[64]

From the above theories on ethnicity one may ask whether for an ethnic group to exist all these elements have to be fulfilled at the same time or whether one element is enough to qualify a group as an ethnic group. If in the former case it is difficult to qualify Hutu, Tutsi and Twa as ethnic groups, in the latter this qualification becomes easier. Taking for example the community of memories as the central element of ethnicity, one could be brought to see—in the context of post-genocide Rwanda—the Tutsi as an ethnic group. Although it is difficult to determine when exactly the common history began, according to the above hypothesis, one may argue that the killings in 1959 which were directed against Tutsi, those of 1973 and the ultimate genocide in 1994 created common memories and conscience among

Tutsi. Those forces transformed the Tutsi into an ethnic group.[65]

Ethnicity in Rwanda's pre-colonial institutions

Many have argued that the terms 'Hutu,' 'Tutsi' and 'Twa' that are often referred to as ethnic groups are as old as Rwanda itself.[66] The two main theses so far developed by historians, sociologists and anthropologists on the origins of these groups, although divergent, agree that all these groups existed before colonisation.[67] The first thesis argues that Rwanda was initially populated by the Twa as the very first occupants in the same family of those people known as the 'pygmies.'[68] The Hutu—identified as belonging to the Bantu ethnic group—were the second group to populate Rwanda. They came from the regions neighbouring the present Lake Chad and began clearing the forest and cultivating to organise the country into decentralised kingdoms. The Tutsi identified as belonging to the Hamitic ethnic group, were the third group to populate Rwanda. They came from the regions neighbouring Ethiopia with their cattle and defeated the Hutu kingdoms and began organising Rwanda into a centralised kingdom.[69]

The second thesis argues that the Hutu, Tutsi and Twa are one ethnic group. The supporters of this thesis base their arguments on the fact that these groups share the same language and territory. In the words of one author, it is wrong to consider the Twa as pygmies because they have nothing in common with the pygmies living in forests or even bushmen, as the Twa are much taller than other pygmies.[70] Moreover, Kashamura argues that there are no important morphological differences between Hutu and Tutsi.[71] If there is any difference of an essential character between the three groups, it should rather be found in the social stratification of Rwandan society.[72] Accordingly, Tutsi, Hutu and Twa correspond to certain social classes, with the Tutsi generally forming the nobility, the Hutu being equivalent to the middle class and the Twa making up the lower classes. These classes were not static: a rich Hutu could rise to become a Tutsi.

Whatever thesis of relevance to this discussion, it all leads to the conclusion and justification that the Tutsi dominated pre-colonial Rwanda.[73] This could have resulted from being the nobility or from the domination they exercised as 'conquerors.' Nevertheless, it is worthwhile highlighting the fact that there was no polarisation between the Hutu and Tutsi as ethnic groups in pre-colonial Rwanda.   Instead, what was relevant during that period was the clans to which one belonged.[74] The institutional structure of the kingdom and the ubuhake brought the individuals in the system to be considered as the source of law or channels through which the law passed to reach the citizens and as agents of its execution. In this system citizens could not or were discouraged from verifying the source of the law applied to them. Following this situation the population was brought to look at authorities as incarnating the law. As most of them in this hierarchy were Tutsi it is obvious that for ordinary citizens, the Tutsi was the group representing this power and therefore responsible for their happiness or misery.

Ethnicity in colonial institutions

As in many African territories, the colonisers sought to use existing traditional chiefs as agents of their rule in Rwanda. Such a system of indirect rule preserved existing structures. The most striking fact, however, is how the Germans and then more systematically the Belgians transformed the existing Hutu and Tutsi groups into radical and rigid ethnic groups. The first step in this radicalisation resulted from the Hamitic theory.[75] According to this theory the Hamites—allegedly being a branch of the Caucasian race—are more intelligent than the rest of the African ethnic groups and therefore born leaders.[76] Everything of value found in Africa was imported to the continent by the Hamites.[77] Basing their arguments on more subjective criteria, the colonialists designated the Tutsi as belonging to the Hamitic race,[78] while the Hutus were declared to belong to the Negroid or Bantu race.[79] From this assertion they confirmed that Hutu were naturally supposed to serve Tutsi. This theory prevailed with little difficulty as it matched well with the collaboration with the monarchy and with the ego of Tutsi nobles.

However, the theory reached its apogee in the 1920s and 1930s when colonial powers undertook administrative reform. Under this reform, traditional structures of land, pasture and army chiefs were abolished and replaced by a single chief with a certain number of sub-chiefs under his authority.[80] In doing so, the administration removed all Hutu chiefs from any centres of power.[81] The responsibility of sub-chiefs was granted almost exclusively to the Tutsi.[82] Another important step towards the establishment of Tutsi exclusiveness was the creation of schools for the sons of chiefs. The most important was the school of Nyanza that was founded in 1919 and replaced in 1935 by the *Groupe Scolaire d'Astrida* (presently *Groupe Scolaire de Butare*).[83] Up to the eve of the 1959 revolution, the majority of students in those schools were Tutsi and the sub-section for candidate chiefs admitted only the sons of chiefs and registered Tutsi children exclusively.[84] During the years 1933-4 a census was conducted and identity cards issued to all the citizens. These cards specified the ethnic identity of the bearer and it was not legally possible to change it.[85] Colonial rule also extended the institutions of clientship to all the peripheries of Rwanda and most particularly to the north where Hutu principalities or *abahiza* enjoyed independence from the court.[86]

To sum up, one could say that instead of creating a society based on the rule of law and which was favourable to the development of constitutionalism, colonial rule radicalised the Hutu-Tutsi relationship and empowered the latter to exploit and abuse the former. Wherever it tried to reserve advantages to the Hutu, it appeared biased to the extent that it was likely to further radicalise the relationship between Hutu and Tutsi rather than bringing them closer together.[87] Under this institutional arrangement, individuals kept their central role in the development of the constitution of Rwanda. It is under this influence that in the eyes of ordinary people, the Tutsi came to be equated with arbitrary administrative power, while the Hutu were left powerless. This collective subordination undermined existing clan ties and created a new sense of 'pan-Hutu identity.'[88]

Ethnicity and constitutionalism in independent Rwanda

The road to the independence of Rwanda was violent and resulted in turning Tutsi supremacy into Hutu supremacy. The Hamitic theory—long supported and perpetrated by the colonial power—and Tutsi elitism became a serious threat to Tutsi dominance when in the late 1950s the colonial power suddenly shifted its support to the Hutu.[89] With this shift, Hutu leaders began to reject the Tutsi as 'foreign invaders.' The opposition by the colonial administration against the Tutsi elite and a corresponding increase in support to the Hutu elite became wide open in 1957, when the mostly Tutsi-dominated National High Council[90] addressed a note, *mise au point*, to the visiting UN mission demanding immediate independence.[91] In reaction to this note a 'Hutu Manifesto' was released, highlighting the social aspects of the indigenous racial problem in Rwanda and denouncing various aspects of the feudal system, notably the Tutsi monopoly in the political and economic life of the country.[92] Following this manifesto, twelve high officials at the royal court signed a letter denying any blood links between the Hutu and Tutsi and declaring Hutu as an inferior race. This essentially meant that the Hutu should be deprived of any right to power.[93]

In addition to the above escalation in tensions, the mysterious death of King Rudahigwa in Bujumbura in neighbouring Burundi and the peasant uprising ignited by the beating of Mbonyumutwa—one of the few Hutu sub-chiefs—by the youth of UNAR,[94] led to the abrupt and violent end of Tutsi rule. It also signified the beginning of Hutu domination. It has been asserted that following the termination of Tutsi rule in 1959, at least ten thousand Tutsi were killed. It has also been alleged that the revolution left no single Tutsi habitation in the prefecture of Ruhengeri.[95] All of them were burned to the ground.[96]

Rwanda's three post-colonial constitutions
The first but largely ineffective constitution in the post-colonial period was

known as the 'Constitution of Gitarama.'[97] This constitution was adopted following a meeting of all *bourgoumestres* and *conseillers communaux* held in Gitarama on 28 January 1961.[98] The main objective of the meeting was to abolish the monarchy and install a republic. This resulting instrument— which was neither published in the *Bulletin Officiel du Rwanda Urundi* nor in the *Journal Officiel du Rwanda*—was considered invalid by the monarchists and more significantly by the trusteeship authorities, i.e. Belgium. The Belgian authorities declared that the constitution had no legal force as it was not legalised by any legislative act,[99] and it was not formally endorsed by the Rwandese people.[100] As a consequence, unlike other African countries that gained independence by having their own constitutions, Rwanda had no constitution at the time of its independence on 1 July 1962. The constitution of Gitarama which was supposed to replace that of the colonial regime was in fact null and void on the day Rwanda gained its independence.

The constitution of 24 November 1962 became the first constitution of the Republic of Rwanda. The draft of this constitution was presented on 4 October 1961 by the parliamentarians of the PARMEHUTU and APROSOMA parties. It was inspired by the constitutions of France, the Republic of Guinea, Senegal, Madagascar and the then Haute-Volta (today Burkina Faso).[101] It was, however, the constitutions of France and Senegal most significantly influenced first Rwandan constitution. In this regard it is argued that the constitution of Rwanda literally repeated the provisions of the constitution of Senegal on civil rights.[102]

Article 1 of the 1962 constitution declared Rwanda a democratic, socialist and sovereign republic while Article 2 abolished the monarchy and stipulated that it could never be reinstated. The constitution of 1962 has been praised for having embodied a complete list of human rights as defined by the Universal Declaration of Human Rights including rights that are traditionally considered difficult to implement such as economic rights.[103] In Article 3, the constitution obliged the Republic of Rwanda to ensure equality for all citizens without any distinction on grounds of race, origin, sex or religion. In Article 16 it stressed that all citizens were equal before the law without any distinction based on race, clan, colour, sex or religion.

The adoption of the constitution of 1962 did not, however, bring about any fundamental changes in the relationship between the citizens and political authorities and in particular in the relationship between Hutu and Tutsi. Article 15 of the constitution obliged every citizen to know the law. The question remained, however, how this could be possible in a country where the only way the citizens could know the law was through the official Gazette and where ironically, close to 90 per cent of the populace was illiterate? This situation has been the most challenging obstacle to the realisation of progressive constitutionalism in Rwanda since independence. On the other hand, and despite the overwhelming support given to the constitution, it was argued that in reality the new political system simply replaced one set of Tutsi-dominated institutions with another set of Hutu-dominated ones.[104]   In other words, it was the reversal of Tutsi hierarchy with a Hutu one, where ethnic identity served as the basis for systematic discrimination against Tutsi in education, the civil service and the armed forces.[105]

The violation of the right to life also remained frequent. This violation became even more serious when exiled Tutsi formed guerrilla bands and started attacking Rwanda from the neighbouring territories of Zaire (the present Democratic Republic of Congo), Burundi, Uganda and Tanzania in the hope of returning home by force.[106] These attacks led to ferocious and indiscriminate reprisals against Tutsi within the country. It is argued, for example, that following a guerrilla attack of 20 December 1963 organised from Burundi, which progressed up to 20 km of the capital Kigali, an estimated ten thousand Tutsi were massacred while 15 leaders of Tutsi-dominated political parties were arrested, tortured and barbarously killed.[107]

By the end of the 1960s dictatorship in Rwanda had been fully reinforced. The multiparty system was abolished and a one-party system installed. Terrorism orchestrated by the state against any opposition became frequent and sometimes resulted in massacres against the Tutsi and their Hutu collaborators. The Hutu group also became divided between those from the north and those from the south.[108] It was with the objective of putting an end to this injustice and to restore peace and national unity that on 5th July 1973 a group headed by Major Juvenal Habyarimana took power through a military coup.[109] The most striking fact relating to these developments is, however, that the proclamation following this military coup suspended the constitution of 1962.[110] Until December 1978, the time of adoption of a new constitution, Rwanda was governed without any constitution. Executive and legislative powers were placed in the hands of the president of the republic.[111]

The constitution of 1978 was adopted three years after the creation of the *Mouvement Revolutionaire National pour le Developpement* (MRND) and its imposition as the only framework within which political activities could be carried out.[112] This constitution installed a system of one party (MRND) with leaders who, in the name of the constitution, controlled every structure (legislative, executive and judiciary) of the state and who were empowered to give or take away any of the political and economic rights of any citizen. Like that of 1962, the constitution of 1978 guaranteed most human rights as defined by the Universal Declaration. And yet, ethnic and regional discrimination, as well as favouritism continued to characterise those holding the reins of power. The regime installed the policy of ethnic and regional 'equilibrium' which established quotas for ethnic groupings and to regions that were proportional to their representation in the population.[113]

Following the winds of change for democratisation that swept Africa on the heels of the struggle for democracy in Eastern and Central Europe, and following the attack of the RPF (Rwandese Patriotic Front) in October 1990,[114] the Habyarimana regime ended up by giving in and accepting a multiparty political system. This was expressed in the constitution of 1991, which as was the case with its predecessors, also guaranteed political, social and economic rights to every citizen.[115] However, not much changed. Indeed, one may conclude that the existence of the new constitution had little influence on the way political power was exercised. Instead of being a document of reference, providing supreme guidelines on the exercise of power and serving as a point of departure with respect to human rights, the constitution became an instrument to be used as a booster to state authority, and to be ignored whenever it did not accommodate the interests of those in power.[116]

In a country where the majority of the populace was illiterate and where each new regime designs its own constitution reflecting its own political goals, one may even wonder about the raison d'être of having a written constitution. The fact that despite the absence of a constitution between 1973 and 1978 Rwanda was no worse governed, demonstrates how much political regimes underestimated the value and the meaning of a formal constitution. This can be further illustrated by how power is referred to with reference to ethnic group: Tutsi regime, Hutu regime, Kiga[117] regime, Nduga[118] regime, and individuals: the reign of Kayibanda (*ku ngoma ya Kayibanda*), Habyarimana (*ku ngoma ya Habyalimana*) etc. All this clearly demonstrates how power was understood not by reference to the constitution but by reference to the leaders.[119] This would not have been problematic , however, if it was not accompanied by changes in the behaviour of the leaders and that of the governed. This approach brings us back to the distinction between the formal constitution and the real constitution. The former, lacking legal or historical background and continuity in Rwanda remained an alien source of power and authority. The latter, although not formally binding, was accepted and served as an authoritative reference in the exercise of power. It is in the latter wherein we can also discern some ethnic features, and where also the roots of genocide can be found.

Constitutionalism in the post-genocide period

The fundamental law in the post-genocide period is composed by the constitution of 1991 as modified[120] and the Arusha Peace Accord signed on 3 August 1993.[121] Being a product of lengthy negotiations, the negotiators took time to analyse the problems of Rwanda and to propose a means of solving the old, and preventing the eruption of new problems. A comprehensive attempt in this regard can be found in the Protocol Agreement on the Rule of Law.[122]   In its preamble, this protocol stresses that the rule of law is grounded in national unity, democracy, pluralism and respect for human rights. According to Article 1, national unity should be based on the equality of all citizens before the law, equal opportunities in all activities as well as respect for the fundamental human rights as defined, among others, in the Universal Declaration of Human Rights and the Africa Charter on Human and Peoples' Rights.[123]

To render effective the objective of the protection of human rights, the Protocol on the Rule of Law prescribed the setting up of an independent national commission on human rights.[124]   The basic function of this commission is to monitor the violation of human rights committed on Rwandan national territory by any person and particularly by state organs, individuals or diverse organisations acting under state cover. The field of investigation of this commission shall be unlimited and its results used to sensitise and train people in the field of human rights on the one hand and to induce judicial action when necessary on the other.[125]   Stressing that national unity also means the indivisibility of the Rwandan people, Article 2 of this protocol stressed the necessity to combat all obstacles to national unity and most importantly the fight against ethnicity. To achieve national unity, Article 3 of the accord calls for the rejection of all kinds of discrimination and particularly of ethnic discrimination. In order to achieve the above goals, the protocol agreement on power-sharing established efficient mechanisms to ensure the separation of powers. It also set up a number of special commissions that were designed to achieve several different objectives.[126]   The first commission is that on unity and national reconciliation that has the double mission of preparing a country–wide debate on national unity and national reconciliation, and to prepare and distribute information aimed at educating the population and achieving national unity and national reconciliation.[127] The Legal and Constitutional Commission is the second commission which also has a double mission, namely drawing up a list of legislative provisions to be abrogated or amended in conformity with the provisions of the peace agreement, in particular those provisions relating to the rule of law. It must also prepare a preliminary draft of the constitution which shall govern the country after the transitional period. An electoral commission which shall be responsible for the preparation and organisation of local, legislative and presidential elections is also prescribed by the Protocol on Power Sharing.[128]

At the time of writing, the National Commission on Human Rights, the Commission on Unity and National Reconciliation and the Legal and Constitutional Commission have all been set up and began their respective activities. These important steps towards the development of constitutionalism in Rwanda follow the decision to remove the mention of ethnic affiliation from identity cards. It should be remembered that this card served as evidence of an ethnic identity and was used during the genocide to identify who was Tutsi and who was Hutu; in other words who should die and who should not. To end the culture of impunity that has characterised the political history of Rwanda and to bring about justice while creating an enabling environment for reconciliation, a number of steps have been adopted. It is within this framework that an organic law on the crime of genocide and crimes against humanity was adopted in 1996 to punish the crime of genocide and other crimes against humanity.[129] Furthermore, a system of participatory justice known as *Gacaca* has been installed. This system allows the citizens to know the truth about the genocide and massacres of 1994, to contribute in the trial and judgment of those suspected of genocide and other crimes against humanity and to set solid grounds for reconciliation.

Constitutionalism in post-genocide Rwanda suffers, however, from a number of setbacks. First of all, the consequences of genocide which is itself the expression of the failure of the harmony between the formal and the real constitutions are difficult to heal. Forgive and forget is hardly observable in the Rwandan situation and it may need time and hard work to reach a complete reconciliation. Another element affecting the process of developing progressive constitutionalism in Rwanda is the security concerns which take the first priority of the government. Threats from *interahamwe* and soldiers from the defeated army undermine or risk making fragile the democratic process as an expression of sustainable constitutionalism. Furthermore, the government has been very slow in putting into place the Legal and Constitutional Commission. So far, this commission provided by the Arusha Peace Accord of 1993 only recently became operational and given the time left before the end of the transition[130] and considering how long the constitution making process can take, it is worth underlining that there is still much to do.

Conclusion

If the larger rubric of constitutionalism is constituted by the simple making of a constitution, understanding and utilising the document and making it accessible to the citizenry, it still requires a constitutional ethos that in turn results from a variety of elements such as symbols, history and shared values. The constitutional ethos should precede and develop into the normative comprehensive constitution which in turn must be invested with an authority beyond the government, guarantee the rule of law, protect human rights and support democratic procedures.

As reviewed in this chapter, the biggest challenge to constitutionalism in post-genocide Rwanda remains the lack of a comprehensive constitution bringing together 'normalised behaviour' with a formal constitution. The former was developed throughout the long and ethnically coloured history of Rwanda while the latter is a recent product copied largely from outside. The confusion between the law and authority, and the source of law, has developed into normalised behaviour in Rwandan political history. Such development would not of itself be dangerous if this authority was considered outside an ethnic framework. In other words, citizens fear more the authority than they do law. What the law can do, even when positive, does not matter; what matters instead, is what the authority says. This is what people mostly perceive as law. In a country where the authority has been perceived as either Hutu or Tutsi and where the advantage of one corresponded to the disadvantage of the other, the perception of the norm-receiver (the people in general) is different, depending on the ethnic group of the norm-sender (either Hutu or Tutsi authority).

To avoid the manifest pitfalls of this situation, any new approach to constitutionalism should take into consideration the above contradictions. The first step should be the drafting of a comprehensive constitution bringing together universal constitutional values and national ones. Such a constitution should also provide for a framework for the management of ethnic conflict. The second step should be to put the law above the authorities and closer to the people. This undertaking implies the development of good governance and a sound civil society in an environment of the rule of law. This means that in addressing the people the authority should always make reference to the constitution. The constitution should be the first and final reference point for any political activity. On the other hand, the participation of all Rwandans in the decision making process and in political, economic, social and cultural activities should be strongly encouraged. As participation implies knowledge, the government should promote the right to information and particularly knowledge of the law. Only then will Rwanda be able to extricate itself from its ethnically–charged history and embark on the path to progressive constitutionalism.

Notes

1.   Reyntjens, (1994): 21-30.
2.   Staatslehre (1963) quoted by K. Ginther, (1998): 85-86.
3.   *Ibid.*
4.   Page (1993): 105.
5.   *Ibid.*
6.   Bourgois quoted by D. Murego (1975): 88.
7.   Murego, *ibid:* 117.
8.   *Ibid:* 117.
9.   The term's 'law' and 'decree' should not be understood here in the sense by which they are known today. Writing and the system of parliament did not exist, unwritten laws and decrees were in use.
10.   Hagenimana (1990): 18.

11. Kagame, Article 331.
12. *Ibid.*
13. Nkurunziza (1988): 20.
14. Kagame, *supra,* note 11, Article 79.
15. This is confirmed by the Rwandan saying *ugutwi k'umwami ntikunena*, which literally translated means, the ear of the king does not discriminate or in other words the king listens to everybody.
16. Kagame, supra note 11, article 71.
17. *Ibid.,* article 71.
18. Nkurunziza (1988): 24.
19. Murego (1975) *supra,* 121.
20. The queen mothers could only come from two clans; *abega* and *abakono.*
21   Murego *op.cit.*, 121.
22. *Ibid.*, 123.
23. Hagenimana (1990): 21.
24. Murego (1975): 122; Hagenimana, *supra.*
25. Perugia: 243-44.
26. *Ibid.:* 246.
27. Paternostre de la Mairieu (1972): 123.
28. Murego, *op.cit.*, 91-92.
29. See Kayumba (1998): 42.
30. Kagame quoted by Kayumba.
31. Maquet (1961); see also Kayumba, *supra.*
32. Murego, *op.cit.:* 49
33. Murego, *supra:* 48; Overdulve (1997): 25-32.
34. Mbolongo (1980): 41.
35. Murego op.cit,: 329.
36. *Ibid.*
37. *Ibid.*
38. *Ibid.*
39. See Lugan (1997): 269-83.
40. *Ibid:* 329.
41. See Bulletin Officiel (1950): 87.
42. See Basomingera (1986) at 60, and (1916) *Bulletin Officiel du Congo Belge*, (4), 248 and 250.
43. See *Bulletin Officiel du Rwanda-Urundi* (1925), (5), 1 November.
44. Basomingera (1986) *op.cit:* 61.
45. See Article 7, *Colonial Charter*, 18 October 1908, *loi sur le gouvernement Belge; Bulletin Officiel* (1908), 65.
46. *Ibid.* Article 7.
47. See article 22, para. 3-5 of the law of 29 March 1911, *Bulletin Officiel du Rwanda-Urundi,* No 7 –1911 of 31 March 1911:358.
48. Reyntjens (1984): 45-46.
49. *Ibid:* 55.
50. Article 4 of the *Ordonnance-Loi* No 2/5 of 6 April 1917, in *Bulletin Officiel* (1917): 49.
51. See Nkurunziza, *op.cit.*, 38.
52. Hagenimana (1990) *supra:* 30.
53. Desforge (1972) quoted by F. Reyntjens, *supra:* 132.
54. Kagame (1975) 175-176; Reyntjens (1985): 79.
55. *Ibid.*
56. See for example Breton (1981), Eriksen (1993); Young: 421-495; Roosens (1989).
57. Eriksen *ibid.*

58. Breton (1981) *supra:* 26.
59. *Ibid.*
60. *Ibid.*
61. *Ibid.*
62. Sevo and Mountali, 106.
63. *Ibid.*
64. *Ibid.*
65. See also Kornblum (1988): 290-311, and Goldhagen (1996).
66. *Ibid.*
67. *Ibid.*
68. See Harroy, *op.cit,* Prunier, *op.cit,* and Reyntjens.
69. *Ibid.*
70. Kashamura quoted by P. Erny (1994): 27-28.
71. *Ibid.*
72. *Ibid.*
73. See *supra*
74. Rwanda counted 18 clans (*siinga, siindi, zigaaba, gesera, nyiginya, eega, baanda, cyaaba, uungura, shaambo, tsoobe, koono, ha, shiingo, nyakarama, siita, oongera, eenengwe*). These clans were composed of Tutsis as well as Hutu. For more details on these clans and the percentage of Hutu and Tutsi in each clan see: Hertefelt (1971), and Kayihura (1998).
75. Sanders (1969) quoted by. Reyntjens, *supra: 1*03.
76. *Ibid.*
77. *Ibid.*
78. *Ibid.*
79. *Ibid.*
80. Hertefelt, in Reyntjens.
81. *Ibid.*
82. *Ibid.*
83. National University of Rwanda (1998).
84. *Ibid.*
85. Africa Rights (1995): 6.
86. The attempt to extend Tutsi supremacy to the northern principalities was not however, an easy task as it was strongly resisted. On this question see DesForges (1986).
87. This is the case for example of the decision contained in letter No 791/A/53 which rendered punishable the deprivation by a Tutsi of the property of a Hutu as if the deprivation between Tutsi or Hutu was legitimate. Reyntjens *supra:*131.
88. See Newbury (1988): 116, 178-9.
89. Lugan (1997) *supra* at 300; see also Murego (1975) *supra.*
90. The National High Council was the highest level of political structure of the country. It was created by a colonial decree to booster political development through democratisation and indigenous political participation.
91. National University of Rwanda, *op.cit,* 18.
92. *Ibid.*
93. For more details on the content of both the Hutu manifesto and the letter of the 12 high officials see Reyntjens, *supra*, annex.
94. Subsequent to the *Ordonnance* No 11/234 of 8 Mai 1959 that was rendered in execution by the *Ordonnance du Rwanda-Urundi* No111/105 of 15 June 1959, political parties were created. The Union Nationale Rwandaise (UNAR)—a monarchist Tutsi-dominated party was created on 3 September 1959. It was followed on 14 September 1959 by *Rassemblement democratique Rwandaise* (RADER), then the *Partie du Mouvement de l'Emancipation Hutu* (PARMEHUTU) was created on 9 October 1959. *Association pour la promotion sociale de la Masse* (APROSOMA) has existed since 15 February 1959.

95. See Linden (1977): 267-68.
96. *Ibid.*
97. Reyntjens (1985): 321.
98. *Ibid:* 293-321
99. See A.L. Doc. No 4 session of 23 February 1961, 1, quoted by Reyntjens (1984) *supra* 325.
100. In adopting the constitution of 1962 considered as the legitimate one, no reference to the constitution of Gitarama was made.
101. See Reyntjens (1984) *supra:* 358-64.
102. *Ibid.,* 364.
103. Durieux (1973): 310.
104. See African Rights (1995) *supra:* 12.
105. *Ibid*
106. See Nkunzumwami (1996): 88-89.
107. *Ibid.*
108. Lugan (1997) *supra:* 442-56.
109. See 'Communiqué du 5 juillet 1973,' in B. Lugan, ibid: 443-45.
110. Reyntjens, supra: 508.
111. For details on the constitutional gap between 1973 and 1978 see, Basomingera (1986): 65-68.
112. Article 7 of the constitution of 1978, in Reyntjens and Gorus *supra, 6.*
113. See National University of Rwanda (1988) *supra,* 28.
114. The Rwandese Patriotic Front (RPF) was an organisation composed mostly by Rwandans in exile who decided to take arms and began their attack from Uganda.
115. Articles 12-33 of the 1991 constitution, in F. Reyntjens and J. Gorus (eds.) *supra note* 1:24.
116. This is mostly illustrated by the case of suspension of the constitution in 1973 as well as 1978 constitution which was fashioned to serve the regime in place.
117. Kiga is usually used to refer to the northern regions of Rwanda (Gisenyi, Ruhengeri, and Byumba).
118. Nduga usually refers to those regions of south and sometimes the centre of Rwanda (Gitarama, Butare Gekongoro.)
119. *Paternostre de la Mairieu* (1972) *supra,* 250.
120. This constitution was modified by the law No 18/83 of 3 August 1993. Following the Arusha Peace Accord also a number of articles were abrogated or replaced by those of the Arusha Peace Accord.
121. The Arusha Peace Accord was signed between the Rwandese Patriotic Front (RPF) and the then Government of Rwanda. It contains the Agreement on Cease Fire, the Protocol Agreement on the Rule of Law, the Protocol Agreement on Power-Sharing within the Framework of a Broad-Based Transitional Government, the Protocol Agreement on the Repatriation of Refugees and the Resettlement of Displaced Persons, the Protocol Agreement on Integration of Armed Forces of the Parties and the Protocol Agreement on Miscellaneous Issues and Final Provisions. The Arusha Peace Accord was signed in Arusha on 3 August 1993.
122. The Protocol on the Rule of Law was adopted on 18 August 1992, See Reyntjens and Gorus *supra,* 8.
123. *Ibid.*
124. Article 15, *Arusha Peace Accord,* the *Protocol Agreement on the Rule of Law.*
125. *Ibid.*
126. See article 24, *Arusha Peace Accord, the Protocol Agreement on Power Sharing.*
127. See article 24, *Arusha Peace Accord, Protocol on Power Sharing;* Reyntjens and Gorus *supra,* 12.
128. *Ibid.*

129. Organic law No 08/96 of 30 August 1996 on the organisation of Prosecution for offences constituting the crimes of genocide or crimes against humanity committed since 1 October 1990; J.O. No 17 of 1 September 1996.
130. The period of transition which started in July 1994 ended in July 1999 but it was extended for 4 more years and is thus scheduled to end in July 2003.

References

Africa Rights (1995) *Rwanda, Death, Despair and Defiance*, (Revised Edition).

Basomingera A., (1986) *Cours de Droit Constitutionnel*, (2ᵉ serie) Butare.

Breton, R., (1981) *Les ethnies, Collection Que-Sais-Je, No 1924,P.U.F.* Paris.

Desforge, A. (1972) *Defeat is the only bad news: Rwanda under Musiinga 1896-1931,* Yale: Yale University, Ph.D Thesis (unpublished).

_____. (1986) 'The Drum is Greater than the Shout; the 1912 Rebellion in Northern Rwanda,' in D. Crummey (ed.) *Banditry, Rebellion and Social Protest in Africa*, London.

Durieux, A. (1973) 'Les libertés bubliques de la République du Rwanda,' in *Revue Juridique et Politique*.

Eriksen, T.H.M. (1993) Ethnicity and Nationalism: Anthropoligical Perspectives, London: Pluto Press.

Ginther, K. (1998) 'Civil Society and Development,' in *Institute for Scientific Co-operation, Law and State: A Biannual Collection of Recent German Contribution to these Fields*, (58) Tubingen, 85-86.

Goldhagen, D.J. (1996) *Hitler's Willing Executioners, Ordinary Germans and the Holocaust*, New York: Alfred A. Knopf.

Hagenimana, F.X. (1990) *La Séparation des Pouvoirs et Histoire Constitutionnelle Rwandaise, Mémoire*, Kigali: UNR.

Hertefelt M. (1971) *Les clans du Rwanda. Ancien-Elements d'Ethnosocologie et d'Ethnohistoire* No 70;

Kagame A., (1975) *Un Abrégé de l'Histoire du Rwanda de 1853 a 1972*, Butare; Editions Universitaires du Rwanda.

_____. *Code des institutions du Rwanda précoloniale.*

Kayihura, M. (1998) 'Composantes et relations sociales au Rwanda pre-colonial, colonial et post-colonial: Hutu,Tutsi, Twa, lignages et clans,' in *Rapport de synthese du seminaire sur l'histoire du Rwanda,* Butare, 14-18 decembre.

Kayumba, C. (1998) 'Le système de clientélisme pastoral (ubuhake),' in *Rapport de Synthèse du Séminaire sur l'Histoire du Rwanda, Butare*, 14-18 December, 42.

Kornblum, W. (1988) *Sociology in a changing world*, New York: Holt.

Linden, F. (1977) *Church and Revolution in Rwanda*, Manchester: MUP.

Lugan, B. (1997) *Histoire du Rwanda, de la Préhistoire à nos jours, Bartillat*, Paris.

Maquet, J. (1961) *The premises of inequality in Rwanda*, Oxford: Oxford University Press.

Mbolongo E., (1980) *L'Afrique au XXe Siecle: Le Continent Convoite, Etudes Vivantes*, Paris.

Murego D., (1975) *La Revolution Rwandaise 1959-1962, Thèse de Doctorat*, Louvain; Institut des Sciences Politiques et Sociales.

National University of Rwanda (1998) *Comprehending and Mastering Conflicts: The case of Genocide in Rwanda: Genesis, Consequences and Action Proposals*, October, 12.

Newbury, C. (1988*) The Cohesion of Oppression: Clientship and ethnicity in Rwanda, 1860-1960*, New York: Colombia University Press.

Nkunzumwami E., (1996) *La Tragédie Rwandaise, Historique et Perspectives*, l'Harmattan.

Nkurunziza, C., (1988) *Histoire des Institutions Politique du Rwanda*, Course Notes, Kigali: unpublished.

Overdulve, C.M. (1997) *Rwanda, un peuple avec une histoire*, L'Harmattan.

P. Erny (1994) *Rwanda 1994, Clés pour comprendre le calvaire d'un peuple*, Paris: Editions l'Harmattan.

Page, A. (1993) *Un royaume hamite au centre de l'Afrique*, I.R.C.C.B. (I) Bruxelles.

Paternostre, B. de la Mairieu (1972) *Le Rwanda, son effort de développement*, Bruxelles.

Perugia, P.D ,*Les derniers rois mages*, Paris: Editions Phebus.

Reyntjens F. (1985) Pouvoir *et Droit au Rwanda, Droit public et évolution politique, 1916-1974*, Bruxelles; Musée Royale de l'Afrique Centrale.

_____. (1984) *Pouvoir et Droit au Rwanda, Envers.*

_____. (1985) *Pouvoir et Droit au Rwanda, Droit public et évolution politique 1916-1973*, Tervuren; Musée Royale de l'Afrique Centrale, 79.

_____. (1994) 'The 1991 Constitution of Rwanda,' in F.Reyntjens and J. Gorus (eds.) *Codes et Lois du Rwanda*, (I) 21-30.

Roosens, E., (1989) *Creating Ethnicity: The Process of Ethnogenesis*, Newbury Park: Sage Publications.

Sanders, E.R. (1969) 'The Hamitic Hypothesis: Its Origin and Functions in Time Perspective,' *Journal of African History*, 521.

Sevo K. and G. Mountali, 'L'Anthropologie contemporaine et la remise en cause du concept d'ethnie,' in C. *Coauery Vidrovitch, Histoire démographique, concept d'ethnie, Recherche diverse, Groupe de recherche Afrique Noire*, Cahier No 8 Université de Paris VII.

Young, Crawford 'Nationalism, Ethnicity and Class in Africa: A retrospective,' in *Cahier d'Etudes Africaines*, (XXVI-3)103.

8

Constitutions, Law and Civil Society: Discourses on the Legitimacy of People's Power

Willy Mutunga

The right to rebel and to change or overthrow a dictatorship are both constitutional and legal. The constitutionality and legality of peaceful mass action means that civil society becomes an arena of contesting political power with the capacity of capturing the state. Many civil society activists have argued, that such a capture of the state by the forces of civil society, must be interim. However, this need not be the case because political parties may emerge from such social movements (without divorcing themselves from them) and continue holding political power. What the social movements in civil society must establish in the politics of each African country is the role of effective checks and balances and the readiness to contest for and secure political power.

   Civil society must re-examine its positions on the principle of non-partisanship that has been invoked to de-legitimise political action and the contest for political power. Civil society must furthermore perceive their alliances with political parties as necessary for their political expression and contestation of political power. The debate whether opposition political parties are part of civil society is irrelevant for these alliances to occur. [1] Indeed, such alliances between opposition political parties and the various sectors of civil society against African dictatorships are becoming common. The examples of Kenya, Zimbabwe and Côte d'Ivoire most readily come to mind. [2]

   The argument here is that what has been waved by staunch positivists as the law on political activities by various sectors of civil society is open to challenge. A further argument is that the courts of law can positively invoke the legal theories we discuss here in order to broaden the democratic space that is opening up in Africa. In turn, this will promote democratisation by de-legitimising the criminalisation of politics through the use of criminal charges such as treason or sedition that still exist in the outdated statute books of numerous African countries. Fortunately for East Africa and perhaps the rest of Common Law Africa, the courts can adopt such theories as Sir

Udo Udoma Uganda's first African Chief Justice did. The precedential value of such theories and, indeed the case law is of persuasive authority.[3]

The concept of popular sovereignty justifies the right of people to overthrow tyrannical, oppressive and despotic governments. This concept has been exercised throughout history by both the bourgeoisie and the working class. The Americans used it to throw out the British in 1776, as did the French to create a republic. South Africans used it against apartheid and the Mau Mau against the British in colonial Kenya. The essence of the concept is that all sovereignty comes from the people, not the state, or an elite class of privileged social groups. That state must serve the people's interests and not the reverse. In their clauses on political participation, the Universal Declaration of Human Rights (UDHR) and the International Covenant on Civil & Political Rights (ICCPR) assume that sovereignty belongs to the people. Common Article one of the ICCPR and the International Covenant on Economic, Social and Cultural Rights (ICESCR) on self-determination are also based on this concept. Democracy would not be possible without it. This essay is concerned with explicating the concept of 'popular ownership' of the state and demonstrating how constitutional reform processes and even extra-constitutional seizures of power must respond to the urgings of common people with regard to reform. Its main point of reference is the case of Kenya, although the issues at hand are of continental application.

Ex parte Matovu's case and the relevance of Hans Kelsen to civil society

In the famous case of *Uganda v. Commissioner of Prison, ex Parte Matovu*[4] the facts were that the applicant, Michael Matovu, was arrested on 22 May 1966 under the notorious Deportation Ordinance. Following a court nullification of the ordinance, he was released, rearrested and once again detained on 16 July 1966 under emergency legislation that had been brought into force immediately after his first arrest. Between 22 February and 15 April 1966 a series of events took place in Uganda which culminated in the overthrow of the 1962 independence constitution of Uganda and its replacement by another called the 1966 'interim' constitution—a new constitutional instrument enacted to defuse what was perceived to be a crisis. Among other changes the 1966 constitution set up the office of the president with executive powers. Under this constitution a state of public emergency was declared and the Emergency Powers (Detention) Regulations 1966 were enacted. Michael Matovu took out *habeas corpus* proceedings in the High Court.

The case discussed various technical issues, but for our purposes it is important to note that the-then chief justice of Uganda, Sir Udo Udoma held that the series of events that took place in Uganda from 22 February 1966 to 15 April 1966, were law-creating facts appropriately described in law as a 'revolution.'[5] Relying on the positivist jurist Hans Kelsen, Udoma and his colleagues on the bench were of the view that this revolution resulted from an abrupt political change not contemplated by the independence constitution. Furthermore, this change destroyed the entire legal order and ushered in a new constitution that overthrew the 1962 instrument.

For our purposes, it is also important to recall that the decision also accepted Kelsen's proposition that the factors that cause political change are irrelevant. Rather, it is the effect of the political change and the satisfaction of the criteria Kelsen gives for what constitutes a revolution that are important to decide whether a new revolutionary social order exists. Kelsen also anticipated a replacement of the status quo '... through a movement emanating from the mass of the people...'[6] If this movement satisfied his criteria then in law there was a revolution and consequently a new social order had come into existence.

Civil society constitutes organisations that have been crucial and fundamental pillars to peaceful and non-violent mass action. Organisations of students, workers, the youth, women, people with disabilities, religious associations, NGOs, community-based groups, minorities and non-profit making organisations in the private sector, continue to play crucial political roles in African countries. We have witnessed the phenomenon of 'people's power' in Benin, Côte d'Ivoire, the Philippines and Indonesia. In Africa, the decade of the 1990s has witnessed movements of the people in support of the so-called 'second liberation.' Constitution-making projects have included mass action in their strategies for reform.[7] Africa has also witnessed the violent overthrow of governments in Ethiopia, the former Zaire and Sierra Leone among others. There have continued to be military coups d' etat, with the example of Côte d'Ivoire as the most recent. There have also been negotiated settlements which have resulted in new societal orders. South Africa still remains the best example of this last experience.

Despite resistance, dictatorships in Africa continue to rear their ugly undemocratic heads. The institutions of recolonisation and the interests they represent have surfaced.[8] However, recolonisation can no longer take cover under the discourses of independence and national development. It is not that foreign interests had gone underground. Instead, we have simply stopped engaging in the discourses of imperialism, foreign domination, social-imperialism and the other revolutionary discourses of the 1960s, 1970s and 1980s because of the intellectual surrender that was reflected in the end of the Cold War. The new discourses of 'globalisation,' 'the New World order,' and the 'free market' also reflect this intellectual surrender. We all seem to accept that communism and socialism are indeed dead!

The seizure of political power and the resultant capture of the state in Africa has, therefore, largely been accomplished through elections, successful votes of no-confidence, the peaceful sharing of political power, military take-overs, palace coups, foreign interventions (including mercenary activities) and revolutionary armed struggles. In cases where the capture of state power has not occurred through legal means laid down by the status quo, Kelsen's theory has been invoked to legitimise a new revolutionary social order.[9]

There are, however, activities that take place before the invocation of Kelsen's theory that are close to what the various sectors of civil society do. These activities, which constitute the exercise of people's power (demonstrations, processions, boycotts, strikes and others that have collectively been called peaceful, non-violent civic action or simply mass action or civil disobedience) may be outlawed through constitutional and legal instruments, administrative fiat, and state violence. These activities constitute the right to rebel and to change or collectively overthrow such governments through peaceful mass action. This latter right can be called the right to revolution.

Staunch positivists invoke the dictum: 'the law is the law is the law.' Such theorists declare activities of the kind listed above as subversive and punishable. African legal theorists who support the status quo and advise African dictatorships to outlaw and hang dissidents invoke similar legal arguments and theories. Reformists use the same bourgeois theories to legitimise their activities. These arguments by African reformists warrant discussion because they are currently the life-nerve of the struggles that are taking place in many parts of the continent. They are also relevant because the middle class (the *Walalaheri*)[10] in these countries have posed the problem in such terms. They have likewise based their support of the struggles of the mass of the people, the *Walalahoi* (the exploited, the oppressed, or Frantz Fanon's 'wretched of the earth')[11] against their national exploiters and oppressors, the compradors, the *Walalahai,*[12] and the support of the compradors by the international ruling classes of the global socio-economic systems, the *Walalahaihai.*[13]

There is no need to rationalise the legitimacy of people's power. The argument that the exercise of people's power has a sound constitutional and legal basis can and must be made. The argument demands that the events taking place before Kelsen's revolution are neither illegitimate nor illegal. Where do we look for such constitutional and legal basis? We will find it in the legal theories of the feudalist era of the emerging bourgeoisie. These legal theories formed a formidable legal arsenal against backwardness and oppression. And so we revisit Kelsen, Locke and Rousseau for the constitutional and legal justification of mass action, the right to rebel, the right to change and overthrow dictatorships, the political impact of social contract theory, and the right to self-defence.[14] We revisit Montesquieu to justify civil society as a fourth arm in the separation of powers because the three arms of government have consistently usurped the people's powers as evidenced by presidential authoritarianism, legislative chicanery and judicial incompetence.

Reconceptualising the overthrow of dictatorships

In an issue of this nature, analysing the Marxist theory of state and law would be the obvious commencement point because of its specific treatment of the subject. The theories analysed here are what Karl Marx[15] and his adherents would describe as bourgeois, because they reflect the interests and rule of the bourgeois ruling class. These theories also describe the bourgeois state as 'collective capitalist' and clearly view the overthrow of that state by violent revolution as inevitable and necessary. Marxist analysis and its developments by other theorists such as V.I. Lenin,[16] Mao Zedong,[17] Enver Hoxha,[18] Antonio Gramsci,[19] and East African scholars such as Issa Shivji,[20] Mahmood Mamdani,[21] Yash Tandon,[22] Dani Wadada Nabudere,[23] Issa Khamis,[24] and Ngugi Wa Thiong'o,[25] is, in our opinion, still on the agenda of liberation. What is investigated here are the positive aspects of bourgeois legal theory and law in a revolution that emerges out of a peaceful, non-violent mass action: this is a contradiction in terms of Marxist discourse. It cannot be denied, however, that movements of the mass of people have carried out revolutions peacefully in cases where the state doubted whether its own machinery of violence would not be met by a more powerful people's power.[26]

Social democrats and various sectors of civil society have popularised the theory of social contract. It has been emphasised that when a government is no longer able to perform its terms of the social contract (key among them being the protection of life, freedom and property) it has no legal or moral legitimacy to stay in power. Such government should therefore resign. If it fails to do so, the people have the right to recall and overthrow it. John Locke advanced this theory and his argument—in a language that is clearly not gender sensitive—is well paraphrased by R.W.M. Dias:

> Executive powers were regarded as natural powers of a quasi-judicial character. To remedy this flaw Man entered into the social contract by which he yielded to the sovereign, not all its rights, but only the power to preserve order and enforce the law of nature. The individual retained the rights to life, liberty and estate, for they were the natural and 'inalienable rights of Man.' This was an innovation of significance inasmuch as the idea of a natural law of society as transmuted into one of the individual natural rights which could be used to resist social control. The purpose of the government was to protect these; it has no other end than 'to preserve the members of that society in their lives, liberties and possessions.' Its

function is in the nature of a trust; Locke put it, all this 'is limited to the public good of the society.' So long as the government fulfils this purpose, its law should be binding. But when it ceases to protect or begins to encroach on these natural rights, laws lose their validity and the government may be overthrown.[27]

On this basis Dias observes that Locke[28] was able to champion the 'Glorious Revolution' in England in 1688-1689, and his idea of the supremacy of natural law over positive law was invoked by the American colonists against the laws passed by the British parliament in the years 1775-1781.[29] In both cases, the resistance faced feudalist authoritarianism, absolute monarchism and the denial of bourgeois freedoms as we understand them today. And it is from here that we draw clear political parallels between the feudal systems of the West and the post-independence dictatorial regimes of Africa. The difference that has to be emphasised is that the autocrats, dictators and oppressors who rule in Africa today have generally operated Westminster or Elysée-style constitutions—a contradiction that the feudalist absolute and enlightened monarchs did not have to contend with. It is this contradiction that reflects the positive use of bourgeois rights and laws to resist authoritarianism.

The theory of social contract reflected the struggles to resist an oppressive system headed by an oppressive monarchy. The social contract theory was further developed by Jean-Jacques Rousseau.[30] Again, Dias paraphrases Rousseau in these terms:

> Rousseau set out to evolve a community in which the community as such would protect the individual; but which at the same time the individual would remain free from oppression. All should participate in policy-making. Accordingly, he argued that in the original contract the individuals did not surrender their rights to any single sovereign, but to society as a whole, and this is their guarantee of freedom and equality. Society, having come into being for this purpose, is expected to restore these rights to its members as civil liberties. Their basis is a moral one. Each individual is not subject to any other individual, but to the 'general will' and to obey this is to obey himself. Government and law are both dependent upon general will, on popular as distinct from parliamentary sovereignty, which may revoke or overthrow them.[31]

Dias observes that this theory was utilised as the philosophy of the French revolution of 1789.[32] In both Locke's and Rousseau's expositions people's power is supreme. That power has distinct features of self-help and self-reliance in its resistance to authoritarianism, exploitation and oppression. In exercise of this supreme power, the people can use a continuum of strategies: ranging from the peaceful overthrow of the government and the law, to violent revolution. It can also be argued that the principle of self-defence that justifies resistance against authoritarianism and oppression is based on these theories. Civil disobedience is yet another strategy that can be informed by these theories. [33]

Lloyd and Freeman[34] argue that '...social contract is a wholly formal and analytic construct that can be used as a means of presenting conflicting political ideals.'[35] They argue that many liberal theorists emphasise the theory either in terms of consent theory or, borrow from John Rawl's theory of justice:[36] 'At root, the political theory is that' no man can be subjected to the political power of another without his own consent.' Obedience to authority is thus legitimated by voluntary submission to those who exercise authority.'[37]

In *ex-Parte Matovu's* case, then Chief Justice Sir Udo Udoma accurately reproduced the theory from Kelsen's book and held that coups d'etat are recognised in international law as a proper and effective legal means of changing governments or constitutions. [38] The learned Chief Justice discussed the principles of legitimacy, the change of the basic norm (the *Grundnorm*) and the birth and death of the state as a legal problem.[39] Kelsen argued that:

> A revolution, in this wide sense, occurs whenever the legal order of a community is nullified and replaced by a new order in any illegitimate way, that is, in a way not prescribed by the first order itself. It is in this context irrelevant whether or not this replacement is effected through a violent uprising against those individuals who so far have been legitimate organs competent to create and amend the legal order. It is equally irrelevant whether the replacement is effected through a movement emanating from the mass of the people, or through the action from those in government positions.[40]

Kelsen's theory clearly makes the point that if the new order fails to materialise and the old is preserved, the authors of the new revolutionary order commit treason and can be prosecuted for that high crime. The basis of this argument arises from what he calls the '...illegitimate way, that is, a way not prescribed by the first order.' In most African countries the Westminster and Elysée style constitutions have bills of rights incorporating the bulk of bourgeois rights.[41] These bills of rights have also been dubbed 'Bills of Exceptions' in which fascist and oppressive colonial and neo-colonial laws have negated the enjoyment of the rights ostensibly protected. In Kelsen's theory these exceptions are part of the law. What the theory does is to criminalise democratic struggles at the altar of staunch positivism: 'the law is the law is the law.' Kelsen's theory reflects an established conservative bourgeois order that staunch positivism serves.

The theories of Locke and Rousseau reflect a revolutionary bourgeois project, challenging the backward feudal order and its autocratic monarchy. In answer to Kelsen, both Locke and Rousseau would have argued that people's power and the people prescribe the first order or the community determines the terms of the contract. The people decide what power they concede to the sovereign, governments and to the law. The theories of Locke and Rousseau can be utilised to legitimise activities that emanate from the people's movement. People's power can overthrow the constitution and the law. The controversy is, of course clear: the reformists will be accused of stating what the law ought to be.

The reformists, however, have an argument that is invoked to justify their struggle for the attainment of bourgeois rights. Bourgeois rights must be demanded and, once given, protected in authoritarian countries. Dictatorships find these rights revolutionary and unacceptable. The international community that takes bourgeois rights for granted, can be mobilised to fight for these rights for the rest of humanity. The international community has not abandoned the project of civilising the 'native'; although, in the case of bourgeois rights there are arguments by the same international community that the native does not deserve them. The hypocrisy, perfidy, double standards and paternalism displayed by the international community are part of the challenges reformists must contend with. The autocrats and their international masters—the international bourgeoisie—therefore, deny the protection and defence of bourgeois rights. The latter and their agents, the autocrats, face a challenge from the entire peoples of the world whose rights are constantly denied.

In countries with relative independence of the judiciary, the reformists may want to take the theories of Locke and Rousseau to court and invoke them in the defence of peaceful, non-violent mass action. The dangers are obvious. In authoritarian countries, staunch positivism could be positive because the law may not be followed. Again this issue falls within the area of discretion. Consequently, conservative judges may view these arguments as raising the spectre of anarchy. We should, however, not forget that the judiciary, like the religious organisations and the international community, normally back the winners. The argument could be politically timed in the way that Kelsen's theory was utilised in the context of post-revolutionary Uganda. What discretion did Sir Udo Udoma have in the matter after he had sworn to defend the 1966 Constitution?

The French philosopher, Montesquieu, theorised the doctrine of separation of powers: 'The secret of its [the English constitution] success … lay in the fact that power was not concentrated in the hands of an individual or group. Unless power be made to check power, it will be abused.'[42] The guarantee against that abuse of power by the sovereign lay in the establishment of mutual checks between the three arms of government, the Executive, the judiciary and the legislature. The danger, therefore, was the absolute union of these functions in one person or body. Again, the mischief here was clear: the absolute monarchy. The mischief in most authoritarian countries is the executive or 'imperial' presidency that in effect operates like a monarchy.[43] The separation of powers while clearly stated on paper in the constitutions of most African countries, is in practice actually the union and the culmination of all powers in the Big Man (or rarely, the Big Woman).

The judiciary is supposed to check the powers of the executive and parliament in the name of the people and to protect their rights: 'Having one's day in court,' became a sword for the emerging bourgeoisie against feudal authoritarianism. The separation of powers as a doctrine consolidated bourgeois rule by giving it decentralised and democratised structures. In most African countries, the judiciary is not independent. It has either succumbed to the influence of the executive or the moneybags of the *Walalahais*.

An argument has also been advanced by members of parliament and elected councillors that parliament is the voice of all the people. Once elected, councillors and members of parliament become 'people's representatives' by acquiring the voices of their constituents in all national matters. This is the fallacy behind the call by certain authoritarian African leaders that the constitution-making project is rightly a task for parliaments.[44] Once the autocrats buy the parliamentary voice, the people's voice ceases to exist.

Demystifying the separation of powers is a project in which Locke and Rousseau can be utilised to full effect. The people have the right to recall their powers from all the arms of government. Indeed, it can be argued that the people are recalling these powers from the executive where they are concentrated. Checks and balances on the separation of power have to emanate from the people and their organisations. The demand by the various sectors of organised civil society to be recognised as an arm of government is yet another demand that civil society should represent the people. Again, as a concept of self-government by the *Walalahois* may not exist, the dangers of the people's voices being captured by this fourth arm of government are real. The 'anti-power movement' as Ifi Amadiume calls it,[45] is still in danger of being captured and held prisoner.

Civil society as an arena for contesting political power

The state, civil society and the seizure of political power

Conceptualising civil society is a task undertaken elsewhere and will not be revisited in this essay.[46] The doctrine of checks and balances and the manner in which various sectors of civil society can invoke it to hold the three arms of government accountable has already been alluded to. Various sectors of civil society have invoked this doctrine and played the role of check and balance when the state has allowed them to do so. The sectors have been allowed to generally represent the people when this representation has not challenged the powers of the state. The representation has also been tolerated when it has challenged the political power of the ruling classes.

One doctrine that has kept the various sectors of civil society in check is the doctrine of non-partisanship that such sectors have uncritically accepted. At its most conservative, this doctrine demands that the various sectors of civil society be apolitical. What this means in practical terms is support of the status quo. The middle ground of this doctrine is the argument that civil society has political views, but these views are not to be perceived as supporting any partisan political interests. The radical view of this doctrine is argued as follows: Non-partisanship—the sacred principle in the voluntary sector— must be demystified. The principle, it has been argued, does not mean that the various sectors of civil society do not have political views. Nor does it mean that these sectors are barred from political participation. What the principle implies is that these sectors should shun being appendages, departments or being directly or indirectly integrated to partisan interests. It has never been argued that members of institutions in the various sectors of civil society should not be card-carrying members of political parties or of the political movements of their choice. And this is not the end of the debate. Partisan interests share some of the views of these sectors. These sectors are themselves nurseries for alternative political leaderships. The contest for political power is seen as the business of all and not exclusively that of political parties. No wonder there have been suggestions that opposition political parties be described as part of civil society.[47]

Some discussion has been conducted about social movements and civil society.[48] A number of these movements have struggled to change the status quo.[49] Others have the distinct objective of capturing political power.[50] Yet others struggle for broad changes in society and convert themselves into political parties on the eve of elections. A category of social movement that does not convert itself into a political party, but allows such a party to have a base in the movement—which the movement does not disband—and continues to direct the political party so formed has become the subject of some debate in Kenya. The political party becomes the political expression of the movement and is politically subordinated to it. Here, civil society is being urged to play the role that the private sector plays in directing and controlling political parties to ensure that the interests of the private sector are not jeopardised. Civil society has the intellectual and material resources to pursue the projects of the private sector in the contestation for political power.

The participation by the sectors of civil society in interim governments is yet another crucial issue in this debate. The principle of non-partisanship would demand that civil society participate in interim governments as a matter of national interest. Civil society does so on an interim basis because it aims at preparing an environment for the partisan interests to contest political power in a fair environment. Having done that for any nation, it is argued, civil society has to give up power to avoid the charges of partisanship.[51] Thus, it is further argued, civil society can set a great precedent of cleaning up the politics of the nation, much in the same vein as the military claims to do. The difference between the military and civil sector in issues of leadership, it has been argued, need not be labored.[52] Here, the theories of Locke and Rousseau beg the question: Who will lead the movement of the mass of the people against the authoritarian sovereign or the union of the separated powers? Such leadership will always come from civil society, and various sectors of civil society must take this project aboard in their objectives.

On the subject of collapsed, collapsing or failed states,[53] the question posed by Professor Ali Mazrui: 'What is the solution in situations of acute state-failure or political collapse?' has drawn various solutions and options.[54] In none of these possible options has the role of civil society in capturing state power been discussed. Various sectors of civil society have a broader perspective of national interest than political parties, who by their very nature and calling are formed to struggle for the narrow confines of political power while paying lip service to national issues. It is also from the sectors of civil society that international solidarities that demand the survival of humanity the world over will be forged.

Some lessons from Kenya

On August 26, 1997 the question of the legitimacy of people's power in the context of Kenya came up in one of the plenary sessions of the National Convention Assembly (NCA)—a grouping of civil society organisations that has recently led the opposition to the government of President Daniel arap Moi and his Kenya African National Union (KANU) government.[55] It was argued that the Moi-KANU regime had ceased to have the constitutional, legal and moral power to rule the country. The regime had, it was further contended, failed to carry out economic, social, cultural and political reform. The regime was oppressive, corrupt and dictatorial. The new forces assembled at the convention it was argued had the credibility of a moral government. These forces, therefore, needed to discuss how they would contest political power through mass action. The debate on these issues was not informed by the legal technicalities of the theories of either Locke or Rousseau. The lawyers in the movement, quite rightly, did not seek to complicate the debate by bringing in such technicalities. However, the theory of social contract was articulated in a manner that the convention understood. It was argued that the Moi-KANU regime had violated all its terms under the social contract, and it left the people with no option but to disobey it. The question then was: *what had to be done?*

It should be stated here that there were those who argued against the invocation of the social contract theory. The majority of those who articulated views against this theory were simply afraid of sedition or treason charges. They sought to discredit the theory. Others who supported the opposition to the social contract theory were simply afraid of taking up the mantle of leadership coupled with the realisation that while their criticism of the regime was easy, inheriting its problems was not a palatable option. Yet others revived the debate of one presidential candidate for all the opposition parties to sidetrack the discussion on seizing political power. If the idea of one presidential candidate was accepted, then the convention was going to await the general election that was around the corner and expected before the end of the year.

There was, however, overwhelming support for the social contract theory. It was proposed that there be a presidency that rotates among the leaders of the opposition political parties and the leaders of civil society. All opposition political parties were represented in the convention, and the discussions on taking power from the Moi-KANU regime were indeed serious. The compromise reached was a relief to the middle class initiative that did not want to take over power through a people's initiative. It was decided that if the regime did not pass the minimal reforms before the general election, then the National Convention Assembly (NCA) would convert itself into a Constituent Assembly—a parallel parliament; not a parallel government.[56] At the time of the compromise, the government was already aware of the deliberations at the convention and had stated that the convention was out to overthrow the government.[57] These threats must have been taken seriously by the majority of the delegates and may explain the comprise arrived at.

As the crises in Kenya deepened, it became clear that the obvious leaders of the convention were not acceptable to some of the leaders of the political parties.[58] Rather than sort out these differences the 'KANU deserters' (as the Kenyan opposition is called) trekked back to KANU. What came to be called the Inter-Parties Parliamentary Group (IPPG) came into existence.[59] The Moi-KANU regime regained its political initiative and gave the country extremely minimalist reforms in the constitutional arena.

One of the crucial consequences of this discussion was the death of the distinction between convention and conference. It has been argued by constitutional lawyers that the French model of change was unacceptable in Kenya because at no point did the movement intend to overthrow the government.[60] Such constitutional lawyers were basically informed by staunch positivist principles. Following the convention proceedings, the distinction was not necessary any more. The movement had discussed the taking of political power and the state on the basis of social contract theory. It would appear that in the case of Kenya, both Locke and Rousseau have had their theories popularised and justified in political rather than legalistic terms. That is an important lesson for contemporary struggles against dictatorship and the resilience of broad concepts of inclusion.

Conclusion

Africa is experiencing a new political cycle. Recolonisation is fast becoming a new reality on the continent. African dictatorships never lose elections because such elections are neither peaceful, free nor fair. Military interventions are unacceptable. Naked foreign invasion and occupation are likewise unpalatable. And yet, democratisation will not come from periodic elections which political parties viewed as their exclusive domain of operation. One view is that the various sectors of civil society are nurseries for alternative political leadership and clean politics. This is, of course, debatable. What must be thrust into the dustbin of legal history is the argument that the right to rebel and overthrow governments does not have valid constitutional and legal foundations. Such a legal position inhibits the roles which the sectors of civil society can play in effecting political change in contemporary society.

The Kenyan experience very clearly illustrates that the issue here is political. Legal theories legitimise political positions that the reforms invoke to resist authoritarianism and dictatorship. The reform movement will only successfully use the legal theories when victory is on the horizon and when it can argue that it leads the people's power against authoritarianism. The utilisation of courts as arenas of struggle cannot be ruled out. *Ex-Parte Matovu* teaches us that these theories can be utilised to legitimise new social orders. Such theories can also be invoked as a defence to charges of treason or sedition which invariably can be used by the state to crack down on the forces of reform. The use of courts is thus a double-edged sword that would require proper timing if the authoritarian blade is not to mutilate the reformist hand.

The various sectors of civil society will have to accept this new role and struggle for it. The Kenyan experience illustrates that this is no easy task. The civic sector is not homogeneous. It has secular and religious components in which the latter has a broad popular base. Key groups in civil society— most notably the youth, women and workers—have to be mobilised to create the necessary popular base for the reformists to achieve this mission of contesting political power. The Kenyan experience shows that relying on the popular parties or the religious groups is unreliable at the best of times.

Finally, what will emerge as people's power in civil society must be clearly identified and analysed? The people's power is still crying to be allowed to have its voice heard. There are so many groups speaking in the name of the people that the use of bourgeois theories will only legitimate the contestation of political power between the social groups that are involved and in the result exclude the people themselves. It is important to note that under such circumstances bourgeois theories have their limitations which have to be rescued by other theories that will bring about the realisation of people's power. As these theories are similarly under interrogation, the intellectual challenge of the new millennium is the crafting of a theory that will guarantee the survival of humanity.

Notes

1. For arguments that support the proposition see, Akiiki B. Mujaju (1997); Folson (1993) and Abatudu (1995).
2. The Kenyan story is recounted in detail in Mutunga (1999). In Zimbabwe the movement called the National Constitutional Assembly (NCA) was such an alliance until the Movement for Democratic Change (MDC), a political party, delinked from the NCA to contest political power. In the new arrangement it became clear that MDC was championing the NCA's ideology and politics as reflected in the movement's agenda and policies. Other political parties sought the support of the movement in the elections of mid 2000.
3. *Dodhia v. National Grindlays Bank* [1970] E.A. 200.
4. [1966] E.A. 514.
5. Kelsen (1961): 117-18, 120.
6. *Ibid.*
7. Examples include Kenya, Zimbabwe and Nigeria.
8. The IMF and the World Bank are clearly such institutions. The international trading, manufacturing and other financial institutions (other than the IMF and World Bank) are part of the institutions of recolonisation.
9. Sir Udo Udoma followed the Pakistani case of *State v. Dosso* (1958), S.C. Pak. 533. It is worth noting that the *Dosso* case was overruled by *Jilani v. Government of Punjab* Pak. L. D. (1972) S. C. 139. Dias correctly notes that 'the point, however, is that this decision [*Jilani*] was given after that revolutionary regime had itself been overthrown so that the declaration that it was illegal *ab initio* was retrospective.' Dias (1976): 105-106. Dias also discusses the case of *Madzimbamuto v. Lardner-Burke* where Rhodesian courts accepted the legality of Ian Smith's Unilateral Declaration of Independence (UDI) while the English courts did not.
10. The *Walas* are Kiswahili words, popularised in part in Tanzania that describe these social classes—means those who get some comfortable sleep.
11. Those who sleep hungry and tired
12. Those who sleep alive, meaning full (of food, drink and other comforts) and are comfortable in their sleep.
13. Those who sleep always alive and happy and beat the *Walalahais*.
14. See, Kibwana (1996), at 362. At page 366 Kibwana concludes: 'In Jurisprudence or Legal Theory, it is accepted that citizens can justifiably resort to collective self help or civil disobedience to dislodge an authoritarian regime or to ensure change of policies and laws.'
15. See, Marx & Engels (1988); Hampstead & Freeman (1985) especially, Chapter 11.
16. Lenin (1970): 666.
17. Mao Zedong's works are published by Foreign Languages Press, Beijing. Publications of this press are still banned in Kenya.
18. Hoxha (1979).
19. Gramci's *Prison Notebooks* were published posthumously.
20. Shivji (1976); Shivji (1986).
21. Mamdani (1976); Mamdani (1997).
22. Tandon (1982).

23. Wadada Nabudere (1977); Wadada Nabudere (1986).
24. Khamis (1983).
25. Ngugi wa Thiong'o (1979).
26. Some examples to consider are Philippines, Indonesia and Benin.
27. See Dias (1976): 95-96.
28. *Ibid.,* 1632-704.
29. Dias, *op cit.,* 96.
30. *Ibid.,* 1712-778.
31. Dias, op.cit., 98.
32. *Ibid., op.cit.,* 98.
33. Kibwana, *op.cit.*
34. *Ibid.,* 115-116.
35. *Ibid.* Lloyd and Freeman state that the social contract theory was rejected by Hume and Bentham.
36. *Ibid.,* 116.
37. *Ibid.,* 116.
38. This argument was derived from Kelsen's book *General Theory of Law and State.*
39. Judgment in *Ex Parte Matovu,* 534-37.
40. *Ibid.,* 535-36.
41. It is also a truism that except for South Africa none of these countries can claim to have a modern Bill of Rights, i.e. is one that has domesticated the whole gamut of human rights and all the international covenants on human rights.
42. Dias, *op cit.,* 97.
43. In Kenya it is persuasive to argue that President Moi enjoys the powers of the President of the US, the prime minister and queen of Great Britain, and perhaps the pope!
44. The examples are Kenya and Tanzania.
45. Amadiume (1995): 35.
46. See, Mutunga, op.cit., 15-19.
47. *op.cit.*
48. *op cit.*
49. Amadiume, *op.cit.*
50. See generally Mamdani & Wamba-dia-Wamba (1995).
51. *op cit.,* 15.
52. Mutunga.
53. See Mazrui (1995), and Mutua (1995): 1113.
54. Professor Mazrui gives the following possible solutions: unilateral intervention by a single neighbouring power, intervention by a single power but with the blessing of a regional organisation, inter-African colonisation and annexation, regional integration, the formation of an African Security Council and the establishment of the Pan-African Emergency force.
55. NCA is a movement of the main organizations of Kenyan civil society.
56. This was a resolution by the NCA in its second plenary. See, Mutunga, *op.cit.*
57. The threat came from Mr J.J. Kamotho, the secretary-general of KANU.
58. Kivutha Kibwana was the leader of the civic arm of the convention while James Orengo (MP) was clearly the leader of its political arm.
59. This was a pact of by members of parliament that President Moi ingeniously manipulated to seize the political initiative on constitution making from the NCA.
60. This is a position that Dr Gibson Kamau Kuria has articulated in the concept paper drawn by the National Convention Planning Committee (NCPC) called *Njia ya Kufika Katiba Mpya* (Nairobi: NCPC: 1996).

References

Abatudu, M. I. M., (1995) *The State, Civil Society and the Democratisation Process in Nigeria,* Dakar; Codesria, Monograph Series 1.

Amadiume, Ifi (1995) 'Gender, Political Systems and Social Movements: A West African Experience,' in M. Mamdani & E. Wamba-dia- Wamba (eds.) *African Studies in Social Movements and Democracy,* Dakar: CODESRIA.

Dias (1976) *Jurisprudence* (Fourth Edition), London: Butterworths.

Folson, K.G., (1993) 'Political Parties and the Machinery of Democratic Government,' in K. A. Ninsin & F. K. Drah (eds.) *Political Parties and Democracy in Ghana's Fourth Republic,* Accra: Woeli Publishing Services.

Hampstead & Freeman (1985) *Lloyd's Introduction to Jurisprudence* (5th Edition), London: ELBS with Stevens.

Hoxha, Enver, (1979) *Imperialism and Revolution* Tirana: Nentori Publishing House.

Kelsen, Hans (1961) *General Theory of Law and State,* (translated A. Wedberg, 20th Century Legal Philosophy Series, 1).

Khamis, I. (1983) *Imperialism Today,* Dar-es-Salaam: TPH.

Kibwana, Kivutha (1996) 'The Right to Civil Disobedience,' in Kivutha Kibwana, Chris Maina Peter and Joseph Oloka-Onyango (eds.) *In Search of Freedom and Prosperity: Constitutional Reform in East Africa,* Nairobi: Claripress.

Lenin, V.I. (1970) *'Imperialism the Highest Stage of Capitalism',* in *Selected Works,* Moscow: Progress Publishers.

Mamdani M., (1976) *Politics and Class Formation in Uganda,* London: Heinemann.

_____. (1997) *Citizen and Subject: Contemporary African and the Legacy of Late Colonialism,* Princeton: Princeton University Press.

Mamdani M., & Wamba-dia-Wamba, (eds.) (1995) *African Studies in Social Movements and Democracy,* Dakar: CODESRIA.

Marx, K. & F. Engels (1988) *Selected Works in One-Volume,* London: Lawrence and Wishart.

Mazrui, Ali (1995) 'The African State as a Political Refugee: Institutional Collapse and Human Displacement,' *International Journal of Refugee Law,* (Special Issue) July.

Mujaju, Akiiki B., (1997) 'Civil Society at Bay in Uganda,' in G. Nzongola Ntalaja and Margaret Lee (eds.) *The State and Democracy in Africa,* Harare: APPS Books, 42.

Mutunga, Willy (1999) *Constitution-Making from the Middle: Civil Society and Transition Politics in Kenya, 1992-1997,* Nairobi & Harare: Sareat & Mwengo.

Shivji, Issa (1976) *Class Struggles in Tanzania*, London: Heinemann.

_____. (1986) *Law, State and the Working Class in Tanzania*, London: James Currey.

Tandon, Yash (1982) (Ed.) *The Debate on Class, State and Imperialism*, Dar-es-Salaam: TPH.

wa Mutua, Makau (1995) 'Why redraw the Map of Africa: A moral and Legal Inquiry' *Michigan Journal of International Law* (16): 1113.

wa Thiong'o, Ngugi (1979) *Detained*, Nairobi: Heinemann.

_____. (1976) *Petals of Blood*, Nairobi: Heinemann.

_____. (1987) *Matigari*, London: Heinemann.

Wadada Nabudere, Dani (1977) *The Political Economy of Imperialism*, London: Zed Press.

_____. (1986) *A Critique of the Political Economy of Social Imperialism*, unpublished Manuscript, Harare/Helsingor.

PART III

GENDER STRUGGLES AND CONSTITUTIONAL REFORM

9

Culture, Gender and Constitutional Restructuring in Nigeria

Charmaine Pereira

For most of Nigeria's post-colonial history, military regimes have usurped and dominated the political space. In the forty years since flag independence was attained, a mere ten have been governed by civilian administrations. Military regimes, marked by their arbitrary and coercive rule, have brought about a simultaneous decomposition of the economy and the polity.[1] Prolonged military rule has unleashed new torrents of authoritarianism and violence, whilst compounding tendencies in these directions. Authoritarianism, both military and civilian, constitutes a most pervasive influence on state and society. Ever-widening categories of people exert little control over their lives, can expect little justice from and even less respect for the rights and dignity of all human beings.[2] This state of affairs bears little resemblance to the promises inherent in successive constitutions, guaranteeing fundamental human rights for all categories of Nigerian citizens, women as well as men.

The reality for most categories of women is more likely to be characterised by the continued existence of gender inequity and women's subordination, a phenomenon widespread across the continent, and indeed, internationally. In Nigeria, this takes the form of pervasive beliefs that women are (men's) 'property', and by extension, minors, whose adult status is mediated via men, primarily the father or husband, but also uncle, brother and so on. A range of oppressive and inhumane practices, that do violence to women's bodily integrity and their humanity, are justified through recourse to a complex that variously combines 'culture/tradition/religion'. In the main, dominant constructions of 'culture' work against women being viewed as autonomous agents, unlike the situation of men. Whilst it is true that culture is a multifaceted realm,[3] the amalgamation of diverse practices in ways that pay scant attention to history or politics, produces a monolithic version of 'culture' that obscures more than it explains.[4]

As a result, the historical variations, complexities and differentiations among varying cultural practices are often less recognised. The wide range of practices justified in 'cultural' terms includes degrading widowhood rites, taking differing forms in the southern, eastern and northern states of Nigeria;

female genital mutilation, also differing in form, intensity, significance and regional differentiation; and child marriage, predominantly in the northern states.[5] In addition, there is the widespread denial of education, land and property rights and access to credit.[6] The prevalence of these practices can rarely be appropriately explained solely in terms of culture, however, since they are embedded in relations of power, as well as historical and social change. Yet 'cultural' practices tend to be spoken of as inherently unchanging and as essential to the sense of definition of a group of people. Mainstream representations of practices justified in cultural terms tend to ignore shifting historical and political contexts, and therefore ignore the possibility of change in the face of continuity.

An alternative understanding of culture would draw on the Gramscian theorisation of culture as conceptions of the world, which encompass ideas and philosophies, embodied in the social practices of individuals and the institutions within which these practices take place.[7] Implicit in this is the notion of culture as a site of contestation, marked by multiplicity and power relations which constitutes the terrain for organising consent for (as well as resistance to) existing hegemonies.[8] Such an understanding of culture allows us to broaden our conception of what practices and processes count as culture, and help us go beyond the fixation on 'tradition' and 'custom' to include some very modern practices and processes.

Broad reflections on the relation between gender and culture

The contentiousness of the assertions made to justify the status quo is underpinned by a powerful tendency to conflate 'culture' with gender. Why it is that when there is any suggestion that existing gender ideologies should be changed, there are romanticised notions of the past, notions that seldom surface at other times? Static notions of gender, bearing essentialised depictions of women at their heart, combine with similarly static conceptions of 'Culture' in defining the identity of a given group. Contemporary resistance to recognising the anti-women character of the 'traditions' thought to be central to 'culture' has meant that feminists attempting to engage in cultural transformation face an uphill task.

The feminist analyses and activism of the international women's movement, coupled with the attention drawn by UN agencies to women's greater participation in development, have combined to put pressure on reluctant governments to show some commitment to greater gender equity and the implementation of women's human rights. For their own part, African women have increasingly voiced their dissatisfaction with their marginal involvement in decision making and the denial of constitutional rights.

Sixteen years after marking the end of the UN Decade for Women (1975-85) with the United Nations conference in Nairobi, African women rightly expect more than has so far been acceded to them. The ultimate goal is the full realisation of their human rights[9] and more central involvement in the making of decisions that affect people and the trajectories of national development.[10] Against this background, calls for constitutional restructuring have come from a range of sources—feminist and mainstream.

In Nigeria, the current interest in federalism, for example, reflects a concern with the unity of the country and the consequences of its regimes of rule, in the aftermath of the Ibrahim Babangida (1985-93) and the Sani Abacha (1993-98) military regimes in particular. Nigeria's status as a federal polity reflects the history and geography of colonial rule, given additional twists by the interventions of an array of military regimes. Debates in the 1980s centred on ways of promoting greater local autonomy and equality of access to power and resources by federating units, in the context of considerable reduction in the powers of the federal government. This line of argument has been counterpoised to the more recent focus on the creation of new states and local governments.[11]

Whilst the general debate has been referred to in some quarters as the 'national question', there is little recognition of the virtual invisibility of women in this Question. Despite their active participation in anti-colonial and nationalist struggles,[12] women's unequal status in postcolonial Nigeria remains, as do the structural relations that support their subordination. This begs the question of whose 'nation', what 'question' and on what terms women are to be integrated, if at all, into the nation. The substantial feminist literature on gender and the nation appears to have bypassed mainstream discussions of the so-called national question.[13]

Women's serious marginalisation from governance in the period following flag independence, coupled with the denial of women's constitutional rights, has fuelled calls for constitutional restructuring from other quarters. Nina Mba's overview of women and the military regime in Nigeria poses the question of whether military government alters the legal and administrative systems in ways that enhance or diminish the status of women.[14] Mba concludes that women were marginally represented, if at all, in the bureaucratic centralism characteristic of militarised states. Such centralism greatly increased the power of the federal government in relation to state governments and society, and generally served to alienate government from the people. More recent work has examined the gender dynamics operating under specific regimes. Such work has focused on state structures for women, the ways in which processes of governance and discourses of democracy have been gendered, and notions of femininity which have shaped processes of incorporation into militarism and its consolidation.[15]

As for the state and the constitution, addressing the tensions between difference and universality on the one hand, and between autonomy and co-ordination, on the other, remains one of the overall goals of constitutional restructuring in the direction of democracy. In what ways, for example, have assumptions about *universal* interests, needs, experiences and rights mitigated against the recognition of specific interests, needs, experiences and so on, on the basis of differences such as gender? The cultural, social and political dimensions of such questions are manifold.

Federalism and the emphasis on territoriality

The traditional notion of federal polities is one of a territorial matrix, organised in that manner in order to take account of issues such as the regional concentration of particular ethnic groups. From this perspective, the traditional practice of federalism would tend to be oriented towards structures that accommodate territorially based groups rather than those more broadly diffused throughout the federal political system.[16] Women are a prime example of the latter, and they will necessarily be composed of a multitude of ethnic groups, not to mention religious ones and so on. My argument is that protection for non-territorial groups is more likely to be achieved through the implementation of basic rights, as for example in Canada's 1982 Charter of Rights and Freedoms, than through political structures based on territoriality.[17]

The arguments for territoriality, however, are generally made on the following grounds:

> While in theory the constituent units of a federal system can be nonterritorial, in fact it is the area of division of power that is the most common and successful form of federalism. Apparently only a territorial division can accommodate the two forms of the division of power necessary for a successful polity: 1) a division designed to recognise pre-existing groups ... and 2) a more neutral division based upon who occupies a particular territory at any given time ... [18]

Although the boundaries of constituent states or regions in Nigeria cannot be said to have recognised pre-existing groups, they can neither be described as 'neutral' demarcations of group entities. The pre-1967 regions were arbitrary units that effectively established the hegemony of the three majority ethnic groups over the minorities.[19] The state-creation exercise of 1967 was aimed at promoting greater equity by accommodating minority groups within the federal system. Subsequently, however, state creation has been largely about satisfying distributive pressures arising from the dominant ethnic groups.[20] The process has resulted in homogenous ethnic groups being subdivided (and thus multiplied) while minority communities have been simultaneously enclosed in multiethnic states. Many of the states have since turned into crucibles of conflict and conflagration. Territorial reorganisation has far too often been pursued as an easy means of gaining access to federal revenues as opposed to a serious avenue for addressing the problems faced by ethnic minorities.[21]

A more useful approach to safeguarding the rights of the less powerful sections of society would be to think in terms of creating and strengthening democratic and accountable institutions of governance targeting social inequality and unequal development. Specific structures would need to be established in order to monitor and evaluate policies and practices impinging on the rights of diverse groups of women as well as the rights of men from minority ethnic, religious and other groups. With respect to gender equality, there is much to be learned from recent developments in South Africa. Through an internally driven process of consensus building facilitated by the emergence of the Women's National Coalition, a high level of agreement was reached about the need for national machineries for women and the nature of such structures. In South Africa, these include a co-ordinated set of structures within government dedicated to gender policy issues; a statutory Commission for Gender Equality (CGE) funded by, but independent of, government; and a mechanism that ensures the representation of women within the legislature.[22]

In Nigeria, the continual spate of state creation witnessed under military rule has been premised on an ostensibly more equitable distribution of national development patronage.[23] Whilst that principle has not been realised, the way in which this has happened has not been the same for women relative to men. State creation has subjected most groups of women to further forms of discrimination. Ironically, whilst the creation of new states officially occurs to create more space for 'others', the space available for women subsequently shrinks. The dynamics of this shrinkage are shaped significantly by women's class positioning, both independently and as mediated by marriage. For most categories of men and women, state creation places tremendous strains on marriage.

There are instances when couples from the same state, but different areas, have to make a choice of where to relocate after a new state is created out of the parent state. The expectation generally is that female partners automatically follow their male counterparts to the new state. When this happens, however, women are not always able to get new jobs at the same level as their previous ones and so tend to take up inferior positions.[24] This contrasts sharply with the situation for women married to men who take up official positions in the new state. The material conditions and status for these women are very likely to improve. This is as much a result of their husband's greater access to state resources as it is a reflection of the heightened significance attached to wifehood under the Babangida and Abacha military regimes. The increased visibility of first ladies, as well as the wives of senior state officials, and their easy access to resources via 'state' programmes and structures for women are manifestations of this phenomenon.[25]

During the political debates held following the inauguration of the Political Bureau under Babangida's regime, women demanded a redefinition of the federal structure. They were concerned about the implications of state creation, referred to above. They were further worried about the discrimination inherent in the application of the criterion of 'state indigeneity' in relation to claims on the state. However, discussions on the federal structure in the Constituent Assembly were terminated. These issues were declared 'no go areas' by the military regime because a 'national consensus' existed on them. As Shettima points out, how the 'national consensus' was arrived at was not explained.[26] And yet, the possibility of debate has to be considered and addressed on its own terms, rather than being automatically treated as a challenge to existing authority and, therefore, inherently subversive.

Claims on the state have analytically been considered under the rubric of citizenship. National citizenship for Nigerian women and men is formally constructed as guaranteeing fundamental human rights through the provisions of the constitution.[27] No distinction is made between men and women thus providing—in formal terms at least—complete equality for women. The implementation of the constitutional prohibition against discrimination is another matter altogether, one that is thrown into sharp relief by the prolonged misrule of military regimes whose habit it was to suspend the constitution each time they intrude into the body politic.

Aside from this, the reality is that women face an array of legal and administrative barriers to the realisation of gender equality. Married women have to obtain the consent of their husbands when applying for passports, when they want to travel, and in many cases, when they want to use health and contraceptive services. In practice, women are not allowed to stand surety for bail, they are discriminated against in taxation assessments and women in the civil service receive half the annual leave allowance of their male counterparts.[28] Since male citizens are regarded as the norm, and women as minors whose adult status is mediated by men (whether father or husband), citizenship for women is experienced more often in the denial of rights considered 'natural' for men, than in their realisation. The denial of women's rights occurs in specific ways, sometimes overlapping but not reducible to the generalised denial of the fundamental human rights of all citizens that has been evident under prolonged military rule in Nigeria.

Local state citizenship, like national citizenship, means not only different things for women relative to men but subordinate (and sometimes indeterminate) status as well as unequal rights. Women face particular problems when married outside the state in which their father was born (generally referred to as their 'indigenous' state). The federal government, as a means of fostering national unity encourages, marriage across ethnic, religious and linguistic groups.[29] Members of the National Youth Service Corps who marry during their one-year of national service are awarded prizes for inter-state marriage.[30] However, since most marriages are patrilocal, women in 'mixed' local state marriages end up living in states where they are viewed as 'non-indigenes'. Consequently, they are likely to have problems when seeking employment, scholarships, loans, land, admission to schools, in either their indigenous states or in the states where their spouses are indigenous. When they seek access to such resources in the state where their spouses are indigenous, they are asked to apply for them in their indigenous states. The converse also applies.[31]

Clearly, the criterion of 'state indigeneity' for claims on the state is, in its conception, a partial one. It excludes any recognition of claims that women, as opposed to men, may make on the state. Women in 'mixed marriages' often find it difficult having their children accepted as indigenes of their states of origin. Worse still, whilst not having gained the status of indigene in their husband's state, women in this position are often treated as having 'lost' indigeneity of their own state of origin. Ironically, whilst remaining Nigerian citizens, they lose the ability to make claims on the local state, unlike men in 'mixed marriages'. Insistence on state 'indigeneity' clearly discriminates against categories of women, as well as men, who may have resided, worked and paid taxes for considerable periods of time in a given locality. In the process, the development of equal citizenship is undermined.[32]

The discussion so far has highlighted the need to clarify and reconcile divisions of power with the rights of citizens. The debate in modern democratic theory over the respective value of territorial and functional divisions of power is one frequently engaged in by federalists and pluralists. Pluralists argue that the territorial division of powers is unnecessary to preserve liberties and may very well interfere with their protection. Territorialists, on the other hand, argue that: '... the deficiencies of territorial democracy are greatly outweighed by the advantages of a guaranteed power base for each group in the political system....'[33]

In the Nigerian context, the emphasis on territoriality has only selectively provided guaranteed power bases. Paradoxically, however, this has strengthened the appeal of territoriality in the form of renewed calls for state creation, particularly under military rule. At the same time, the emphasis on 'indigeneity'—and thereby on 'origins'—as the basis for claims on the state is at odds with the reality of the ever changing boundaries of one's 'state of origin', as well as people's social mobility and migration. The interpretation of the significance of territoriality is thus contradictory, validating change in the continual process of state creation whilst advocating stasis and the permanence of 'origins' for citizens.

More significantly, such a contradictory understanding of territoriality misses its real significance for the vast majority of the poor, and poor women in particular. It is neither state creation nor an emphasis on 'origins' that will benefit the majority of the rural-based population, but a concerted effort at land and agricultural reform, in the context of the broader initiative of finding ways to implement rights effectively. Such a programme would need to address land distribution, sustainable land use and the establishment of tenure security for all within the context of gender equality. The commitment to gender equality would have to be grounded in the recognition that male supremacist structures of authority, whether in kinship structures or in the name of 'tradition', often act to marginalise women systematically from access to and control over land.[34] The significance of such access and control is located in the relationship between land rights, property rights and the sustainability of livelihoods. Without land or property rights, women are unable to provide collateral for bank loans or formal credit schemes. This undermines their ability to sustain livelihoods that are not, in themselves, dependent on land usage.

Implementing women's human rights

What kinds of understandings of human rights and the processes required for the effective implementation of human rights, would aid us in the quest for greater gender equality? Feminists increasingly speak not only of women's rights in the context of human rights, but of women's empowerment and thus of changes in the cultural and social arenas that are necessary for women to be able to *claim* their rights. The United Nations' adoption of the Convention on the Elimination of All Forms of Discrimination against Women (CEDAW) in 1979 represented a positive development in the international protection of human rights. It is now recognised by the world community that human rights protection requires not only regional initiatives, such as the African Charter on Human and People's Rights, but other forms of protection for specific groups primarily within the given constitutional and legal frameworks of individual countries. Whereas the specific protection of women's human rights is to be welcomed, it is important to go beyond this because women are not politically, economically or culturally homogeneous. The implications of this diversity are that it is necessary not only to examine women's problems specifically, but also to examine the assumptions of the provisions of the convention in order to see how they can be applied within this variable context.[35]

Awe sets out the case for viewing women's rights as human rights, pointing out that despite the provisions of CEDAW and the African Charter for Popular Participation, Development and Transformation, 'all is not well with women as far as the recognition of their rights is concerned.'[36] Other analysts have been more optimistic about some of the international and domestic legal developments concerning the rights of women and children in Nigeria.[37] Osinbajo states that 'giant strides have been taken since independence in establishing a framework for the eradication of discrimination against women'.[38] He nevertheless notes the failure of human rights legislation to have created a system of what we now call reproductive rights.

It is hardly surprising that the terrain of human rights is characterised by tensions and multiple perspectives. Women's status is inextricably linked to a wide range of rights that may or may not be theirs to exercise. We can restate that in the sense that women's human rights should encompass such rights as legal rights, economic rights, political rights, bodily rights as well as reproductive rights, even if in practice they do not. Struggles have taken place over the legitimacy of rights such as reproductive and sexual rights, in the context of debates about the impact of population policies on women.[39] On the opposing side, there are religious fundamentalists as well as those against the notion of human rights in general, who associate human rights with individualistic tendencies arising from Western capitalism.[40]

Criticisms of human rights discourse abound. First, there is the point that the value and meaning of rights are contingent upon the socio-political context.[41] Yet notions of human rights and duties prevail in even the most authoritarian, patriarchal and traditional regimes. Such notions may be manipulated by the state and corporate powers to serve their own interests and perpetuate the burdens of citizens in general, and those less privileged, in particular. A second criticism is that the language of human rights is indeterminate.[42] Women may want to claim their reproductive rights but then so could men and the same is true for foetal advocates, clinicians and pharmaceutical companies to mention only a few possible candidates.[43] Thirdly, there is the issue of abstract individualism and universality that is generally attributed to the discourse of rights. The classic liberal model presupposes equal individuals, bargaining for the satisfaction of their rights. Differences on the basis of class, gender, race, ethnicity and other social dimensions structuring power relations and unequal access to resources are completely ignored.[44] There is also the point that international law accords priority to civil and political rights—rights that may have very little to offer women generally. The major forms of women's oppression operate within the economic, social and cultural realms. However, economic, social and cultural rights are generally regarded as a lesser form of international right and as much more difficult to implement.[45]

and as much more difficult to implement.[45]

Correa and Petchesky point out that:

> While these criticisms are theoretically compelling, they offer no alternative discourse for social movements to make collective political claims. Whatever its theoretical weaknesses, the polemical power of rights language as an expression of aspirations for justice across widely different cultures and political-economic conditions cannot easily be dismissed ... In practice, then, the language of rights remains indispensable but needs radical redefinition.[46]

Feminists have been prominent in spearheading efforts to rid the human rights discourse of its problems of indeterminacy, abstract universality and individualism. The aim has been to transform the classical liberal rights model in a number of ways. This is done first, by stressing the social, not just the individual nature of human rights. In this way, the corresponding duties can be seen to lie not so much with individuals alone as with public agencies. Secondly, it is emphasised that individuals act to exercise their rights in relational contexts, that is as human beings with connections to others in the family, community and so on. Thirdly, the substantive basis of rights is embedded in human needs and a redistribution of resources. Finally, human beings—the primary and traditional bearers of rights—are recognised as having multiple self-defined identities that encompass dimensions such as their gender, class, race, ethnicity and religion.[47]

For those who have never had the power, status and privilege of being recognised as agents with human dignity, the discourse of human rights can be extremely empowering. Human rights can be an important tool in conscientisation as well as in mobilising marginalised groups of women. A transformed notion of human rights embodies two fundamental properties: personal liberties—domains where people are empowered to exercise their rights—and social justice, i.e. arenas where affirmative public action is required to ensure that rights are attainable by everyone. In this sense, the notion of rights necessarily implies public responsibilities and renewed emphasis on the linkages between personal well being and social good.

It is social rights—also referred to as enabling conditions—that create the foundation of rights in general. They include material and infrastructural dimensions, such as reliable transport, childcare, shelter, financial subsidies or income supports, and welfare services that are accessible, humane and well staffed. Social rights also include cultural and political dimensions, such as access to education, earnings, and the channels of decision-making. Such enabling conditions directly entail the responsibility of states and mediating institutions for their implementation.

Nigeria today is characterised by the absence of the enabling conditions mentioned above, and in many cases, by the denial of women's human rights.

With regard to reproductive rights, the 'modern tradition', to use Whittaker's words, of denying women safe contraception is a case in point. The effects of compulsory and repeated childbearing in terms of exhausting and damaging women's health are well known. Women have no right to refuse sex with their husbands. Furthermore, rape within marriage is not recognised under the law. Effectively, married women have no right to refuse to be impregnated. The denial of reproductive rights to women often makes it more likely that they will use damaging, but hidden, forms of contraception. These include the long-acting hormonal injectables that have been banned in the countries of their production.[48] Many women have no other option but to use the 'services' of unsafe and unsanitary backstreet abortionists, resulting in the ensuing trail of damage and destruction for which such practitioners are notorious.[49]

More recently, there has been a convergence of women's human rights and empowerment discourses. A telling illustration can be drawn from the final declaration of the Fourth World Conference on Women, adopted in Beijing in September 1995,

> The objective of the platform of action, which is in full conformity with the purposes and principles of the Charter of the United Nations and international law, is the empowerment of all women. The full realisation of all human rights and fundamental freedoms of all women is essential for the empowerment of women.[50]

The above excerpt raises the question of the relationship of women's human rights to empowerment. To what extent can either be pursued relatively independently of the other? Under what circumstances does the pursuit of women's empowerment overlap the pursuit of women's rights? Does a relationship of contingency or dependence exist between the two, as implied in the above excerpt? Whilst the realisation of all human rights for women will no doubt result in the empowerment of women, is it not also the case that it is only when women are empowered in particular ways that they can claim their rights? Differing understandings of women's empowerment, women's rights *and* the relations between them are significant since they will have differing strategic implications.

Perspectives on empowerment

Afshar poses the following question: "...what must be defined are the questions: what is empowerment, and who empowers whom?"[51] The inquiry highlights one of the contemporary appropriations of the concept of empowerment, namely, that it is something 'done to' a particular grouping or individuals 'by' others. This appropriation is particularly evident in the pronouncements by First Ladies, during both the Babangida and Abacha regimes, instructing women on how to 'empower' themselves. This top-down, authoritarian approach runs completely in the opposing direction to the liberative aspirations embedded in more progressive understandings of 'empowerment'.

For example, Paulo Freire's realisation that the ignorance and lethargy of the poor were direct results of their economic, social and political domination propelled his praxis in the direction of 'the practice of freedom.'[52] What Freire described as the 'culture of silence,' is a serious obstacle to the ability of the dispossessed to resist their domination and disadvantage. Conscientisation, as a process of naming the world in order to transform it, therefore became a necessary precursor to the goal of human liberation. 'Empowerment' here is conceived as occurring primarily through the power of thought and collective, dialogical action aimed at transcending accepted limits and paving the way to a new future.

The linkages between knowledge and power underlying such praxis are evident in several other movements of liberation, including radical anti-colonial and nationalist movements in erstwhile colonies as well as movements for women's liberation. Frantz Fanon pointed out that decolonisation never took place unnoticed: 'For it influences individuals and modifies them fundamentally. It transforms spectators crushed with their inessentiality into privileged actors, with the grandiose glare of history's floodlights upon them.'[53]

In similar ways, the nature of the relations between knowledge and experience has been of particular concern to feminists. For example, Patricia Hill Collins has observed that

> Offering subordinate groups new knowledge about their own experiences can be empowering. But revealing new ways of knowing that allow subordinate groups to define their own reality has far greater implications.[54]

The starting point for a number of feminist analyses of empowerment has been conceptions of power—since it is around this term that the discourse is built and differentiations drawn between the exercise of different types of power. Many feminists have drawn on Foucault's notion of power as productive and intimately bound up with knowledge.[55] A significant feature of his conceptualisation of power is its location in multiple sets of social relations, which are rooted in systems of social networks.

In the post-colonial era, the question of how to continue 'the process of building political consciousness without the spur of a visible enemy or of dramatic victories' remains.[56] The multi-faceted nature of such struggles, made manifest by the need to address the various obstacles arraigned against women, is aptly summed up below:

> ... the failure to confront the sexual division of labour in the home limits a woman's potential, and keeps her locked into old patterns of overwork and subordination. These limits on women's ability to become literate are another sharp reminder of the need for gender struggle, a struggle waged in the context of literacy that will assist the quest for self-empowerment.[57]

Apart from highlighting the need for women to become empowered at the individual level, feminists have drawn attention to the collective dimension of empowerment. In DAWN's feminist visions of the achievement of a new world order, the emphasis is on women empowering themselves through organisations, since these are viewed as the channel through which change is most likely to occur.[58] The strategic importance of women's organisations is thought to be twofold. First of all, it is women's organisations that are viewed as capable of developing the political will for the major changes that are needed in order that feminism may be realised. Secondly, the need to prioritise the fulfilment of basic survival needs is most likely to be met with the involvement of poor women's organisations.

> Empowerment of organisations, individuals and movements has certain requisites. These include resources (finance, knowledge, technology), skills training, and leadership formation on the one side; and democratic processes, dialogue, participation in policy and decision making, and techniques for conflict resolution on the other. Flexibility of membership requirements can also be helpful, especially to poor working women whose time commitments and work burdens are already severe. Within organisations, open and democratic processes are essential in empowering women to withstand the social and family pressures that result from their participation. Thus the long-term viability of the organisation, and the growing autonomy and control by poor women over their lives, are linked through the organisation's own internal processes of shared responsibility and decision making.[59]

It is women's organisations that have been in the forefront of advocacy and activism vis-à-vis women's rights and empowerment. As Rowlands points out, the implications for activists of a clearer understanding of empowerment processes are considerable, and require further exploration.[60]

Women's organisations, women's rights and empowerment

Discourses of women's 'rights' and 'empowerment' have, in some cases, been used independently of one another and in other cases, as overlapping configurations. My concern here is to address some of the discursive and strategic issues arising from this scenario. How have the discourses of 'women's rights' and 'women's empowerment' been used; to address what kinds of issues, from what kinds of ideological perspectives and using what kinds of strategies? The section begins by examining the conceptions of women's rights and women's empowerment held by women in organisations active in this arena. The work of three women's organisations based in Lagos is highlighted. This necessarily limits the scope of the discussion, which is, in any case, not intended to be exhaustive but rather to highlight some of the issues around which women have organised and the strategies that they have used. The second part of the section examines the ways in which the organisations have attempted to promote women's rights and empowerment within the context of constitutionalism.

Conceptions of empowerment and rights in women's organisations

Women, law and development centre of Nigeria (WLDCN)

Set up in 1993, WLDCN undertakes advocacy on women's rights, offering free legal services (guidance and counselling) to poor women. The organisation also carries out research on women's rights. WLDCN networks with a number of organisations, including Baobab, Women In Nigeria (WIN), Legal Research and Resource Development Centre (LRRDC), Civil Liberties Organisation (CLO), Girls Power Initiative (GPI) and Women, Law and Development in Africa (WILDAF) to mention several. At the time of writing this chapter, these organisations had formed a coalition to carry out 16 days of activism against gender violence.

One of the cases that WLDCN were working on involved counselling a woman who had received a seven days eviction notice to leave her accommodation where she lived with her three children.[61] Her husband had been living with the family until he moved to a house elsewhere, where he was living with a mistress. From that point onwards, he stopped paying the rent for the family accommodation and was refusing to house his wife and children. WLDCN were about to write to the husband, threatening him with legal redress if he failed to act. At the same time, they were putting the woman in touch with shelter rights organisations.

What about those instances where women did not think in terms of 'rights'? The deputy director made the following observation:

> Yes, some women come here, especially women who have been abused violently. They don't want to assert their rights. They just want somebody to hear them, someone to talk to them. When we then say, look, this man has no right to do this to you, this is what we should do to them ... It is then they will say, 'Ah, where would I get the money to do that or this!'

> You find that for many of them - it is not that they don't have the notion of rights. They know their rights, it is just that they feel that economically they are disempowered. Many of them, even the most illiterate of them, know their rights.

Implicit in the above is the connection between the realisation of women's rights and empowerment, which is referred to in economic terms. How exactly is empowerment understood here?

> Empowerment to me is all encompassing … I think knowledge is power, and if you know your rights, if you are … literate, numerate, and have access to information, that to us is empowerment. … trying to make people aware. Where you can … get information, develop yourself, this is empowerment. Empowerment to us in this Centre is like sustainability. … We also want to make people economically viable, how you can help yourself. Then you are empowered for life, because you will never go hungry and nobody will trample on your rights and get away with it. You will find ways and means of redressing it because you have knowledge.

The failure of the state to provide adequate welfare services is evident in the terms in which encounters with such agencies are referred to below. Consequently, it is not surprising that women prefer to approach women's organisations when they need help.

> … it is not that they don't know their rights, it's (a question of) how they can go about it, having somebody to talk to, an organisation to talk with other than social welfare, because social welfare will treat them the same as any government ministry would … And you feel, unless you are in a position of power you feel that you cannot even get to that government. They want somewhere, some organisation, especially (women's organisations) where they feel they will be understood better, so they come to us, they talk to us.

Regarding the impact that women's organisations may have had on expanding the notion of human rights to include women's rights, the deputy director of WLDCN referred to the question of what criteria might be used for assessing such change. She pointed to the increased presence and visibility of women in public life, for example in local government elections, as indicative of women's greater awareness of their rights. Moreover, women's level of preparation for the Dakar regional and Beijing conferences was more intensive than had been the case for previous UN international conferences on women.

Baobab – for women's human rights

Baobab is a women's human rights organisation that focuses on legal literacy. It does this by addressing issues concerning women's legal rights under the multiple legal systems operating in Nigeria: customary, statutory and religious.

Baobab formally came into being in 1996. Many of those involved, however, had previously worked together on an action research project on women and laws in Nigeria, part of a 26-country project run under the auspices of the International Solidarity Network Women Living Under Muslim Laws (WLUML).[62]

Baobab's objectives include raising awareness about women's rights, abuse of these rights and other legal issues affecting women; research and documentation; the promotion of women's human rights through a variety of means, including popular education and training, interdisciplinary teaching, exchange of ideas and resource development in Nigeria.

Information about women's human rights is disseminated in a number of accessible ways, such as pamphlets and leaflets in indigenous languages. The concept of 'women's rights' is not easily translated into many languages, raising the question of how one gets people to talk about 'rights':

> We approach it in indirect ways. We talk about what kinds of things do you think should happen, what happens to you when this and this happens, and then you introduce the concept and let people take it from there. I mean one of the things that we found for instance, when we were trying to find what was our original idea for the name (of the organisation), which was 'women's rights' in a number of different indigenous Nigerian languages, that it in fact provoked a lot of consciousness-raising discussion. We'd ask people, well how do you say this in your language? And then we would get into discussion about whether or not it was possible to say it, what did it mean, what applicability did it have in their own particular cultural context ...[63]

Three differing aspects of rights are referred to here: a normative dimension (what should happen); an expressive dimension (how you say it); and the applicability of rights, given multiple and potentially contradictory cultural standpoints. More research on the overlapping and interrelated aspects of these dimensions of rights is clearly needed. One wonders how successful, generally speaking, the attempt to expand the notion of human rights to encompass women's rights has been? Imam provides an answer:

> Well, I think that some progress has been made. First of all, in having thought of the notion at all, that human rights as presently defined, don't encompass all human beings. I think that there are some ways in which there have been successes, in for example, pushing for rape [in the context of war] to be recognised as a war crime in itself, and not simply a criminal issue that has nothing to do with war. So there has been some practical progress as well as conceptual progress but clearly it's not sufficient ... The slogan for next year is 'There are no human rights without women's rights', which clearly indicates that it's not yet enough.

Baobab networks with a number of organisations in an effort to build on each other's strengths rather than compete with one another. For example, they have a broad understanding with Legal Research and Resource Development Centre (LRRDC) that Baobab will make an input into the latter's paralegal training, rather than carry out such training themselves. LRRDC has been carrying out training on statutory laws for some time but knows less about Muslim and customary laws. This is the area in which Baobab contributes.

In March 1997, Baobab initiated a network of women's and human rights organisations in an effort to build solidarity and mutual support. The network organised a week-long programme of activities around International Women's Day on the theme 'Towards Women's Empowerment'. Empowerment was interpreted here in a broad sense to mean enabling women to take more power. Whilst Baobab was able to network with other organisations on this general theme, empowerment was viewed as a distinct arena of work relative to women's rights, not one in which Baobab was itself engaged at the time.

> I don't think that either within the office or within what was the Women and Laws scheme as a whole, that we have actually ever specifically discussed the concept of 'empowerment'.[64]

Although the concept of 'empowerment' had not been discussed explicitly in relation to the setting up of the Women and Laws project, the language of empowerment has since pervaded its definition. Baobab's 1998 annual report describes the project's aims as:

> directly assisting grassroots and activist women by providing a better understanding of the multiple forces that define the parameters of their lives, thereby equipping them to strategize for their own empowerment. Hence women can use [Women and Laws] derived knowledge to strategize and campaign around defining and pressing for the enforcement of women's rights in the family, as citizens and over their own selves and bodies.[65]

Moreover, the links between knowledge, power and the capacity to exercise rights are referred to explicitly below:

> For the research to be useful, the knowledge generated needs to be translated into workable outreach, empowering people to know, exercise and develop their rights. During the process of research itself, state teams engaged in networking with communities and their organisations, and [worked] on developing a sense of the felt needs of each community, regarding legal and women's human rights knowledge.[66]

Women Empowerment Movement (WEM)

WEM was set up in 1995 after the founding members returned from the

Fourth UN World Conference on Women in Beijing. The aims are to empower women socially, politically and economically. In 1997, its focus was on political empowerment and enabling women to participate in the political 'transition' from military to civilian rule.

> We did a lot of research into the participation of women in democracy and realised that compared with other African states, Nigeria is very backward in projecting the image of women. They've been saying that the constraints among other things were low education and cultural inhibitions, which are still on, but we realised that if women are more (prominent) in the political field, the percentage of women involved in democratization, in decision-making (bodies) would be higher than hitherto.[67]

WEM's engagement in women's political empowerment took the form of participating in the voters' registration exercise and organising workshops and seminars on the issues. In conjunction with the federal Ministry of Women Affairs, they developed a radio jingle that was used during the registration exercise to encourage people to come out and vote. WEM was also active in urging NECON the Nigerian Electoral Commission to ensure that the affirmative action based on the Beijing Declaration would be put in place. They urged NECON to ensure that the political parties registered should have in their constitutions and manifestos, the reservation of at least 30-40 per cent of their positions for women. Men and the general public virulently attacked this stance on the grounds that women should go out and fight with the men rather than having positions reserved for them.

> We've been fighting with the men but if you look at it critically, you'll see in Nigeria that what really happens is selection, not election. That is why we were crying out at that point in time because they did not go by election ... Now if you have to select about ten men, why don't you select four women?[68]

The politics of military 'selection, not election' are not challenged here. What is advocated, instead, is that women should be part of the 'selection' exercise, rather than 'selection' by the military being questioned as an undemocratic practice.

One of the obstacles faced by women who want to participate in politics is the problem of money.

> You see a typical Nigerian thinks that when (civilian) politics is around, the politicians must spread money around ... They are clamouring for this because they are poor, because of the poverty. They want you to give them something in return for the votes they want to cast because they think it is our men who spoiled the system. They think that once the men

get there, they won't remember them. ... In the rural areas, they don't have potable water, they don't have electricity, the roads are bad, they don't have the necessities of life.

Women's greater participation in politics is justified not via the discourse of rights, but by recourse to an essentialist notion of 'women'.

Nigerian women being very compassionate, being very accountable, being very critical and meticulous would be able to put sanity into the system. Throughout the First and Second Republics, we had the men dominating the affairs; they have not performed well. But we realised that we have qualified women who can go in there and be able to fight for the cause of women and when we are talking about the cause of women, we are talking about the cause of the whole family. Because Nigerian women are those who are always at home when the men are out, looking after the children, ensuring that they get good education, good moral upbringing and if they can inject this in to the larger society, by putting them in decision making bodies, by making them determine the destiny of the people of this country, we think we shall be better off.

The notion that 'women are always at home' is one that cannot readily be reconciled with the realities of women's work inside as well as outside the home, in farming, production, trade, the labour market and/or work in the informal sector. Nor is it clear how women who are 'always at home' would be free to govern the country. The ideology that women should be domesticated beings, tied to the home, is a relatively recent one introduced and reinforced by the experience of colonialism and military rule.[69]

Promoting women's rights and empowerment

Whilst the formal presence of women's rights in constitutional arrangements is a necessary precondition to the realisation of rights, it is clearly not sufficient to bring about that realisation. For this to happen, other processes—located in the terrain between social relations and cultural dynamics—are involved. At least two arenas can be identified in which women's organisations have been active: consciousness raising and the transformation of 'culture'. These domains tend to blend into one another as opposed to being mutually exclusive.

Consciousness raising

Particularly prominent in this area has been the work addressing violence against women, in view of the breadth and intensity of such violence, which appears to be on the increase. Nigeria is a signatory to international conventions such as CEDAW whose provisions are aimed at protecting women from such abuse. In this context, the state's direct and indirect complicity in the perpetration of violence against women[70] is a serious abdication of responsibility and should be a matter of grave concern to all. The need to promote women's rights and empowerment, under deteriorating social, economic and political conditions, has never been greater. This need was clearly recognised by UNIFEM in its Campaign to Eliminate All Forms of Violence Against Women and Girls in Nigeria, launched in July 1998, in which several organisations working in the arena of women's human rights participated.

Another area in which women's organisations have been prominent in consciousness raising is in the production of *Shadow Reports* on the implementation of CEDAW. At least two such reports were produced, one by a coalition of seven organisations, co-ordinated by Baobab,[71] and the other produced by the Kaduna chapter of Women in Nigeria.[72] Shadow reports provide a useful mechanism for highlighting areas where women's rights are neither recognised nor enforced. They are particularly important in view of the problems inherent in the official report presented by the Nigerian government to CEDAW. These problems included inaccuracies in the depiction of the status of Nigerian women as well as in the implementation of CEDAW:

> The Nigerian government CEDAW report ignores or downplays the all important problem of the wide gap between laws as written in the books and their enforcement (or lack of enforcement) in practice by state agents. It also omits consideration of the Nigerian State's responsibility to eliminate contradictions between broad statements of principle, and the many statute, common law, religious and customary laws, as well as the administrative practices, which continue to discriminate against women. It further downplays Nigeria's responsibility under the Convention to find means of specifically affirming women's status and rectifying their disadvantaged position in political, social and economic life.[73]

The report was well received by the CEDAW committee who used it to formulate questions and recommendations for the Nigerian government.

The transformation of 'culture'

The second area of work, the transformation of 'culture' has involved a range of strategies. These include critiques of mainstream, gender-neutral discourses on human rights, some of which were referred to earlier in this chapter. Conservative interpretations of 'culture', 'tradition' and 'religion' very often deny rights to certain groups of people, particularly women. In addition, there is a need to recognise that it is not only states that violate rights but also individuals and members of 'civil society'. The aim is to deepen the understanding of the multiple ways in which gender, alongside other power structures, mediates the recognition and strengthening of some rights, or rights for some people, as well as the denial and abuse of rights for others. Ultimately, such understanding is intended to serve as a prelude to supporting women's capacity to exercise their rights.

Other strategies have involved organising and engaging in cultural events that aim to popularise a more inclusive notion of human rights. Such a notion would be one in which the gender-specific abuses of rights are acknowledged and incorporated into strategies for change. An example is that of the commemoration of the 50th anniversary of the Universal Declaration of Human Rights in 1998. On this occasion, Baobab initiated and co-ordinated a process of collaboration with other organisations working on women's human rights.[74]

The anniversary was marked by a series of joint activities on the theme 'Building a Culture of Women's Human Rights in Nigeria'. A range of activities were organised, including the production of a Newssheet, an exhibition, a press conference, seminars, workshops, signature and poster campaigns, as well as advocacy events with public agencies. Baobab itself organised a poster competition for young people, on women's human rights in Nigeria. In all, these events represented an attempt to intervene in the dominant political culture in which human rights are embedded and transform that culture so as to recognise the dignity and rights of all human beings, women as well as men.

Conclusion

This chapter has highlighted some of the issues and processes concerning constitutional restructuring in the direction of gender equity and social justice. My focus has been on some of the tensions between difference and universality, and the ways in which they have been addressed with respect to the state and the constitution. Proponents of federalism have treated the rubric of difference and universality in contrasting ways, on the one hand, and women's rights advocates, on the other. Whilst these two camps are not entirely exclusive to one another, it is also true that they have generally been differentiated by gender as well as in terms of priorities, arguments and areas of interest. Despite this, both camps have found common ground in the need for constitutional restructuring.

An important impetus here has been the restructuring of the state, in the wake of the overcentralisation and destabilisation incurred by the military rule of Generals Babangida and Abacha, in particular. State restructuring has been conceived primarily in territorial terms, whether in terms of the creation of new states or the regulation of existing ones. The current emphasis on territoriality has been contradictory, however, and in itself, will undoubtedly fail to address the marginalisation and discrimination experienced by diverse groups of women as well as men. For rural women living in poverty, it is likely that a concerted effort at land reform would be more useful. For most groups of women, an approach that relies less on state creation and more on the use of alternative institutional frameworks, such as the implementation of basic rights, is likely to be more effective. My short point is that the successful implementation of basic rights for women, and men, will depend on processes and relations that are largely extra-constitutional. These include processes operating within the realms of social change and cultural relations, such as empowerment, consciousness-raising and the transformation of political culture. Women's organisations active in this area have used a number of strategies to carry out such work. The dynamic and contradictory character of co-existing cultures means that the range of positive cultural options and possibilities cannot be circumscribed, nor would it be desirable to do so. However, it ought to be possible to delineate the minimum criteria for the unacceptability of actions justified as 'culturally' based (the 'bottom line', as it were). Arriving at this position will require engaging with the perspectives and involvement of the very many diverse organisations involved in the promotion of women's rights and empowerment, in the long-term process of building a democracy. Constitutional restructuring will form just one of the many dimensions necessary for this to happen.

Notes

1. Beckman (1996).
2. See e.g. Effah, Mbachu and Onyegbula (1995); Civil Liberties Organisation (1993).
3. I have used the term 'culture' in inverted commas, to indicate a malestream, monolithic construction as opposed to an understanding of culture that recognises diversity and contestation.
4. See e.g. Ranger (1989), Chanock (1982), and Narayan (1997).
5. Osakue, Usuman and Osagie (1995).
6. See Effah *et al.*, (1995).
7. Gramsci (1971).
8. Foucault (1982).
9. See Baobab (1998).
10. See ABANTU (1994).
11. Olukoshi and Agbu (1996).
12. Mba (1982); R. Shawulu (1990).
13. See, Yuval-Davis (1997); McClintock (1993); Enloe (1990); Yuval-Davis and Anthias (1989), and Jayawardena (1986).
14. Mba (1989).
15. See, Abdullah (1993); Mama (1995); Mama (1997); Shettima (1995); Imam (forthcoming), and Pereira (forthcoming).
16. See Watts (1994).
17. Brown-John (1994).
18. Elazar (1995): 17.
19. Suberu (1996).
20. These pressures have been to increase access to central government funds, state office and the privileges and resources associated with the latter. Attempts to meet these pressures have been effected by the creation of new states.

21. Suberu (1996).
22. Hassim (1998).
23. Suberu (1995).
24. Shettima (1995): 90.
25. Mama (1995, 1997) discusses the female power structures, predicated on marital relationships, installed by the First Ladies of the Babangida and Abacha regimes.
26. Shettima (1995).
27. See Chapter 4, sections 33-43 of the 1999 Constitution of the Federal Republic of Nigeria.
28. Effah et al (1995).
29. See section 15(3)(c) of the 1999 Constitution of the Federal Republic of Nigeria.
30. Shettima (1995).
31. Imam (forthcoming).
32. Ibid.
33. Elazar (1995): 7.
34. See Walker (1998): 4, for a discussion of the South African case. The latter is marked by its explicit commitment to gender equality as well as by the tensions between central government policy and the resistance to change from 'traditional' quarters.
35. See Armstrong, *et al* (1993).
36. Awe (1984): 7.
37. Osinbajo (1989).
38. Osinbajo, n.d.: 239-240.
39. See Correa & Reichmann (1994), and Pitanguy (1994).
40. See Kapur (1992) and Lessellier (1991).
41. Correa & Petchetsky (1994).
42. Ibid.
43. See, Freedman and Isaacs (1993): 18-30.
44. Correa and Petchesky (1994).
45. Charlesworth *et al* (1991).
46. Ibid., 4.
47. Correa and Petchesky (1994): 4.
48. See e.g. Ogbuagu (1985).
49. Pittin (1985).
50. 'The women's platform for action (i).' *Today*, 22-28 Oct. 1995: 18.
51. Afshar (1998): 1.
52. Freire (1972).
53. Fanon (1963): 28.
54. Hill Collins (1990): 222.
55. Foucault (1982).
56. Urdang (1989): 18.
57. *Ibid.*, 233.
58. Sen and Grown (1987).
59. *Ibid.,* 89.
60. Rowlands (1998).
61. Personal interview with Dr Awoshika, Deputy Director, Women, Law and Development Centre of Nigeria, Lagos, 13 November, 1997.
62. Baobab (1998): 3-5.
63. Personal interview with Ayesha Imam, Executive Director, Baobab, 13 November 1997, Lagos.
64. Personal interview with Ayesha Imam, Executive Director, Baobab, 13 November 1997, Lagos.
65. Baobab (1998) *supra* 4.
66. Baobab (1998) *supra* 4.

67. Interview with Mrs Onikepo Oshodi, President of Women Empowerment Movement (WEM), 5 December 1997, Lagos.
68. *Ibid.*
69. See, e.g., Mama (1997), and Pereira (forthcoming).
70. See, e.g., WIN [Kaduna] (1998).
71. Nigerian NGO Coalition (1999).
72. WIN [Kaduna] (1998).
73. Imam, *et al* (1999): viii-ix.
74. The following organisations were involved: Women's Health Organisation of Nigeria (WHON), Gender and Action Development (GADA), Action Health Incorporated (AHI), Constitutional Rights Project (CRP), Women Justice Programme (WJP), Inter-African Committee (IAC), the Lagos State Council of the Nigerian Association of Women Journalists (NAWOJ), Women Health Programme (WHP), Shelter Rights Initiative (SRI), Community Life Project (CLP), Social and Economic Rights Action Centre (SERAC), Women, Law and Development Centre (WLDCN), Civil Liberties Organisation (CLO), Legal Research and Resource Development Centre (LRRDC), the Lagos State chapter of Women in Nigeria (WIN), and Amnesty International Nigeria.

References

ABANTU (1994) African *Women and Governance: Towards Action for Women's Participation in Decision-Making* Seminar and Training Workshop held at Entebbe, 24-30 July 1994, London: ABANTU.

Abdullah, H. (1993) 'Transition Politics and the Challenge of Gender in Nigeria.' *Review of African Political Economy 56.*

Afshar, H., (1998), 'Introduction: Women and Empowerment: Some Illustrative Studies,' in H. Afshar (ed.) *Women and Empowerment: Illustrations from the Third World*, Basingstoke: Houndmills, Macmillan.

Armstrong, A., Beyani, C., Himonga, C., Kabebeberi-Macharia, J. Molokomme, A. Ncube, W., Nhlapo, T., Rwezaura, B., and Stewart, J., (1993), "Uncovering Reality: Excavating Women's Rights in African Family Law," Vol.7 *International Journal of Law & the Family.*

Awe, B. (1994), 'Women's Rights are Human Rights,' Keynote address delivered at the Women in Nigeria (WIN) conference, Katsina, 13 April.

Baobab, (1998), *Annual Report,* Baobab for Women's Human Rights, Lagos.

Beckman, B. (1996) 'The Free Fall of the Nigerian State'. Paper presented at workshop on The State of Nigeria, St. Peter's College, Oxford, 30 May 1996.

Brown-John, L. 1994 'Asymmetrical Federalism: Keeping Canada Together?' In B. De Villiers (ed.) *Evaluating Federal Systems* Dordrecht: Martinus Nijhoff.

Chanock, M (1982), 'Making Customary Law: Men, Women and the Courts in Colonial Rhodesia,' in M.J. Hay & M. Wright (eds.) *African Women and the Law: Historical Perspectives*, Boston: African Studies Centre, Boston University.

Charlesworth, H., Chinkin, C., and Wright, S., (1991), 'Feminist Approaches to International Law,' *American Journal of International Law* Vol.85.

Civil Liberties Organisation (1993) *Human Rights in Retreat* Lagos: Civil Liberties Organisation.

Correa, S. and Petchesky, R. (1994) 'Reproductive and Social Rights: A Feminist Perspective.' In G.Sen, A. Germain and L. Cohen (eds.) *Population Policies Considered* Cambridge, MA: Harvard University Press.

Correa, S. & R. Reichmann, (1994), *Population and Reproductive Rights: Feminist Perspectives from the South*, London/New Jersey/New Delhi: Zed Books/Kali for Women/DAWN.

Effah, J., Mbachu, D. and Onyegbula S. (1995) Unequal *Rights: Discriminatory Laws and Practices Against Women in Nigeria,* Lagos: Constitutional Rights Project.

Elazar, D. (1995) *Federalism: An Overview*, Pretoria: HSRC Publishers.

Enloe, C. 1990 Bananas, *Beaches and Bases: Making Feminist Sense of International Politics,* Berkeley: University of California Press.

Friere, P., (1972), *Pedagogy of the Oppressed*, Harmondsworth: Penguin Education.

Foucault, M., (1982), 'The Subject and Power,' in H. Dreyfue & P. Rabinow (eds.), *Michel Foucault: Beyond Structuralism and Hermeneutics*, Chicago: Chicago University Press

Freedman, L. and Isaacs, S. (1993) Human Rights and Reproductive Choice Studies *in Family Planning 24* (1).

Gramsci, A. (1971), *Selections from the Prison Notebooks of Antonio Gramsci*, London: Lawrence & Wishart.

Hassim, S. (1998) 'Gender Institutions in South Africa: New Forms of Politics.' In D. Bach (ed.) (1998) l'Afrique *Politique: Femmes D'Afrique,* Paris: Centre D'Etude D'Afrique Noire, Karthala,.

Imam, A. forthcoming 'I wan bi President ...': Gender Politics and Discourses of Democracy in Nigeria.' In P. Robinson, C. Newberry and M. Diouf (eds.) *Political Transitions in Africa*

_____., Williams, O. and Onyegu, R. (1999) 'Introduction'. In *NGOs CEDAW Report for Nigeria*   Nigerian NGO Coalition for a Shadow Report to CEDAW

Jacobson, R. (1997 'Gender and Democratisation: The Mozambican Election of 1994.' *Internet Journal of African Studies:* 1.

Jayawardena, K. (1986) Feminism *and Nationalism in the Third World,* London: Zed Press.

Kapur, R., (1992), 'Feminism, Fundamentalism and Rights Rhetoric in India,' Special Bulletin on Fundamentalism and Secularism in South

Asia, in WLUML, Women Living Under Muslim Laws, Coordination Office Asia, June.

Lesselier, C., (1991), 'Apocalypse Now,' *Apres-Demain*, No.30. Mama, A. (1995) 'Feminism or Femocracy? State Feminism and Democratisation in Nigeria.' *Africa Development XX* (1).

_____., (1997) 'Khaki in the Family: Gender Discourses and Militarism in Nigeria.' Paper presented at the Centre for Research and Documentation (CRD) Workshop on Women's Rights, Politics and Democratisation, 26-28 November 1997, Kano.

Mba, N. (1982) Nigerian *Women Mobilized: Women's Political Activity in Southern Nigeria, 1900-1965* Institute of International Studies (IIS), Berkeley: University of California.

_____, (1989) 'Kaba and Khaki: Women and the Militarised State in Nigeria.' In J. Parpart and K. Staudt (eds.) *Women and the State in Africa* Lynne, Boulder: Reinner.

McClintock, A. (1993) 'Family Feuds: Gender, Nationalism and the Family.' *Feminist Review 44*, 61-80.

Narayan, U., (1997), *Dislocating Cultures: Identities, Traditions and Third World Feminism*, New York/London: Routledge.

Nigerian NGO Coalition (1999) NGOs *CEDAW Report for Nigeria* Nigerian NGO Coalition for a Shadow Report to CEDAW, Lagos.

Ogbuagbu, S., (1985), 'Depo-Provera—A Choice or an Imposition on African Women: A Case Study of Depo-Provera Usage in Maiduguri,' in A. Imam, R. Pittin & H. Omole (eds.), *Women and the Family*, Zaria: WIN.

Olukoshi, A. and Agbu, O. (1996) 'The Deepening Crisis of Nigerian Federalism and the Future of the Nation-State.' In A. Olukoshi and L. Laakso (eds.) *Challenges to the Nation-State in Africa* Nordic Africa Institute, Uppsala/ Institute of Development Studies, University of Helsinki.

Osakue, G., Madunagu, B., Usman, H. and Osagie, J. (1995) Voices! International Reproductive Rights Research Action Group (IRRRAG) Nigeria.

Osinbajo, Y., (n.d.) 'Epilogue: International and Domestic Legal Protection for Women: Landmarks on the Journey So Far,' in A.U. Kalu & Y. Osinbajo (eds.), *Women and Children Under Nigerian Law*, Federal Ministry of Justice, Lagos.

Pereira, C. forthcoming 'National Council of Women's Societies and the State, 1985-1993: "A Woman's Place".' In A. Jega (ed.) *The Transformation of Popular Identities under Structural Adjustment in Nigeria*, Uppsala: Nordic Africa Institute.

Pitanguy, J., (1994), 'Feminist Politics and Reproductive Rights: The Case of Brazil,' in G. Sen & R. Snow (eds.) *Power and Decision: The Social Control of Reproduction*, Boston: Harvard School of Public Health.

Pittin, R., (1985), 'The Control of Reproduction: Principle and Practice in Nigeria,' in A. Imam, R. Pittin & H. Omole (eds.), *Women and the Family*, Zaria: WIN.

Ranger, T. (1989) 'The Invention of Tradition in Colonial Africa'. In E. Hobsbawm and T. Ranger (eds.) *The Invention of Tradition*, Cambridge: Cambridge University Press.

Rowlands, J., (1998), 'A Word of the Times, but What Does it Mean? Empowerment in the Discourse and Practice of Development,' in H. Afshar (ed.), *Women and Empowerment*, op.cit.

Sen, G., and Grown, C., (1987), *Development Crises and Alternative Visions: Third World Women's Perspectives*, London: Earthscan.

Shawulu, R. 1990 The *Story of Gambo Sawaba* Echo Communications Ltd., Jos.

Shettima, K. (1995), 'Engendering Nigeria's Third Republic.' *African Studies Review 38* (3).

Suberu, R. (1995), 'The Politics of State Creation.' In S. Adejumobi and A. Momoh (eds.) *The Political Economy of Nigeria under Military Rule: 1984-1993*, Harare: Sapes Books.

_____., (1996), Ethnic *Minority Conflicts and Governance in Nigeria*, Ibadan: Spectrum Books Ltd/IFRA.

Tedheke, M. and Ishaya, D. (eds.) (1995), Problems *of Early Marriage in Nigeria* Proceedings of Seminar organised by Women in Nigeria (WIN) Kaduna branch, held 21 January 1995 at the British Council Hall, Kaduna. Women In Nigeria, Kaduna.

Urdang, S., (1989), *And They Still Dance: Women, War and the Struggle for Change in Mozambique*, London: Earthscan.

Walker, C. (1998), 'Land Reform and Gender in Post-Apartheid South Africa.' *UNRISD News No. 18*, 4.

Watts, R. (1994), 'Contemporary Views on Federalism.' In B. De Villiers (ed.) Evaluating Federal Systems, Dordrecht: Martinus Nijhoff.

Women in Nigeria (WIN) Kaduna (1998), *Nigeria's Compliance with its Obligations under the Convention on the Elimination of All Forms of Discrimination Against Women* WIN Kaduna Chapter

Yuval-Davis, N. (1997), *Gender & Nation*, London: Sage.

_____, and Anthias, F. (eds.) (1989), *Woman-Nation-State*, London: Macmillan.

10

Equality, Discrimination and Constitutionalism in Muslim Africa

Ola Abou Zeid

Concepts of human rights have been a significant preoccupation of Islamic political thought since the nineteenth century when the East came into contact with the West after centuries of isolation behind the 'iron curtain' which the Ottoman Empire had dropped between its provinces and the West. Concepts of human rights were deeply related to the different political and legal changes that liberal Islamic thinkers wished to see imported to Muslim societies from the West.[1] Prominent among the institutions that were brought about by the modernisation process was the nation-state. It was inevitable that, in time, other institutions and ideas that accompanied the state would also be transplanted. Among these was the notion of constitutionalism which can be described as an institution closely tied to the development of legal protections of the rights of citizens. Because this actually meant imposing legal constraints on the power of evolving nation states, many governments of Islamic countries tended to reject the adoption of constitutional safeguards for individual rights and freedoms. In doing so, such governments argued that the concept of constitutionalism is incompatible with the *Sharia*.

Needless to say, the governments of Islamic countries have of recent become more aware of the rising popularity that human rights have come to enjoy mainly on account of various internal and external factors that have been at play since the 1980s. Concerned about their own popularity, governments in the Muslim world have developed new tactics in response to these developments. The ratification of the major international human rights conventions is one measure adopted to modify their image as repressive governments. This is despite the fact that they do not have an even record of ratification.[2] Of even greater importance are the attempts by such governments either to sponsor or to formulate Islamic human rights constitutions.

Instead of undertaking a detailed study of actual constitutions that are in force in varying African Islamic states, I have opted for an examination of some proposals of such Islamic human rights constitutions. I adopt this approach for several reasons. For one thing, serious differences exist among the various African Islamic states with regard to their national constitutions. This is despite the claim that all these constitutions are derived from the

Islamic *Sharia*.[3] Secondly, drafters of the Islamic constitutions proclaim that these instruments convey the authentic Islamic position on human rights, which they would like to see incorporated in the constitutions of Islamic countries around the world.[4] Three such constitutions will be examined in this Chapter. These are the 1979 al-Azhar draft of the Islamic constitution,[5] the 1981 Universal Declaration of Human Rights in Islam (UDHRI)[6] and the 1990 Cairo Declaration on Human Rights in Islam.[7] These are selected because they represent approaches to human rights adopted by influential Islamic figures and major Islamic institutions, that either represent governments of Islamic countries or have a deep influence over their policies.[8]

This chapter is mainly concerned with the principle of equality embodied in the human rights provisions in the proposed Islamic constitutions. I also set out to determine their relationship to fundamental international human rights principles. The aim is to discern the prospects of endorsing equal legal protection of human rights in the countries of the Muslim World in general, noting that Muslin Africa is also part of this world.

Two preliminary remarks are warranted in this regard. First, it must be emphasised that this chapter is not concerned with discussing human rights as enshrined in the Islamic divine sources i.e. the Qur'an and the Sunnah. I am instead interested in analysing three humanly-contemplated documents that expose the formal and intellectual endeavour of some Islamic governments and figures regarding their personal viewpoint about human rights in Islam. Second, comparing the principle of equality within Islamic human rights schemes with the international context would not have been necessary if the authors of the Islamic schemes had simply stated that they were deriving the human rights provisions solely from the *Sharia*, that it is incompatible with the international schemes and that it is impermissible to judge the Islamic schemes by the criteria of international law. However, this is not the case. Rather, the authors of the Islamic constitutions explicitly proclaim their desire to produce human rights schemes that correspond to internationally accepted ones. They were basically concerned with demonstrating how international human rights provisions are compatible with Islamic human rights norms. However, such attempts have largely stumbled on a major obstacle, namely, their view of the *Sharia* regarding the status of women, on the one hand, and of non-Muslims, on the other. Both these subjects seriously injure the principle of equality as contemplated in international frameworks of human rights law.[9]

Three Islamic constitutions: A broad overview

The earliest of the three examined constitutions is the al-Azhar Draft of the Islamic constitution. It was published in 1979 in volume 51 of the al-Azhar journal by the Islamic Research Academy which is an institution affiliated to al-Azhar University, based in Cairo, Egypt. This draft constitution appears to represent the official position of that institution as to what rights should be recognised in a political system based on Sunni Islamic principles.[10] Taking into account the fact that al-Azhar University is not simply a Cairene institution, but is rather the most prestegious institution of higher education in Sunni Islam and a centre of conservative Islamic thought in which a great number of Muslim Africans receive training, one can appreciate the importance of including the al-Azhar draft constitution in this study.[11]

The 1981 UDHRI was prepared by intellectuals of conservative religious inclination from different Islamic countries such as Egypt, Pakistan and Saudi Arabia which convened in Paris in September 1981 under the auspices of the International Islamic Council.[12] This council is affiliated to the Muslim World League—an international non-governmental organisation headquartered in Saudi Arabia and known to represent the views of conservative Muslims. Despite the fact that the UDHRI was a wholly non-governmental initiative, it was presented to the United Nations Educational, Scientific and Cultural Organisation (UNESCO) in a ceremony attended by prominent Islamic figures including several Africans. Among them were Ahmed ben Bella and Mukhtar Ould Dada, the former leaders of Algeria and Mauritania, respectively.[13]

The Cairo Declaration was endorsed in August 1990 by the foreign ministers of the Organisation of the Islamic Conference (OIC)—the accredited international organisation of Islamic governments. The Cairo Declaration thus appears to embody a consensus, at least at the governmental level, of the fashion in which Islam perceives human rights. To be sure, when the declaration was presented at the 1993 World Conference on Human Rights in Vienna, the Saudi foreign minister declared that it embodies the consensus of the Muslims of the world on human rights issues.[14]

These documents are conceived to respectively represent the non-governmental and governmental positions on human rights issues in Islamic countries. It is true that none of these documents has imposed any obligation of a legal nature on the Islamic countries in order to enforce the observance of the human rights norms included in them. However, their study and analysis can prove to be of great importance. On the one hand, they reveal the points of consensus on which the governments of Islamic countries agree concerning the notion of human rights. On the other, it is expected that they will act as the starting point for any upcoming governmental effort to enact an Islamic scheme of human rights. Because the national constitutions of all Islamic countries declare that the *Sharia* is a main source, if not *the* main source of their legal systems, and because the views endorsed in these Islamic schemes represent the conservative Islamic trend which existing Islamic governments prefer for different reasons, it is expected that if they choose to endorse human rights provisions in their constitutions the Islamic governments will be following the guidelines of these documents.[15]

The principle of equality in Islamic human rights schemes

The treatment of the principle of equality in the Islamic human rights schemes examined in this chapter is generally characterised by ambiguity and inconsistency. For while it is obvious that the drafters of these constitutions do not undertake any serious attempt to abide by the principle of equality as set out in international human rights law, at the same time they appear rather reluctant to acknowledge their unwillingness to respect this principle.[16] Scholars contemplate that this stems mainly from the ambivalence which the drafters of these schemes feel about the principle of equality. On the one hand, it appears that they believe that distinctions made between different groups of persons in Islamic law are but natural and essential and that Islam treats as equal all those who should be so treated. From this perspective *Sharia*-based discrimination is compatible with the principle of equality. On the other, however, they realise that this belief does not stand up against the test of international human rights standards on equality which utterly reject any regime of discrimination against women and non-Muslims no matter the justification.[17]

Because the Muslim nation joined the international community of nations formed under the auspices of the UN, Islamic states have agreed to be bound by international law. To be sure, the 1972 Charter of the Organisation of Islamic Conference (OIC) proclaims in its preamble the commitment of its members (i.e. all Islamic countries) to international law and fundamental human rights. This amounts to the formal acceptance that the conduct of Islamic states is subjected to regulation by international human rights principles.[18]

This reality led the drafters of the examined Islamic constitutions to be cautious enough not to explicitly condemn the principle of equality as espoused in the international scheme. However, in practice, they sought to circumvent it. One device used do so is to proclaim that the *Sharia* constitute the sole source of contemplation and interpretation of the rights and freedoms included in the Islamic constitutions. By this they apparently want to convey that the Islamic *Sharia*, like international human rights law, endorses the principle of equality but arrives at it via a different path. However, because the *Sharia* is divinely revealed, Muslims do not have the right to alter its dictates.[19]

Evasiveness is another device used by the drafters to confront their explicit confusion. For example, the al-Azhar draft constitution tried to completely avoid the issue of equality. It simply refrains from discussing those categories of human rights on the basis of which it is impermissible to discriminate. It is true that Article 28 states that justice and equality are the basis of rule, but this does not actually denote that all persons are equal before the law.[20]

Instead of avoiding the issue altogether, the UDHRI and the Cairo Declaration opt for disturbingly evasive formulations of the provisions relating to equality. Thus, while Article 1 (a) of the Cairo Declaration states that all human beings are equal, it fails to stipulate that they are equal in 'rights'. It states instead that they are equal in human dignity. Likewise, the preamble to the UDHRI states that people are all equal, not in rights, but because of the fact that they all emanate from the same human origin. Article 3 (b) that comes under the rubric 'Right of Equality' further emphasises the notion by stating that people are equal in terms of their human value.

By refraining from openly endorsing the international principle that human beings are equal in human rights and electing to say that they are equal in dignity and value, one could say that such formulations are disturbingly evasive. Apparently, for the authors of these documents, this equality in human value or dignity does not necessarily mean that human beings should enjoy equal rights. To be sure, the UDHRI includes the Qur'anic verse 10:19 'Mankind was a single nation, but differed later.' Such reference illustrates that the authors of the Declaration are influenced by the juristic traditional interpretation usually given to this verse, namely, that the single origin of humankind did not stop human beings from leading different ways of life. According to this interpretation, these differing life patterns become a means of grading people using various criteria, prominent among them being piety. In the highest rank of piety would reside those who truly believe in one God and accept the guidance of Prophet Muhammed (i.e. Muslims). According to this line of thought, such people would enjoy more rights than people in other ranks.[21]

This stance of the UDHRI is further fortified by examining the wording of Article 3(a). This article stipulates that people are equal before the *Sharia* and that no distinction is made in its application to them or in their protection under it. However, as several researchers correctly observe, *Sharia* is not a neutral law.[22] Rather, it is a law that favours the model of the male, free, sane, adult Muslim in a number of areas. The farther the individual is from this model, the fewer rights he (or she) is to enjoy. To be sure, the *Sharia* establishes separate categories of human beings. Muslims differ from non-Muslims and men differ from women. According to this value system, equality, which is to treat equally the persons within each separate category, is the only rightful path to achieve justice which is the highest Islamic value.[23] Taking into consideration this concept of equality and its relation to the value of justice, the claim of Article 3(a) of the UDHRI that people are equal would fail to stand up to the standard of equality contemplated in international human rights schemes. This is because equality of people before the *Sharia* would fail to guarantee women and non-Muslims the legal protection of their rights on an equal footing with Muslim men. It explicitly violates international human rights law which demands that a neutral law be applied to all citizens of a country.[24]

Likewise, Article l9(a) of the Cairo Declaration which refers to the equality of all individuals before the law, is no less evasive. For one thing, taking into account the context of the document, the law meant here would be *Sharia* law. If we apply the above discussion concerning doubts about the neutrality of the *Sharia* law we can arrive at the same conclusion drawn before. Moreover, the equality referred to in the article was immediately qualified by the statement 'without distinction between the ruler and the ruled.' Some researchers read this as meaning that discrimination in applying the law to rulers and the ruled is the only discrimination that this article rejects. In their opinion, this qualification amounts to the denial of equal rights or equal protection of the law to women, non-Muslims and Muslim men.[25]

In fact, none of the examined documents ever fully and unequivocally endorses the principle of equality and the basic idea that no sexual and religious discrimination is permissible as reflected in the international human rights conventions. An examination of the articles in these documents that deal particularly with women's and non-Muslim's rights will further expose the various restrictions and the actual denial of many of their rights that are otherwise protected under the international human rights framework.

Islamic human rights schemes and women

Despite the fact that these documents do not explicit admit that women are to be accorded second class status, they actually deny women a number of rights and freedoms under the guise of applying Islamic *Sharia*.[26] For example, while all three documents allow women the right to marry, all of them qualify the right. It is true that the UDHRI abhors forced marriage for girls and boys alike as Article l9(i) states that no boy or girl may be married against his or her will. However, if the woman's right to marry the partner of her choice is guaranteed, her right to dissolve this marriage at will is not equally protected. According to Article 20(d), the woman can dissolve the marriage only via consensual agreement with her husband or through the court. One should note that the husband is not obliged to grant her request.

Furthermore, the court seeks various requirements in order to dissolve the marriage against the husband's will. If we recall the fact that the husband can dissolve the marriage on his own will and without resort to court, one can see that the application of the Islamic view point endorsed in the document allows for serious discrimination to be applied against women. It might be useful to mention that the family laws that are in force in the various Islamic states make the dissolution of a marital relationship at will an absolute right of the husband.[27] Even in Tunisia, where the most progressive 'Islamic' family laws are in force, this right is not given to the woman, but rather to the judge.[28]

The UDHRI seems to further relegate women to second class status. For, after stipulating to all human beings the right to marry in article 19(a), and after stating that husbands and wives enjoy equal rights and obligations, the text incorporates the Qur'anic verse 2: 228 to the effect that men are a degree above women. This verse is traditionally used by conservatives to establish male superiority,[29] and this conveys the view that the inequality of husbands and wives in a marital relationship is the underlying assumption of the UDHRI.

More serious still is the formulation of Article 5(a) of the Cairo Declaration to the effect that the enjoyment by men and women of the right to marry should not be restricted by race, colour or nationality. The failure to mention religion means that the authors of the declaration expect that the enjoyment of this right could, and should, be restricted by rules of the *Sharia*. The superficial reading of the provision might convey equality in imposing this restriction on both men and women. However, a more careful scrutiny of the provision will reveal discrimination against women in particular—a situation that is unacceptable according to international human rights norms. For one thing, under this provision Muslim women will not be allowed to marry non-Muslim men because the rules of *Sharia* simply do not allow it.

This is not the case with Muslim men who are not restricted by *Sharia* only to marry Muslim women and can marry women from any religious belief. Moreover, Muslim women are restricted by this article to marry one husband at a time. In contrast, Muslim men can marry four wives simultaneously. It should be noted that the *Sharia* rules mentioned here refer specifically to the traditional juristic interpretation of the divine sources. In contrast, some scholars read the Qur'anic verse 1: 221 concerning the marriage of Muslims to non-Muslims as addressing Muslim men and women alike meaning that both are allowed to marry from a different religious belief.[30] Moreover, they believe that the restriction of polygamy is originally discerned by the *Sharia* to be applied to men and women alike.[31] It should be noted that the Tunisian family law treats polygamy as a crime to be punished by imprisonment.[32]

The Al-Azhar draft constitution does not only uphold the traditional image of the nature of the spouses' relationship which preserves the upper hand for the husband and keeps the wife in a subordinate position, but it also appeals to the state to intervene and legalise this situation. Article 8 of the draft constitution calls upon the state to use its power to enforce the right of the husband to his wife's obedience and to accord primacy of place to her duties as mother and housewife.

If the al-Azhar draft constitution is direct and bold in demanding the enforcement of male authority as an absolute right to be enjoyed by husbands over wives, the Cairo Declaration adopted a more evasive route to arrive at the same end. Article 6(a) stipulates that women are equal to men in human dignity, but not equal in rights. Sub-section (b) of the same article fortifies the inequality of men and women by stating that it is the responsibility of men to provide the family with maintenance. By this, the authors of the Cairo Declaration are apparently upholding the traditional Islamic view which undertakes that because men are burdened by the duty of providing for the family they are to enjoy rights of control over the wives. In other words, the duty of being the family 'bread-winner' imposed on the husband is balanced by the duty of subordination expected of the wife.[33]

Portraying men as the sole providers directly supports the perception of a system where men work outside the home while women concentrate only on their domestic role. Therefore, one can expect that the drafters' treatment of women's right to work will not be less biased. To be sure, article 38 of the al-Azhar draft constitution while providing that women have the right to work, states that this right will be enjoyed within the limits of the precepts of the *Sharia*. Despite the fact that the article does not discern the limits imposed by the *Sharia* on women's ability to work, it is presumed that the husband's permission and the nature of the job and its milieu are among these restrictions. None of these restrictions apply to men.

Likewise, Article 13 of the Cairo Declaration which starts by stating that everyone is free to choose the work that suits him or her best, proceeds to qualify this right by providing that the work 'freely chosen' must serve the interests of the society and that no one should be assigned work beyond his capacity. These qualifications are expected to serve mainly to limit the fields in which women are permitted to work on the ground that the demands of the job were beyond their capacity or that the interests of the society impose their exclusion.

To be sure, the traditional Islamic stance prohibits women from undertaking jobs that are considered, by men, to be beyond their physical or mental capabilities. Working in mines and fighting in the battlefield are two examples given for the first kind of restricted employment. Leadership of the state and judgeship are two types of employment from which women are exempted because of the second set of restrictions.[34] It should be mentioned here that some researchers reveal that there is no verse in the Qur'an that denies women the right to rule. On the contrary, several verses in the Qur'an praise the leadership of women rulers like Sheba. According to these researchers, the prophetic anecdote which is usually employed by conservatives in this regard is categorised as weak.[35] They are keen to attract attention to the fact that Muslim women were free to work and to move during the time of the prophet and up to the medieval ages. They undertook all kinds of jobs including the jobs from which they were later deprived when the conservative juristic interpretation of the divine sources prevailed starting from the medieval ages onwards.[36]

Discrimination against women continues with regard to the freedom of movement. Article 12 of the Cairo Declaration again conditions the right to freedom of movement within the framework of the *Sharia*, a condition which, in practice, applies specifically to women. According to conservative interpretations of the Islamic sources, women should not be allowed to travel unchaperoned. Moreover, they should not be allowed to leave their homes without their husbands' permission.[37] Property rights for women are violated in Article 20(d) of the UDHRI which, while stipulating the right of the wife to inherit from her husband, also incorporates the Qur'anic verse 4:12 that determines the Qur'anic scheme for inheritance. Without indulging in a discussion about the enforceability of Qur'anic orders and regulations from an Islamic perspective, from the viewpoint of international human rights law, this article fails to afford the protection for women's human rights as it confirms discriminatory rules of inheritance. It might be revealing to mention that Tunisia is now applying non discriminatory rules of inheritance.[38]

The above analysis reveals beyond doubt that the Islamic human rights schemes examined here discriminate against women and restrict many of the rights that women have been granted in international human rights documents. One can easily point to the violations of the guarantee to equality in article 1 of the Universal Declaration of Human Rights (UDHR) and Articles 3 and 26 of the International Covenant on Civil and Political Rights (ICCPR) and Articles 1 and 2 of the Convention on the Elimination of All Forms of Discrimination Against Women (CEDAW); the guarantee against discriminatory treatment in article 2 of the UDHR and Articles 2 and 26 of the ICCPR and Articles 2 ,7 and 11 of the CEDAW; the guarantee of equal protection of the law in articles 7 of UDHR and Article 26 of ICCPR and Article 15 of CEDAW; the guarantee of equal treatment in marital relationship in article 16 of CEDAW and the guarantee of liberty of movement in article 12 of the ICCPR and Article 15 of CEDAW.[39]

It is quite revealing to know that the reservations made by Islamic governments to CEDAW outnumbered all the reservations made by such governments to all other human rights instruments. The reservations were directed mainly to Articles 2, 7, 9, 15, 16 and 29 of the convention. However Article 16, which discusses the marital relationship, received the highest number of reservations. It is significant to know that when justifying their reservations to Article 16 of CEDAW, all states referred to the Islamic *Sharia* emphasising their belief that the article violates the teachings of the *Sharia* with regard the rights of women in the marital relationship.[40]

Islamic human rights schemes and non-Muslims

Just as it is not permissible in international human rights law to deny people equal protection of the law or to discriminate against them on the basis of sex, it is equally impermissible to do so on the basis of religion. However, as in the case of women, the Islamic human rights schemes examined in this chapter provide no real protection for religious minorities against discrimination and from deprivations of their rights established in international law.

Thus, although the guarantee of equality in basic human dignity in Article 1 (a) of the Cairo Declaration prohibits discrimination on the grounds of religious belief, this same article appears to be constructing a system of discrimination against non-Muslims. This is because the article closes by stating that true faith is the guarantee for enhancing dignity along the path to human perfection. The wording betrays the author's conviction that this human dignity which is supposedly the basis of equality of all people differs drastically in its quality. Moreover, this quality is determined by nothing but true faith, i.e. Islam. In other words, human dignity is treated as a means of grading people in different ranks culminating to perfection, true faith being the tool of polishing this dignity. This discrimination on the basis of religion is further emphasised in Article 1(b) which states that no one has superiority over another except on the basis of piety.

The same notion can be discerned in Article 3(b) of the UDHRI which likewise states that all people are equal in human value. The provision then goes on to state that people attain superiority over each other because of their good deeds. Consulting the traditional Islamic attitude one can presume using this criteria that good pious Muslims will be superior over unpious Muslims. Further it can be surmised that all Muslims will be superior over non-Muslims.

The Islamic human right schemes not only differentiate between Muslims and non-Muslims on the basis of piety, but they also discriminate between non-Muslims who are people of the book, i.e. Christians and Jews and non-Muslims who are not Christians or Jews. Although Article 10(b) of the UDHRI gives religious minorities the right to choose either to be governed by Islamic law or by their own laws on personal status and civil matters it actually confines the enjoyment of this right to the people of the book. This means that members of the communities of non-Muslims who are not Christians or Jews have to be subjected to *Sharia* law. This is a sharp violation of the international human rights law which holds that a neutral, non-discriminatory law must be applied to all citizens of a country.

The evasive treatment of the principle of equality and equal protection accorded to non-Muslims is quite clear in Article 10(a) of the UDHRI which incorporates the Qur'anic verse 2:256 proclaiming that there is no compulsion in religion. At first glance, this article seems to be offering a basis of protection for the religious rights of non-Muslims. However, non-Muslims have a different opinion. They believe that this bar against forced conversion does not by itself guarantee that non-Muslims will not be subjected to discrimination based on their religion.[41] The other article of the UDHRI 12 (e) which holds that no one should ridicule the religious beliefs of others does not help much in this regard. As Mayer rightly observes, it is more of an ethico-moral injunction than an enforceable legal right.[42] To be sure, the article addresses the 'Muslim' i.e. the private individual and not the government or the legal authorities that act as the sources of infringements of liberty.

Article 10 of the Cairo Declaration which apparently endorses protection for freedom of religion, limits this protection, in practice, to Muslims only. The article which prohibits any form of compulsion or exploitation of one's poverty or ignorance in order to convert him (or her) to another religion or to atheism starts by declaring that Islam is the religion of unspoiled nature. Various scholars believe that this article is biased against non-Muslims because, as they read it, it would not ban the use of the same techniques as long as they are applied to convert people to Islam.[43]

The UDHRI is no less evasive than the Cairo Declaration on the issue of protection for freedom of religion. For, while Article 13 which comes under the rubric 'Right to Freedom of Religion' reads that every one has freedom to believe and to worship according to the Qur'anic principle 'you have your religion, I have mine' (109:6), other articles of the UDHRI put restrictions on the rights enjoyed by non-Muslims. One might contemplate that this could practically form a limitation on the right to freedom of religion. This is because it could create a situation in which non-Muslims are forced to convert to Islam in order to enjoy the rights which they are otherwise deprived because of their religious beliefs. Thus, we find Article 12(a) allowing the enjoyment of freedom of thought, belief and speech as the individual obeys the limits set by the *Sharia* while 'freely' thinking, believing and expressing him or herself. Limitations on such freedoms using the criteria of one religion violate the rights of followers of other religions to fully enjoy them.

Likewise, Article 14 of the UDHRI which, on its face, treats the right to freedom of association granting it equally to all people, again qualifies this right by requiring that such associations must enjoin the good and forbid the evil. This requirement relates to the Qur'anic command in 3: 104. One can conclude that the freedom of association meant here is one that includes Islamic activities or at least does not violate Islamic rules. The right to propagate religions other than Islam or to disseminate philosophies of secularism or atheism cannot be accommodated within the scope of this article. This article therefore violates the principle of equality between Muslims and non-Muslims regarding the right of association and expression.

Even the enjoyment of the right to life is restricted by the power of the *Sharia*. While Articles l(a) of the UDHRI and 2(a) of the Cairo Declaration proclaim the sanctity of human life, they both state that life could be taken by the power of *Sharia*. The al-Azhar draft constitution is more explicit in discerning in Article 71 that the death penalty would be applied for apostasy. One can expect that in a system governed by *Sharia* norms the apostasy that will call for execution would only refer to conversion from Islam.[44]

It becomes obvious from the above discussion that the Islamic human rights schemes examined here violate the international human rights law which prohibits religious discrimination and guarantees religious freedom. The principle prohibiting religious discrimination is enshrined in Articles 2 of the UDHR, 2 and 26 of the ICCPR and Article 2 of the 1981 Declaration on the Elimination of all forms of Intolerance and of Discrimination Based on Religion or Belief. Article 2:2 of the last mentioned document defines impermissible discrimination as '...any distinction, exclusion, restriction or preference based on religion or belief and having as its purpose or as its effect nullification or impairment of the recognition, enjoyment or exercise of human rights or fundamental freedoms on an equal basis.' Unqualified religious freedom is enshrined in Article 18:1 of the ICCPR and Articles 1:1 and 1:2 of the 1981 Declaration and Article 18 of the UDHR which reads: 'Every one has the right to freedom of thought, conscience and religion; this right includes freedom to change his religion or belief...'.[45]

Revisiting the debate on Islam, constitutionalism and human rights

From among the many serious shortcomings of the Islamic human rights schemes examined here, the most disturbing is their insistence that the revealed sources enjoy primacy over reason as the source of law in general, and of human rights law, in particular. The UDHRI explicitly states in its preamble that reason is inadequate to discern the best plan for human life as long as it is unaided by God's guidance and inspiration. Unfortunately, this claim is inaccurate. What these Islamic schemes consider as revealed, divine sources are actually nothing but the medieval traditional school of Islamic jurisprudence which offer a conservative interpretation of the divine sources (the Qur'an and the Sunnah) particularly with regard the personal status law and the laws that govern non-Muslims. It is my considered opinion that this is an interpretation that violates the principle of equality and of equal protection of the law.[46]

According revelation the central role in discerning human rights norms within an Islamic context, makes it easy for the authors of the Islamic human rights schemes to sanctify them and hence to demand unwarranted respect and acceptance of these norms. To be sure, the preamble to the UDHRI and the forward to the Cairo Declaration both state that the human rights norms being derived from the Islamic divine sources are not susceptible to alteration, modification, neglect or curtailment. The inevitable consequence of such position is to rule out any challenge that might be made to such schemes on the grounds that they deny human rights protected under international law.

International human rights law is meant to serve as a model for the schemes of human rights to be endorsed in the constitutions and legal systems of the countries that form the international community. This is important because the actual implementation of international human rights law depends on the degree it is exemplified in national laws and constitutions. The treatment of human rights in the Islamic constitutions examined here conveys the intention of their drafters to make the rights provisions in the legal systems of the Muslim countries conform to international standards, but only to a certain degree. The application and extension of these rights is determined by a divine, unquestionable source.

To be sure, Muslim African countries have a poor record of ratifying international human rights conventions and have made numerous reservations to the instruments they have ratified. These actions have always been justified by the claim that the main source of their national constitutions and laws is divine. But this is not true. Suffice it to point to the wide differences that exist between the national constitutions and laws of the African Islamic states and also to the amendments that affect the national law and constitution of the same country from time to time in order to prove the falseness of the claim that they all derive from divine sources. Their source is rather the widely various juristic interpretations of those divine sources.[47]

The scenario described above creates a very serious situation in the Muslim world, in general, and in Muslim Africa in particular. For whether these states are representing repressive one-party systems, or military dictatorships, or whether they endorse imported western constitutional models, they have always been ready to utilise the notion of cultural relativism, namely, the denial that there are universal standards by which all cultures may be judged, to restrict internationally guaranteed human rights. To be sure, the African Charter on Human and People's Rights was itself drafted to expose the African concept of human rights and to demonstrate that African values and morals have a prominent place in African societies.[48]

It is true that the argument of cultural relativism is employed by relativists from all cultures to condemn using western values to judge the institutions and practices of non-western cultures.[49] However, the seriousness of the problem within the cultural context of Muslim Africa arises from the fact that the institutions and practices which they seek to defend are identified as Islamic and the cultural system they claim to guard is equated with Islam. Hence, Muslim African cultural relativists deny the legitimacy of any evaluative comparisons of Islamic right norms and international ones. They argue that such comparisons involve making judgments about Islamic beliefs using the criteria of international law. However, the relativists claim that international law is not only an alien system but is also atheistic, and undivine. In this respect, the Islamic limitations on human rights will be considered by many of the governments of African Islamic countries as an application of the African notion of cultural relativism that allows the state almost unbounded discretion in using the notion to restrict internationally-guaranteed rights.

The second most striking feature in all the Islamic human rights schemes reviewed in this chapter is the use of Islamic criteria to qualify human rights principles. Throughout our examination of the studied documents we noted that their authors are consistent in limiting the international human rights provisions they include by imposing restrictions which they represent as being inherent in the Islamic *Sharia*. Nevertheless, the authors do not precisely delineate what limits they envisage the Islamic criteria would impose on the human rights afforded by international law. The very disturbing result of using unidentified Islamic legal standards to restrict internationally-guaranteed human rights principles is to reduce the protections which these rights actually afford. Such a situation leaves unlimited discretion to states in deciding what the scope of the affected rights should be.

If we remember that the studied constitutions act as models of what their authors want to see in Muslim countries, and if we observe that these schemes broadly reflect the ideas of conservative Muslims that are traditionally aligned with repressive governments, the seriousness of the problem becomes obvious. If these constitutions, or the ideas that underlie them, will be incorporated in the constitutions of Muslim countries, Islam will be used as a device for restricting the individual's rights and freedoms, and thereby keeping the individual in a subordinate status vis-à-vis the state. It should be remembered that the *Sharia* criteria employed to restrict human rights are not only demanded to be unquestionable, but they are also vague, general and uncertain. This means that they can be defined in widely varying ways. To be sure, they can always be defined so as to conform to the demands of the governments for obedience and submission—impositions that may have nothing whatsoever to do with the true spirit of the religion.

This might prove seriously critical in the case of Muslim African countries. One should remember that African governments have a record of curtailing the human rights of citizens employing apparently benign criteria such as law and order. These criteria are recurrently used to deprive religious minorities of the enjoyment of the right to religious freedom, as well as various other civil and political rights, mainly rights of expression, association and participation in political life using domestic legal standards.[50] One can expect that the infringements on these rights by governments in Muslim African countries will be dangerously augmented if the 'uncertain, unquestionable' *Sharia* restrictions are added to the application of law and order. It should also be noted that governments in Muslim countries, in general, and in Muslim Africa, in particular, feel uncomfortable with the intellectual foundation that underlies the western philosophy of rights. The international human rights standards rest on the assumption that rights of the individual are of primary concern and must be protected against any infringements either by the government or the society. This would entail that the individual must not be denied his or her rights even if this would be in the general interest.

In contrast, the Islamic historical experience shows that the individual and the state have sometimes had conflicting interests which have usually been resolved at the expense of the individual's human rights and freedoms. Authors of the Islamic human rights schemes examined here, have failed to endorse the international human rights standards regarding the relation between the individual and the state, that conforms with the true spirit of the teachings of Islam as embodied in the divine sources. Instead, they have yielded to a certain trend within the medieval juristic heritage and hence downgraded the significance of protections for individual rights.[51] The endorsement of such a scheme by Muslim African countries would prove critical because of the enormous increase in the powers wielded by central governments prevailing in Africa and the vast disparity in power between these and the position of the individual. Significant also in this regard is the fact that the African Charter on Human and Peoples' Rights is formulated to stress the duties, rather than the rights of each person towards the state. This has been considered as one of the features peculiar to the African Charter and one which presents numerous problems.[52]

It is important to emphasise that the Islamic international human rights schemes examined in this chapter represent the ideas of the conservative Muslim position that—although apparently tolerating international human rights—imposes restrictions on them to bring them into conformity with Islamic standards as they understand them. However, Muslims in this trend do not constitute all Muslim opinion on human rights issues. One very important position is that of liberal Muslims who favour the perpetuation of modern norms of constitutional government and the unqualified endorsement of international human rights standards.[53] Such scholars seek to distinguish between sources of the *Sharia* (Qur'an and Sunnah) and the *Sharia* law which they conceive as the accumulated intellectual endeavour of Muslim jurists to understand the sources. This is an endeavour which, for them, has produced widely diverging interpretations of the divine sources.[54] They proceed from this stance to demand a serious reappraisal of *Sharia* law with the final aim of discarding many of the traditional interpretations.[55] They also believe that the Islamic law position on human rights is one of the domains that requires a fresh approach to the Islamic divine sources in order to resolve the pressing problems at hand.[56]

To start with, such scholars reject the notion that the existing *Sharia* law should act as a source of limitations on the enjoyment of human rights guaranteed by international law.[57] They refer to the fact that the Islamic criteria used to impose restraints on rights and freedoms are themselves a source of great disagreement.[58] They are specifically concerned about the status of non-Muslims and of women under the *Sharia*-imposed restrictions. For instance, they deeply protest the current *Sharia* rule on apostasy. They repudiate the death penalty for apostasy insisting that the traditional juristic interpretations in this regard are unwarranted by the Islamic sources, as there is no verse in the Qur'an that stipulates any earthly penalty for apostasy. Scholars advocate that this penalty violates the principle of tolerance of religious differences which figures in the Islamic value system. They emphasise that centuries of accumulated prejudices and wrong practices lead to the erroneous belief that conversion is a one way traffic, i.e. to Islam, and that one is not free to walk in the other direction. The solution they pose for this problem is to revive the authentic Islamic belief which they conceived, namely, that religious adherence should be left as a private matter of conscience. One is then at liberty to select alternative interpretations of the Islamic rules on apostasy that are more in keeping with the spirit of the Qur'an and with modern human rights norms on religious freedom.[59]

In the same vein, liberal Muslims place the blame for the inferior status of women on the distorted juristic interpretations of the original sources augmented by the social practices of many diverse cultural traditions.[60] According to such scholars, these traditions must be distinguished from Islam whose original message was to improve the status of women and to preach equality of the sexes. In this respect, they draw attention to the fact that the status of women in the period of early Islam was much better compared to their status in modern Islamic societies.[61] They call for a re-examination of the sources which they believe when properly understood, will reveal that authentic Islam actually supports equal rights for both sexes.[62]

Conclusion

The conservative and liberal Islamic trends are both interacting on the political scene in Islamic African states: Algeria, Tunisia, Egypt and Sudan are only a few examples to be mentioned in this regard. Both trends are pressing the governments of these states to constitutionally endorse their viewpoints regarding human rights and freedoms. To be sure, the conservative, violent Islamic movements are quite active in this regard. In Tunisia, for example, they are pressing hard to alter the personal status laws so as to conform with *Sharia* law as they conceive it. In particular, they are demanding a restoration of polygamy, divorce to be an absolute right of the husband and women's deprivation of their equal inheritance rights to cite a few examples.[63] Likewise, the conservative Islamic movements of Algeria boldly proclaim that once they arrive in power, the 're-formation' of family laws following the lines discerned by the Islamic *Sharia* as they understand it, will be their primary concern.[64] In the Sudan, where the conservative Islamic trend has held power since the late 1980s, women's rights were viciously crushed. The liberal Islamic trend is working hard to re-establish concepts of equality.[65]

In fact, governments in power might actually prefer to endorse the conservative position as exposed in the Islamic human rights schemes examined in this chapter. Its ideas serve their political aspirations, compromise the rising Islamic tide and might help in solving pressing economic problems. But, on the other hand, the human rights movement is now powerful enough at the grass-roots level to be a factor to be reckoned with in politics. Figures of the liberal Muslim stance are prominent human rights activists. The concessions made recently by governments of more than one African Muslim state to growing public opinion and liberal Muslim activists demanding the observance of international human rights standards, provides some hope that a bright future for the promotion and protection of human rights in Muslim Africa is under formulation.

Notes

1. The Egyptian Rifa'ah al-Tahtawi and the Tunisian Khayr al-Din al-Tunisi, both of the nineteenth century, discussed notions of human rights known in the west praising them, while declaring their admiration of constitutionalism and constitutional goverment. See, al-Tahtawi (1993), and al-Tunisi (1972).
2. While a state like Djobouti, for instance, had ratified only two of the main international human rights conventions, others like Egypt and Tunisia had ratified all these conventions with the exception of the Optional Protocol to the International Covenant on Civil and Political Rights. Huquq al-Insan fi al-Watan al-Arabi (Human Rights in the Arab World) (1997).
3. Khidr (1998): 221-22.
4. The preamble to the UDHRI and the Cairo Declaration explicitly state that they are intended to act as guide to the Islamic leaders and rulers. The al-Azhar draft constitution directly address the Islamic governments in more than one article calling upon them to endorse these articles in their national constitutions and laws.
5. All references in the chapter to the al-Azhar draft constitution will be given to the Arabic version published in *Majalat al-Azhar*, the al-Azhar journal (Vol. 1, 1979).
6. All references in this chapter to the UDHRI are from the Arabic version published in: al-Ghazali, (1993): 241-62.

7.   All references to the Cairo Declaration are to the Arabic version published in *Dirasat Dawliyyah* (International Studies) Oct., 1992: 26-31.

8.   These three documents represent the most prominet jurisprudential contributions to the field of Islamic human rights at the governmental and non-governmental levels. The first level is represented by the Organisation of the Islamic Conference (OIC), while the second level is represented by the International Islamic Council (IIC) and the al-Azhar University. See, Awad, (1999): 15-16.

9.   Fodah, (1994): 199-200.

10. The two major sects in Islam are the Sunni and the Shi'i sects. As early as the 5th century AD both started to develop schools of jurispruduce. Co-existence was not impossible though. Rejection and hostility started around the 10th century AD, when both sects started to develop political theories of state, government and leadership. The cornerstone of the Shi'i political theory is that the Imam of the ummah (leader of the nation of believers) is divinely chosen. Hence, total obedience and the denial of political participation on behalf of the ruled are but natural. The Sunni theory of state and government is based on the notion that the ruler is freely chosen by the ruled. Hence, at least theoretically speaking, participation, accountability and peaceful replacement by the opposition are acceptable. For a detailed illustration of the Sunni and Shi'i political theories see, Lambton, (1981).

11. One can view the al-Azhar draft constitution as a new circle in the chain of confrontations between Sunni and Shi'i sects with regard to political theories. Ann Mayer correctly observes that the al-Azhar constitution appeared at the time when the Iranian constitution was drafted by the leaders of the Iranian Islamic revolution. By this draft constitution, al-Azhar— being the most prominent centre of learning in the Sunni Muslim world—might have been responding to the political repercussions of the Iranian Shi'i Revolution. The al-Azhar draft constitution was meant to address Islamic governments in general, and Sunni ones in particular. It was an attempt to demonstrate that Sunni Islam was not bereft of sources to forumulate a constitition for a modern government that takes into consider internationally recognized human rights. See, Mayer (1997): 22.

12. Awad, *op. cit*, 16.

13. Mayer, *op. cit.*, 22.

14. *Ibid*, 23-24.

15. Awad, *op.cit.*, 16-17.

16. Mayer *op. cit.*, 79-80.

17. al-Sharafi, (1995): 158-59.

18. The OIC Charter is published in al-Ahsan (1988): 127-34.

19. Mayer, (1995): 276.

20. Mayer, (1997): 80-83.

21. This is a well established Islamic position. It usually employs prophetic anedotes such 'as the best among you is the most pious.'

22. The term Shari'ah is used here not to denote the Islamic divine sources, namely the Qur'an and the Sunnah, but to point specifically to the different juristic interpretations of these divine sources.

23. Mayer, (1997), *op.cit.*, 84, al-Sharafi, *op.cit.*, 158-59.

24. Fodah, *op. cit.*, 204-05.

25. Mayer, (1997) *op. cit.*, 82.

26. Abbas (1998): 201-02.

27. Radi (1995): 71-75.

28. Khidr, *op.cit.*, 228.

29. Wafi (1979): 99-107.

30. Khidr, *op. cit.*, 225.

31. See, Al-Sharafi, *op. cit.*, 158, who provides the legal opinion of Muhammed Abdu the Great Ima of al-Azhar at the turn of the twentieth century against polygamy.

32. Khidr, *op. cit.*, 226.
33. Wafi, *op. cit.*, 103-107.
34. al-Ghazali, (1990), 40 ff.; Huquq al-Insan, *op. cit.*, 120-21, and 125-31. Note that in Tunisia and Morocco women can work as judges in civil courts, but not in religious courts. In Egypt they are denied this right altogether. Khidr, *op. cit.*, 223.
35. Al-Sharafi, *op.cit.*, 154-55.
36. See for example, Shuqah (1990).
37. Most Islamic countries include this traditional conservative Islamic view in their family laws and give the husband the right to prevent his wife from travelling, working and leaving the home altogether. See, al-Sayegh (1995): 104.
38. Mayer, (1995) Istratijiyat, *op. cit.*, 285.
39. For the texts of these documents see, Centre for the Study of Human Rights (1992).
40. Khidr, *op. cit.*, 220-221.
41. Mayer, *Islam and Human Rights*, *op. cit.*, 131.
42. Ibid. 133.
43. Ibid., 159-60. See also Galal, (1994): 39.
44. Fodah *op. cit.*, 199 and 204.
45. Examine these documents in Centre for the Study of Human Rights, *op. cit.*
46. Abbas, *op. cit.*, at 201-202.
47. Khidr, *op.cit.*, at 221-22; Mayer, Istratijiyat, *op. cit.*, 276.
48. Ojo and Sesay (1986): 93-94.
49. Awad in al-Hasan, *op. cit.*, 55-56.
50. Amnesty International (1991): 28-30.
51. For the relationship between the ruler and the ruled in traditional Islamic schools of jurisprudence see: Abouzeid (1992).
52. Amnesty International *op. cit.*, 12-13; Ojo and Sesay, *op. cit.*, 94-95.
53. Badriyyah al-'Awadi of Kuwait, Fatimah Marnisi of Morocco, Abdullah an-Na'im of Sudan, Fawzi al-Najjar and the late Faraj Fodah of Egypt are but a few examples.
54. Abbas, *op. cit.*, 201-02; Sha'ban (1995): 23. Sha'ban was eager to include the phrophetic anecdote to the effect that the shari'ah law is to be found in the Qur'an and Sunnah only, not in the juristic interpretations that have no sanctity whatsoever.
55. See for example al-Ghazzali, *op. cit.*, 56.
56. See for example al-Sharafi, *op. cit.*, 155-59; an-Na'im (1984): 75-89.
57. See for exmaple Fodah, *op. cit.*, 205-06.
58. See for example Galal, *op. cit.*, 40.
59. Fodah, op. cit., 203-04.
60. See for example Abbas, *op. cit.*, 201-02; Abu Shuqqah, op. cit., 5 ff, and Khidr, *op. cit.*, 221-22.
61. See for example al-Ghazzali, *op. cit.*, 49 ff., and Abu-Shuqqah, *op. cit.,* 5 ff.
62. See for example an-Na'im, *op.cit.*, 82.
63. al-Sharafi, *op.cit.*, 155.
64. Sa'uli, (1995): 131-32.
65. Ibrahim (1995): 140-41.

References

Abbas, Abdul Hadi (1998) 'al-Mar'ah wa Huquq al-Insan' (Woman and Human Rights) in *al-Nahj*, no. 13.

Abouzeid, Ola A. (1992) 'Wajib Ta'at al-Hakim wa ilaqatihi bi mafhum al-musharakah al-siasiyyah fial-islam' (The Duty of obeying the ruler and its relation to the concept of political participation in Islam), Political Research Series, Cairo: Centre for Political Research and Studies.

al-Ahsan, Abdullah (1988) *The Organization of the Islamic Conference: An Introduction to an Islamic Political Institution* (Herindon: The International Institute of Islamic Thought.

al-Ghazali, Muhammad (1990) 'al-Sunnah Bayn al-Fiqh wa al-Hadith' (Sunnah between Jurisprudence and Anecdotes), Cairo: Dar al-Shuruq.

_____, Muhammad (1993) Huquq al-Insan Bayn Ta'alim al-Islam wa I'lan al Ummam al-Muttahidah (Human Rights Between the Tenets of Islam and the U.N. Declaration) (Alexandria: Dar al-Da'wah).

al-Sayegh, Mai (1995) 'al-Mar'ah al-Arabiyyah: al-Waqi' wa al-Tatalu'at' (The Arab Woman: Realities and Aspirations) in *al-Nahj*, no.5.

al-Sharafi, Salwa (1995) 'al-Sukut fi muwagahat al-'Unf: al-usus al-thiqafiyah lil 'unf did al-Mar'ah' (Silence facing violence: the cultural foundations for violence against women) in *al-Nahj*, no.5.

al-Tahtawi, Rifa'ah Rafi' (1993) Takhlis al-Ibriz fi Talkhis Paris (Mining the Gold while Roaming Paris) (Cairo: al-Hay'ah al-Misriyyah al-'Ammah lil kitab).

al-Tunisi, Khayral-Din (1972) Aqwam al-Masalik fi Ma'rifat Ahwal al-Mamalik (The most rightful path to learn about states), in al-Munsif al-Shanufi (ed.) Tunis: al-Dar al-Tunisiyyah lil Nashr.

Amnesty International (1991) Dalil ila al-Mithaq al-Afriqi li-Huquq al- Insan wa al-Shu'ub (A Guide to the African Charter on Human and People's Rights), London.

an-Na'im, Abdullahi, (1984) 'A modern approach to human rights in Islam: Foundations and Implications for Africa,' in Claude Welch, Jr. and Roland Meltzer (eds.), *Human Rights and Development in Africa,* Albary: SUNY Press.

Awad, Muhsin' (1999) 'al-Mawathiq al-Islamiyyah wa al-'Arabiyyah li Huquq al-Insan' (The Islamic and Arab conventions of Human Rights) in Yusuf al-Hasan (ed.), *al-Imarat al-Arabiyyah al-Muttahidah wa Huquq al-Insan* (The United Arab Emirates and Human Rights) (Sharijah: Markaz al-Imarat li al-Buhuth.

Awad, Muhsin (1999) 'Mafhum Huquq al-insan fi al-Watan al-Arabi Bayn al-'Alamiyyah wa al-Khususiyyah' (The concept of Human Rights in the Arab World: Between Universalism and Relativism) in al-Hasan, *op. cit.*

Centre for the Study of Human Rights (1992) *Twenty-four Human Rights Documents,* New York: Colombia University Press.

Fodah, Faraj (1994) 'al-Aqaliyyat wa Huquq al-Insan fi Misr' (Minorities and Human Rights in Egypt) in 'Huriyyat al-Ra'y wa al-Aqidah' (Freedom of Thought and Belief), Cairo: al-Munazammah al-Misriyyah li Huquq al-Insan.

Galal, Muhammad Nu'man (1994) 'Jami'at al-Duwal al-'Arabiyyah wa Huquq al-Insan' (The Arab League and Human Rights). Political Research Series, Cairo: Centre for Political Research and Studies.

Huquq al-Insan fi al-Watan al-Arabi (1997) (Human Rights in the Arab World) Cairo: al-Munazamah al-Arabiyyah li Huquq al-Insan.

Ibrahim, Fatimah Ahmad (1995) 'al-Harakah al Nisa' iyyah fi al-Sudan wa Aqsar al-Turuq lil-Musawah' (The Feminist Movement in Sudan and the Shortest route to Equality) in *al-Nahj*, no. 5.

Khidr, Asma (1998) 'al-Mar'ah wa al-Ahwal al-Shakhsiyyah fi 'Adad min al-Tashriat al-'Arabiyyah' (Woman and Personal Status law in some of the Arab legal systems) *al-Nahj*, no.14, Spring.

Lambton, Ann K.S. (1981) *State and government in Medieval Islam*, Oxford: Oxford University Press.

Mayer, Ann Elizabeth (1995) 'Istratijiyat Kalamiyah wa siyasat Rasmiyyah hawl huquq al-Nisa' (Verbal strategies and formal policies regarding women's rights) Nawal Layqah (tr.in *al-Nahj*, no5.

Mayer, Ann Elizabeth (1997) *Islam and Human Rights: Traditions and Politics* London: Westview Press.

Ojo, Olusola and Amadu Sesay, (1986) 'The OAU and Human Rights: prospects for the 1980s and Beyond,' in *Human Rights Quarterly*, Vol..

Radi, Hasan Ali (1995) 'Nahdrah fi Ittigahat al-Tashri'at fi qawanin al-ahwal al-Shakhsiyyah fi al-Duwal al - Arabiyyah' (An Overview of the personal status laws of the Arab States) in *al-Nahj*, no.5.

Sa'uli, Murad (1995) 'Bism al-Mar'ah al-Jaza'iriyyah' (In the name of the Algerian Woman) in *Al-Nahj*, no.5, 1995.

Sha'ban, Buthaynah (1995) 'al-Mufasirat al-Mukammamat' (The Female Interpreters who are Silenced) in *al-Nahj*, no5.

Shuqah, Abdul Halim Abu Tahrir (1990) 'al-Mar'ah fi Asr al-Risalah' (Emancipating women during the time of the prophet's message), Kuwait: Dar al-Qalam.

Wafi, Ali Abdul Wahid (1979) *Huquq al-Insan fi al-Islam* (Human Rights in Islam), Cairo: Dar Nahdat Misr.

11

Women, Politics and Gender Politicking: Questions from Kenya

Kivutha Kibwana

This chapter examines the impact of gender politicking on the relationship between women and politics. Using the Kenyan case as an example, it adopts an historical perspective and begins by defining gender politicking and developing a criteria by which the nexus between women and politics can be evaluated. This allows for a critical evaluation of the women's movement before proceeding to thematically consider the history of the movement in Kenya. Finally, the subject of women, politics and gender politicking in contemporary Kenya is given specific treatment. The analysis reveals that there has been historical continuity in the unfolding of Kenya's women's movement. During colonial times the movement was constructed on 'apoliticism'—the belief that gains could be achieved for women through co-operation with the government of the day. Unsurprisingly, the gains that were made were minimal and served to further entrench the situation of women's marginalisation.

Maendeleo ya Wanawake Organisation (MYWO) was Kenya's first formally organised women's organisation. Its goal was to improve the lives of women by equipping them with modern skills of house keeping and health care. They were not to engage in politics but were to, in the words of Lady Baring (the wife of the then governor) '...be devoted to social justice and humanity and not politics, race or religion.'[1] The independence era—up to the 1990s and beyond—has seen the women's movement attempt to shun political feminism. This apoliticism mostly translates into conformist politics. The conformity saw at one time the MYWO affiliate itself to the Kenya African National Union (KANU), the party that has been in power in Kenya since independence in 1964. This meant that male politicians in the ruling party KANU would define the agenda of MYWO, and consequently that of the entire women's movement as MYWO is an umbrella body. On 30 May 1982, KANU's National Governing Council ruled that MYWO would remain a welfare organisation.[2] KANU secretary general, Joseph Kamotho is quoted as having warned that 'KANU MYWO is not a political body. Its goals are to promote the socio-economic status of women.'[3] This conformity has on occasion taken the form of open support for the ruling party and President Moi even though MYWO formally delinked itself from the ruling party. During the December 1997 elections, MYWO chairperson, Mrs. Zipporah Kittony asked women to vote for President Moi. This was despite the fact that a woman was running as presidential candidate.[4] It also followed her call to women in 1996 to vie for all parliamentary seats and civic seats save for the presidency.[5] This clearly undermines goal of the women's movement's politically empower women.

This conformity has also been demonstrated by the movement's lethargy to women's leaders who do not tow the line. For instance, Alicen Chelaite, the former Mayor of Nakuru, was replaced in a coup as Rift Valley MYWO chairperson. Her election was read to mean that she was sympathetic to the opposition as Nakuru is viewed as opposition dominated. Her replacement was Margaret Kamar—the wife of the powerful government minister and Moi associate, Nicholas Biwott.[6] Mrs Grace Ogot, a key MYWO leader asked women to only elect women loyal to Moi and KANU as MYWO officials. 'Don't elect rebels,' she said.[7] A bad precedent had been set much earlier in 1989 when on 15 December MYWO asked KANU to expel Prof. Wangari Mathai form KANU because of her opposition to the construction of the Kenya Times Media Trust Complex at Uhuru Park. Wangari was opposed to the construction as the Park was used by the city poor for recreational purposes as well as maintaining an environmental balance within the city.[8]

Evidence illustrates that the women's movement has not scored the success it deserves. In my considered opinion this failure or shortfall is explained by the movement's fraternisation with 'apoliticism.' In agreement with the scholar Maria Mies, it is my view that if women are to benefit from the practice of politics in Kenya, they and their male collaborators must not be afraid to 'take sides' because:

> The women's movement does not address its demands mainly to some external agency or enemy, such as the state, the capitalists, ...but addresses itself to people in their most intimate human relations, the relationship between women and men, with a view to changing these relations ... Every person is forced, sooner or later, to take sides. And taking sides means that something within ourselves gets torn apart, that what we thought was our identity disintegrates and has to be created anew. This is a painful process.[9]

Without taking sides in favour of gender equality and women, nothing or little of value will be harnessed in the gender struggle.

Women, politics and gender politicking: A theoretical perspective

Gender politicking refers to the deliberate use of politics and social activism by a multiplicity of actors including governments to reverse gender discrimination so as to achieve pervasive gender equality. Hence gender politicking as a genre of politics enhances the promotion of human rights and democracy—*gendermocracy*—since these can only thrive where society recognises the equality and complimentarity of both genders. Gender politicking thus refers to equality-of-the-sexes politics and subsequently legitimises the right of women to practice and benefit from politics.

Gender politicking can—at the behest of male chauvinism and patriarchal domination—be employed against the female gender although ordinarily the politicians and others who engage in gender politicking aim to uplift the lives of women. Gender politicking is characteristically the articulation of political feminism because the struggle for women's rights in particular (and human rights in general) is decidedly a political struggle waged squarely in the political arena.[10] Gender politicking and thus gender politics involve a redefinition and reordering of societal values, shift and redistribution of resources from male to females in society.

Apolitical feminism,[11] which is the ideological position that women can improve their lot without dirtying themselves in the world of politics, consciously or unconsciously advocates the politics of undermining women's rights and the women's movement. In the political world, no rights are conceded without struggle. Hence the line drawn between apolitical and political feminism and gender politicking is merely a nuance about how the game of politics is played and lived. It is not about the avoidance or bypassing of politics on the one hand and the immersing of oneself in politics on the other. Between 'noisy' politics and 'low-key' politicking, the two apparently contradictory positions seek to describe the result that is to be expected by women and society from the practice of non-confrontational quiet diplomacy, versus advocacy or confrontational, independent politics.[12]

The claim by apolitical feminists that the pursuit of women's welfarism is usually jeopardised by the unsettling of the status quo fails to appreciate the fact that welfare rights (which are substantial economic rights) can only and must be negotiated politically. Precisely only by the shaking of male hegemony is the securing of such rights guaranteed from the knowledge by the political establishment that a sector will politically struggle for them, their maintenance and enhancement. Cajoling the political or other dominating class to concede rights from altruism gives them the golden opportunity to prioritise only the needs of those sectors engaged in struggle, while neglecting the rest.

Although gender politicking concerns affect both men and women, it is often employed to address the subordinate status of women in what are male-dominated, patriarchal societies. For this reason, gender politicking tends to be largely practised by feminists or women's rights activists as one type of politicking or politics in pursuit of placing the gender question on the national agenda. Understandably, as Sylvia Tamale has established in her seminal study *When Hens Begin to Crow,*[13] gender politicking directly threatens male dominance in society. Gender politicking is thus roundly but sometimes subtly challenged by the male political establishment even if seemingly liberal political frameworks recognise the principle of gender equality. The establishment of the Women's Bureau and the MYWO was in itself a recognition of the role of women in Kenya's national life. The Constitution of Kenya Review Act recognised the principle of gender balancing by providing that a third of the review organs would be made up of women. In the same vein parliament passed a motion asking the government to establish a Gender Equality Commission.[14] Despite this recognition, the male politicians have systematically undermined the principle of gender equality by firstly keeping the movement under male leadership and secondly by trivialising the content of the women's rights movement.

The movement is firmly under male leadership as demonstrated by the often too obvious interference in the affairs of women. For a long time the elections of MYWO have been controlled by the government with the president or minister setting dates of elections, putting them off, and even by preferring candidates. The officials that win must be acceptable to the male leadership of the country. Usually it is the wives of status quo politicians who win the elections.[15] This interference demonstrates the male leadership's discomfiture when women enter the political arena. On 28 June 1999, Hon. Shariff Nassir, minister for culture and social services (the ministry registers women's groups) is reported to have denounced the Kenya Women's Political Caucus (KWPC) and noted that the ministry only recognised MYWO. This was prompted by the KWPC's stated goal to have women meaningfully participate in the constitutional review process—a process that the country's leadership does not support.

On 7 November 1989 John Keen warned politicians whose wives had been elected into Maendeleo leadership that they should hold their seats tightly because 'very soon' they will lose those same seats to the same people they patronised.[16] On the content of the women's rights discourse the male leadership in Kenya attempted to delegitimise the movement by casting it as a sexual liberation movement led by elite women. While reacting to the reforms packaged by the International Federation of Women Lawyers—Kenya (FIDA—KENYA), President Moi reduced it to a campaign for the legalisation of lesbianism and abortion in Kenyan society. The two are taboo subjects for both the leadership of the state and the religious sector.[17]

Gender politicking has the potential to dismantle the benefits that accrue to men *qua* men in society due to their subordination of the female gender. When men deny women the right to participate in politics, this is not simply because they need women in the kitchen or to rear their offspring. Men know that gender politicking will free women from male shackles just as slaves and serfs were liberated pursuant to their political struggle. Gender politicking, *inter alia*, can potentially strengthen the women's movement and thus the role of women in politics and society.

Over time certain criteria[18] have developed to discern or measure the robustness of the women's movement among them, the following are questions that require consideration in the process of examining the efficiency of the movement. These are:

- The extent to which a consciousness of gender equality and women's rights has permeated in the entire society, that is among women of all levels including elite and grassroots women, between both genders and as far as both the unofficial and official institutions are concerned.
- The level of participation of both men and women in activities that promote the equality of the sexes.
- The degree to which official and unofficial institutions have a gender policy.
- The existence of institutions whose functions and roles are to protect gender rights and to ensure responsibilities and duties of promoting gender equality are undertaken.
- The extent of theoretical clarity within general society and among public decision-makers in terms of the gender question.
- The availability of leadership at all levels to carry the women's movement countrywide.
- The movement's legal and official recognition?
- The level of programmatic expression of the women's movement both at the local and national levels. What is the gender agenda?
- Is the movement independent and autonomous so that the state or other societal actors do not capture it? Does it have the ability to network without risking co-optation?
- The capacity of the movement change the lives of both men and women and especially the political, socio-cultural and economic lives of women.
- The extent to which the principle of gender equality and the women's movement in general gained national acceptance. To what extent do men accept the women's movement?
- The volume and vitality of both secular and religious civil society that promotes gender rights and equality.
- The level of historical richness of the women's movement and the extent to which lessons of history are applied in the present to address the present and the future.
- The degree to which the international and regional women's movement acknowledged and domesticated in the national arena.

The above criteria and prior theoretical exposition will be employed in the ensuing discussion of the question of women, politics and gender politicking in the specific case of Kenya

Women and politics in Kenya: An historical survey

History is the unravelling of important facts from which the human race can either learn or choose to ignore. Instead of sequentially documenting the factual history of gender relations in Kenya from pre-colonial times to the present, a thematic approach is preferred. A good point of commencement is to consider Chiekh Anta Diop's understanding of the position of women in pre-colonial Africa:

> A study of our past can give a lesson in government. Thanks to the matriarchal system, our ancestors prior to any foreign influence had given women a choice place. They see her not as sex object but as a mother. This has been true from the history of the Pharaohs to our time. Women participated in the running of public affairs within the framework of a feminine assembly, sitting separately but having the same prerogatives as the male assembly. These facts remained unchanged until the colonial conquest, especially in such non-Islamed states as the Yoruban and Dahomean...Black Africa had its specific bicameralism, determined by sex. Far from interfering with national life by pitting men against women, it guaranteed the flowering of both. It is the honour of our ancestors that they were able to develop such a type of democracy.[19]

Chiekh Anta Diop's assertion clearly contradicts a host of analyses that reach the conclusion that in pre-colonial Africa women were routinely subordinated to the male gender. Either his exposition applies to a specific region or time, or the historical gender equality he describes was eroded as a consequence of the changing nature of patriarchy within colonialism.[20] The marginalisation of the African man by colonialism seems to have deepened the marginalisation of the African woman by the man and colonialist enterprise—by subjecting her to so called double exploitation.[21]

However, elements of gender recognition of women which survived (and continue to exist until the present day) are the veneration of motherhood; the dominance of women in matrilineal societies, the right of women to exploit the property of the houses to which they belong; recognition of leaders such as Wangu wa Makeri, Me Ketilili, and Mary Nyanjiru;[22] society's acceptance of senior women citizens as decision makers; the consultation of women for their input in dispute resolution; and egalitarianism of communal society which guaranteed sustenance for women. We are in support of Chiekh Anta Diop, suggesting that a subtle and incisive analysis of pre-colonial Africa could reveal that there are dormant themes about the status of women that require academic revisiting. Having subjugated and impoverished the African woman, capitalism spawned colonial anthropological propagandist literature that exaggerated the cultural dominance of women by men.[23] This literature tended to obscure the real causes of latter day gender inequality.

Educational and religious enlightenment and colonial-based opportunities gave rise simultaneously and paradoxically to domesticated women, but also to some of the most liberated women of modern Kenyan history. Pioneer women leaders exist in many fields of endeavour.[24] At the same time, although providing these openings, educational institutions encouraged women to pursue what were regarded as 'feminine' careers such as sewing, nursing, teaching, knitting and home science. To this day, many donors unwittingly or otherwise support sewing and knitting projects for women thereby perpetuating the stereotype of what women should do in their professional lives. Science and the professions were 'temples' for men.[25] Only wayward girls and women could stray into this so called 'male' territory. Female students who crossed the rubicon were desexed, and described as men!

Pre-colonial organisation of the women's movement was anchored in social points such as the water-well, the forest where firewood was collected, hair-plaiting sessions and collective work in polygamous homes. The movement was thus a horizontal phenomenon. Colonialism gradually dichotomised it into grassroot and elite streams[26] thereby shattering its harmony. *Maendeleo ya Wanawake* Organisation (MYWO) began as a welfare organisation catering for the wives of the white ruling elite. The bulk of African women continued to be organised in grassroots women's groups and networks. Within colonialism, the primary objective of the women's movement was to promote welfarism and mutual socialisation. Predictably, one of its hallmarks was the shunning by its membership of politics. When the women's movement drew its leadership from African women both in MYWO and the National Council of Women of Kenya (NCWK), the organisations continued—as was the case with the grassroots women's groups—the theme of welfare goals as they worked with and protected the political incumbency. However, dominant welfarism has been qualified by a counter trend in which rebel politically-inclined women such as Me Ketilili, Mary Nyanjiru, the Mau Mau women fighters, Mothers in Action and the women leaders of the National Convention Executive Committee (NCEC) have emerged over time.

From pre-colonial times until the present, the female gender has been the most organised of all the units of Kenyan civil society. Women have organised themselves for both social and economic reasons. By 1998, 97,317 women's groups had been registered by the government.[27] This figure is only a fraction of the existing women's groups as the majority remain unregistered. And yet, this organisational strength has been largely at the disposal of male politicians such as when MYWO was annexed to the ruling party KANU during the era of the one-party state. This point is illustrative of a broader development, namely, the fact that the women's movement has usually been designed by men. Its leaders are ordinarily the spouses, relatives, or close supporters of the political elite.[28] In this way, men indirectly and often directly define the women's agenda such as when MYWO was affiliated to KANU. The history of the Kenyan women's movement is thus one of co-optation and the '*male*streaming' of its agenda.[29]

Historically, only a small number of women have occupied office and other public decision making offices in Kenya. Between the years 1963 to 1969, no woman was elected to Kenya's parliament. In 1969, only one woman was elected, while another was nominated by the President.[30] The period 1992-97 witnessed the highest number of women elected into parliament with the total standing at six (6). The elected number declined to four in the 1997 elections while five of them were nominated by their respective political parties. Kenya's current parliament has 222 members, meaning that the percentage representation of women stands at a minuscule 4 per centof the total.

Kenya's leaders have not allowed the women's movement to flourish, despite the fact that in 1985 Nairobi hosted the UN End of the Decade Women's Conference. There has also not yet been significant internationalisation and regionalisation of the women's movement within Kenya. The state has resisted such a trend because if rigorously pursued, it would free the women's movement from the clutches of political leadership. However, even when the women's movement is led apolitically, women as a mass have always engaged in silent struggles against male domination. During colonialism as men became immigrant workers, women stayed at home to tend the land and raise families. The Mau Mau rebellion of the1950s occasioned an exodus of men either into the struggle or into detention. Once again, women stayed at home and became more independent. The urban migration of men in search of work led to the same result. The more women became producers of sustenance and wealth (and despite all the odds staked against them) the more they incrementally won the gender war. Kenya's political and tribal leaders tend to agree that support of women's gender struggles for emancipation would lead to incremental equalisation of the sexes and a loss of a buffer category which men of all classes have a 'right' to exploit.

Despite the multiple wars against it, the women's movement has continuously survived since the pre-colonial period. Other movements e.g. political movements were undermined by the authoritarianism of the system of one party rule. It is a credit to the women's movement that it was not suspended or seriously sabotaged by politicians even during the dark days of extreme authoritarianism. Whatever setbacks the movement suffered especially affiliation to KANU, it has survived well enough to further build on its numerous strengths.

Whither women and politics in contemporary Kenya?

It is trite to note that the women's movement in Kenya has developed from the 1960s in faithfulness to its historical past. Put another way, the movement has witnessed change without substantial change. Its greatest challenge is therefore that it strategically abandons its past apoliticism. At the close of the last century, the women's movement had grown considerably for a variety of reasons. The most obvious is the explosion of both the elite type of women's groups (comprising in the main the ubiquitous NGOs), as well as the grassroots organisations.[31] Since the transition to multipartyism in 1992, the movement has consciously focussed ensuring that women are represented in the political arena and in other public decision-making fora.[32] In 1992, Maria Nzomo's National Committee on the Status of Women (NCSW)[33] mobilised women to field both parliamentary and civic candidates with the result that the highest number of women to date won political seats in the elections of that year.

However, the movement is yet to achieve a fusion or partnership of both its elite and grassroots components. Elite women's groups including MYWO continue to operate without identifying and implementing an agenda for grassroots women. Many such elite groups hesitate to pervasively organise grassroot's women without government approval; they are also wary of seriously identifying an agenda encompassing disadvantaged women which they may not articulate and satisfy. The leadership of the women's movement has expanded in numbers and vision, especially as a consequence of the proliferation of NGOs dealing with women's issues and a sizeable number of women interested in politics. In 1997, the first woman presidential candidate was fielded. Charity Kaluki Ngilu of the Social Democratic Party (SDP) emerged fifth. Unfortunately, the women's movement did not universally support her candidature. This is largely because most women voters— especially in the rural areas of the country—have been socialised to believe that leadership is a male preserve. As yet, adequate civic education for women to erase such prejudices has not been facilitated.

In terms of organisational capacity, women have since 1997 come together under the Kenya Women's Political Caucus—a loose federation of 43 women's organisations and 23 individuals including 6 MPs. The chief objective of the caucus is to pressurise the state for full recognition of the equality of the female and male genders in the social, economic and political spheres. The forerunner to this caucus was the NCSW, that organised women for the 1992 elections after both MYWO and NCWK failed to collaborate for the purpose.[34]

The potential of the caucus is immense. However, it must urgently determine the minimum agenda acceptable to its membership. Its members are diverse, and often espouse contradictory objectives. Some are pro-government; others advocate non-partisan, while a few are intent on discarding the movement's previous apoliticism. A common programmatic and pragmatic agenda may therefore be difficult to build. Currently, however, such agenda seems to be unfolding in terms of increasing the numbers of women in all public decision making fora.[35] If the caucus comprehensively addresses the content of the agenda these women should pursue, this could break the frail gender partnership. Hence, it is perceived that numbers are critical for the caucus as it seeks to negotiate a women's agenda that will change the lives of women. However, even this minimalist agenda is not politically acceptable to several key caucus members. Membership strength for the caucus definitely gives a boost to the women's movement. However, there exists the danger that the agenda of progressive groups may be neutralised in pursuit of an elusive consensus. The question: *'unity for what?'* must always be honestly addressed.

Until the present time, the Kenyan government has not committed itself to a gender policy although relevant work is ostensibly in progress.[36] Each successive development plan has a paragraph or two on women's issues. The same trend is followed when government develops papers on other issues such as poverty eradication, HIV/Aids, and micro-enterprise, to mention but a few. Following the 1997 elections, the government created a ministry to deal with women's issues in which a man was appointed minister. The following day, the ministry was mysteriously scrapped.

The women's movement itself is yet to develop a gender agenda that reasonably addresses the interests and expectations of women of all classes. In this regard, the agenda of the Pan-African Association of African Women for Research and Development (AAWORD) based in the Senegalese capital, Dakar, could form the basis of this discussion within the Kenyan context.[37] Perhaps this is the most urgent task that the Women's Political Caucus could undertake. A compass for the women's movement is badly needed. To arrive at this point, research should be undertaken whose purpose is to supply a theoretical framework for understanding and contextualizing the struggle for women's rights. Plentiful current research exists which can form the basis for such work. Without a clear theoretical exposition of the issues, a vision and an agenda that are broadly shared by the caucus membership and women of Kenya, the push for policy, unity and gender responsive programmes will continue to be elusive. A movement is less about the physical unity of its members and more about ideological and philosophical coherence.

Although the Women's Political Caucus ignited the promise of unity and common purpose among women's groups, its role in the negotiations for constitutional review that have been underway since 1997 also introduced fragmentation and threatened the continued existence of the caucus.[38] Women who argued that they were members of minority tribes advocated that representation to the constitutional commission be sourced on a provincial basis.[39] The reasoning informing this position was that the elections to the commission by women had favoured urban-based elite women from the major ethnic groupings. The controversy ended in court. Furthermore, a splinter group sought to officially register the caucus and thereby to exclude key actors from leadership positions. For the time being a truce has been declared by the warring factions. The caucus is uneasily and loosely united while internal dissension, e.g., in the NCWK and MYWO, is rife. The NCWK's 1999 elections that had previously aborted were declared rigged by some of the contestants. The above evidence suggests that unity in the caucus is for the time being more apparent than real.

In the late 1990s, the women's movement received support through the work of the National Conventional Assembly (NCA) and its National Convention Executive Council (NCEC). In its constitutional gender reform crusade NCA/NCEC agitated, *inter alia*, for the outlawing of sex discrimination as well as increasing the number of women in parliament through the nomination process. The NCA declared that at least each of its organs should have one-third membership from each gender.[40] Opposition political parties similarly adjusted their policies.[41] However, both the NCA and the opposition parties have not succeeded in implementing their gender quotas. Women are yet to come forward especially pursuant to the organisation's conducting vigorous search campaigns.

Notes on the constitutional context

The legal and constitutional recognition of the women's movement in Kenya is hopelessly inadequate. In 1997, section 82 of the constitution was changed to outlaw sex discrimination. However, section 82(4) remained unaltered. The relevant text of this provision is as follows:

> Subsection (I) the law against sex discrimination shall not apply to any law so far as that law makes provision-
>
> (a) ...
> (b) with respect to adoption, marriage, divorce, burial, devolution of property on death or other matters of personal law.
> (c) for the application in the case of members of a particular race or tribe of customary law with respect to any matter to the exclusion of any law with respect to that matter which is applicable in the case of other persons....

The essential effect of this stipulation is that women can be discriminated against if such discrimination is sanctioned by personal or customary law.[42] Can Sections 82(1) (2) and (3), which outlaw sex discrimination, be interpreted to contradict Section 82(4)? What happens if constitutional provisions contradict each other? Sloppy drafting of constitutional provisions has made this contradiction possible. It must be removed either by judicial interpretation or the long-anticipated process of constitutional review.

The struggle for enhancing women's representation in parliament in the short term was based on the demand that of the 12 nominated members, at least 6 should be women. The eventual constitutional amendment, which conceded this demand, was legislated as follows:

> The persons to be appointed shall be nominated ... taking into account the principle of gender equality. (Section 33(3) of the constitution.)

In this way, the language adopted avoided explicit use of the mathematical ratio 6:6 which would have meant gender parity in the representation of nominees. Although a task force on legal reform of women's law has been established since the early 1990s, it is yet to complete its work. Therefore the reform of marriage law and other laws that promote gender inequality which stalled on two occasions in 1976 and 1979 has not yet been completed.[43] The women's movement still has a full plate of legal reform ahead.

Perhaps one of the most significant achievements of the women's movement in Kenya was its ability to be reasonably represented in the organs of the constitutional review process that has been through considerable twists and turns. The movement was able to secure at least one-third membership in the drafting committee of the review law. The same applied for the constitutional commission, the district forum and the national forum.[44] Unfortunately, the KANU government has stalled the review process. When and if the 1997 review law is improved through re-negotiation, women will have a significant representation in the organs and will consequently be able to articulate, *inter alia*, constitutional issues that address the status of women. The women's movement—especially the Women's Political Caucus—has adopted a strategy of closely working with the government in the hope that government will concede changes to them. Often, leaders in the women's movement advise against an alliance with radical forces since such a move would obviously distance the movement from the government. And yet the government, especially of recent, has shown itself utterly contemptuous of women and their issues. For example, a minister in the Office of the President Julius L. Sunkuli has clearly stated that women's civil society groups should not be part of the constitution making process.

Revisiting the challenges facing women's civil society

Numerous civil groups working on women's issues have mushroomed throughout Kenya. They are now poised to conduct countrywide civic education on the constitutional and gender issues under the auspices of the caucus. The work of these groups in the past has been absolutely critical in terms of placing the issues of most interest to the women's movement squarely on the national agenda. Unfortunately, the presidential candidature of Charity Ngilu was not used to adroitly promote women's issues. Her party, the SDP, was careful to package Ngilu as a national as opposed to sectoral candidate. Both goals need not have been conflictual, but the calculations of male politicians obviously called the shots.

Many groups in the women's movement endeavour to claim for themselves the gains achieved from the struggle. There is hardly any recognition of the role played by non-women groups. Often these 'outsiders' are antagonised by being described as groups that are opposed to the women's struggle. Some leaders in the women's movement have advocated a separatist approach in which they advise against networking with male counterparts in the democratic struggle. In response, a new network called Men For Equality with Women (MEW) led by Rev. Timothy Njoya whose aim is to influence men so that they promote gender equality has been established. MEW hopes to particularly focus on and reach out to those men who insulate themselves against the messages of women groups as well as to network in the women groups.

Since the 1997 constitutional change outlawing sex discrimination, not enough work has been done to change the laws and the practices that are discriminatory. There is a shortfall between agitating for legal change and calling for their implementation. Furthermore, when one examines each sub-sector in the economic and social sphere, women's involvement is still extremely low and various constraints account for this. Legal changes are meant to lead to the transformation of the status of women especially in relation to their capacity to access the economy, natural and public resources, education, health services and other basic needs.[45] It is only when women access such economic and social advantages in a significant fashion that the principle of gender equality can be said to have been fully recognised. As it is, there is still a great need for serious campaigns that will lead to the domestication of international and regional standards of gender equity. There is not doubt that the contemporary debates about constitutional reform and constitutionalism will play a significant role in this regard.

Conclusion

The Kenya women's movement, as expected by liberal feminists, has proceeded on the basis that it can achieve socioeconomic and political gains in collaboration with and not in contradiction to the status quo. Hence, the majority of the leaders of the movement have largely confined their gender politicking to apolitical feminism. We have seen that the success of the women's movement has still been limited. What is clear from the preceding analysis is that unless the women's movement embraces a healthy radicalism that weans it from nestling with the status quo, the gains for women in the political and other arenas will be minimal.

If reform forces unite to face the KANU hard-liners in the 2002 elections—women will be better served if they join hands with reformers rather than remain subservient to the status quo. Gender politicking that embraces apoliticalism or some form of non-partisanship will continue to seriously undermine the women's struggle for gender equality. The Kenyan women's movement has made important strides that can only be consummated by the movement taking sides on behalf of the discriminated, down trodden and toiling women. A movement that is simply the appendage of a conservative status quo represents a women's movement created by men and for men. For a movement to mature, it must go through a painful process. To create a new woman, and a new man something within ourselves must be torn apart. Women more than men should know: to every birth, there must be blood.

Notes

1. See the *East African Standard*, 21 February 1957.
2. See the *Daily Nation*, 31 May 1982.
3. See the *East African Standard* 3 April 1991.
4. The *Daily Nation* on the 16 February 1997, quotes her as saying that 'voting for Moi is voting for peace.'
5. See the *Daily Nation* 10 October 1996.
6. See the *Daily Nation* of August 21 1996.
7. See the *Daily Nation* 3 March 1996.
8. See the *Daily Nation* 16 December 1989.
9. Mies (1986): 6.
10. See Mute (1997): 403-19.
11. For an elaboration of apolitical and political feminism see: Wanjiru Muigai (1999).
12. The movement is hostile to women who confront the government on key issues of the day. As seen earlier MYWO asked KANU to expel Prof. Wangari Mathai after confronting the government with a key environmental question. The same organisation severely, perhaps more than the government, criticised women strippers at the Freedom Corner who were agitating for the release of political prisoners, in Kenya. See the *Daily Nation*, March 10th 1992.
13. Tamale (1999).
14. See the *Daily Nation*, 13 May 1999.
15. See the *Daily Nation*, 29 January 1995, 1 February 1995, 10 March 1996, 17 March 1996 and 18 March 1996.
16. *The East African*, 7 November 1989; see also Catherine Gicheru, 'Male factor adds a new twist to Maendeleo Polls,' *Daily Nation*, November 7 1989, 15.
17. See the *Daily Nation* 17 and 19 of March 1999.

18. I have developed these criteria from my research in the women's rights area. See Kibwana (1996a); Kibwana (1996b); Kibwana (1995), Nzomo and Kibwana (1993); Kameri-Mbote and Kibwana (1993), and Nyamu, Makome & Kibwana (1996).
19. Diop (1978): 33.
20. See Mbilinyi (1983).
21. See Ramazanoglu (1989) who argues that women who belong to exploited groups are exploited doubly in comparison to their male counterparts. See also Mies, *supra*.
22. wa Thiongo (1983).
23. For a survey of such literature see Etiene and Leacode (1980).
24. Among the most prominent was Margaret Kenyatta who was the first African mayor of Nairobi, and had been educated in the all-boys church-established Alliance High School.
25. Obura (1991): 41.
26. See Muigai *supra* 77-80, Adhiambo Mbeo (1989): 123-29, Kabira & Nzioki, (1993, 1994), and also Mazingira Institute (1992).
27. See Lewa (1999): 6. For comprehensive information on women groups up to 1991 see, Women's Bureau (1992).
28. The current Chairman of *Maendeleo ya Wanawake* is Zipporah Kittony, a nominated KANU Member of Parliament. The chairperson of the National Council of Women of Kenya (NCWK) is Jane Kiano, a former chairman of Maendeleo. She is a KANU activist and her husband Dr Julius Gikonyo Kiano has been one of KANU's intellectual leaders.
29. *Supra*.
30. See Nzomo *supra*, 5-15.
31. See Muigai *supra*.
32. See Kabira and Wasamba (1988). See also AAWORD (1997). Most recently, a coalition of women from the Democratic Party (DP), KANU, the National Democratic Party (NDP) and the SDP formed the Political Women Mobilisation Network which targets to get at least 30 per cent women representation in parliament in the year 2002 elections. See the *Daily Nation* 20 September 1999.
33. Later to be renamed the National Commission on the Status of Women (NCSW). See Nzomo and Kibwana *supra*.
34. Both MYWO and NCWK themselves umbrella groups are members of the Caucus.
35. *Supra*.
36. AAWORD has tried to prompt the government to come up with a gender policy. See their 1997 publication, *The Kenya Women's Election Manifesto: Towards Gender Equity*.
37. *Ibid*.
38. See the *Daily Nation* 16 1999, 4; *Sunday Nation* 24 1999.
39. Delegates from the North Eastern Province, the Rift Valley and the Coast provinces argued that they wanted their provinces represented in the Review Commission. See the *Sunday Nation* 24 January 1999, 28.
40. See NCA First Plenary Declaration and Resolutions, Limuru, Kenya, April 1997.
41. See especially the constitution of the Democratic Party, Nairobi, Kenya.
42. In a 1986 case, Wambui Otieno was not allowed to bury her husband as the court held that this right belonged to his clan under customary law. See Ojwang and Mugambi (1989).
43. See Phoebe M. Asiyo (1989), 41-52.
44. See Constitution of Kenya Review Act, 1997.
45. See Kibwana (1995).

References

Adhiambo Mbeo, Mary (1989) 'Mobilizing Women Groups.' in *Kenya Perspectives and Emerging Issues*, Nairobi Public Law Institute,Anta Diop, Chiek, (1978) *Black Africa: The Economic and Cultural Basis for Federated State* (New Expanded Edition) Westport, Connecticut: Africa World Press Edition, Lawrence Hill and Company.

Association of African Women for Research and Development (AAWORD) (1997) *The Kenya Women's Election Manifesto; Towards Gender Equity*, Nairobi: AAWORD.

Etiene, Monna and Eleanor Leacode (eds.) (1980) *Women and Colonisation: Anthropological Perspectives*, New York: Praeger.

Kabira, Wanjiku and Peter Wasamba (1988) *Reclaiming Women's Space in Politics*, Nairobi: The Collaborative Centre for Gender and Development.

Kameri-Mbote, Patricia A. and Kivutha Kibwana (1993) 'Women, Law and Democratisation Process in Kenya,' in Wanjiku M. Kabira, Jacqueline A. Oduol and Maria Nzomo (eds.) *Democratic Change in Africa: women's Perspective*, Nairobi: Association of African Women for Research and Development (AAWORD) & Acts Gender Institute.

Kibwana, Kivutha (1996a) 'Family Rights in Kenya: A Preliminary Examination of the Legal Framework' in Rajni Palriwala and Carla Risseeuw (Eds.) *Shifting Circles of Support: Contextualising Kinship and Gender in South Asia and Sub-Saharan Africa*, New Delhi: Sage Publication.

_____. (1996b) *Law and the Status of Women in Kenya*, Nairobi: Faculty of Law, University of Nairobi.

_____. (1995) *Women and Autonomy in Kenya: Policy and Legal Framework*, Nairobi: Claripress Ltd.

Mlewa, Rhoda (1999) 'Women Groups and the Law in Kenya,' Nairobi; Centre for Law and Research International [Mimeo]

Mazingira Institute, (1992) *Women and Development: A Kenya Guide* Nairobi: Mazingira Institute.

Mbilinyi, Marjorie (1983) 'Where do we Come From Where are We Now and Where Do We Go From Here?' in Achola Pala, Thelma Awori and Abigail Krystal (eds.) *The Participation of Women in Kenyan Society*, Nairobi: Kenya Literature Bureau.

Mies, Maria (1986) *Patriarchy and Accumulation on a World Scale: Women in the International Division of Labour*, London: Zed Books Limited.

Muigai, Wanjiru (1999) 'Apolitical versus Political feminism: The dilemma of the Women's Movement in Kenya' in E.K Quashigah and O.C Okafor (Eds.) *Legitimate Governance in Africa*, Netherlands: Kluwer Law International.

Mukabi Kabira, Wanjiku & Elizabeth Akinyi Nzioki, (1993, 1994) *Celebrating Women's Resistance: A Case Study of Women's Groups Movement in Kenya,* Nairobi: New Earth Publications

Mute, Lawrence M. (1997) 'Gender and African Politics: The Paradigm of Property,' in Kivutha Kibwana (ed.) *Readings in Constitutional Law and Politics in Africa: A Case Study of Kenya,* Nairobi: Claripress and Faculty of Law, University of Nairobi.

Nyamu, Celestine I., Anne N. Makome & Kivutha Kibwana (1996) 'The Role of Pressure Groups in the Promotion and Preservation of Democracy in Kenya: The Case of The Women's Movement.' in the *University of Nairobi Law Journal,* Issue (1).

Nzomo, Maria 'Engendering Democratisation in Kenya: A Political Perspective,' in Wanjiku M. Kabira, Jacquiline A Oduol and Maria Nzomo (eds.).

_____ and Kivutha Kibwana (Eds.) (1993) *Women's Initiatives in Kenya's Democratization: Capacity Building and Participation in the December 1992 Multiparty General Elections,* Nairobi.

Obura, Anna P. (1991) *Changing Images: Portrayal of Girls and Women in Kenyan Textbooks,* Nairobi.

Phoebe M. Asiyo (1989) 'Gender Issues and the Legislative Process in Kenya,' in Mary Adhiambo Mbeo & Oki Ooko-Ombaka (eds) *Women and Law in Kenya, Perspectives and Emerging Issues,* Nairobi: Public Law Institute, 41-52.

Ojwang, J.B. and J. N.K. Mugambi (1989) *The S.M. OTIENO CASE: Death and Burial in Modern Kenya,* Nairobi: Nairobi University Press.

Achola Pala, Thelma Awori and Abigail Krystal (eds.) (1983) *The Participation of Women in Kenyan Society,* Nairobi: Kenya Literature Bureau.

Ramazanoglu, Caroline (1989) *Feminism and the Contradictions of Oppression,* London: Routledge.

Tamale, Sylvia (1999), *When Hens Begin to Crow: Gender and Parliamentary Politics in Uganda,* Kampala: Fountain Publishers.

wa Thiongo, Ngugi (1983) 'The Changing Image of Women Over Three Crucial Historical Phases,' in Achola Pala *et al.*

Women's Bureau (1992) *National Census of Women Groups in Kenya,* Nairobi; Women's Bureau.

12

Gender and Affirmative Action in Post-1995 Uganda: A New Dispensation, or Business as Usual?

Sylvia Tamale

Even as we embark upon a new millennium of human history, many Africans will argue that 'sex discrimination' is a fictitious invention of western feminists. They argue that the sex differentials that exist in our societies are 'natural' and/or flow 'naturally' from the biological differences between men and women. *Ergo*, we cannot do much to change the status quo. However, a growing number of people now recognise the concept of sex discrimination and are devising means to address its debilitating consequences. The 1995 Ugandan constitution recognises this concept in several of its articles. But recognising women's rights formally through the letter of the law is one thing. For women to substantively realise such rights is quite another.

Take one example; Article 33(4) of the constitution clearly states as follows: 'Women shall have the right to equal treatment with men and that right shall include equal opportunities in political, economic and social activities.' However, such a formal statement does not guarantee women a just and fair share in the political, economic and social life of our society. In other words, removal of the legal obstacle will not magically remove centuries-long gender discrimination that has slowly become part of the lifestyle and culture of Ugandans. Thus, the question of implementation of the general principle of equality becomes extremely crucial. One of the ways that the law has proactively moved from a conception of formal equality to one of substantive equality—a way that positively enhances the chances of women achieving equity –is through affirmative action programmes. Thus affirmative action is one way of moving from the instrument of the constitution towards the road to constitutionalism.

The 1995 constitution provides, *inter alia*:

- *Objective VI: The* State shall ensure gender balance and fair representation of marginalised groups on all constitutional and other bodies.

- *Article 32(1): Notwithstanding* anything in this Constitution, the State shall take affirmative action in favour of groups marginalised on the basis of gender, age, disability or any other reason created by history, tradition or custom, for the purpose of redressing imbalances which exist against them.
- *Article 32(2):* Parliament shall make relevant laws, including laws for the establishment of an equal opportunities commission, for the purpose of giving full effect to clause (1) of this article.
- *Article 33(2): The* State shall provide the facilities and opportunities necessary to enhance the welfare of women to enable them to realise their full potential and advancement.
- *Article 33(5):* Without prejudice to article 32 of this Constitution, women shall have the right to affirmative action for the purpose of redressing the imbalances created by history, tradition or custom.

In effect, the above provisions furnished constitutional backing to existing affirmative action policies, thereby elevating gender equity to greater heights.[1] Furthermore, the constitution opened the door for the introduction of more extensive affirmative action programmes for marginalised social groups.

Making a case for gender-based affirmative action

The term affirmative action is often misconstrued to mean 'reverse' discrimination. 'The answer to discrimination is not new discrimination'; 'two wrongs do not make a right,' the arguments go. The tendency is to perceive affirmative action as a one-time occurrence, isolated from the process of struggle within the wider social movement to emancipate oppressed groups. Schreiner[2] explains that affirmative action 'is a political strategy of a *transition* period, along the way from relations established by centuries of oppression and inequality to a future of truly *equitable* relations (my emphasis).' The transient nature of Uganda's affirmative action policy is endorsed by Article 78(2) where it is stated that the policy shall be reviewed by parliament every ten years 'for the purposes of retaining, increasing, or abolishing' it. The term 'equitable' is used deliberately to connote fairness, justice and rightfulness, embodying more than mere equality in terms of value and law (*ibid.*). Defining affirmative action in the United States, Mullen wrote:

> Attempts to make progress toward *substantive*, rather than merely formal, equality of opportunity for those groups, such as women or racial minorities, which are currently under-represented in significant positions in society, by explicitly taking into account the defining characteristic – sex or race – which has been the basis for discrimination (my emphasis).[3]

The analogy of a running race is often evoked to demonstrate what affirmative action attempts to achieve:

If a race has started between two runners, and one is shackled, simply removing the chains and allowing the runners to continue is insufficient, because one runner has had a head start. The race must be started again, or more realistically, the previously chained runner must be moved up to an equal position.[4]

This analogy portrays affirmative action as a means of giving the traditionally disadvantaged that indispensable first leg. It captures the lingering and pervasive effects of discrimination on account of sexism or racism. It also demonstrates the need to achieve a balance of social groups in significant positions in society.

Most scholars erroneously trace the origins of affirmative action to the United States in the aftermath of the Black civil rights movement of the 1960s.[5] However, the fact is that such programmes had been used in the twilight of colonialism and termed 'indigenisation' or 'Africanisation'.[6] They sought to incorporate indigenous peoples in those areas of the civil service and elsewhere from which they had been historically excluded. Interestingly, the same men who defended Africanisation programmes in the 1950s and early 1960s practice double standards today when they argue that gender-based affirmative action is unfair and unjust treatment because it amounts to reverse discrimination. In other words, it was okay for offsetting the legacy of racial discrimination but unacceptable for reversing inequalities based on gender; what's good for the goose is apparently not good enough for the gander.

In order to appreciate the principle behind preferential treatment it is imperative to make sociological analyses of social realities. Discrimination, for example, should not be viewed through an 'individualistic lens' but through a 'social' one. Hence, we often hear the argument that individual rights cannot be overridden by group rights. Such opponents of affirmative action are quick to point out that not all members of supposedly disadvantaged groups have in fact been disadvantaged. That a privileged female may benefit from affirmative action 'merely' because she is a woman. They argue that it is only disadvantaged individuals that should benefit from affirmative action.[7]

Such arguments bring into bold relief the notion of Western democratic philosophy which espouses individual rights. This is in contrast with the African ethic underpinning the notion of rights which is more communitarian. Fasil Nahum, for example, hits the nail on the head when he argues: 'African humanism does not alienate the individual by seeing him as an entity all by himself... the individual does not stand in contradistinction to society but as part of it.'[8] Even the Organisation of African Unity (OAU) recognised the philosophy of individualism as being inherently un-African as is reflected in the 1981 African Charter on Human and People's Rights where group rights are given special status.[9] Why then are the same African men who espouse the ideals embedded in African human rights reluctant to apply such a reconceptualisation to the status of women? Again we see the deployment of double standards when it comes to women's rights.

True that some women in Uganda, because of their privileged positions are better placed than some men. But it is also true that *every* woman in Uganda, regardless of her social class, suffers discrimination, directly or indirectly, simply because of her gender. When one looks beyond 'individual rights' and understands that sexism is institutionalised into the wider social and political apparatus, one can then comprehend their pervasiveness which directly or indirectly affects *all* members of the disadvantaged group.[10] While the former lens will focus on individual atoms that make up society, the latter will clearly reveal the hierarchical world system based on capitalist, patriarchal values.

Others shun affirmative action because they believe that it 'dilutes' the quality and standards of those institutions where it is applied;[11] that affirmative action offends the principle of meritocracy which requires the best qualified person to hold a contested position. At another level it is argued that recipients of preferential treatment tend to suffer from a serious, and in many cases, irrevocable, decline of self-respect which Nacoste characterises as the 'impostor syndrome.' Nacoste goes on to explain that 'the impostor syndrome can develop among minority members and women working in organisations that have affirmative action policies.' Such people, he argues, 'tend to overcompensate for imagined inadequacies so that they are initially productive but frazzled in the long run'.[12]

In the first instance, such arguments ignore the fact that all affirmative action programs require minimum qualifications for its beneficiaries. Secondly, such an argument ignores the legacy of discrimination suffered by designated groups which was well captured in the 'shackled runner' analogy. Mullen[13] dismisses such perceptions as irrational given that affirmative action is not, in fact about preferring the unqualified. He also argues that it would be unduly pessimistic to conclude that the stigma will be so prevalent as to destroy the point of affirmative action. Arguing that prejudice is something that minority groups have lived with irrespective of affirmative action, Mullen concludes that affirmative action would in fact improve minority representation in untraditional positions.[14]

Apart from the 'obvious' reason of effecting equitable gender relations, affirmative action holds additional advantages. By including members of groups which have hitherto been excluded from certain institutions, jobs and professions, it provides social benefits of increased diversity. For example, by proactively involving women in decision-making at all levels from the grassroots to parliament, the country is assured of substantively new perspectives and a robust exchange of ideas. Moreover, affirmative action is a means of levelling out the effects of stereotyped perceptions. Koggel[15] justifies affirmative action on the ground that it offsets the biased beliefs or stereotypes that are held against members of disadvantaged groups in the context of historically entrenched discrimination. But, most importantly, by facilitating women's active involvement in all spheres of society, affirmative action contributes to the development of the entire society.

In a nutshell, positive discrimination for women is a short-term strategy for creating more equitable gender relations in society. Despite the backlash and fierce reactions against the policy, it only represents a drop in the ocean in the struggle for breaking the institutional aspects of patriarchy and sexism. Affirmative action, therefore, can achieve little without the support of other policies directed at reducing disparities in wealth, status and power.

The historical and societal context

In order to appreciate the need for gender-based affirmative action programmes in Uganda, it is imperative to understand the historical structures and societal contexts of the country. Ugandan society may generally be characterised as a patriarchy[16] operating under a form of under-developed capitalism.[17] These two elements constitute the fountain spring that nourishes Ugandan gender relations. Patriarchy and capitalism collectively produce and maintain sexism in Uganda.

Male dominance or patriarchy existed in Uganda even prior to the coming of the British colonialists in the late nineteenth century. However, the subtleties and inner workings of the pre-colonial system of patriarchy reveal some differences from what one may refer to as classic patriarchy. The cultural and gendered relations in most Ugandan societies during the pre-colonial era offered women some degree of autonomy and allowed for them to indirectly/ informally participate in the decision-making process of their societies.[18] Ugandan women, like elsewhere in Africa, were never confined to the private/ domestic sector. Rather, their lives were also shaped by their participation in the economic and political-juridical spheres. However, with the advent of colonialism, clear policies and structures were put in place that removed such limited autonomy and excluded women from decision-making, thereby entrenching their total subordination to men.[19] Such policies and structures were mainly reflected in the law (customary, common and statutory), the economy, religion and the educational systems.

To illustrate how colonialism entrenched women's subordination in Uganda, let us consider its policy on formal education. Educational policy was especially significant because it had far-reaching implications on other sectors of society including economics and politics. One's educational level/ content, for example, determines one's level of participation in the civil service, politics and even business. The colonial policy on education, implemented through missionary schools, not only provided disproportionate opportunities to males but also offered gender-based curricula. While men's education prepared them for work in the civil service, law, politics and business, education and training offered to women was primarily geared towards molding good housewives and homemakers.[20]

When Makerere University was established in 1922 only men were enrolled. Indeed its guiding motto at the time was 'Let's be Men!'[21]. It was not until 1945 that the first female students enrolled at Makerere College (as it was called then). But even then, the courses that women could enrol for were restricted to the 'soft' Arts-based 'traditional' female ones such as Home Economics, Hygiene and Teaching. One of the pioneer females, Mrs. Sarah Ntiro (née Nyendwoha) recalls:

> I had wanted to do mathematics but there was a problem; the tutors of mathematics did not think that girls could do this subject. This was a big disappointment for me... and I had been warned that I would not be accepted in the class.... But I felt that I had to make a statement. I went to the first class and when I got there the White professor asked me, "Where are you going?" I said, "here." "Do you think this is a maternity ward?" I answered, "Obviously not" (laughs). He went and stood near the window with his back to the class... you could have heard a pin drop. When he turned round, I was still there so he collected his books and marched out of the classroom.[22]

The goal for women's education was basically to bridge the intellectual gap between husbands and wives and to breed chaste and obedient wives for the sons of chiefs and clergy.[23]

More importantly, the colonial policy on education worked to delineate the boundary between the public and private spheres. Thus, where such distinction had been blurred in pre-colonial Ugandan societies, a bold line was drawn to distinguish between 'public' (political) men and 'private' (domestic) women. Such artificial separation is engineered to serve both patriarchy and capitalism. Naila Kabeer[24] describes families in precapitalist societies such as those that existed in precolonial Uganda and the changes that were brought on by the introduction of capitalism:

> In pre-capitalist societies, kinship was the key idiom of social interaction, organising economic, cultural and political activities as well as sexual and reproductive practice. Clearly, in such contexts, the domestic domain was the primary site of most social relations, including those of gender. By contrast, one of the pivotal features of contemporary market-based societies has been the institutionalized separation of the 'private' domain of family and kinship from other 'public' institutions of the market and state.[25]

The artificial separation of the 'public' and 'private' realms serves to undermine women's position within Ugandan society. This is clearly seen from the fact that society and the state apportion more power and privilege to the public sphere than to the private one.

The relationship between domestic life and the political/economic order should be clearly recognised.[26] There is a direct connection between the seemingly apolitical 'private' realm of the family and the "public" political realm of the state. The patriarchal state depends on the patriarchal family to consolidate its own authority. As the people with the primary responsibility for food crop production and as the primary caretakers and nurturers in the home (all of which are done gratuitously), women provide the strengthening qualities necessary for social units to survive under exploitative conditions. It follows therefore that as the primary caretakers of home and family, women are key levers in securely harnessing the family to state goals.[27] Through their food production, child rearing and other production activities that ensure the reproduction of the labour force, women subsidise capital (albeit underdeveloped), making it possible for the state to pay low wages and prices.[28]

Using the traditional colonial tactic of "divide and rule," the British played off different communities against one another other, favouring and 'developing' certain regions at the expense of others. Buganda, being the biggest of the collaborators and most politically organised, became the hub from which the colonial power spread its stranglehold across the rest of the country. On the other hand, Bunyoro and the northern region which put up the toughest resistance to colonial hegemonic expansion saw the least 'development' during the colonial period. Such region-based disparities in in the allocation of socio-economic resources persist to the present day. This means that the historical location of women from Buganda and those from say northern Uganda greatly influenced the degree of gender oppression that they suffer today. It is therefore important to understand that in addition to class, religion, culture and age, the impact of gender oppression is also regionally differentiated.[29]

Even with thirty-seven years of formal independence, the colonial legacy continues to impact Uganda's gender relations. Although colonialism did not introduce patriarchy to Uganda, it doubtlessly redefined, modified and significantly altered Uganda's gender relations. Such changes did not remain only at the level of the socio-political strata but also within the consciousness of the people. Through socialisation and the power structure of Ugandan society, the ideology of patriarchy inculcates in the minds of men and women that the public/private divide is natural and that men are naturally superior to women.

Some elementary statistics about Uganda will place the plight of women in better perspective: (a) women constitute 51 per cent of the total population of 22 million; (b) women account for 60 per cent of cash crop production and 80 per cent of food production; (c) women bear the primary responsibility for nurturing and raising the people of Uganda and future generations; (d) the illiteracy rate of women is one and a half times higher than that of men; (e) the female composition of people's representatives in the highest national decision-making body constitutes only 18 per cent; (f) women represent only 20 per cent of total formal sector employees with a negligible number occupying high level posts in their organisations; and (g) there are relatively more women-headed households living below the poverty line than households headed by men.

Against this backdrop of Uganda's socio-political context, it should be easy to understand that women's subordinate position is socially-constructed through a distinct historical process. It should also point to the necessity for an interventionist strategy to remove the gender inequities that exist in Ugandan society.

From theory to practice: The impact of affirmative action

Affirmative action for Ugandan women has been introduced in the spheres of politics and education but is yet to be introduced in the economic sphere which is the arena of social existence that is of fundamental importance to the transformation of the status of women. Below, I assess the impact of the policy on each area in turn.

Politics

The NRM administration became the first post-colonial government in Uganda to take proactive measures to include women in formal politics. Affirmative action for women in politics started in a limited fashion at the level of popular democracy introduced in the form of a five-tier local council (LC) system.[30] One out of the nine executive committee member seats at each LC was reserved for a woman. However, this initial attempt at affirmative action for women was not only skewed but also tokenistic. In the overwhelming number of councils, the one seat reserved for women became the upper limit as women were discouraged and/or prohibited from offering their candidature for any other position on the executive committees. Moreover, the role of female councillors who occupied the reserved seats tended to be apolitical and often limited to organising entertainment and refreshment for council functions.[31]

Following the spirit of the 1995 constitution, the Local Governments Act of 1997 expanded the women's quota at all LCs to one-third. In theory, this improved the situation somewhat as it guaranteed the necessary critical mass for women to substantively influence council deliberations and policies.[32] But even then, there are certain loopholes in the law that seriously limit LC women's participation in decision-making. When central government decentralised its powers, functions and services to local governments, most authority and resources were placed at the sub-county (LCIII) and district (LCV) levels.[33] Whereas the composition of women on the executive committees of the less powerful administrative units (i.e., LC I and II) are defined as one third, this quota does not extend to the executive committees of the sub-county and districts where real power lies.[34] Indeed, current statistics show that in 69 per cent of the 45 districts of Uganda only one female (secretary for women) sits on the district executive committees. This is a serious defect in the law because it is these sub-county and district (LC V) executive committees which that and formulate policies.

Moreover, despite the fact that the law reserves one-third of the council seats for women at the sub-county and district levels, many of these seats remain vacant to-date, especially at the sub-county level. This is because the mandatory non-refundable nomination fees required of each candidate is way beyond the financial means of the majority of women who wish to stand at this level. Hadija Miiro–one of the commissioner of the Uganda Electoral Commission—noted that this problem was very real for the majority of women at the sub-county level during the 1997-98 LC elections.[35]

A related financial problem that affects women's participation in local government is a direct result of the nature of their elections. Women councillors who are supposed to fill the one-third quota at all levels are elected by the electorate lining up behind the candidate of their choice. But because it is not practically possible for one candidate to appear at the numerous polling stations allocated to each electoral area, women have to incur the additional cost of printing posters bearing their portrait or paying agents to 'stand in' for them. By contrast, councillors who are elected into office by secret ballot in the direct elections do not incur any such costs as all ballot papers are printed by the electoral commission.

Furthermore, many female councillors still face the expected teething problems associated with the new roles have assumed. Even in those councils where the quotas have been completely filled, women are yet to find their footing in the unfamiliar 'public' context of formal politics. At a national conference for women councillors held in August 1998, there was consensus among the participants that the participation of women in councils left a lot to be desired.[36] Part of the reason is the cultural upbringing which requires women not to speak out in public. These are just a few of the constraints that women who wish to participate in politics at the local level have got to overcome.

In 1989, government extended affirmative action for women to the parliamentary level when it accorded mandatory seats to at least one woman from every district.[37] Female membership in the national legislature was significantly boosted by the new policy. Between independence and 1986 female representation to the national assembly never exceeded two.[38] During the first three years of NRM rule there were only four women in the National Resistance Council.[39] This means that until affirmative action policy was introduced, the total number of women in any given post-independence legislature was never higher than four. The 1989 sex-quota is evaluated experiment comprehensively elsewhere.[40]

There have been both positive and negative effects of affirmative action at the parliamentary level. On the positive side, the culture of formal politics is beginning to register some modest changes. The presence of such an unprecedented number of females in an institution that was traditionally dominated by men has, for example, introduced a gendered perspective to the law-making process. The women's caucus in parliament often makes it its business to analyse bills and policies for their gender sensitivity or otherwise. Thanks to the affirmative action policy, more and more women have been exposed to the 'public' sphere, thus empowering themselves in the face of patriarchy and underdevelopment. Moreover, the increased visibility of women in positions of leadership is slowly changing the attitudes of Ugandans (both men and women) towards women's presence in the political arena. This new consciousness forms the crucial basis for a new kind of political self-organisation for women and for a more radical transformation of gender relations in Ugandan society.

Perhaps the place where affirmative action registered its most visible gains was in the 1994/95 Constituent Assembly which debated and passed the 1995 constitution. On account of the significant caucusing efforts by female delegates with the strong backing of the women's movement, the 1995 constitution contains strong pro-women provisions.

Yet the advances noted above have only made a marginal dent on the overarching dominance of patriarchal forms of doing politics; women are still considered intruders in a preserve that was previously almost exclusively male. Some of the limitations associated with affirmative action policy are historical, others relate to actual implementation.

First, prevailing gender relations together with the underdeveloped economy (rooted in neocolonialism and imperialist domination) operate to limit or otherwise shape the performance of women legislators. Unless the underlying structural problems of the system are addressed, the beneficiaries of affirmative action will continue to operate under conditions of sexism, power imbalance, sexual harassment and gender violence. Uganda may have a woman vice-president and witnessed a higher number of female appointments to high positions such as cabinet, the judiciary and government commissions, but the status of the majority of womenfolk remains constant. Cultural socialisation which moulds 'public (political) men' and 'private (domestic) women' as well as the gendered order of state institutions and ideologies jointly operate to ensure the perpetuation of the status quo. Thus, culture and morality, aided by the male-dominated media, still form a considerable tool for men's domination over women and continue to act as a caveat hindering women's participation as autonomous political actors.

Secondly, the policy of affirmative action introduced the phenomenon of double representation. Every constituent in the country has at least two representatives in parliament—the affirmative action district woman representative and the regular county representative. This is significant in that it raises the potential for a clash between the two representatives, particularly because the affirmative action legislator does not (despite the prevailing belief) represent women alone. Potentially and in fact the issues addressed by the two representatives are the same. In order to avoid alienation and competition, the affirmative action MPs have to be careful not to step on the toes of their county colleagues. This fact, together with the fact that they operate in a much wider area of operation with limited allowance or facilitation from government, creates real limitations on the kind of work affirmative action MPs can do. They tend to focus on the 'safer' and 'nonthreatening' agenda of dealing with women's community-based organisations and groups and/or children's issues and only obliquely tackling with other issues concerning county constituencies within the district.

Thirdly, the benefits that women extracted from the affirmative action experiment are also limited by the fact that it was a top-down policy imposed by the state.[41] This meant that the recipients of affirmative action were not involved in devising the rules and procedures of participation. Instead, most of the beneficiaries feel beholden to the NRM government for 'giving' them access to the political arena; we often hear them thanking the NRM for 'delivering' them from the bondage of oppression. Perceiving affirmative action as a favour, and not a right, has engendered complacency and self-satisfaction in many affirmative action MPs.

Fourthly, no one—either inside or outside the state—seems to link affirmative action to broader social, political and economic transformations that would ensure a radical alteration in gender relations. This is hardly surprising given that at independence, Uganda inherited a state structure whose ideology was designed to systematically promote male privilege and power while solidifying women's subordination. Both government and civil society seem to be contented with bureaucratically putting women in places of leadership and authority without any attempt at simultaneously removing the practical and structural obstacles that stand in their way to effective involvement in this arena.[42] Simply 'adding women' to existing social and political structures and 'stirring' can do little in removing the discrimination and inequities from which they perennially suffer.[43]

Unless the NRM government exhibits a real political commitment to roundly remove patriarchal inequalities, affirmative action may prove much more of a burden than a blessing to Ugandan women. While it is wonderful to have women participating in formal politics from the grassroots to the highest level of decision-making, we should not lose sight of the fact that it creates yet one more responsibility to the full-time tasks that women perform in the domestic/economic arena. Thus, as Schreiner[44] correctly points out, without looking into the democratisation of the domestic tasks, affirmative action demands that women become 'superpeople.'

A fifth limitation lies in the provisions of article 80(1) of the constitution. This article lists 'a minimum formal education of advanced level standard or its equivalent' as one of the prerequisites for a potential parliamentarian. Imposing such qualification for eligibility to stand for a parliamentary seat (i.e., credentialism) benefits only the elite. To this end, affirmative action at the highest decision-making institution has proved to be class-centric, largely benefiting a minority of an educated élite group of Ugandan women. By eliminating almost 90 per cent of the female population from the status of member of parliament in this way, the policy perpetuates the characteristic of mainstream post-colonial politics which has excluded the voices of the largest section of the peasant population.

Finally, the work of female politicians in Uganda is in many ways a reflection of the constraints and contradictions arising out of a patriarchal sociopolitical setting existing in a peripheral area of the global economy. On the one hand, traditional gender roles and basic issues related to daily survival give shape to their political work. On the other, their contradictory status as marginalised women in positions of power sets them apart from the masses of Ugandan women. Luckily, it is these very contradictions that are likely to foster further action for social change by female legislators; the sense of incongruities for these women is bound to precipitate into a particular form of political consciousness.

Education

Article 30 of the 1995 Constitution states that 'All persons have a right to education.' Given the illiteracy level of women in Uganda, affirmative action within the formal educational sector is crucial if they are to fully enjoy their human and constitutional rights. As the old adage goes, 'knowledge is power;' indeed one's literacy, intellectual skills and formal schooling greatly determine one's social, political and economic status. Preferential treatment for women in education has been in place on an informal and ad hoc basis since the 1970s. This was especially at the point of entry from primary to secondary schools. Thus co-educational high schools such as King's College, Buddo would admit females at slightly lower points than males.[45] More recently, with the introduction of universal primary education (UPE) in 1997, government insists that out of the four children from each family that benefit from UPE, two must be girls.

In July 1990, government, through the Makerere University Council, formally introduced an affirmative action policy for female applicants to state-funded tertiary institutions. This was to be done by weighting the grade points of each female applicant with an additional 1.5 points. The sole purpose of this policy was to increase female enrollment in the various courses at Makerere University and other public institutions of higher learning.

The backlash to the policy was immediate; beneficiaries of the 1.5 points were stigmatised and derogatory terms such as '1.5' and 'concessionary' graduates came into use and were especially associated with the first batch of women entrants, irrespective of whether or not the additional points enhanced their chances of admission. Local newspapers were inundated with letters disparaging the policy: One Kakande described the 1.5 policy as 'not serious, discriminative and a sign of government failure to comprehend social problems.'[46] Oduman believed that it was 'a sign of sectarianism invading education.'[47] Mugyenyi argued that the policy would water down the standards of Makerere and 'eventually undermine the few genuinely qualified students.'[48] Three years after the policy was introduced Olive Birabi interviewed several male university students who indicated 'bitterness and rage towards the 1.5 girls.' A patronising George Lugalambi thought that the policy would kill the confidence and self-esteem of female students.[49] Male students felt that undeserving girls benefited while innocent boys were victimised by the policy.[50] But Birabi's study found no evidence to show that beneficiaries of the preferential treatment policy performed poorly academically.

Table 1 gives the data of total admissions of female students into various courses at Makerere University over a period of eleven years (1987-1998). The figures allow us to assess the ratio of female to male 'freshers' and to determine whether the 1.5 policy had any significant effect on the total number of entrants in each course. The year 1990 is presented in bold to signify the year that preferential treatment was introduced. When one looks at the total number of females admitted in each year for all the twenty-one courses sampled in the table, one notes that there was a boost in the overall number of females admitted to Makerere University after the introduction of the 1.5 points. The total number of female entrants increased by 5 per cent in the year that the policy was introduced. In 1997 there was an increment of 9 per cent in the total number of female entrants, but this may have been a result of more self-sponsored females taking advantage of the more liberalised education system in place at Makerere at the time.[51]

Table 1: Admission of female students to selected courses at Makerere University (1987 - 98)

Course	1987 A	1987 B	1987 C	1988 A	1988 B	1988 C	1989 A	1989 B	1989 C	1990 A	1990 B	1990 C	1991 A	1991 B	1991 C	1992 A	1992 B	1992 C
Medicine	16	73	22	20	71	28	19	70	27	17	87	20	26	93	28	31	92	34
Vet. Medicine	04	40	10	01	37	03	05	40	13	05	49	10	03	39	08	03	39	08
Engineering	02	55	04	05	44	11	03	46	07	05	49	10	06	56	11	13	59	22
Agriculture	25	96	26	31	100	31	16	80	20	23	86	27	10	81	12	19	81	23
Forestry	04	30	14	04	34	12	05	30	17	04	34	12	05	35	14	05	29	17
Statistics	07	47	15	04	33	12	05	51	10	03	59	05	18	69	26	10	64	16
Commerce	11	79	14	08	74	11	26	89	29	16	98	160	29	100	29	24	99	24
Social Works & Admin.	09	45	20	14	44	32	16	46	35	24	55	44	21	50	42	31	49	63
Law	11	51	22	14	54	26	17	52	33	24	58	41	30	61	49	27	62	44
Fine Art	11	32	34	08	21	38	13	29	45	19	39	49	12	41	29	05	30	17
Science	28	251	11	36	272	13	34	268	13	62	301	21	52	300	17	67	286	23
Arts	41	141	29	61	209	29	76	266	29	126	311	41	124	339	37	137	354	39
Social Sciences	68	350	19	71	296	24	39	252	15	121	361	34	87	287	30	123	309	40
Dental Survery	01	10	10	01	10	10	02	09	22	07	10	70	01	10	10	02	09	22
Pharmacy	-	-	-	04	10	40	03	10	30	04	11	36	03	10	30	04	10	40
Food Science & Technology	-	-	-	-	-	-	02	15	13	10	26	38	09	22	41	08	19	42
Library Information Science	-	-	-	-	-	-	11	32	34	14	37	38	22	45	49	19	46	41
Mass Communication	-	-	-	07	21	33	09	20	45	11	17	65	10	19	53	13	20	65
Architecture	-	-	-	-	-	-	00	07	0	01	10	10	01	11	9	02	07	29
Arts (Educ.)	52	130	40	53	122	43	78	189	41	10	201	54	103	198	52	94	196	48
Science (Educ.)	05	88	06	03	65	5	44	110	40	20	188	11	18	102	18	18	67	27
Total	**295**	**1518**	**19**	**345**	**1517**	**23**	**423**	**1711**	**25**	**625**	**2087**	**30**	**590**	**1968**	**30**	**655**	**1927**	**34**

(Tabe 1 continued) Admission of female students to selected courses at Makerere University (1987-98)

Course	1993			1994			1995			1996			1997*			1998*		
	A	B	C	A	B	C	A	B	C	A	B	C	A	B	C	A	B	C
Medicine	25	89	28	29	89	33	25	97	26	22	88	25	32	110	29	43	93	45
Vet. Medicine	03	41	7	00	38	0	02	40	5	03	40	08	03	42	07	03	40	08
Engineering	08	71	11	14	62	23	14	80	18	14	84	17	31	164	19	34	181	19
Agriculture	24	83	29	29	81	36	09	79	11	17	77	22	18	86	21	15	91	16
Forestry	04	25	16	03	30	10	02	31	6	04	30	13	12	52	23	05	41	12
Statistics	13	74	18	08	56	14	09	61	15	18	57	32	19	57	33	16	68	24
Commerce	30	96	31	21	110	19	25	02	25	30	93	30	41	121	34	37	114	32
Social Works & Admin.	43	62	69	20	47	43	23	51	45	19	50	38	34	62	55	33	57	58
Law	18	65	28	21	59	36	36	70	51	30	74	41	133	244	55	159	328	48
Fine Art	13	41	32	11	38	29	19	40	48	13	39	33	32	84	38	35	66	53
Science	71	335	21	78	297	26	65	375	17	69	350	20	77	369	21	55	306	18
Arts	124	332	37	116	309	38	128	385	33	132	338	39	275	652	42	302	651	46
Social Sciences	120	292	41	126	295	43	109	285	38	105	298	35	469	1050	45	382	883	43
Dental Survery	05	11	45	07	10	70	03	10	30	02	10	20	03	14	21	06	15	40
Pharmacy	02	08	24	01	10	10	03	10	30	02	10	20	05	15	25	07	17	41
Food Science & Tech.	07	16	44	05	15	33	08	19	42	08	21	38	10	31	32	10	28	36
Library Info. Science	28	51	55	16	37	43	24	40	60	22	37	59	35	47	74	33	48	69
Mass Communication	20	20	100	11	19	58	11	20	55	13	17	76	34	73	47	56	92	61
Architecture	01	08	13	06	10	60	02	12	17	02	14	14	07	20	35	10	16	63
Arts (Educ.)	129	218	59	114	232	49	121	235	51	132	338	39	231	410	56	304	555	55
Science (Educ.)	19	63	30	23	76	30	17	85	20	11	93	12	20	104	19	12	83	14
Total	707	2001	35	659	1920	34	655	2127	31	668	2158	31	1521	3807	40	1556	3773	41

A = No. of admitted females   B = Total no. of admitted students   C = Percentage of females admitted

* Data for this year reflects the total number of registered (as opposed to admitted) students in the first year of each course.

Source: Academic Registrar's Office, Makerere University, Kampala.

A closer analysis of the individual courses reveals a general pattern whereby the 1.5 policy seems to have had a greater impact on Arts-based courses than Science-based ones. Take the two examples from the faculties of Veterinary Medicine and Arts. The only time that the percentage of female entrants to the course in Veterinary Medicine exceeded 10 per cent was in 1989 (i.e., 13 per cent). Ironically, the percentage dropped to 10 per cent the following year when preferential treatment was introduced. Indeed, four years later, the course admitted no female at all. In contrast, the Faculty of Arts recorded a 12 per cent increment from 29 per cent to 41 per cent in the year that preferential treatment was introduced and the ratio never fell back to the pre-1990 figures throughout the eleven year period. Mass communication is another course which had a significant positive effect from the 1.5 policy, recording a 20 per cent boost in 1990 from the previous year. This trend was generally maintained to the extent that in 1993 course entrants were exclusively female.

In spite of some erratic figures here and there, preferential treatment has, over the years, steadily raised the proportion of females to an average ratio of 50:50 in the following courses: Law, Arts (Education), Mass Communication, Library & Information Science, and Social Work & Social Administration. But the table also shows some 'freak' figures in certain courses where female representation is abnormally high in specific years. These include: Dental Surgery in 1990 (70 per cent); Architecture in 1994 (60 per cent) and again in 1998 (63 per cent); and Medicine in 1998 (45 per cent). Explanation for such anomalies would require a more comprehensive study into the individual faculties.

Are there any significant changes after 1995—the year that the women-friendly constitution was promulgated? The post-1995 years coincide with increased liberalisation of higher education in Uganda. This means that the opportunities for women to join tertiary institutions increased, especially for those who had minimum academic qualifications with the capability to pay for their studies privately. Although there is no cogent evidence to support the view, it is likely that the liberalised atmosphere towards gender issues contributed to more women pursuing higher education in the years from 1996 to 1998.

Preferential treatment in higher education largely benefits privileged children. For example, in 1990 admissions where the policy was first implemented no females from Kotido, Moroto, Bundibugyo and Kapchorwa were admitted to the university.[52] Most beneficiaries of this policy emanate from 'grade one' schools. Very few if any from 'grade three' ('third world' in local parlance) schools benefit from it.[53] Indeed, the benefits of the 1.5 policy can be assessed regionally in the following descending order: central, western, eastern and northern.[54]

In sum, the 1.5 policy at the largest and oldest university has to a small extent realised its purpose in arts-based courses but is yet to influence female in-take in the Sciences. This points to an inherent problem underlying preferential treatment in the education sector. By placing emphasis on higher education, government in effect addressed the symptom and largely ignored the fundamental causes that lead to the disproportionate numbers of female degree holders. Gender-based affirmative action in education must begin at the lower echelons of the formal education structure. It is not enough to simply state that half of the UPE recipients must be girls as such a condition can be easily manipulated by chauvinist parents and guardians. Moreover, the policy should address the high female drop-out rate in both primary and secondary schools. The appalling attrition rate of girls from the school system is directly linked to socio-cultural influences that encourage girls to perfect themselves in the domestic arena, get married and start their own families by sixteen.

Conclusion

As a redress policy, affirmative action in Uganda stands as a beacon light on a distant island surrounded by a turbulent sea of regressive waters. While the policy provides space for Ugandan women's increased entry into politics and education and a potential for change, its implementation is dogged by too many contradictions. Affirmative action alone cannot promise a democratic, nonsexist political economy without effectively dismantling the hierarchical institutions that exist in the patriarchal status quo. Indeed, it would only amount to a cosmetic measure, a hollow victory that has little potential to shatter the institutional aspects of sexism in Uganda.

The policy must be extended in a comprehensive fashion to the lower levels of the formal educational system as well as in adult education programmes. State members of the Southern Africa Development Community (SADC) region have gone a long way to close the enrollment gender gap in both primary and secondary schools.[55] Meaningful affirmative action in the educational sector would afford free schooling to *all* girls at primary and secondary levels as is presently the case in Malawi. Angola also introduced a positive discrimination quota system to guarantee women's access to its free education scheme. In addition to a free education policy, government should also undertake a review of school curricula and texts that portray women and girls in a stereotypical sexist manner. In Zambia and Zimbabwe all texts and supplementary materials have already been replaced with those that portray females positively.[56]

Uganda still faces the enormous burden of introducing affirmative action in the employment/economic sector. Currently, the workforce is extremely gendered with women occupying the lowest ranking and least-paying jobs. As the people who shoulder the greatest responsibility for the country's cash and food crop production, women must be empowered to contribute to the national economy in a more significant and dignified manner. We could borrow a leaf from the South African Employment Equity Act which compels designated employers to undertake organisational audits and to institute affirmative action policies for, *inter alia*, women.

It is significant that out of the twenty or so commissions established by the 1995 constitution to implement various tasks, only the Equal Opportunities Commission (EOC) has not been instituted to date.[57] Establishment of the EOC is long overdue since it is the body with a special mandate to implement specific nondiscrimination legislation and to open up more opportunities for vulnerable marginalised groups to participate in the political, economic and social spheres of our society. In post-apartheid South Africa the Commission on Gender Equality (CGE) was established to promote respect for gender equality and included in its various tasks is the function of monitoring the affirmative action policies of government and the private sector.[58] The statutory powers of the EOC would allow it to successfully advise, campaign, implement and monitor affirmative action programmes for women in all spheres of Ugandan society.

For affirmative action to achieve its primary goal of redressing historical and socio-political imbalances that exist in society, a multi-layered agenda involving an altering of gender relations must be adopted. It will take a total transformation in prevailing ideologies as well as social and political structures to confer substance and power to women's participation in the different sectors of our society; in sum, a redefinition of power and equality. This can be accomplished through: the state acknowledging and gainfully rewarding the productive and reproductive labor of Ugandan women; sharing of domestic labour between men and women; promoting gender-awareness for men and women through education (formal and informal), the media, popular theater, and so forth; legal reform to scrap all forms of male oppression and dominance; and, to establish and consolidate links between women in policy-making, feminist (male and female) activists, women in academe, and grassroots women.[59] Obviously, all these goals cannot be achieved in a short period. Uganda must therefore draw a time schedule for herself, clearly spelling out the target period within which to achieve specific goals towards gender equity.

If the current add-women-and-stir conception of affirmative action persists, then the policy shall lose its transient nature and become a permanent fixture on the Ugandan political scene. In other words, redistributing positions of leadership within the same patriarchal structures will not change the status quo. The end formula will be affirmative action *plus* business as usual. That is no recipe for the evolution of a genuinely progressive and gender-sensitive culture of constitutionalism.

Notes

1. Prior to 1995, the NRM government had introduced affirmative action in politics (1986) and in state-funded public institutions of higher learning (1990).
2. Jenny Schreiner (1996): 81.
3. Mullen (1988).
4. Love (1993): 492.
5. For e.g., see Fullinwider (1980); Combs and Gruhl (1986); Turner (1990); Sikhosana (1996).
6. Adedeji (1981).
7. Evans (1983); Goldman, (1979).
8. Nahum (1982) at 2 & 5, quoted in Howard (1990): 162. See also Mutua (1995): 339-80;
9. See The African Charter on Human and People's Rights, 27 June 1981, OAU Doc. CAB/ LEG/67/3/Rev.5 (1981) which entered into force on 21 October 1986.
10. The 'individual rights' argument seems to have gained the upperhand in countries like the United States. For example, on July 20, 1995, the board of regents of the University of California voted to dismantle all racial- and gender-based affirmative action programmes at all its nine campuses. This decision, which was taken amidst intense protests and demonstrations, affected hiring, contracting, and student admissions at the university (see Yoachum, Susan and Edward Epstein (1995), 'U.C. Scraps Affirmative Action,' *San Francisco Chronicle*, 21 July:A1).
11. Heins (1987): 15.
12. Nacoste (1989): 104.
13. Mullen (1988).
14. Ibid., 251.
15. Koggel (1994).
16. The term 'patriarchy' as used in this chapter refers to male dominance within the specific cultural and historical arrangements of Ugandan gender relations. Patriarchy in the Ugandan context is grounded in the institution of polygamy—the practice of a man taking on multiple wives. Under this system, men are the dominant sex, having control over women and the management of gender relations (see Tamale, 1999: chap. 1).
17. This form of capitalism (as opposed to classic capitalism) is based on pre-capitalist elements located in the peasantry (e.g., kinship structures and relations of production). Stamp (1986: 30) explains, 'The key to underdeveloped capitalism is that subsistence activities are more important than wages or the returns from cash crops in the reproduction of labor power.'
18. See, Kandiyot (1988); Stamp, (1986); Tamale (1999).
19. Uganda was declared a British Protectorate in 1894.
20. See, Staudt (1981); Tamale and Oloka-Onyango (1997).
21. Hansen and Twaddle (1988).
22. Interview with the author, 24 September 1998.
23. Wandira (1974).
24. Kabeer (1994).
25. Ibid., 57.
26. See, Molyneux (1985) and Shanley (1995).
27. Molyneux, ibid.
28. Stamp supra 30; Gordon (1996): 28-32.
29. Tamale supra 12-13.
30. First known as Resistance Councils (RCs), the LC hierarchical structure consists of the village council (LC I), the parish council (LC II), the sub-county council (LC III), the county council (LC IV), and the district council (LC V).
31. Ddungu (1989).
32. Some scholars argue that for tokens to be able to influence the culture of any institution, their representation must attain a certain ratio (critical mass). Such ratio varies from 15 to 35 per cent (See, Kanter (1977); Dahlerup (1988).

33. Under the 1997 Local Governments Act, local councils at the village (LCI), Parish (LCII) and county (LCIV) levels are merely administrative units with minimum power and resources to make important decisions (see Part II of the Act).

34. The one-third quota at the levels of LC III and V applies to the entire council but not the executive committee membership of the councils.

35. Author's interview with Commissioner Hadija Miiro, 24 August 1998.

36. National Conference organised by Forum for Women in Democracy (FOWODE) on the theme, 'Setting the Agenda for Women's Economic Empowerment,' International Conference Centre, Kampala, 27-30 August 1998.

37. There existed 39 districts in Uganda at that time. Today the number of districts has expanded to 45.

38. Female representation in the national assemblies prior to 1986 was as follows: 1962-1971 – Florence Lubega and Sugra Visram; 1979-1980 – Rhoda Kalema and Geraldine Bitamazire; 1980 - 1985 – Theresa Odongo-Oduka.

39. These were, Victoria Ssekitoleko, Gertrude Njuba, Betty Bigombe, and Oliva Zizinga. The original 74-member NRC (which acted as the interim legislature) was primarily made up of so-called 'historicals' members of the NRA/M.

40. See Tamale supra.

41. Elsewhere I argue that at the time the NRM assumed power in Uganda, the women's movement was in the process of re-organising and brushing off cobwebs that had grown as a result of years of dictatorship, instability and civil strife that dogged post-independent Uganda for decades. Thus, although women's groups would demand for greater political participation at every opportunity, no significant grassroots pressure group existed to pursue this agenda exclusively (see Tamale, 1999).

42. cf. Schreiner supra, 82.

43. Harding (1991).

44. Schreiner supra, 83.

45. Birabi (1993).

46. See 'Makerere Not Serious,' *Weekly Topic*, 24 August 1990: 34 (quoted in Birabi, *ibid.*).

47. See 'Sectarianism Invades Education,' *New Vision*, 3 October 1990: 5 (quoted in Birabi, *ibid.*).

48. See 'Equality Front is Elsewhere,' *New Vision*, 19 October 1990: 5 (quoted in Birabi, *ibid.*).

49. See 'Makerere 1.5 Scheme Kills Female Confidence,' *Weekly Topic*, 25 October 1991 (quoted in Birabi, *ibid.*).

50. Olive Birabi *ibid.*, 66.

51. In 1992, the Faculty of Law pioneered the introduction of evening class programmes whereby students who qualified and could afford to pay tuition and other fees privately got opportunities to study. Other faculties followed over the years, peaking in 1996/97.

52. Birabi supra, 37.

53. *Ibid.*, 55-57.

54. *Ibid.*, 62.

55. This is especially true for Zambia, Zimbabwe, Tanzania, Malawi, Angola, Mauritius and South Africa. See *SADC Gender Monitor*, Issue 1, February 1999, Gaborone: Southern African Development Community (SADC) Gender Unit.

56. South Africa is currently undertaking a similar exercise. See *SADC Gender Monitor*, Issue 1, February 1999, Gaborone: Southern African Development Community (SADC) Gender Unit.

57. See article 32(2) of the 1995 constitution.

58. Similar commissions have operated with significant success in countries like Australia, Sweden and Canada.

59. Tamale supra.

References

Adedeji, Adebayo (Ed.) (1981), *Indigenization of African Economies*, London: Hutchinson University Library for Africa.

Birabi, Olive (1993), 'The Impact of the Female Weighting Admission Policy on the Enrolment and Status of Female Students in Makerere University,' M.A Thesis, Makerere University.

Combs, M. and Gruhl, J. (eds.) (1986), *Affirmative Action: Theory, Analysis and Prospects*, Jefferson N.C: McFarland & Co.

Dahlerup, D. (1988) 'From a small to a large minority', *Scandinavian Political Studies* 11:275-99.

Ddungu, Expedit (1989), 'Popular Forms and the Question of Democracy: The Case of Resistance Councils in Uganda,' Working Paper No. 4, Centre for Basic Research, Kampala.

Evans, Bette (1983), 'Thinking Clearly About Equality: Conceptual Premises and Why They Make a Difference,' in James Foster and Mary Segers (Eds.), *Elusive Equality: Liberalism, Affirmative Action, and Social Change in America*, Port Washington, NY: Associated Faculty Press.

Fullinwider, Robert (1980), *The Reverse Discrimination Controversy*, Totowa, NJ: Rowman and Littlefield.

Goldman, Alan (1979), *Justice and Reverse Discrimination*, Princeton, NJ: Princeton University Press.

Gordon, April (1996), *Transforming Capitalism and Patriarchy: Gender and Development in Africa*, Boulder, CO: Lynne Rienner Publishers.

Hansen, Holger and Michael Twaddle, (eds.) (1988), *Uganda Now: Between Decay and Development*, London: James Currey.

Harding, Sandra (1991), *Whose Science? Whose Knowledge? Thinking From Women's Lives*, Ithaca, NY: Cornell University Press.

Heins, Marjorie (1987), *Cutting the Mustard: Affirmative Action and the Nature of Excellence*, Boston: Faber and Faber.

Howard, Rhoda (1990), 'Group Versus Individual Identity in the African Debate on Human Rights,' in Abdullahi Ahmed An-Nacim and Francis Deng (Eds.), *Human Rights in Africa: Cross-Cultural Perspectives*, Washington D.C.: The Brookings Institution.

Kabeer, Naila (1994), *Reversed Realities: Gender Hierarchies in Development Thought*, London: Verso.

Kandiyoti, Deniz (1988), 'Bargaining with Patriarchy,' *Gender and Society* 2(3): 274-90.

Kanter, Rosabeth (1977), *Men and Women of the Corporation*, New York: Basic Books.

Koggel, Christine (1994), 'A Feminist View of Equality and Its Implication for Affirmative Action,' *Canadian Journal of Law and Jurisprudence* 7(1):43-59.

Love, Buchan (1993), 'Justifying Affirmative Action,' *Auckland University Law Review* 7(2): 491-99.

Molyneux, Maxine (1985), 'Mobilisation Without Emancipation? Women's Interests, the State, and Revolution in Nicaragua,' *Feminist Studies* 11(2): 227-54.

Mullen, Tom (1988), 'Affirmative Action,' in Sheila McLean and Noreen Burrows (Eds.), *The Legal Relevance of Gender*, Atlantic Highlands, NJ: Humanities Press International.

Mutua, Makau (1995), 'The Banjul Charter and the African Cultural Fingerprint: An Evaluation of the Language of Duties,' *Virginia Journal of International Law* 35(2): 339-80.

Nacoste, Rupert (1989), 'Affirmative Action and Self-Evaluation,' in Fletcher Blanchard, and Crosby Faye (Eds.), *Affirmative Action in Perspective*, New York: Springre-Verlag.

Oloka-Onyango, J. (1996), 'The Plight of the Larger Half: Human Rights, Gender Violence and the Legal Status of Refugee and Internally Displaced Women in Africa,' *Denver Journal of International Law and Policy* 24(2/3): 349-94.

Schreiner, Jenny (1996), 'Affirmative Action and Reconstruction: A Basis for Changing Race, Class and Gender Inequalities,' in Blade Nzimande and Mpumelelo Sikhosana (Eds.), *Affirmative Action and Transformation*, Durban: Indicator Press.

Shanley, Mary (1995), 'Father's Rights, Mother's Wrongs? Reflections on Unwed Father's Rights and Sex Equality,' *Hypatia* 10(1): 74-103.

Sikhosana, Mpumelelo (1996), 'Affirmative Action: Possibilities and Limitations,' in Blade Nzimande and Mpumelelo Sikhosana, (eds.), *Affirmative Action and Transformation*, Durban: Indicator Press.

Stamp, Patricia (1986), 'Kikuyu Women's Self-Help Groups: Toward an Understanding of the Relation Between Sex-Gender System and Mode of Production in Africa,' in Claire Robertson and Iris Berger (Eds.), *Women and Class in Africa*, New York: Africana Publishing Company.

Staudt, Kathleen (1981), 'Women's Politics in Africa,' *Studies in Third World Societies* No. 16:1-28.

Tamale, Sylvia and Joe Oloka-Onyango (1997), 'Bitches at the Academy: Gender and Academic Freedom at the African University,' *Africa Development* 22(1): 13-37.

Turner, Ronald (1990), *The Past and the Future of Affirmative Action*, New York: Quorum Books.

Wandira, A. (1974), *Indigenous Education*, Entebbe: Government Printers.

PART IV

BEYOND THE HORIZON: TOWARDS A NEW AFRICAN CONSTITUTIONALISM

13

Constitution-making in Eritrea: Democratic Transition through Popular Participation

Bereket Habte Selassie

On 23 May 1997, a Constituent Assembly ratified the draft constitution of Eritrea prepared by the Constitutional Commission.[1] The ratification marked the climax of a process of three years of intense public debate and consultation. That debate was itself the fulfilment of a long struggle for national self-determination and independent statehood. A thirty-year war of independence fought with Ethiopia ended in Eritrean military victory in May 1991. Two years later, Eritreans of voting age chose independence rather than association with Ethiopia in an internationally observed referendum. The government of the Eritrean People's Liberation Front (EPLF) then embarked on a transition process culminating in the adoption of the constitution. A crucial part of the transition was the establishment in March 1994, of the Constitutional Commission of Eritrea (CCE). The CCE was mandated to draft a constitution on the basis of wide ranging public debate on the matter and through expert consultations.

The Eritrean experience of constitution-making occurred—as did those of other African countries in recent years—in the context of a democratic awakening (or re-awakening) in the African continent. Following more than three decades of political and socio-economic crisis, the African peoples were seeking to embark upon a new path. These crises must themselves be placed in perspective. Though crisis-ridden, Africa is by no means a hopeless continent; on the contrary, by and large, the people of Africa have historically struggled without losing hope during a century of wrenching colonial rule. They struggled for their freedom and, after independence they suffered with dignity and hope as their own governments wreaked havoc on them.

The post-Cold War era has ushered in a period of transition whose clear and universally-supported objective is democracy, stability, and the rule of law. Authoritarian regimes that used to receive massive military aid by the protagonists of the Cold War have suffered a marked decline in external support. The proxy wars in which African regimes squandered scarce resources are becoming a thing of the past.[2] Popular pressures have been building up with increasing demands for democracy, the rule of law, decentralisation of political power and accountability and transparency in government at all levels. The decision by Kenya's ruling party—the Kenya African National Union (KANU) and President Moi to accept the demands of opposition groups for a constitutional amendment to create a fairer electoral system illustrates that popular pressures can force the hand of even the most recalcitrant of governments.[3]

In connection with the political transition, note must also be made of the economic transition from centrally planned economies to ones based on the market. The causes of the political crises of the past were inextricably linked with those of the economic debacle that had led to stagnation. A rigid, centralised bureaucracy, was reinforced by the one-party centrally-controlled and planned economy. Instead of the era of freedom and plenty promised at independence, Africa for the most part, endured over three decades of repressive regimes ruling over impoverished populations.[4] Nonetheless it is worth issuing a note of caution not to view the market as the panacea to all Africa's problems; indeed, there are risks that go with it, risks that were dramatically illustrated by the financial crisis that afflicted the Asian economies at the end of the last century.[5] In sum, democratic transition has not always been a peaceful affair. In some instances, the transition was preceded or accompanied by armed struggle; some of these transitions were encouraged or supported by 'donor' governments, including the government of the United States.

Against the above background it is trite to note that constitution-making is invariably a crucial moment in any nation's social and political history. The aim of this chapter is to describe and analyse the process of constitution making that culminated in the adoption of a new constitution in Eritrea. It outlines the principal elements of the process, mentions the actors and mechanisms involved, and briefly examines some of the most controversial issues that were raised and debated during the process.

Transition and the clash of values...or interests

Underlying the process of transition are two related assumptions. First of all, there is the assumption that a new generation of leaders has emerged, chastened by the tragedies of the past and, with clearer vision and more coherent programs, are now steering Africa in new directions. Second, this transition to democracy is part of a world-wide phenomenon in which there has been a movement away from autocratic and repressive regimes towards constitutional democracy and transparent governance. It is further assumed that the trend for more democracy and the rule of law is irreversible and that the new brand of leadership is keenly aware of this fact. There is also an emerging consensus that any resistance to the trend enjoys neither broad internal public support nor external backing. All these factors present an extraordinary challenge, intellectually as well as in practical, political terms.

Concerning the above challenge, two scenarios alternate to engage the political imagination of scholars and politicians alike, occasionally spilling over into public discourse. The first and most sanguine scenario is one in which there is a meeting of minds—a shared perspective on the meaning and implication of universal principles such as democracy and human rights. This meeting of minds—between the West and 'the rest'—proceeds from an assumed collective consciousness of a chastened, post-Cold War world community in which there is general agreement to promote universally accepted values such as democracy and human rights. It is a fair assumption to make; after all, no nation has voted against the Universal Declaration of Human Rights or the 1966 covenants on political, civil, social, economic and cultural rights. And every leader, on all occasions, pays rhetorical homage to human rights and democracy. Nearly all world constitutions have incorporated these and other universal values into their substantive provisions.

The other scenario is not so optimistic. It involves the use of human rights and democratic values to advance the foreign policy interests of powerful nations. To take a well-known example, the American and European (especially Franco-Belgian) support of Mobutu Sese Seko for over three decades, was a travesty of democracy and human rights. The Cold War rationale of an anti communist ally was wearing thin long before the fall of the Soviet empire, and yet the support, or tolerance of Mobutu continued until his overthrow. Such indisputable historical facts tend to diminish the effect of well-meaning and well-conceived policy pronouncements on human rights and democracy. Ironically, it also plays into the hands of dictators or would-be dictators who cite them in defense of their own anti-democratic tendencies or practices.[6] Constitution making thus acquires added significance as a testing ground for the 'war of visions' that has replaced the ideological war of past years.

Constitution making in Eritrea: A needs based approach

The Constitutional Commission of Eritrea began its work by posing a series of questions—questions that it set itself the task of answering before drafting the constitution. The essence of the questions may be summarised as follows:

- What lessons, if any, do historical experiences offer in this respect?
- Do such experiences yield helpful models or guidelines?
- Is it desirable, or practicable, to use models: are they transferable like some form of technology?

- What, after all, are the values and goals that a nation needs most emphatically to promote, nurture and protect?, and how should these be incorporated into a constitution?
- Should such values and goals be so incorporated, or should they be left for determination in the crucible of political and social interaction.[7]
- What form of government is best suited for Eritrea?
- What degree of centralisation should there be?
- Should there be an official language, or languages and: if so, which ones do we select and Why?

There were numerous other questions of detail, including some pertaining to technicalities such as the size of the constitution; and whether it should be long or short? In particular, how detailed should the chapter on human rights be? All in all, the commission listed 23 questions for consideration.

The commission reached a consensus at the outset that it should not rely on a ready-made model, whatever its source. It began instead by taking stock of the historical reality and paramount needs of the country. It designed and organised its research and public consultation activities on that basis. Furthermore, the commission used its statutory mandate to organise and conduct wide ranging public debates. The commission thus attached critical importance to the process; in its estimation, the process was as important as, if not more important than, the product. Another way of putting it is: the end (the constitution) prescribes the means, but the means shape the end.[8] This may be described as a new politics of constitution making. In a nutshell such an approach seeks to involve the public in the act of creation, while at the same time adopting and adapting universally-applied institutions and values. Its underlying philosophy proceeds from the conviction that Africans know what they want, and what will work for them. In effect Africans are saying: 'we don't indulge in blind imitation, but we don't have to reinvent the wheel.' The Eritrean experience exemplifies this new politics, with similar experiences in South Africa and Uganda, to mention two recent examples.

The historical and theoretical context: A brief history

The country now known as Eritrea—as was the case with most of Africa—is a creation of colonialism. In pre-colonial times the territory was known by various names, experienced different systems of government and was subjected to population migrations in which there was an intermingling and the development of different cultures. Historical records show that as early as the third century BC, the port of Adulis, near present day Massawa, was frequented by ships sailing from Greece and Egypt.[9] Christianity was introduced to the area early in the fourth century AD specifically into Axum which was the centre of the region of present day Eritrea and Tigray. Following the advent of Christianity which shaped the ideology of the Axumite state and defined its culture, the rise of Islam gradually laid the foundation for a competing faith and a corresponding culture and way of life. The two religions lived side by side, at times giving rise to strife and religiously-inspired wars. By and large however, they co-existed in remarkable harmony. The periodic strife was driven by external powers such as the Ottoman Empire and its nineteenth century Egyptian successors under Khedive Ismail.[10]

Italian colonial rule began in 1890, five years after the Treaty of Berlin which carved up Africa into different European colonial dominions. The Italians introduced different infrastructures and a typical colonial system of government in which the indigenous inhabitants had no say. The colonial state and its laws were superimposed over native traditional laws and institutions which were, however, left intact after earlier attempts at suppression failed.[11] After the Second World War, the fate of the former Italian colonies—Eritrea, Libya and Somalia—was decided differently due to strategic and geopolitical reasons. In 1950, a US-sponsored resolution of the UN disposed of the matter by joining Eritrea with Ethiopia in a lopsided federal arrangement under which Eritrea was given local autonomy just short of sovereignty. Eritreans thus became the subjects of His Imperial Majesty—the Ethiopian emperor—to whom they were required to owe allegiance. But that was not to be.

The Emperor gradually destroyed even the limited autonomy granted by the UN. Indeed, in November 1962, he abolished the federation, declared Eritrea the fourteenth province of Ethiopia and sent in an army of occupation. Eritreans had seen the writing on the wall before that event; a year earlier an armed liberation group had announced the start of armed struggle which was to last 30 years. Perhaps the most important legacy of the long struggle concerns the social revolution that was carried out throughout the last two-thirds of the thirty-year war. This is amply reflected in the draft constitution and came out clearly throughout the public discussions on the constitution making process. The victories achieved in the social revolution are part of the irreversible legacy of the Eritrean liberation struggle. The question of women's equality is one such irreversible legacy, as is social justice, democracy and human rights. There is therefore a sense in which the constitution making process is critically influenced by the values acquired during the long armed struggle. It became clear during the course of public debate over the constitution that the instrument was perceived as the fulfillment of the liberation struggle, and thus also as vindication of the enormous sacrifice that the struggle involved.

Revisiting the theoretical framework

Constitution making is a process that brings people and their governments together to shape their future political life. It is a meeting point between the past, the present and the future. It is an historic rendezvous between state and society, if one may be permitted a hyperbole. The history of the great charters of the world attest to this conclusion, and one common feature of such charters is the principle that there must be certain limits to governmental power; the nature and extent of the limits differ from place to place and from one period to another. The conflicts between king and barons that produced the Magna Carta gave more power to the barons. The strife between the king and his aristocracy on the one hand and the commoners on the other that broke out some five centuries after Magna Carta was resolved in favour of the commoners represented by the ascendant English bourgeoisie.

In our own time, the struggle between autocracies and the common citizens demanding democracy is going on all the time. All these struggles are concerned essentially with the limits to government. The concept of constitutionalism expresses rule with appropriate limits placed on government. The oldest method devised to achieve constitutional rule, with certain limits placed on those who govern, was to make the latter answerable to some outside group such as a priesthood. This practice was gradually extended to the public in general through the principle of universal suffrage and other democratic devices such as term limits to elective office, the separation of powers and federalism. This limit on government lies at the heart of a democratic system of government, and since it is best guaranteed in the constitution, the process of constitution making becomes crucial. For this reason the method of constitution making has been the subject of continual debate and theorising.

Historically, three main approaches to modern constitution making can be identified. There is first, what may be called the Philadelphia model. Then, there is the Westminster model which may also be called the parliamentary method. Thirdly, there is the constitutional commission approach which combines aspects of both. The governing principle common to all three is that of legitimacy, namely the requirement that the constitution must be ultimately approved by an entity or entities in which sovereignty resides. The Philadelphia Convention of 1787 debated and drafted the US constitution. Thereafter, the state legislatures legitimised it in the act of ratification. In the Westminster model, a committee of parliament is formed to draft a constitution which is thereafter approved by parliament in plenary session.

The difference between the two lies in the fact that the legislative body appoints a committee to report to it after an inquiry on the need for reform and on the content or extent of the proposed reform. Parliament has control over the process, because sovereignty resides in parliament, at least in the case of Britain. Nonetheless, the committee has power of initiative and control over the investigative process which involves research and public hearings during the parliamentary debates. The final report can of course undergo changes, and the government of the day can rely on its majority in Parliament to introduce any changes that it deems necessary. Clearly, the Philadelphia model is more complicated and difficult to implement compared to the parliamentary model. This is borne out by the many failed attempts at constitutional amendments in US constitutional history. The difficulty flows from the nature of the US system as contrasted to the simpler and easier method used under the parliamentary model. It also relates to the existence of a written, fairly rigid constitution in the US in contrast to the 'unwritten' flexible British model.

What about the new approach that relies on a constitutional commission with a clear mandate to organise public debates and draft a constitution on the basis of such debates, while also taking expert opinion into account? How different is this from the other two? The critical difference is that in the new approach the public is directly and actively involved. Another difference lies in the use of a constituent assembly to ratify what parliament has already approved which is primarily a function of the principle of legitimacy. It may be pointed out that this was also the case in the United States, but there is a difference in that the ratifying entities in 1787 were the state legislatures which had been elected with a larger mandate. In the new approach a wholly new entity is elected specifically to debate and approve the constitution; this function is the sole purpose for which it is elected, except in the Namibian case. In Namibia, the first (independence) parliament turned itself into a constituent assembly to ratify the constitution drafted by a constitutional commission.

In analysing these various approaches and their differences, the criterion for judgment on choosing one or the other is basically the following: to what extent has the method helped to achieve the desired end i.e. optimal public participation? On the face of it, the new approach seems to be a better method. Its validity will depend, however, on the quality of participation and on the extent to which the constitutional commission concerned actually takes the public opinions into account in drafting the constitution.

As the twentieth century drew to a close, two African governments, having accepted the importance of popular participation in principle, were involved in contestation with organised members of their civil societies as to the means of achieving popular consultation. These were the governments of Kenya and Zimbabwe. In Kenya, the dispute turned in one respect around the question of whether the reform of Kenya's constitution should be made through the appointment of a constitutional commission, as was done in South Africa, Uganda and Eritrea. On the other, the question was whether the reform process should be transformed into a national conference of representatives of all the 'stakeholders.' The Kenya government stated its preference for the commission model, whereas the representatives of civil society demanded that a constitutional conference be held embracing all the stakeholders. At the time of writing, the stalemate in perceptions still remains, although some progresss has been made in arriving at a compromise.

Similarly in Zimbabwe, the government appointed a 400-member constitutional commission to collect the views of Zimbabweans and to draft a constitution that was submitted to a controversial referendum in mid-2000, which the government lost. About half the commission's membership was drawn from parliament, with the majority coming from the ruling Party— the Zimbabwe African National Union—Patriotic Front (ZANU-PF). The National Constitutional Assembly (NCA)—a civil society coalition that had championed the cause of constitutional reform since 1992—refused to be part of the process. Instead, it decided to draft its own 'people-oriented' constitution in a parallel process.

The relevance to our discussion of this dispute on the choice of the entity to draft the constitution lies in the fact that it involves both principle and politics. The issue of principle lies in the fact that the entity designated with the task has to be representative of the various interest groups of the nation concerned—the stakeholders. Public participation in the process is a categorical imperative; consequently, the manner and extent of public participation is of crucial importance. The connection between principle and politics is also of relevance because the political leaders of a country have the right to decide on the appointment and function of such an entity. That is provided, of course, that the basis of their own power is legitimate. Where there is a lack of legitimacy in their power base, there is bound to be contestation.

Assuming legitimate political authority, a political leadership can appoint a commission and assign it the task of drafting a new constitution. For such a constitution to be widely supported, however, the participation of the citizens of the country concerned in its making needs to be ensured in a wide-ranging public debate or consultation.

Constitutional theory and the Eritrean experience

With these considerations in mind, let us now focus on the Eritrean experience and inquire about the extent to which the new method has been of value and whether it has enabled Eritreans to respond adequately to the challenges of citizenship in establishing constitutional government. In this respect, it seems that in order to assess the value of the new approach, particularly in the African context, three principal requirements have to be satisfied. I intend to discuss the Eritrean experience in constitution making, in light of these requirements by focussing first, on the process of constitution making, and secondly, on the substance of some of the most controversial issues raised during the public debate.

The three requirements are:

- The existence of government wedded to the ideal of a democratic constitutional order.
- A sufficiently sensitised public that is aware of such an ideal and is willing, if not entirely able, to play a role in its realisation.
- An entity—by whatever name known—with a clear legal mandate to organise, with complete autonomy, the reception of public views on the basis of widely held debates and other forms of popular consultation. Those views must be seriously considered for possible incorporation in the constitution.

An additional requirement that is implied by the third concerns the quality of the membership of the entity. The members of the constitutional commission must be selected to reflect not only political considerations of religious, ethnic and/or regional representation, but also professional competence.   In the following section of the chapter, we will explore the Eritrean experience through the application of each of the above requirements.

The Eritrean government and constitutional order

The government of Eritrea was formed in May 1991 by the EPLF immediately after the liberation of the country from Ethiopian military occupation. The EPLF-based government was designated, under Proclamation No.1. of 1991, as a provisional government, pending the formal independence of the country which came two years later. Formal independence which could have been declared almost immediately, was delayed at the insistence of the EPLF leadership that wanted an internationally-observed referendum to be held two years following military victory.

This path was chosen—despite the obvious cost implied—not only out of considerations of international law and the desirability of consummating military victory by a formal legitimising process, but above all, out of the confidence of the leadership that the people would choose independence. Such popular expression would be a signal to a hitherto skeptical, or largely indifferent, world that theirs was a legitimate and just struggle fought with the full backing of the people. It reflected a devout wish—some might even say an impish desire—on the part of the leaders for poetic justice. At any rate, it was amply rewarded by the outcome of the referendum of April 23-25, 1993 in which 99.8 per cent of Eritreans of voting age voted for independence.[12]

Under Proclamation 37/1993, the provisional administration was renamed the Government of the State of Eritrea. The same law charged the government with the responsibility, inter alia, of preparing the ground for laying the foundation for a democratic system of government. The Constitutional Commission of Eritrea was established a year later in fulfillment of this responsibility. The preamble to the law establishing the commission is worth citing here because it conveys the sense of commitment of the governing party (the EPLF, now renamed Popular Front for Democracy and Justice— PFDJ) and the government to a democratic, constitutional order. The preamble to the law provides that the government of Eritrea was established under Proclamation No. 37/1993 with the responsibility, inter alia, of maintaining the unity and territorial integrity of Eritrea; of guaranteeing the fundamental rights of its citizens; of planning, organising and directing the reconstruction and rehabilitation of the war-ravaged economy; and above all, of preparing and laying the foundation for a democratic system of government.[13]

The paragraph that follows refers to the provision of Proclamation No. 37 which requires the National Assembly (the transitional parliament) to establish a constitutional commission 'comprising experts and other citizens of proven ability to make a contribution to the process of constitution making, and charged with the responsibility of drafting a constitution and organising popular participation in such a process of constitution making...'[14] It should also be noted that the government passed other laws that signified its overall commitment to democracy and constitutional rule. One of the most important was Proclamation No.26, providing for the establishment of regional government.[15]

The commitment of the new government leadership to the democratic ideal and constitutional government was expressed at the party level by the issuance of a charter approved by the Third Congress of the EPLF in February 1994. The charter was published as the National Charter for Eritrea, and subtitled: 'For a Democratic, Just and Prosperous Future.' The charter expressed the vision of the Front for the future of the country. The constitutional commission used it as a principal source of national consensus and as a point of departure for national debate in the course of constitution making.

Dealing with the issue of citizen participation

As noted earlier, citizen participation in constitution making—including the quality of such participation—is of the essence. As such, it became the cornerstone of the commission's strategy. To that end, the commission started its work, as already noted, by drawing up a comprehensive list of questions defining the parameters of its research and study. This approach also helped in organising public debate and in soliciting expert opinion on the experience of other countries.

The question of organising public debates and making the necessary preparations to that end is thus not merely a technical, logistical matter. It involves issues of substance concerning the most appropriate literature that must be procured, translated and distributed to the public, and the best way of communicating the essence of the ideas about democracy and constitutional rule to them. Due attention was thus paid in preparing the public to enable them to make the best possible contribution to the debate. This was also true in the reverse process of recording, collecting, collating and eventually analysing the views of the public. This careful processing of public views was a matter of the utmost importance: in the first place, those views might be used in drafting the constitution. Secondly, it has an empowering quality in that the people feel a sense of ownership of the constitution.

There are a number of conditions that make for optimal citizen participation. In the first instance, citizens have to be aware of their rights and responsibilities. Secondly, and related to the first, they have to be literate. The Jeffersonian adage that democracy depends for its success on a literate citizenry cannot be overstressed. However, it raises the fundamental question: how does one address the problem in countries like Eritrea where there is 80 per cent illiteracy?

Under the law, the Constitutional Commission of Eritrea was required to draft a constitution following extensive public debate and then to present the draft for parliament's approval. After submission to parliament there was further public debate on the approved draft. At the end of the final public debate, the commission would prepare a final draft, taking into account public opinion, where deemed necessary. Then the final draft would be presented to parliament and, through it, to a Constituent Assembly. It was understood that the parliament represents the government of the day whereas the Constituent Assembly represents the nation at large. The first draft was approved by parliament with a few amendments and debated by the public in late 1996 and early 1997. The final draft was ready for submission to the Constituent Assembly in the spring and ratified on 21 May 1997.

The composition and work of the CCE

The commission comprised fifty members of a policy making council and a ten member executive committee drawn from the council, including a chairperson, a vice and a secretary. Both the council and the executive committee were chaired by the same individual. The commission members represented a cross-section of Eritrean society, including twenty-one women, the majority of whom were liberation fighters. All nine ethnic groups of Eritrean society were represented as well as the business community and the professions.

The commission divided its three year mandate into four phases. The first phase, running from the first quarter of 1994 to the end of the year involved the establishment of a headquarters and branch offices. It also involved other logistical matters such as raising money and organising introductory seminars. The second phase began with a well attended international symposium in early January, 1995. Thereafter a civic education campaign was launched and the members of the commission and over four hundred specially trained teachers instructed the public on constitutional issues and related political and social questions. To that end, the commission prepared pamphlets and translated several international legal instruments into local vernaculars. Among them were the Universal Declaration of Human Rights, and the 1966 international covenants on civil and political, and that on social, economic and cultural rights. Over half a million Eritreans were reached in this civic education exercise, which proved a turning point in the public attitude towards the constitution making process.

The third phase commenced in the last half of 1995 with the preparation and wide distribution of a set of proposals prepared by the commission. The proposals which contained most of the major constitutional issues of contention helped in clarifying and focusing attention on the most salient issues of concern. Extensive public debates were organised on the basis of the proposals, between September and December, 1995. At the end of the debates the commission collected and analysed the questions raised and opinions expressed by the public and sat down to write the first draft of the constitution. The fourth and final phase was in the first quarter of 1997 and led to the presentation of the draft to the appropriate bodies.

Organisational framework

At the outset, the research work of the commission was organised to be performed by four ad hoc committees that carried out their duties under the general guidance and supervision of the executive committee. There was also a standing committee on civic education and public debate. The four research-oriented committees were:

- Committee on Governmental Institutions and Human Rights;
- Economic Committee;
- Social and Cultural Affairs Committee; and
- Committee on Governance and Related Issues.

The four committees were mandated to establish sub-committees and solicit expert views and research assistance from Eritrean professionals in particular.

At the end of the first phase, it was decided to combine the four research committees into one and concentrate on the production of issue papers on the basis of the previous research, as well as on the outcome of the civic education seminars and the international symposium. The issue-by-issue discussion strategy was replaced by aggregating the issues into major questions. Issue papers covering various topics, such as legislative, executive and judicial powers, electoral systems, decentralisation, fundamental rights and freedoms, social, economic and cultural rights, and equality guarantees were also written.

One outcome of the research—of critical importance to the success of the public debate—was that it enabled the commission to focus on the most important constitutional issues and simplify them for the purpose of easier communication to the public. The proposals formula contributed to that end in that it simplified and concentrated the basic issues. The proposals prepared for public debate were themselves based on issue papers that were the outcome of the research work of the various committees.

In sum, the task of painstakingly working to sharpen the focus on the basic issues, simplify them and articulate them in a manner and language that was easily understandable to the average member of the public was accorded top priority. Additional mechanisms of effective communication such as songs, poems, short stories and plays in the various vernaculars were utilised. Artists, poets and playwrights were invited to compete towards these ends. A great deal of money, skill and other resources were spent in this fashion. The broadcast media was also utilised to these ends with satisfactory results. Public seminars, debates, mobile theatre and other aspects of national culture were employed to enhance the people's awareness of the fundamental principles of democratic constitutional government, including citizens rights and duties, the scope and limits of government, and government's responsibilities to its citizens. It is believed that all these efforts succeeded in instilling in Eritreans a sense of engagement with, and ownership of, their constitution.

The autonomy and quality of the commission

The law establishing the commission (Proclamation No. 55/1993), laid down the structure, composition and mission of the commission. As already pointed out, the law provided for a ten person executive committee, drawn from the larger body of the council of the commission, to act as the principal directing organ of the commission in between the meetings of the council, running the day to day activities and planning and executing all programs.

There are two main questions that merit special attention in regard to the role of the commission, including the question of its autonomy. One is political, the other legal. The political aspect raises the issue of its composition with the allied question of legitimacy, or at least the representative nature of the commission: what constituencies ethnic, religious, professional groups, gender, did it represent. That the appointing authority was the National Assembly as a presumptive representative of the nation was obviously a step forward in terms of legitimacy. But in a society with several ethnic groups, and a population more or less equally divided between Christians and Muslims, such factors must be taken into account when the candidates are nominated for election by the National Assembly. It can be fairly assumed that they were in fact taken into account, judging by the balanced composition of the council. Although the majority of the commission members were veteran liberation fighters, there was a fair mix of the professions, including lawyers, teachers, social workers and a member of the Eritrean Chamber of Commerce. The majority of the 21 women members were veteran freedom fighters.

Secondly, there is the point in regard to law and its relevance. In the first instance, it is beyond question that in the final analysis, the primary aim of the constitution-making exercise is the establishment of legal principles to govern and guide the life of the nation concerned. Article 4 of the law establishing the commission enjoined the latter to draft a constitution 'on the basis of which a democratic order would be established, and which shall be the ultimate point of reference of all the laws of the country, and the final arbiter of all basic issues in dispute.' The logic of delegating a commission to draft the constitution implied, it may be assumed, that the question as to what legal (constitutional) principles must be incorporated into the future constitution was a matter that should in the first instance be left to the commission to determine.

The point of my insistence on drawing a distinction between law and politics during the constitution making process is principally to establish a basis for fixing responsibilities between the legitimate political authorities, on the one hand, and the entity authorised to draft the constitution, on the other. There are matters on which the legitimate political authorities may be expected to have the last word, although they must take the views of the public and of experts into account. Whether or not an official language should be declared in the constitution, for instance, is essentially a political question. Such an issue must in my opinion, ultimately be determined by the political leadership.

But even in that instance, the commission's role is critical in terms of sounding out the views of the public and of experts, as well as in assessing the political and cultural implications of a decision on such a language policy. In that respect, the ethnic/linguistic representation in the commission is obviously a relevant factor. On the other hand, I believe that in the matter of the law of the constitution which comprises the central principles governing the rights and duties of the citizens of a country and the powers and responsibilities of government authorities, the commission's word should prevail. Assuming that there is adequate national and professional representation in the commission, the latter should enjoy complete autonomy not only in the management of the process, but also in determining the contents of the constitution.

The role of lawyers (as technocrats) is of critical importance in this matter. Politicians, on the whole, tend to approach most issues politically, whereas lawyers view issues through the prism of legal principles. A debate between the two sides in the context of a constitution making exercise can be a fascinating exchange. Finally, the Eritrean political authorities were not only extremely co-operative in making the task of the commission easier, but they generally respected the autonomy of the commission and the integrity of the process from beginning to end.

Democratic transition, and the dialectic of process and substance

It bears reiteration that the task of constitution making embraces both the domain of politics and the realm of law. The term 'law' is used here in the normative sense—the law as a set of norms laying down rules that guide and control behaviour. One could describe law as the frozen politics of yesterday. It is at times difficult to determine where politics ends and law begins, but it is crucial to be clear about the distinction for the establishment and sustenance of the rule of law. Another way of looking at the question is to consider law as value, as the ultimate source of consensus binding society.

Nonetheless, there are other paramount values or primary goals of society that must be reflected in a constitution. In this respect those charged with the task of constitution making must ask at least two sets of related questions. The first concerns the nature of the values and goals that a society needs to advance and maintain, for which the constitution is at once an embodiment and a consequence of society's attachment to them. The second set of questions concerns the issues that a commission and society at large must select for debate and eventual inclusion in the final draft document.

Concerning the first question, the charter of the PFDJ set forth five major national strategic goals which the Constitutional Commission of Eritrea took as a significant source of national consensus and a point of departure for the public debates in which Eritreans were invited to participate beginning in May 1994 until the end of the process. These goals and values are:

- Stability and national unity;
- Democracy;
- Economic development;
- Human rights; and
- Social justice.

No argument is necessary in the affirmation of the validity of these fundamental goals and values. The public debate readily confirmed the initial assumption of a national consensus.

During the many tours that members of the commission undertook organising public meetings of Eritreans abroad, the public was asked whether there were any alternative, or opposed, visions to those on which the debate was premised. None that questioned or challenged the PFDJ vision of a future Eritrean society based on the five fundamental goals were forthcoming. Clearly, a civil order cannot be viable without such central goals and values, and the constitution is the principal instrument of expressing them. There can be no civil order where there is no stability and national unity as the recent history of Somalia, Liberia and Rwanda aptly demonstrate. Nor is there any serious dispute as to the critical link between democracy, economic development, human rights and social justice.

With respect to the second set of questions, i.e., the principal constitutional issues to be debated by the public, the commission launched its work by framing the public debate in terms of such issues. In this regard, it selected twelve key issues for special attention and prepared background papers for expert comments, eventually turning these papers into concrete proposals for public debate. These included: the form and structure of government, separation of powers, the structure and function of the judiciary, the issue of national languages, the electoral system, regional government (decentralisation), the armed and security forces, and fundamental rights.

The commission's mission was designed to ensure maximum public participation, with expert consultation playing a supporting role. The emphasis on extensive and intensive public debate was based on the conviction that such a process involves creativity as well as empowerment. It also involves instilling in the public consciousness of a sense of ownership of the product of the process, namely the future constitution by which they will be governed. The obverse of this is the Lancaster House model, a top-down approach in which the public are excluded. In the course of the public debates throughout Eritrea, a constant reference was made to this deeply flawed model. Indeed, the exclusion of the public from such a process, as from other processes of decision making, represents an important aspect of the 'false start' in the post-colonial misadventure of the African state. The commission hammered this point home, thus enhancing the public's appreciation as to the historic nature of the process and the importance of the people's active participation in it.

There are two reasons—historical and theoretical—which explain the commitment of the Eritrean government to the principle that the constitution must be made with the active participation of the people. Historically, Eritreans owe their success in their lonely struggle against overwhelming odds to the active participation of the people in support of the struggle. Their adversaries, both under Emperor Haile Selassie until 1974, and under the military government of Mengistu Haile Mariam until 1991, were economically, diplomatically, and militarily superior. Furthermore, they were alternately supported by the United States and the former Soviet Union. Moreover, in the referendum of April 1993 to which the governing EPLF submitted the fate of Eritrea, popular participation consummated the military victory and enhanced the role of the public in determining their fate. That historic event proved to the international community that Eritrea was able to win the war not only by military prowess, i.e. by the skill, tenacity and resilience of its fighters, but above all through reliance on the support of the people.

The popular participation of Eritreans in such historical processes relied on the inherent wisdom of encouraging and organising the people to be involved in decisions affecting their lives in all instances. This makes sense theoretically, and conforms to universal principles of democracy. It also accords with the historically evolved system of village democracy in which village communities governed themselves democratically through periodically elected assemblies. This village democracy forms a central part of Eritrean customary law and practice and was preserved, rationalised and utilised during the period of the armed struggle with significant results.

Conclusion

The constitution making experience of Eritrea justifies the assumption of the constitutional commission that the active participation of the population is not only a political imperative of the greatest moment, but that it is a practicable imperative. On theoretical grounds it is a political necessity for legitimacy as well as on the grounds of empowerment of the people who are enabled to develop a sense of ownership of the constitution by being involved in its making. It is practicable on condition that the entity responsible for the process takes all necessary steps to enable the public make their contribution to the process. By all accounts, the Eritrean constitutional commission executed the above with satisfactory results.

A second point emphasised is that, the new politics of constitution making, as exemplified by the Eritrean experience, is a better approach compared to other approaches noted in this essay. Proceeding from the assumption that public participation is a critical condition for good constitution making, the appointment of an independent commission mandated to organise and manage such public participation is a more democratic one. One can argue about details, but the essential consideration is that this approach best serves the desired objective of ensuring maximum participation of the people in the making of the basic law by which they will be governed. It thus creates and reinforces a sense of belonging. In this respect, it can be fairly claimed that the account given in this essay regarding the Eritrean experience bears scrutiny and independent judgment, in terms of satisfying the three requirements—government's commitment, the role of the public, and the role of the commission, including its autonomy. In this respect, the commission launched its historic work with a quantum leap of faith that was later amply vindicated.

The third, and final conclusion flows from the first two, and is related to the challenges faced by the constitutional commission which is indeed implicit in the whole process of constitution making. Among those challenges, ensuring optimal public participation was the most critical. In that respect, the most heartening feature of the Eritrean experience is the extent and quality of the public's involvement. The diffidence observed during the introductory phase of its operation (Spring-Summer of 1994) gradually gave way to more vigorous and candid involvement. During the third phase (Summer-Autumn of 1995) the distribution of the commission's proposals enabled the public to be more focussed, to raise questions, to air their views and express their concerns on a wide range of issues.

Such participation involves the challenge of citizenship which requires the people's engagement with their future constitution, and asserting the principle of constitutionalism which is to bind with government and the governed. Citizenship engagement in such an enterprise requires a measure of trust on the part of citizens who, in the case of Eritrea, undertook the task of constitution making for the first time in their history. The commission preached the gospel of constitutionalism unabashedly, explaining that the concept implies the reign of reason and of the rule of law in which people are the subject of rights and duties and not merely its objects. The commission exhorted citizens to have faith in themselves as active agents of history and not merely as passive recipients of commands. The public response was astounding; the Eritrean people surprised all, including themselves. Needless to say, they cannot afford to sit on their laurels, but rather, should be eternally vigilant.

As for the second challenge regarding personnel and material, it should be remembered that Eritrea suffered enormous loss as a result of the war including death and the mass exodus of its most active populations. The impact of this loss has been felt in all branches of government and society at large. The commission made an effort to augment the work of the trained and experienced human power at its disposal by tapping into all available national human resources. The establishment of two Boards of Advisers and of ad hoc sub-committees helped in meeting the challenge. In terms of equipment and facilities, the commission did not experience any problems. It was adequately prepared, in advance, in terms of defining objectives and preparing budget estimates for submission to international donors. With regard to the collection and analysis of data, the main concern was to make a full and accurate record of all meetings. The outcome of these efforts are the masses of documents now housed in the Centre for Research and Documentation in Asmara.

Nevertheless, it is one thing to write a good constitution; it is quite another to ensure constitutional rule. Looking beyond the time of the promulgation of the constitution of Eritrea what are the prospects for its successful application? How close to the promise will the performance be? What are the chances of it remaining true to the original purpose? As the Constitutional Commission of Eritrea saw it, in order to be effective, a constitution must reflect present day realities as well as be mindful of future developments in society. It must also provide for the existence of institutions that give it life and force, and for interested groups that can defend and enforce it. Such forces must have the requisite interest and capacity. The constitution of Eritrea does all this. But a constitution is only a framework, albeit a crucial one. Great challenges lie ahead to give the instrument life and force. There will have to be a political system that provides the enabling framework for social and political forces to build and develop the necessary institutions to make a constitution a living document. We will also need vibrant civic institutions.

Now the recent history of Africa cries out for balance between state construction and nation building, between state and civil society. The two should go hand in hand; one should not grow at the expense of the other. Constitution makers should be aware of the need for balance. In as much as it may not be constitutionalised, the task would fall on the shoulders of the legislators and the judiciary to maintain the right balance. Each nation may have to work out its own formula in this respect, while looking to the experience of other nations for helpful lessons.

Notes

1. Under Article 4(4) of Proclamation No. 55 the constitutionalism commission, is required 'to present to the National Assembly a Draft Constitution for a final public discussion, and at the conclusion of such public discussion, to prepare a final draft and submit it to the National Assembly for approval and for eventual submission to a democratically formed representative body.'

2. But Somalia today provides an unfortunate example of proxy wars fought by local war lords contending for the conquest of the failed Somali State. In order to achieve their objective, two factions, at least, have accused each other of allying themselves with regional governments that are in conflict, i.e. Ethiopia and Eritrea.

3. See below for the controversies on the different approaches both in Kenya and Zimbabwe.
4. The World Bank annual reports paint a grim picture of economies that are in deficit and, for the most part, debt-ridden. There is abundant literature on Africa's economic debacle, including some insightful studies on how African peoples adopted survival strategies in the face of the failure of their governments in this respect. See generally, Joseph (1999).
5. The exponential growth of businesses financed by irresponsible banks in South Korea and Indonesia have been the cause of these debacles which the IMF has started controlling by imposing strict conditionalities.
6. It is interesting to note that the United States, among other members of the United Nations, insisted that Kabila should hold elections immediately, even though they knew, or should have known, that the country had been destroyed by Mobutu's kleptocratic regime; that the infrastructure was decayed, and that in such a vast country that had been so devastated and ravaged one required a few years to reestablish and sustain law and order and organise a decent government machinery to ensure a fair democratic election. In such circumstances, the shrill insistence on immediate election renders the concerned's party insistence suspect, to say the least.
7. It was apparent at the outset that some things can appropriately be left out of the constitution while others could not, which makes the question susceptible to debate.
8. In a speech that I delivered in January 1996 at the Royal Institute of International Affairs in London (Chatham), I described the constitution making process in Eritrea, under the title 'In Lieu of Lancaster House,' with the subtitle: 'New Politics of Constitution Making.' I chose the title, I informed the audience, to underline the strategic priority the Constitutional Commission of Eritrea ascribed to the participation of the population in creating the constitution of their country. Such a participation was neither envisaged nor permitted under the Lancaster House model of constitution making.
9. See Doresse (1959): 16-18.
10. See Rossini (1937).
11. United Nations General Assembly Resolution 390 (V) of 1950.
12. Mr Samir Samba, the UN observer, solemnly declared that the referendum had been fairly conducted. Soon after the referendum, Eritrea was admitted to membership of the United Nations.
13. Paragraph 3.
14. *Ibid.,*
15. Proclamation No. 26 of 1993.

References

Doresse, Jean (1959) *Ethiopia, Ancient Cities and Temples*, London.

Joseph, Richard (ed.) (1999) *State, Conflict, and Democracy in Africa, Boulder Co: Lynne Reinner.*

Rossini, Carlo Conti (1937) *Diritto Consuetidinaro Del' Eritrea*, Firenze.

14

The National Conference as a New Mode of Constitutionalism

Aminata Diaw

In the preliminary pages of his book, *Mirages of Democracy in Sub-Saharan Francophone Africa,* Francis Akindés takes note of the many-pronged challenges that Africa has had to confront: slavery and colonisation; harmful independence and development ideologies, and democratisation and economic revival.[1] In Francophone Africa, the national conference seemed to provide a solution to at least one of these challenges—namely the challenge presented by the effort to revive run-down national economies, and to democratise the polity, or at a minimum to foster a transition to progressive constitutionalism. Does this suggest that the national conference represents a new mode of indicating Africa's integration into the 'progressive globalisation of liberal constitutionalism ... an important characteristic of democratic civilisation?'[2]

Beyond the participation of Africa in the 'globalisation of constitutionalism,' the challenge that faces African countries today is to strengthen constitutionalism, by placing an emphasis on that which is usually not captured by the mere process of political change. Beyond the myth and ritual, we should find out whether, in the process of constitution making, there's no shifting of the reasoning which demonstrates that the restoration of political legitimacy does not only entail power sharing. Rather, it should be linked to the moment of displacement of authoritarianism and a new structuring of representability. It must also be wary of the imposition of foreign interests in the guise of adopting 'international' standards.

This perspective enables as to guard against any legal oversimplification. Indeed, we could have considered the main characteristic of constitutionalism underscored by Cabanis and Martin: 'Today, it (constitutionalism?) forms the very basis of legitimacy of power. It expresses what the political class believes in, translates power relations and reflects external influences'.[3] In this chapter the concern is with two main points: first, how can the national conference be understood as the representation of the legitimising of power, outside the usual parameters of the law and as the basic constitutional document? Secondly, albeit paradoxically, we will try to see how the constitutional space functions as a space of confrontation between legitimacy and exclusion.

New democratic legitimacies, or old historical paths?

The Cameroonian writer F. Eboussi Boulaga takes note of the philosophy which is at work in the event that constitutes the national conference. For him, 'the national conference seeks to ground itself in liberty as a way of life; it can not evade the responsibility of laying conditions for a political economy of liberty.'[4] In actual fact, it has meant constructing something extra as one works with others. The euphoria of promises of democratisation, retrieved speech, expressed aspirations, all bring hope to the continent. A new dawn seems to be breaking, and with it, the necessity to have new rules for the game, a new institutional framework which will house the wind of legitimacy and lawfulness.[5]

One of the main characteristics of national conferences resides in the constitutional changes that accompany them. In Mali, Togo, Niger or even the Congo (Brazzaville), the will to break away from the old order was translated into the necessity to make a new constitution.[6] Often, draft constitutions have been written by commissions that have had protracted deliberations. These are later subjected to the people's approval, through referenda. Constitution making in fact responds to two major demands: the delegitimisation of the state in Africa and the repeated violation of human rights. In addition, there is a need to define and guarantee the conditions of the state of law, the natural framework for guaranteeing human rights. Decades of authoritarianism on the continent underscored the imperative to control the phenomenon of presidentialism, and to leave presidents with only limited powers. If we analyse the constitution of Mali that was adopted by referendum, we notice that the preamble and the first twenty-four articles all deal with fundamental human rights.[7]

Besides the affirmation of citizen's rights and freedoms and his or her responsibilities, the basic Malien text seeks to mark an irreversible departure from the past. The text recognises the people's right, through Article 21, to use civil disobedience to preserve the republican state: hence, the coup d'etat becomes a crime against the people. This is not the only means of ensuring that constitutional provisions can caution us against history. At the executive level, the president of the republic is eligible for re-election only once. Furthermore, he/she is obliged to declare his or her property and he or she must update this record every year. Through a censure motion the assembly can even countermand decisions that were traditionally even the responsibility of government.[8] The limits of these sanctions are nevertheless undercut by provisions that harken back to the authoritarian past. Thus, the same constitution recognises the powers of the president to dissolve the National Assembly. The executive is the power that determines national policies, and it still controls the army and the administration.

In the process of holding national conferences, there is a clear will to break away from the logic of the arbitrary, which, in the recent past annihilated the participatory capacity of citizens across Francophone Africa. Alongside the effort to design executives characterised by a more limited presidentialism, there was the will to think through the classic institutions in an unprecedented manner. Such was the case with the Constitutional Court in Mali which was conferred with the classic mission of overseeing the constitutionality of laws and ensuring the settlement of disputes between institutions. Other less ordinary institutions cater for a higher degree of representativity by citizens or civil society: for example, the CENI supervises, organises and monitors elections while the Economic, Social and Cultural Council targets a more democratic participation of civil society. The High Council of Local Government must be consulted by the government on all matters pertaining to local and regional development policies. Multipartyism and freedom of expression which are imbedded in the constitution have necessitated the establishment of regulatory bodies such as the High Council of Communication and the National Committee for Equal Access to the Media.

Constitution making in Mali, as was the case in other Francophone African countries, expressed a clear concern not simply with the principle of pluralism, but also for the modalities of its operation. Hence, there is an interdiction against any party identifying itself with a specific ethnic group or region.

Between legitimacy and exclusion: Constitutional space as a point of confrontation

Constitution making which is accompanied by national conferences can often be considered as a process of shaping norms and procedures of political competition, or as a moment of defining the conditions of the state of law and the relationship between the different powers vying for power or its control. This normative perception should not, however, exclude the dynamics of social and political reality. We should also try to observe whether the process of constitution making has not been a means of establishing forced relationships in the political arena—a legalisation of exclusion—by using the game of balancing between the two founding categories of democracy, that is to say, representation and legitimacy.

This hypothesis can be confirmed through the sociography of the new procedures of democratisation that has been elaborated by Francis Akindés.[9] Akindés clearly shows that the national conference can itself prove to be a procedure of exclusion of certain segments of society from political competition, and worse still to ensure that such exclusion is incorporated within the constitutional texts that emerge from the conference.[10] His analysis is based on the Beninoise model, but it is a point that applies with equal validity to so many of the countries that engaged in the process of constitutional reform under the rubric of national conferences:

It is fairly clear that the modelling of democratic transition in Benin was highly influenced by the interests of the former colonial powers. On the other hand, there was the imperious necessity to knock out the Dahomeén Communist Party, (PCD) which had particularly distinguished itself in its unyielding opposition to the Military - Marxist dictatorship of Mathieu Kérékou. This exclusion was facilitated by an international context where bells "were tolling for communist ideas" and especially the obstinate of general armed insurrection, a strategy that was acclaimed by PCD.

The above two elements were to justify the expansion of representation namely, the people, the diaspora, the intellectuals and religious groups among others. In other words, constitutional space was expanded to incorporate the active social and civic forces that were trying to influence the process in Benin. However, the expansion included the return to the political scene, of an old guard that had already held political power and authority in the past. For Akindés, the strategy of the national conference was decided in such a way that it's main political and diplomatic objective was to counter the incisive opposition of the PCD. With the strong support of the media, the return of the old political guard was assured. It is also worth noting that this old guard had friends in influential places elsewhere, such that their links to the Elysée palace (the French ex-colonial power) served them in good stead. There was thus a meeting of the minds between the internal and external actors which served to influence the outcome of the process and ensure a result that led to a reversion of political power to the old guard.[11] This necessity of loyalty to French interests dominated the transition period in Benin. It is no wonder that the formula of the National Conference adopted in Benin was being proposed as a model for Francophone Africa!

Turning more specifically, to the issue of exclusion, the Beninoise process illustrated the subtle manner in which this was executed. Article 44 of the constitution illustrates how the exclusion that we are analysing here found refuge within the constitutional domain. Indeed, the conditions for candidature for the post of president of the republic did not respond to any exclusively normative logic. By affirming that 'no one below 40 years of age or above 70 years at the time of depositing his candidature can present himself for the function of president of the Republic,'[12] conference delegates wanted to eliminate former presidents (like Emile Derlin Zinson) who had demonstrated a certain capacity for mobilisation of the people. While it is true that the age limit can be considered as biologically objective; in the Beninois context, Akindés compares it to the denial of the intelligence of a sovereign people.[13]

The procedure of constitutional exclusion is completed by the argument of physical or mental wellbeing that is not judged by a medical consensus. The fact that the opinion expressed on the candidates by a team of doctors appointed and sworn in by the Constitutional Court is not taken into account, works here as tangible evidence of constitutional manipulation and the reality of political power relations.

One may think that Akindés hypothesis of interpretation makes no concession within the perspective of the procedure of constitutional exclusion. But it seems to be corroborated by the arguments of Richard Banégas, at least in two important respects.[14] Like Akindés, Banégas notes that during the national conference, the PCD boycotted the proceedings and was marginalised, because of its opposition to the Kérékou regime particularly in the 1970s and 1980s.[15] In any case, the hypothesis of a passive revolution as advanced by R. Banégas could be taken into account as ulterior proof of exclusion and the reduction of representation, focusing on the educated elite; the war of quotas for nominating delegates to the national conference has thus contributed to further complicating the regimentation of the elite. In one way or another, it would not be pertinent to limit ourselves to the legal procedure of constitution making: It would be more important to examine the procedure of excluding the past legitimacies and the establishment of new ones who had every reason to find solace in the constitutional text.

In the case of Congo which presents altogether different issues, Charles Bawao demonstrates how the national conference was 'envisaged as a conducive and non exclusive framework, of inventing a new public space from a negotiated consensus in the spirit of republicanism.'[16] Nevertheless, through the process of constitution making, the conference became the space for the confrontation of legitimacies and a place where power relations took shape. He cites several elements of incoherence to elaborate his interpretation of what took place, resulting in what he describes as the 'conceded constitution,' which was founded on the principle of the imbalance of powers. The head of state who convened the national conference was able to retain his position, although the conference forced a reduction of his prerogatives. Indeed, although he continues as president, he does not really govern. At the same time, this reflects how the conference sought to mark some distance from the old order, with the acknowledged intention of establishing a new one. Hence, the head of state retained the responsibility of managing foreign policy and the accreditation of ambassadors, but the power of appointment was devolved to the transitional government. At the same time, this reflected a certain incoherence, and led to the appointment of 'advisory ministers' in all embassies, something which was not provided for in the text of the constitution, but which was clearly an attempt by the presidency to retain certain vestiges of his old authority.

Another instance of incoherence symbolising the confrontation of legitimacies and power relations is contained in the following illustration: although the president of the republic, and no other institution was known to embody national unity, the function of electing the head of state and the transitional government was paradoxically conferred upon the High Council of the Republic. There was no possibility of appeal against its ruling. It is to also be noted that the prime minister of the transitional government was made accountable to the High Council of the republic but has no constitutional obligation to be accountable to the head of state. It would be grotesque to think that these textual incoherencies were unintentional—the mere results of chance; rather, they clearly illustrate the confrontation of legitimacies that came to the fore in the process. It is obvious that the construction of the domain of normative validity of the political order with regards to its organisation and operation, was, in the context of the national conference, more marked by power stakes, rather than by democratic pre-occupation, even though the different stakeholders opposed their democratic sensitivity.

This tug-of-war between political stakes and democratic interests in some cases diverted or perverted the constitution making process. For the rest, C. Bawao notes bitterly about the Congo that: '... the national sovereign conference, basing itself on a legally confused mechanism, did not manage to either pre-figure, nor promote tolerance, respect for others, (or) the right to a difference....' There were further problems, for example, the non-consensual procedure of adopting the Fundamental Act, and especially its spirit, which was intentionally confused, reflect, with no exaggeration, the bad will that existed at the conference. The story which followed the national sovereign conference unfortunately proved C. Bawao right given the breakdown and civil war that followed. Although not as intense, the situation is not only specific to Congo.

Togo is another case illustrating the connection between political space and democratic struggle. The war without concession in which the political actors are involved takes on various forms within the constitutional domain. Article 61 of the draft constitution indicated that the members of the executive during the transitional period—the guarantors of impartial election—couldn't present a candidate for the presidency during the period immediately following the transition. This constitutional provision which aims at guaranteeing only temporary legitimacy to transitional authorities has not left the president of the Republic and the prime minister of the government indifferent: both demonstrated an undeclared objective of going round that provision. The parties were aware of this old principle and as prevention against it, they proposed a supplement to Article 61: a modification in the electoral code fixing the minimum age for candidates at 45 years. However, this was less of a legal provision than a strategy of exclusion since the targeted victim was

Prime Minister Kofi Koffigoh who was 44 years old at the time of the election. We can link this with the 1992 provisional report about the referendum on the new constitution on the one hand, and the fact that the HCR rescinded the draft article of the new constitution which required member of the military to resign before presenting themselves as presidential candidates.

Of course, President Eyadema duly obeyed the edict, resigning from his position as a general and declaring himself a civilian candidate. These elements were indicators of Eyadema's capacity to reverse the situation, through the atmosphere of terror which has been maintained. It also enabled him to retrieve the institutional prerogatives that he had been deprived of. In so doing, he cited the 'mediocrity of the managerial capacity of the political opposition' putting to doubt 'the real capacities of the new political actors in matters of political precasting and strategising.'

The institutionalisation of democracy in Togo (despite the national conference) visibly failed. However, the principal cause of this failure was the fact of an underestimation of what the army was going to lose with this civilian coup d'etat represented by the national conference. Moreover, there was also a failure to answer the unavoidable question for the democratic movement: 'the articulation of global political processes of democratic transition with procedures that are specific to the military institution.'

The pronouncements of President Eyadema to senior officers in his government/army confirms this: 'we must not just let go, at least we must show them that we are still an army in solidarity. We accept to resume taking orders, but we will cease to when we will decide, for the honour of our bodies, our children and to avoid future suffering... Think about your promotion, your own peace, your retirement.' The monopoly of legal violence by the army, the central element of the former party-state, seems not to have been sufficiently addressed by the political actors of the transition period. Beyond the military question, taking into account the way political actors react to constitution making, how they bend the laws by manipulation and adjustment, one cannot help but wonder if the force of law is not just another name for political interest. Mamadou Diouf aptly captures this point with the following trite observation: 'it seems that if we effectively pay attention to the logic applied during crisis management, we note that personal African powers are preoccupied with finding constitutional solutions to social movements and conflicts even if the constitutions are tailored to fit the powers in place.'

In a more general manner, and still in relation to national conferences, the hypothesis of constitutionalism as a space of confrontation for contending legitimacies and for translating power into legal form, enables us to reiterate the fundamental question already posed by Ben Rhomdane. That question is whether the political actors have the capacity to bear the institutionalisation of the democratic process in a sustainable manner given their central or secondary position in social reproduction? What the examples explored in this chapter demonstrate is that there is still a considerable distance yet to be traversed in achieving a resolution to this paradox.

Conclusion

The remark by Achille Mbembe on the non-existence of democracy in Africa is only valid in the sense that it reminds us of the necessity of reference to a democratic culture. Constitution-making emanating from the various national conferences at one time gave us hope. However, the facts have proved that the establishment and guarantee of the state of law or multipartyism, or even of the separation of powers can only be achieved by people who are themselves imbued with the spirit of these institutions. While the sprouting of the phenomenon of national conferences throughout the many Francophone African countries that experienced them was a very welcome development, their outcome can at best be considered mixed. Needless to say, as a study in the paradox of constitutional enactment in a context of serious political contestation, many useful lessons can be discerned. What remains to be witnessed is how long the manipulation of constitutional processes can remain a part of the African political economy without requiring us to revert to the drawing board.

Notes

1. Sindjoum, (1997): 25.
2. cf. Boulaga, (1993).
3. Cabanis, (1999): 10.
4. Mbembe, (1995): 43.
5. Igue (1992).
6. Degni-Sgui (1998).
7. Akindés, op.cit., 53.
8. Bowao (1995): 14.
9. *Ibid.*, 15.
10. *Outre la population, le HCR eu aussi à subir la terreur militaire, le premier ministre en ce qui le concerne finit par rallier le camp presidential.*
11. *Démocraties Africaines, op. cit.*, 24.
12. Akindés, *op. cit.*, 24.
13. Diouf, (1998): 36.
14. *Le Monde*, 10-11 janvier 1993.
15. Diouf, *op. cit.*, 17.
16. Rhomadane, (1992).

References

Boulaga, F. Eboussi, (1993) *Les Conférences nationales en Afrique noire, une affaire à suivre*, Paris: Karthala.

Bowao, C. (1995) *Congo: conférence nationale souveraine, Ethnopartisme et Démocratie. La ruse historique?* in *Démocraties Africaine*, no. 4 oct-nov., 14.

Cabanis, A. et M.L. Martin, (1999), *les constitutions d'Afrique francophone: 2 volution récents*, Paris: Karthala.

Degni-Sgui, R. (1998), *Les droits de l'homme en Afrique francophone*, Abidjan.

Diouf, M. (1998) *Libéralisations politiques out transitions démocratiques: Perspectives africaines*, Nouvelles Pistes, no1, Dakar: CODESRIA.

Igue, J. O. (1992), *Enjeu national, Enjeu démocratique, Septiémen Assemblée Générale du CODESRIA*, Fevrier.

Mbembe, Achille, (1995), *ne semble pas succomber à cette euphorie. Dans sa contributio au colloque Etat, Démocratie, Sociétes et Culture en Afrique en Octobre, il affirmait sans équivoque? contrairement à l'illusion genenerale, il n'existe aucun regime democratique en Afrique noire, editions Democraties Africanines*.

Rhomadane, M. Ben (1992), *Mouvements sociaux et Processus democratiques en Afrique, 7o Assemblée générale du CODESRIA*, 10-14 février.

Sindjoun, L. (1997) 'La formation du patrimoine commun des sociétés politiques-Eléments pour une théorie de la civilisation politique internationale,' *Série des monographies 2*, Dakar: CODESRIA.

15

The Challenges of Constitution-making and Implementation in Uganda

Benjamin J. Odoki

The making of a new constitution in Uganda marked an important watershed in the history of the country. It demonstrated the desire of the people to fundamentally change their system of governance into a truly democratic one. The process gave the people an opportunity to make a fresh start by reviewing their past experiences, identifying the root causes of their problems, learning lessons from past mistakes and making a concerted effort to provide genuine solutions for their better governance and future development. The constitution-making process was thus a major step towards the democratisation of the country which had experienced nearly thirty years of oppression, tyranny and exploitation. It restored Uganda to the constitutional path. The process has been hailed as unique and unprecedented in the history of constitution-making in Africa and elsewhere. It was an epic process lasting over seven years commencing in 1988 when the Uganda Constitutional Commission was established until 1995 when the new constitution was promulgated by the Constituent Assembly. The distinct characteristic of the process was the popular participation by the people that was achieved through wide consultation and national public debate. The process of popular participation contributed to the building of a national consensus on the most suitable form of governance and promoted the general acceptability and legitimacy of the constitution. Such has been the interest in Uganda's constitution making process that it has been the subject of considerable interest and study by scholars and constitutional reformers both within and outside Uganda.[1]

The new constitution enacted in October 1995 was equally a unique and home-grown document deeply influenced by the history, culture, values and aspirations of the people of Uganda and the need to strike genuine compromises between diverse interest groups. The provisions of the constitution were by and large based on the wishes of the people as expressed in their views to the constitutional commission. In the Constituent Assembly, most of the provisions in the constitution were adopted by the delegates through consensus. However, a few controversial provisions were resolved through majority vote and some of these continue to attract controversy, debate, and challenge in courts of law. The controversial provisions mainly relate to the political system especially the issue of suspension of political party activities, the referendum on political systems, the entrenchment of the movement system in the constitution, federalism, and the issue of land.

The implementation of the constitution poses perhaps more difficult challenges than its making. There is a need to make the constitution a dynamic instrument, and a living institution, in the minds and hearts of all Ugandans. The constitution must be internalised and understood in order for the people to truly respect, observe and uphold it. It must be implemented in both the spirit and to the letter. There is a need to establish and nurture democratic institutions to promote democratic values and practices within the country. It is only then that a culture of constitutionalism can be promoted amongst the people and their leaders.

This chapter examines the challenges and problems that were experienced by the major actors in the constitution-making process: the NRM government, the Uganda Constitutional Commission, the Constituent Assembly and the people, including civil society. It also attempts to identify the major challenges facing the country in implementing the new instrument.

Historical background

Uganda has had three constitutions since independence, none of which satisfactorily answered the needs and aspirations of the people. The manner in which the constitutions were made and unmade, the suitability of the institutions and processes that were established, and the extent to which they were viable and acceptable have long been a subject of debate and controversy. The major problem was that Ugandans failed to agree on the most appropriate socioeconomic and political framework for their governance. In the result, the country experienced a crisis of political and constitutional instability that lasted thirty years. To address the above problem the NRM government initiated the constitution-making process in 1988 in order to provide an adequate opportunity for freely determining the system of governance. On 8 October 1995, the process was successfully concluded and the people of Uganda promulgated their fourth constitution after a lengthy and wide consultation.

Uganda as a nation is a creature of British colonial administration. The 56 different indigenous communities now inhabiting the country were brought together during the colonial period following the declaration of a British protectorate over Uganda in 1894. These peoples consisted of four main language groups, the Bantu in the south and west, the Nilotics and Nilo-Hamites in the north and north-east and the Sudanic group in the north-west. These ethnic groups which had reached different levels of political development in their social organisation can be divided into two main categories. The first group comprised the Bantu societies of the lacustrine area which included the Baganda and Banyoro who had highly developed centralised governments under a series of kingdoms. The second group consisted of the segmented non-Bantu peoples who lived to the north of the Nile, where the largest political unit was in general the clan. These societies had different languages, cultures and social systems. The colonial administration imposed its own system of administration on these groups of peoples. A system of indirect rule was established whereby the British administered the protectorate through the local chiefs and kings. In effect the kings surrendered their sovereignty in return for British 'protection.'

Uganda regained her independence on 9 October 1962 with all the trappings of constitutionalism. A constitution had been worked out, the result of negotiation among the major political actors of the day. The constitutional arrangements were aimed at working out political formulae for balancing conflicting interests of the political elite of the day. The constitutional formulae entailed a periodically elected parliament, a cabinet drawn from and responsible to parliament, federal and quasi federal status for Buganda and the kingdom areas, and unitary status for the rest of the country. Powers for the major organs of government were defined. On the first anniversary of independence, the original 1962 constitution was amended to provide for a ceremonial president to replace the governor- general. The Kabaka of Buganda was elected first president.

In 1966, following a confrontation between the then Prime Minister Apolo Milton Obote and Sir Edward Mutesa, president of Uganda and Kabaka of Buganda, the 1962 constitution was abrogated by Obote and replaced by the interim constitution of 1966 which was adopted without protest by members of the National Assembly. This constitution came to known as the 'pigeon-hole constitution.' Obote became president and the post of prime minister was abolished. In 1967 Obote introduced another constitution that was republican in nature. It abolished kingdoms and aspects of federalism and turned Uganda into a unitary state. The president was given excessive powers over appointments and making laws through ordinances and detention without trial. Although the constitution recognised the multi-party system of government, opposition political parties were later banned, effectively transforming Uganda into a single-party state.

While Obote was in Singapore attending a Commonwealth conference in early 1971, General Idi Amin staged a coup d'etat and became President. He suspended the constitution and political institutions and unleashed a reign of terror and murder. Idi Amin was in 1979 overthrown by a combination of forces from Tanzania and Ugandan exiles there who had formed the Uganda National Liberation Front (UNLF). After unsuccessful coalition governments by Yusuf Lule and Godfrey Binaisa a general election was organised by the Military Commission under Paulo Muwanga in December 1980. Four parties namely the Uganda Peoples Congress (UPC), the Democratic Party (DP), the Conservative Party (CP) and the Uganda Patriotic Movement (UPM) contested the elections. The UPC won the elections, but the results were disputed by the other parties. The UPM leadership under Yoweri Museveni went to the bush and waged a guerrilla war against the Obote government for five years.

In July 1985, Obote was overthrown by his two generals, Tito Lutwa Okello and Bazillio Olara Okello. A peace accord was signed in Nairobi between the Okello junta and Museveni, but the agreement failed to halt the war or establish an enduring settlement. In January 1986, the National Resistance Army (NRA) of Yoweri Museveni captured power in Kampala. A broad based government was formed under the National Resistance Movement (NRM). It included various socio-political forces in the country. Its blue print for running the interim administration was the *Ten Point Programme* which included restoration of democracy, security, human rights and economic reconstruction under a mixed economy on its agenda. Political party activities were suspended and a no-party system introduced. Its main organs were the Resistance Councils (RCs) from the village level to the national level with elected committees. These RCs had administrative, political and judicial functions and formed the core of the NRM system of government.[2]

Democratic change and constitutional reform

It is necessary to identify and recognise the need for constitutional change in order to launch it successfully. The objectives to be achieved must be clearly articulated and accepted. People will not support a cause which has not been properly defined. In Uganda, there was general agreement for constitutional reform largely because the three constitutional arrangements had been made with little input from the population, and secondly the provisions they contained were not democratic and modern enough to answer current interests and aspirations. What was not agreed was the nature and extent of reform. Some groups like the monarchists/federalists advocated the immediate restoration of the 1962 constitution that had guaranteed their cherished institutions. The multipartyists especially the UPC advocated for the simple amendment of the 1967 constitution, and not its complete replacement. It was the challenge of those in charge of the process to convince the different forces that ultimately it would be the people to decide.

Democracy is normally achieved after a protracted struggle. Such struggle needs leadership and popular support. The NRM government had gone to the bush to fight for democracy. The government formed the vanguard to champion the struggle for constitutional reform after the NRM had liberated the country. Therefore at the time the NRM assumed power, there was a leadership committed to constitutional reform, as well as popular support for the process. Because the NRM government was committed to constitutional reform, it provided the resources necessary for the exercise and an enabling environment for free public participation and debate.

The preparation of a new constitution that would correct the mistakes of the past as demanded by the people was high on the agenda during the armed struggle by the NRM. Its vision was to see a popular constitution evolved by the people themselves that would consolidate the fundamental change in the politics of Uganda, promised on its capture of power in January 1986. One of the basic objectives of this change was to return power to the people to take charge of their own destiny. Since a constitution was the basic decision of the people on how they wanted to live and be governed, it was absolutely necessary to involve them in the formulation of that socioeconomic and political framework so that it could form a binding and acceptable social contract for their governance. The constitution would institutionalise, regularise and legitimise the use and exercise of state power. Secondly, since the NRM government was an interim administration committed to returning the country to a truly democratic system of government, it was necessary to ensure that a democratic constitution was put in place during the period of transition, to guarantee and promote democratic, as well as other common values and goals, upon which the people could be generally united.

Strategies and models for reform

For any programme to be successfully implemented there must be a realistic and acceptable plan of action to define the strategies necessary for the execution of the programme. The plan of action must be acceptable to the various stakeholders. If it is imposed there may not be full participation in the programme. Neither is there likely to be widespread acceptance of the outcome. Uganda was faced with the challenge of designing a realistic and acceptable plan of action for the constitution-making process.

The Plan of Action was first published in the Uganda *National Resistance News* in 1981 during the early stages of the bush war. The NRM viewed its main political task after defeating Obote as the organisation of a speedy return of democratic government and 'as part of laying the groundwork for returning Uganda to democratic government, the interim administration shall see to it that a new constitution based on popular will is drafted and promulgated by a Constituent Assembly elected by the people themselves.'[3] The consultation was to be carried out by a constitutional committee which would prepare a draft constitution.

Why did the NRM government adopt this model? Three options were open to government. The first was for the government to prepare a draft constitution and present it to the legislative body of the time, the National Resistance Council (NRC)—for debate and adoption. Such an option would have excluded the majority of Ugandans from participating in the process. The second was to convene a national conference of all the significant socio-political forces in the country to draft and adopt the new constitution, as has been done in several Francophone African countries such as Benin, Togo, Congo and Zaire (now the Democratic Republic of Congo). This method would also have excluded the majority of the people from directly participating in the process. The third alternative was to split the process into two stages. The first would be the establishment of a committee of experts to gather the views of the people and draw up proposals and a draft constitution. The second stage would be the establishment of an elected constituent assembly to debate and adopt the constitution. This is the methodology that has been adopted by most Anglophone countries like Nigeria and Ghana and to some extent in Zambia and Tanzania.[4]

The third methodology was adopted in order to give the people of Uganda ample opportunity to formulate and promulgate a constitution of their own choice. The draft constitution would be formulated by a constitutional commission composed of experts, after collecting the views of the people, and it would be adopted by a constituent assembly consisting of representatives of the people. This methodology would achieve two objectives. First, the constitution would be freely negotiated by the people themselves and not merely imposed upon them. Secondly, the constitution would be made not only by a few, but all Ugandans.

Institutional mechanisms to manage reform: The Uganda Constitutional Commission

In 1986 the NRM government established a ministry of constitutional affairs to make appropriate arrangements for the preparation of a new constitution and to oversee the process. The first major institutional mechanism was the Uganda Constitutional Commission that was established by Statute No.5 of 1988. The law set out the purpose for establishing the commission, its composition, and terms of reference. The commission consisted of twenty-one members appointed by the president in consultation with the minister responsible for constitutional affairs.[5] The members were to be appointed on the basis of personal integrity, professional skill and expertise. The commission had a chairperson who was a justice of the Supreme Court, a vice chairperson who was a professor of political science and a secretary who was a professor of history. Other members were highly qualified in various fields and represented the national diversity of Uganda. Two of its members were women. The commissioners were required to perform their functions impartially and in practice enjoyed complete independence from interference from any quarter.

The appointment of the commission by the government did not pass without criticism from several quarters. It was alleged that the members had been hand picked to rubber stamp a constitution already prepared by the NRM government. It was their contention that most members were pro-NRM and not representative of all interest groups. The critics would have preferred members to be nominated by various interest groups. Such a procedure is no doubt more transparent but it can also lead to a stalemate. The government however positively responded to these criticisms by appointing representatives of certain interest groups which felt they had not been represented. The commission therefore appeared fairly representative and balanced. As President Museveni himself has explained on the selection of commissioners:

> They were selected because they represented the broad spectrum of opinions in the country. Some were identified with the idea of a movement structure of governance, some were from the old political parties, some were from the monarchist groups, and some were from the churches.[6]

The functions of the commission were to review the constitution of Uganda with a view to formulating proposals for a new constitution, and to prepare a draft document for debate. In order to do so the commission was required to 'seek the views of the general public through the holding of public meetings and debates, seminars, workshops and any other form of collecting views,' and 'to stimulate public discussion and awareness of constitutional issues.'[7] The commission was required to submit its final report to the minister responsible for constitutional affairs within two years or such further period as the minister found necessary. It was found necessary to extend the period for a total of two years due to the need to give the people adequate time to contribute their views and for the commission to do justice to those views.

Apart from the above operational terms of reference, the statute contained some of the basic objectives that the new constitution should achieve namely to:

- guarantee the national independence and territorial integrity and sovereignty of Uganda;
- establish free and democratic system of government that will guarantee the fundamental rights and freedoms of the people;
- create viable political institutions that will ensure maximum consensus and orderly succession to government;

- recognise and demarcate division of responsibility among the state organs of the executive, the legislature and the judiciary, and create viable checks and balances between them;
- endeavour to develop a system of government that ensures people's participation in the governance of their country;
- endeavour to develop a democratic free and fair electoral system that will ensure true people's representation in the legislative and at other levels;
- establish and uphold the principle of public accountability of all holders of public offices and political posts;
- guarantee the independence of the judiciary.[8]

The above provisions contain the basic principles of liberal democracy and constitutionalism. It was therefore abundantly clear that the new constitution should be grounded on democracy. During the constitutional debate more political and socio-economic goals for the new constitution were identified to include the following:

- restore peace, security and stability in Uganda;
- foster unity and national consciousness amongst the people of Uganda;
- promote socio-economic development and social justice in the country;
- promote regional and international co-operation.

On the basis of the above terms of reference, the commission interpreted its mandate to first of all carry out wide consultations with the people of Uganda and secondly, to formulate a democratic and popular constitution based on national consensus and guarantee the promotion of stability, peace, unity, progress and social justice.

Methodology, programme and activities

The major challenge faced by the commission in designing its methodology was to ensure that the population was given adequate opportunity to participate in the process to produce a constitution of their choice. To do so the people had to be well informed about the nature of the constitution, its content and why a new one was being made so as to contribute from a point of knowledge and make informed decisions. The people had to be given adequate time to discuss the issues involved among themselves and prepare their submissions for presentation to the commission. The second challenge was to collect the views from the entire country and document them, and the third was to carefully study and analyse all the submissions received. The final challenge was to draw up proposals for a new constitution in a final report, and to prepare a draft constitution on the basis of those proposals. In order to carry out its task the commission drew up a programme and timetable of work.[9]

The commission spent the first two months planning the entire programme, holding internal seminars for the commissioners, and preparing materials and the methodology for educating the people. The first education programmes to be held were at the district level. All 34 districts were visited by commissioners and seminars were held for each district for two days. All the leaders–both local and national–representatives of civil society and education institutions attended. A total of over 10,000 participants attended these seminars. This was an important national coverage which proved beyond doubt that the exercise was not only serious but also national. The commissioners also received suggestions on how to improve the organisation and effectiveness of the exercise.

In response to the district seminars the commission prepared information materials to enlighten the people and guide them in discussing constitutional issues. The constitutions of 1962 and 1967 were reprinted. Three booklets, namely, *Guidelines on Constitutional Issues, Guiding Questions on Constitutional Issues, and Brochure on Preparation of Memoranda* were prepared. The documents contained the constitutional agenda for public debate and contribution of views. They listed and explained 29 constitutional issues on which the views of the population were being sought. All these materials were subsequently distributed free of charge to all seminar participants, resistance committee members and other organised bodies, and individuals throughout the country and abroad. The documents supplemented the commission's programmes on the media especially Radio Uganda and Uganda Television in English and local languages.

After the district seminars, the commission conducted sub-county seminars, and these formed the core of the entire exercise of educating and sensitising the people from the grassroots. They were held in the 782 sub-counties throughout the country. Throughout this period and subsequently, the commission organised various seminars for institutions of higher learning and for major social groups in the country. These seminars lasted one or two days.[10] In addition to seminars organised by the commission, many Ugandans of various levels and interest groups organised their own gatherings to educate themselves and enable them to discuss constitutional issues. Finally, to supplement debates and seminars in schools and colleges an essay competition on constitutional issues was organised from May, 1990 to December 1991. Its objectives were to provide an additional channel to the youth in the process of making a new constitution, to stimulate awareness, debate and discussion of constitutional issues, and to encourage the youth to understand their national constitution and to respect it. The students were divided into four categories from primary to university level.[11]

After completing the educational exercise which generated an open public constitutional debate throughout the country, the commission embarked on the exercise of collecting views from the sub-counties and the general public in May 1991. All sub-counties were re-visited, some more than once. People were mobilised to freely submit their views. The commissioners themselves visited the sub-counties to collect the views of the people.[12]

The results of the commission's outreach activities were most encouraging. Of particular interest were the views from the ordinary people at RC I and II, which made up over 10,000 memoranda. Ugandan communities abroad actively participated in the debate and submitted memoranda. Apart from the Uganda People's Congress (UPC) as a party, there was no group in Uganda that refused to participate or had a negative attitude towards the constitution-making process. The submission of memoranda from the various parts of Uganda appeared to be fairly balanced even from areas where there was insecurity.

Study and analysis of views

The task of studying and analysing the submissions received from the public was enormous and challenging, but was necessary if the constitution was to reflect the general views of the people. Therefore the commission had to examine each submission presented to the commission. To do so, many submissions had to be typed out or translated into English to facilitate study by all the commissioners. In addition, the views had to be categorised under each of the twenty nine constitutional issues on which views had been sought. Issues on which there was consensus or which remained controversial also had to be identified. Additional research and the technical staff had to be recruited to speed up research and computerisation of materials, because pressure was mounting to bring the constitution making exercise to an end.

On many issues it was clear from the memoranda that there was a consensus. There was consensus on the issue if it received overwhelming support or rejection in all categories of the various sources received. An issue was supported by a majority when it received majority support from all categories of sources received. A controversial issue was one which received majority support in some categories and a significant minority support in some categories or one with strong minority opposition from all categories.

On the controversial and highly sensitive issues, the commission undertook a statistical analysis to give a picture of the frequency of support for the main viewpoints on each of the controversial issues in the views submitted. The issues on which statistical analysis was undertaken included the adoption of a national language, aspects of citizenship requirements such as dual citizenship; enforcement of human rights; choice of political system;

restoration of traditional rulers; choice of federal or unitary form of government, choice of electoral systems, aspects of legislature, aspects of the presidency, and the issue of safeguards for the new constitution. This elaborate system of analysing people's views was put in place to ally fears that public views would be ignored or rigged out.[13]

The commission first prepared draft chapters of the report based on the constitutional issues identified at the commencement of the exercise. Several committees consisting of a group of commissioners were formed to carry out this task. The draft chapters and recommendations were presented to the plenary session of all commissioners and discussed. Subsequently, the entire report was edited for publication by the commission. It must be emphasised that the recommendations were based on the views of the people not on the preference of the members of the commission. The draft constitution was prepared from the approved final recommendations of the commission. The draft constitution was initially prepared by a team of commissioners and legislative drafting experts. The draft was then discussed chapter by chapter until the final text was approved.

The draft constitution

A constitution is a long-term national strategy for the socio-economic and political development of a country. But it must also address both short-term and medium term objectives. It must balance stability and change, idealism and reality, rights and duties and powers and responsibilities. It must be precise but coherent, comprehensive but viable, and must meet the expectations of a large majority of the people without ignoring the interests of the minority. These concerns affect both the form and the substance of the document. Some challenges of form which the commission faced included how long the constitution should be and how much the constitution should contain. The second issue was whether two documents should be written, one interim and the second permanent. The commission decided to abandon the idea of an interim constitution to cater for the transition to democracy in favour of drawing up a single comprehensive document with interim or transitional provisions included in the transitional chapter. The commission was also initially disposed to writing a short, precise constitution in simple language, but due to the vast number of constitutional issues raised by the people and the need to address them fully, it prepared a fairly long draft constitution.

After studying the main sources of information used by the commission, namely the 25,547 submissions, the commissions observations and analysis of society, including its culture, common history and aspirations, the past three constitutional arrangements since independence, and a comparative study of constitutional arrangements of other countries, the commission deduced the following theoretical or philosophical bases for formulating its recommendations:

- The constitution should provide institutional mechanisms for strengthening national unity taking into account the cultural, religious, regional, gender, class, age and physical diversities of Uganda's peoples.
- While taking into account Uganda's social, cultural and political diversities, the constitution should transcend interests of narrow groups.
- The constitution should identify those Ugandan residual values which can serve as firm foundations for the new constitution.
- There should be efforts to provide for a balance of forces that no one single socio-political force or institutional structure can manipulate such resources as it has to subvert the constitution and dominate other groups and structures
- A new constitutional order should ensure that institutional structures are viable, coherent and integrated to promote a culture of constitutionalism and ultimate socio-economic and political objectives which guide future development.
- There should be constitutional mechanisms for ensuring transfer of power by peaceful and democratic means.
- Since the NRM assumed power, institutional frameworks have been established and appear to be gaining legitimacy. There should be serious evaluation of these to see the extent to which they may be integrated into the new constitutional order.
- The new constitutional order should come to terms with Uganda's past and present and respond to its aspirations for the future.[14]

The commission's mandate was to make constitutional proposals based on the views of the people. However, while on many issues there was national consensus, several others remained a subject of controversy. The commission had to devise a formula that would strike the right balance between conflicting views in order to promote compromise and reconciliation.

The failure to generate adequate consensus on several of the constitutional issues despite a lengthy and serious public debate demonstrated the apparent unwillingness of Ugandans to compromise. This was not a new feature in Ugandan politics. As long as ago as 1961, the *Munster Report* which made proposals for the independence constitution observed as follows:

> No one who examined Uganda's political and social life could fail to be disturbed by one prominent characteristic: The unwillingness to compromise. Many people in Uganda still have to learn that all government, especially democratic governance, depends upon compromise and willingness to see other points of view in matters large and small.

Further the very conception of a united Uganda implies the need for a
wider loyalty to which local loyalties will from time to time have to give
way.[15]

In 1961 the major controversial issue revolved around the position of the
kingdom of Buganda in independent Uganda. The answer to that question
largely affected the ultimate constitutional arrangements adopted in the
independence constitution. The fact that the 1967 constitution abolished
kingdoms and the system of federalism, meant that these issues were to be
resurrected in the constitutional debate but they continued to remain
contentious. The challenge faced by the commission was to make
recommendations that would resolve these outstanding contentious issues.

The views were sharply divided between those for and against the
restoration of traditional rulers. Some viewed the institution of traditional
leaders as archaic while others saw the matter as a cultural right. The
commission recommended the restoration of the institution where the people
concerned so wished, but with the institution restricted to a cultural and
developmental role. It also recommended the return of the properties and
assets. The government decided to restore some traditional institutions and
return their properties before the draft constitution was debated.[16] One
traditional institution—the *Obugabe* of Ankole—remains in limbo even at
the time of writing.

The issue of whether the form of government should be federal or unitary
was also controversial. The monarchists considered it part and parcel of
(*ebyaffe*), 'returning their things' as it was in the 1962 constitution. Those
opposed to this arrangement feared that the 1962 scenario would be recreated
whereby some areas would enjoy this 'privilege' while others had only unitary
status. The commission's compromise was to recommend decentralisation
and the devolution of powers at district level for the whole country. Views on
the question of national language were sharply divided between Luganda
and Kiswahili. There were strong arguments in favour of each. However, the
commission did not consider it viable to recommend one of them but opted
for both together with other major local languages.

The issue which provoked the greatest controversy in the constitution-
making process was the question of the political system. The central issue
was whether or not the country should return to multiparty politics. If not,
what political system should operate? A minority of the populace wanted an
immediate restoration of political parties because freedom of association and
political organisation was a fundamental right which could not be suspended
or curtailed. Moreover, they argued, parties were not the cause of Uganda's
problems. The majority of the people wanted political parties to be suspended
for varying periods from 5 to 20 years because they thought that they had

been responsible for the mistakes of the past. In the meantime, it was proposed that the NRM system of government would continue with some modifications to make it more open, democratic and accountable. To strike a compromise the commission recommended that both political systems should be included in the constitution and that the people should have the right to periodically choose a political system of their choice through referenda until a consensus emerged in future on the most suitable permanent political system. The commission also recommended that if this issue is not conclusively resolved by the Constituent Assembly, it should be resolved by referendum and the outcome be incorporated in the new constitution.[14]

The report and draft constitution were presented to the president of Uganda on 31 December 1992. From that day, the report and draft constitution became public without the need for further action by government. Subsequently, the government published the report and draft constitution to make them easily available to the public. The proposals by the constitutional commission were received with mixed feelings. Commenting on the report of the constitutional commission President Museveni has said:

> I think the final report was quite representative of the peoples views because on some of the crucial points such as whether or not political parties should become fully operational or not, I knew the opinion in the country to be against parties, and this is what the report showed. In fact the Commissioners watered down what the people wanted – the people did not want the return of parties for a very long time – but the Commission compromised on a return to party activity five years from the first elections held under the new Constitution. Therefore the Commission was a temporising force as far as some local and international political thinking was concerned. They gravitated more towards international thinking especially on political parties rather than reflecting the views of the people themselves.

The Constituent Assembly discussion and adoption of the 1995 constitution

The manner in which a constitution is finally adopted by the people is fundamentally important in demonstrating the legitimacy, popularity and acceptability of the constitution. A constitution which is imposed by force cannot form the basis of a stable, peaceful and democratic system of governance. To command loyalty, obedience, respect and confidence, the people must identify themselves with the document through involvement and a sense of attachment.

The issue of which body would discuss and adopt the new constitution was hotly debated throughout the period of the commission's work and immediately thereafter. The legal position at the time the commission was established was that the existing National Resistance Council (NRC) and the National Resistance Army Council (NRAC) would participate in the process of discussion and adoption of the new constitution presumably with other additional representatives.[17]

This provision was made after the constitutional commission was set up but before the members of the NRC had been elected. It was therefore assumed that the members of the NRC had been mandated to adopt the new constitution. Those against this formula contended that the current members had lost their popular mandate by extending their period in the legislature without the consent of the electorate. Another reason advanced against the existing NRC debating the constitution was that it consisted of many members who had not been elected but were simply presidential nominees or were historical members from the 'bush days.' It was also pointed out that the election was not by direct popular mandate but by electoral colleges. The majority of the people therefore wanted fresh directly elected delegates with a special mandate to discuss the draft constitution.

After analysing the views of the people, the commission submitted an interim report on the adoption process which recommended that the draft constitution should be discussed and adopted by a Constituent Assembly consisting of directly elected delegates by universal adult suffrage and interest groups elected by their respective organisations. The main purpose behind this recommendation was to ensure that the future constitutional order enjoyed a wide degree of acceptability among the politically significant forces and that all social forces should participate in the process of adopting the constitution to dispel fears of manipulation or rigging the process and to establish permanent bases for the legitimacy of the new constitution. The government accepted these recommendations and embodied them in the Constituent Assembly Statute 1993[18] which was passed after strong opposition from the members of the National Resistance Council. The Statute established a Constituent Assembly whose functions were basically to scrutinise, debate and prepare a final draft of the constitutional text and to enact and promulgate a new constitution for Uganda.[19]

The commission was to complete its work within 4 months subject to an extension of not more than 3 months. That extension was found necessary and given. The delegates to the Constituent Assembly (CA) [20] numbered 288 in all and were drawn from a cross-section of dominant political forces in Uganda.[21] The CA composition not only ensured direct representation of the population but it also sought broad representation of various interest groups which could otherwise have been left out through direct elections. The result was a large and costly assembly. The statute also established a commission for the CA consisting of a Commissioner for the Constituent Assembly and two deputies appointed by the president on the advice of the cabinet. The functions of the commissioners were to organise and conduct elections for the Constituent Assembly, to administer its deliberations and to conduct any referendum required under the statute.[22]

The constituencies were demarcated, the voters registered and elections held on a non-partisan basis. This meant that every candidate was elected on his or her own individual merit, rather than on the basis of political affiliation. Use of political party, tribal or religious affiliations or other sectarian grounds was prohibited. Campaigning was conducted through candidates meetings organised by returning officers in each parish in an electoral area. The object of the meeting was to enable all candidates to meet together and address voters and answer questions from them, public rallies and public demonstrations in support of candidates were prohibited.

The Commission for the Constituent Assembly and a number of accredited organisations carried out civic education for voters. The major shortcoming in the election campaign was the use of colossal sums of money by candidates dictated by demands from the voters who expected to gain financially from the elections. The candidates were prepared to spend large sums of money in order to invest for the next round of parliamentary elections. Judith Geist decried this worrying practice when she stated:

> the voters took a type of mercenary rationality not known to previous Ugandan elections. While alarming to many, this is more a rational calculus than the response to strictly sectarian appeals that plagued past elections. It carries its own problems. Persons elected because of the depth of their pockets may not be best equipped to discuss and decide constitutional issues.[23]

The elections were held in March 1994. Local and international observer groups were invited by the government to monitor the electoral process to ensure that it was free and fair. The international observers came from 18 countries and organisations. The overall assessment by the observers was that despite some administrative weaknesses like failure to adequately display registers, the electoral process was free and fair and the results reflected the democratic choice of the people of Uganda. The elections represented an important step towards democracy. The OAU report made the following conclusion about the process:

> All international observers were of the opinion that even though there were some inadequacies and minor violations of the electoral laws, the elections were administratively well conducted and that the conduct of the elections was done in an open and fair manner. This is remarkably so considering the background of the 1980 reportedly rigged elections. There was no evidence of deliberate and systematic attempt to influence the outcome or alter the results of the elections. The calm atmosphere that

prevailed on polling day and the extraordinarily good behaviour of all concerned encouraged people to vote and was the factor that underpinned the high turnout. Generally, the elections can be considered as a reflection of the political choice and aspirations of the people of Uganda. The high sense of participation shown by Ugandans is highly commendable.[24]

Nelson Kafir has also observed that:

the Constituent Assembly elections could lay claim to being the most free and fair of Ugandans through nation wide elections since independence. But the elections also posed a challenge by adding a transitional stage in the struggle for power and the return to democracy that will be concluded with the elections to a new Parliament under the rules set by the Constitution produced by the Constituent Assembly. At stake are the questions whether the National Resistance Movement (NRM) will be the dominant political force in the years to come and if it is so whether it will radically restructure Ugandan politics as it had promised when it emerged triumphant in 1986 from its five year guerrilla campaign to overthrow the government.[25]

On the whole, the quality of delegates and the debates in the CA was high. There was a mixture of old and young politicians as well as persons who merely wanted to participate in the discussion and adoption of the constitution. There were some whose contribution was however minimal due to the nature of the subject matter. The NRM had more than two thirds of the delegates in the assembly. The assembly had a chair and a deputy nominated by the president and elected by the delegates of the assembly at its first sitting. The delegates were sworn in on 12 and 13 May 1994 and commenced business on May 18.

The assembly prepared and adopted its own rules of procedure.[26] The quorum of the assembly was agreed at half the members. The CA used to sit for 32 hours a week. Decisions by the assembly were to be by consensus as far as possible. Where consensus was not obtained the matter would be resolved by voting. The motion would be carried if it obtained the support of not less than two-thirds of the delegates voting. The matter was regarded as contentions if the motion was supported by the majority of delegates voting, but did not obtain the required two-thirds. A contentious matter would be referred to the minister who would present it to the nation for resolution through a national referendum. Most of the issues were resolved by consensus or voting and only two issues proved contentious. These were the provisions relating to the movement political system and referendum on political systems and the question of holding presidential and parliamentary elections on separate days. The first issue was resolved after delegates supporting the clauses on the movement and referendum on political parties to be deleted and the presidential and parliamentary elections to be held on the same day, but failed to get majority on both issues had walked out of the assembly and then returned. The second issue was resolved after delegates had been sent to their constituencies for consultations.

The CA established several committees to facilitate its work. The most important were the Business Committee and the Legal and Drafting Committee. The latter dealt with the content and text of the constitution, and assisted in wording and synchronising constitutional amendments during the debate. The debate progressed through several stages. The first was the general debate where each of the delegates addressed the assembly. This was intended to heal wounds of the past, minimise mistrust, build confidence between delegates and lay the foundation for reconciliation, mutual respect and consensus. The second was the consideration stage where the CA began the main task of debating the constitution chapter by chapter. Initially, all the discussions were planned to take place in plenary session. But it was soon realised that the plenary sessions were too slow and this necessitated the formation of five select committees to handle specific chapters of the draft constitution and to submit reports to the general plenary for consideration. This strategy greatly expedited the work of the assembly.

Several caucuses were formed to organise support for various positions in the draft constitution. The main ones were the National Caucus for Democracy (NCD), the NRM caucus and the Buganda Caucus. NCD became the principal platform for the immediate restoration of multi-party politics. The NRM caucus was committed to blocking such immediate restoration and advocated a no-party (Movement) system of politics for the time being. The Buganda caucus was devoted to the restoration of federalism and the consolidation of monarchy in Buganda.

After 16 months of debate the constitution was enacted by the Constituent Assembly on 22 September 1995. It was promulgated by the assembly in the presence of the president and the members of the NRC on 8 October 1995. It is worth noting that more than 80 per cent of the draft constitution was adopted. But the CA did not have the benefit of official representation of the commission to present the proposals in order to guide them nor did they have any white paper or government position on the draft constitution. These omissions could have contributed to the acrimonious debates that took place thus prolonging the process of adoption of the constitution.

Challenges in implementing the new constitution

A constitution is neither self-enacting nor self-executing. Making a constitution is one thing and implementing it is quite another. The implementation of a new constitution poses serious challenges to the government as well as the people to harness the letter and spirit of the constitution and to advance the democratic process and the socio-economic well-being of the people. In order to implement the constitution, appropriate democratic institutions must be established through which the people must exercise power directly or through their selected representatives. Democratic values and practice must be fostered amongst the population to empower them to actively participate in their own governance. Implementing a constitution is an expensive enterprise. Therefore adequate resources must be made available to facilitate the building of strong democratic institutions and pillars of state. Appropriate policies must be put in place to stimulate and promote socio-economic development by attracting local and foreign investment and to enable the people improve the quality of their lives. Government must also create an enabling atmosphere of peace and security to promote the protection of basic human rights and the rule of law.

The greatest initial challenge that faced implementation of the new constitution was the organisation of the presidential, parliamentary and local government elections to return the country to democratic rule after a long period of disenfranchisement. It must be observed that the constitution gave the mandate to the NRM government to manage this transitional process. Elections are an indispensable pre-requisite to democracy. The constitution vests all power in the hands of the people who must be governed through organs created by the constitution only with their consent. As Judith Geist observes,

> An election addresses the issue of periodic reaffirmation of or alteration in the presentation of the public in the institutions of policy making and governance. Elections confer legitimacy on governments by providing a chance for the citizenry to alter the composition of the government. They can also provide channels for citizen input on policy issues directly, through referenda, or in the extreme case to alter the nature of the government itself, through constitutional exercises.[27]

The new constitution preserved the NRM government as the transitional government and it was to remain in power from the time of coming into force of the new constitution until a new government was elected in accordance with the new constitution. The government was required to exercise its functions with such modifications as to bring them into conformity with the new constitution.[28] The government was mandated to make laws to establish an interim election commission whose composition, appointment and functions were to be in conformity with the new constitution, to make interim laws for elections, and tribunals for determination of disputes and appeals.[29] The NRC enacted the necessary legislations to regulate the organisation of the elections. These were the *Presidential Elections (Interim Provisions) Statute* 1996 and the *Parliamentary Elections (Interim Provisions) Statute* 1996. The two elections were to be held separately.

The constitution prescribed the manner in which the President would be elected, the qualifications for office and the procedure for nomination. Article 103(1) of the 1995 Constitution provides that the 'Election of the President shall be by universal adult suffrage through a secret ballot.' The *Presidential Elections (Interim Provisions) Statute* 1996 provided for the manner of holding of public meetings and facilitation of the elections. Presidential elections were held on 9 May 1996. The turn out was estimated at 79 per cent of the registered voters. The elections were won by President Museveni with 74.3 per cent of the votes, Dr Paul Semogerere of the DP with 23.6 per cent and Mr Kibirige Mayanja with 2.1 per cent. The election was viewed by both local and internal observers as free and fair and there were no petitions against the successful candidate.[30] The next challenge was to organise parliamentary elections. The constitution prescribed the composition and different mode of electing each category of members of the legislature. There were directly elected members to represent constituencies to be elected by universal adult suffrage and by secret ballot. Women representatives for each district, and representatives of the army, youth, workers and persons with disabilities were to be determined by parliament.[31] The NRC decided that the army would have 10 representatives, three representatives for workers and five representatives for each of the youth and persons with disabilities.

The procedure for elections of these special interest groups was prescribed by the minister of state for constitutional affairs. They were to be elected by their respective named organisations. The commission had to appoint returning officers for the elections. The country was divided into 214 constituencies for directly elected members, and there were 39 electoral colleges for women. The elections were held on the basis of the no-party system on an individual basis. There were 862 candidates for the 214 constituencies. The campaign period was 45 days and based on joint meetings. Elections were held on different dates for different special interest groups. Although the elections were generally free and fair, there were allegations of intimidation by candidates or their agents, use of abusive language and the ferrying of supporters from one point to another. The international observer group noted some shortcomings on polling day including canvassing by individual candidates, lack of screens around ballot marking tables thus affecting secrecy, illegal cards, and some district officials actively supporting particular candidates especially in the Northern and Western regions, But they concluded,

> The elections we observed from 24th to 28th June were transparent. Despite the deficiencies that we have outlined, the International Observer Group

believes that true Parliamentary elections mark a further positive step within the transition process in Uganda.[32]

Local government elections formed the last stage in the electoral process to return the country to democratic governance in accordance with the new constitution. These elections were conducted over a period of nine months from August 1997 to April 1998. The elections were the first major activity undertaken by the permanent Electoral Commission set up in November 1996, and were conducted after the enactment of the Local Government Act 1997.[33] The process of election was not similar for all units of local government. Secret ballot was used for higher level namely for district/city and municipality chairpersons and councillors other than for special interest groups, and the method of queue-voting was deployed for the election of chairpersons and councillors of units at the sub-county level and below. Organising such elections throughout the country was a big challenge to the Electoral Commission. It had to carry out the demarcation of electoral areas, train officials, carry out voter education and update voter registers.

Conclusion

Every constitution is influenced by what has happened in the past. It is also affected by the present situation and by people's aspirations for the future. The constitution- making process in Uganda attempted to address Uganda's future in light of its past history and more recent developments. The constitutional framework arrived at was based on the views of the people and generally reflected the national consensus of the people of Uganda. The constitution therefore enjoys a high degree of acceptability and legitimacy. This is not to deny that there may be some shortcomings in the document. Nevertheless, the constitution has definitely succeeded in delivering the country onto the constitutional path—a firm but long journey to democracy.

Many people expected that the constitution would solve all their social, economic and political problems. This was one of the motivating forces behind the high response and full participation in the constitution-making process. The people expected the constitution to serve their needs, interests and aspirations. They expect the constitution to promote the principles of unity, peace, equality, democracy, freedom, social justice and progress so that they may live in peace and prosperity. In particular the government has a fiduciary duty to ensure that the constitution is upheld and implemented in a creative and dynamic manner so as to improve the welfare of the people. The constitution is a living instrument which must grow through amendment and interpretation by the courts. Therefore constitutional development must be an ongoing exercise. We must continue the dialogue and consultation amongst the diverse groups and communities so as to build compromises on issues that divide us. In so doing we must develop democratic values of tolerance of diverse views, a spirit of compromise, acceptance of majority views while respecting the minority, and the settlement of disputes by peaceful means.

Some areas which require reconsideration and where dialogue should continue include: the formation of a national government (or grand coalition), introduction of proportional representation, coexistence between movement and the multiparty political system and the future of the movement system, federalism or quasi-federalism, some aspects of land, issues in the bill of rights like the death sentence, the size and composition of parliament, the right to censor or recall members of parliament, the number of constitutional bodies, the effect of the Treaty for East African Co-operation on the constitution and the cost of implementing the constitution. This may call for another constitutional review. Let me conclude with the words of President Museveni at the opening of the Constituent Assembly:

> We must ensure that our political institutions spring from our social structure. If we are to develop, we must evolve constitutional models which liberate us from our backwardness. We must modernise our societies and lay the foundation for industrialisation. We cannot modernise, industrialise or develop without creating an appropriate institutional framework within which to work. It is the historic responsibility of this Constituent Assembly to set our country on the path to development and prosperity.[34]

The Constituent Assembly completed its historic mission over five years ago. It is now the political challenge of the government and the people of Uganda, to commit themselves to internalising, upholding and defending the constitution by creating and sustaining a culture of constitutionalism among the polity.

Notes

1. See, Hansen and Twaddle (1994); Hansen and Twaddle (1992); Mukholi (1995), and Odoki (1993).
2. For a historical introduction to Uganda, see Mutibwa (1993); Hansen and Twaddle (1988), and Museveni (1997).
3. Museveni (1990): 20-21.
4. See further Waliggo (1994): 18.
5. Uganda Constitutional Commission (UCC) Statute 1988, Section 2.
6. Museveni (1997): 193.
7. UCC Statute, section 5.
8. *Ibid.*, section 4.
9. The programme was divided into six phases namely,
   (1) Planning, publicity, and internal seminars;
   (2) Education of the people and discussion of constitutional issues;
   (3) Collection of the people's views;

(4) Analysis and study of the views;
(5) Review of the constitution and comparative study of constitutions;
(6) Preparation of the final report and draft constitution.
10. Seminars were organised for the following groups and institutions: the Uganda Law Society, the police, the prisons, the youth, the women, permanent secretaries, medical doctors, and nurses, engineers, manufacturers, political leaders, national teachers colleges, theological colleges and national colleges of commerce.
11. A total of 5844 essays were received from all over the country.
12. As a result the commission received the following submissions from individuals, groups interest and RCs and educational seminars reports:

(a) District seminar reports	33
(b) Institutional seminar reports	53
(c) Sub-county seminar reports	813
(d) Individual's memoranda	2,553
(e) Group memoranda	839
(f) RC 5 memoranda	36
(g) RC 4 memoranda	14
(h) RC 3 memoranda	564
(i) RC 2 memoranda	2,225
(j) RC 1 memoranda	9,521
(k) Essay competition	5,844
(l) Newspaper articles	2,763
(m) Position papers	290
Total	25,547

13. The list of all persons and organisations which submitted views to the commission and the statistical analysis were published in one volume of the commission's final report entitled *Index of Sources of Peoples Views.*
14. UCC report, 56.
15. Quoted by Waliggo (1994) *op.cit.,* at 38.
16. See Constitution (Amendment) Statute 1993 No.7 of 1993, and Traditional Rulers (Restitution of Assets and Properties Statute 1993 (No.8 of 1993).
17. Statute No.1 of 1989, section 14 B.
18. Statute No.6 of 1993.
19. *Ibid.,* section 8.
20. *Ibid.,* section 4.
21. (1) Directly elected delegates from electoral areas 214

    (2) Representatives from special interest groups as follows:

(a)	One woman delegate from each district elected by electoral college of RC III Councillors and Women Councils	39
(b)	National Resistance Army	10
(c)	Trade Unions	2
(d)	Two members from each of the political parties which participated in the 1980 General Elections namely:	
	(i) The Conservative Party	2
	(ii) Democratic Party	
	(iii) Uganda Patriotic Movement	2
	(iv) Uganda Peoples Congress	2

    (3) The National Youth Council 4
    (4) The National Union of the Disabled Peoples of Uganda 1
    (5) Ten delegates appointed by the President on the advice of cabinet 10

                                   Total 288

22. *Ibid.*, sections 20 – 24.
23. Geist (1994), *op.cit.,* 90.
24. See Report of Constituent Assembly elections 1994, Commission for the Constituent Assembly May 1995: 332.
25. Kasfir, 148.
26. *The Constituent Assembly (Rules of Procedure) Instrument* 1994 S.I 174 of 1999.
27. Guest, *op.cit.,* 90.
28. Article 263.
29. Article 264.
30. See generally the Report of the Presidential and Parliamentary Elections 1996 Electoral Commission, Kampala.
31. Article 78.
32. Report of the Presidential and Parliamentary Elections, 1996, *op.cit.* 153.
33. Act No.1 of 1997.
34. Museveni, (1997) *supra*, 194.

References

Geist, Judith (1994) 'Political Significance of the Constituent Assembly Elections' in Hansen, H.B and M Twaddle (eds.) *From Chaos to Order: The Politics of Constitution making in Uganda,* Kampala: Fountain Publishers.

Hansen, H.B and M. Twaddle (1994), *From Chaos to Order: The Politics of Constitution making in Uganda,* Kampala: Fountain Publishers.

_____. and M. Twaddle; (1992) *Changing Uganda,* Kampala: Fountain Publishers.

_____. and Twaddle (1988) *Uganda Now: Between Decay and Development,* Kampala: Fountain Publishers.

Kasfir, Nelson (1994) 'Uganda Politics and the Constituent Assembly Elections of March 1994' in *From Chaos to Order The Politics of Constitution-making in Uganda,* Kampala: Fountain Publishers.

Mukholi, David (1995) *A Complete Guide to Uganda's Fourth Constitution,* Kampala: Fountain Publishers.

Museveni, Y. K. (1997) *Sowing the Mustard Seed,* London: Macmillan Publishers.

Museveni, Y.K., (1990) *Mission to Freedom: Uganda National Resistance News 1981 –1985,* Kampala: NRM Secretariat.

Mutibwa, P.M. (1993) *Uganda Since Independence,* Kampala: Fountain Publishers.

Odoki, B. J. (1993) 'Writing a Democratic Constitution' *East African Journal of Peace and Human Rights.*

Waliggo, John Mary (1994) 'The Constitution-making Process and the Politics of Democratisation' in *From Chaos To Order: The Politics of Constitution making in Uganda,* Kampala: Fountain Publishers.

16

Ruled from the Grave: Challenging Antiquated Constitutional Doctrines and Values in Commonwealth Africa

Grace Patrick Tumwine-Mukubwa

The word 'constitution' has no precise definition. According to Professor K.C. Wheare, in the widest sense, it refers to the whole system of government of a country, the collection of rules which establish and regulate or govern the government. In the narrow sense it refers to a document having special legal sanctity and setting out the framework and the principal functions of the organs of government.[1] It also declares the principles by which those organs must operate.[2] Such a document must also embody specific values and customs by which the citizens have agreed to be governed. 'Constitution' in its narrowest sense is the most appropriate definition for written constitutions. 'Constitutionalism' then means that the use of governmental power—a process that is essential to the realisation of the values of societies—should be controlled in order that it should not itself be destructive of the values it was intended to promote. Constitutionalism also entails that the citizens must consent to be governed by the assemblage of institutions, rules, values and customs they have voluntarily put in place. In other words constitutionalism is a commitment to be governed by the constitution.

This chapter critically examines the rules, values, customs and influences that have underpinned the constitutions of Commonwealth Africa. The discussion is limited to these countries for a number of obvious reasons. First, because these countries share a common official language, English. Secondly, they share a similar history as former colonies of Great Britain. Thirdly, their independence constitutions have a similar pedigree, and as Professor Gingyera-Pincywa has observed they also have similar features. For example, all had a parliamentary system of government.[3] They vested executive authority in the monarch represented by the governor-general. They had a prime minister and a cabinet to advise the monarch as the chief executive with powers to govern. The prime minister and the cabinet were individually and collectively responsible to parliament. Members of parliament were to be subject to regular elections to renew their mandate. All these features were premised on certain accepted doctrines such as the supremacy of parliament, and the rule of law, which is itself predicated on the doctrine of separation of powers and the notion of fundamental human rights. Other doctrines shared in common are the system of executive prerogatives, the doctrine of sovereignty and even the theory of constitutionalism itself.

The importation of the rules of the British constitution, however, did not incorporate the practices, customs, procedures and assumptions under which it operated. The constitutions were soon either abrogated or amended to fuse the role of the monarch with that of the prime minister to create a president in whom the executive authority was vested. These changes call into question the relevance of the basic doctrinal assumptions and practices of the unwritten British constitution. It will be argued that adherence to these doctrines and practices has stunted the growth of written constitutions and the development of constitutionalism in Commonwealth Africa.

Supremacy of parliament

Professor A.V. Dicey[4] has commented that parliament under the British constitution had a right to make or unmake any law. Nobody had a right to set aside such a law, implying that parliament was the supreme organ of government. The courts in Britain were obliged to apply such a law. The doctrine of the supremacy of parliament was designed to fill a vacuum created by the fact that Britain did not have a written constitution. By contrast, the constitutions in Commonwealth Africa provide for the supremacy of the constitution.[5] They further provided that any law which conflicted with the constitution would have no legal force.[6] This gave courts the power to declare laws made by parliament unconstitutional. Thus, in a number of cases it has been held by the courts that the constitution is the paramount law and any law that conflicts with the constitution is void to the extent of the conflict.[7]

The power conferred upon the courts as interpreters of the constitution has been used by them to declare certain legislation invalid for being inconsistent with the constitution. For example, in *State v. Makwanyane*[8], the South African Constitutional Court held that section 277(1) of the Penal Code which sanctioned the death penalty was inconsistent with the constitution. Consequently, the death penalty for murder, aggravated robbery, kidnapping, child stealing and rape was abolished. In *State v. Vries*[9] the Supreme Court of Namibia struck down a minimum statutory sentence of three years for a subsequent stock theft because it was 'shocking' and therefore unconstitutional. In *Ruto v. Attorney-General & Anor*[10] the Kenya High Court struck down an amendment to the Criminal Code which made drug related offences non-bailable as infringing the right to bail and also as being inconsistent with the unlimited jurisdiction of the High Court. The Court of Appeal of Nigeria in *Agbakoba v. Director State Security Services* decided that all persons had the right to freedom of movement including the right to a passport which cannot be withdrawn by the government.[11]

In *Ibingira v. Uganda*[12] the Court of Appeal for East Africa declared that the Deportation Ordinance at least so far as it purported to affect citizens of Uganda contravened article 28 of the 1962 (independence) constitution which protected the fundamental freedom of movement. Finally, in *Attorney-General v. Abuki*[13] the Supreme Court of Uganda declared s 7 of the Witchcraft Act inconsistent with the constitution and to that extent void, because it authorised the making of an exclusion order which is an inhuman and degrading punishment and in contravention of the provisions of the constitution. All these cases demonstrate that the interpretation of the constitution is primarily concerned with the recognition and application of constitutional values and not with a search to find the internal meaning of statutes. In other words the reasons for legislation may be varied, however the constitution will override individual laws that do not conform to the values in the paramount instrument. Needless to say, the departure from the doctrine of supremacy of parliament to supremacy of the constitution has not been accepted with open arms by all and sundry.

Thus, the deputy chief justice of Uganda held that the constitution does recognise the fact that it is in the public interest to punish criminals who have been fairly tried and found guilty. Relying on Article 23(1) of the 1995 constitution which says that no person shall be deprived of personal liberty except in execution of a sentence or order of the court, the learned judge stated that such sentences may be *cruel, inhuman* or *degrading* but they are lawful. Therefore the exclusion order which violated the right to free movement was justified because Abuki had indeed committed an offence.[14] The learned judge advocated such punishments in total disregard of the non-derogable provisions of the constitution prohibiting such punishments.[15]

This may sound like judicial fascism. However, it would appear that the learned judge was influenced by the doctrine of supremacy of parliament. In his opinion parliament could make or unmake any law. The duty of the courts was simply to apply that law. The judge felt that declaring a law unconstitutional would amount to an unwarranted violation of the powers of parliament and thus of the doctrine of separation of powers. When *Abuki's* case went on appeal to the Supreme Court of Uganda, it was unanimously held that in prescribing the sentence and orders which may be imposed in respect of any criminal offence, every legislative authority is in effect restrained by the constitution not to prescribe any penalty that would subject the person convicted of that offence to any form of torture, cruel, inhuman or degrading treatment or punishment. A court deciding on the sentence to impose on any person convicted of an offence is likewise restrained. The restraint applies not only to the law makers but also to those who interpret, apply or enforce the law. The doctrine of supremacy of parliament also appears to have influenced the decision of the Court of Appeal of Tanzania in the case of *Mbushuu & Anor v. Republic*[16] where it was held that, considered as a whole, the death penalty was cruel, inhuman and degrading. However, the court did not take the next logical step which would have been to strike down section 30 (2) of the Penal Code mandating the death penalty for certain offences. Yet Article 13(5)(e) of the constitution of Tanzania states that '*it is forbidden for a person to be tortured, to be punished unnaturally or to be given punishment that humiliates or degrades him.*' This non-derogable provision should have been invoked to abolish the death penalty in Tanzania where the constitution is declared to be supreme.[17] In *State v. Ntesang*[18] the Court of Appeal of Botswana while upholding the death penalty advised that a large number of countries had abolished this punishment and hoped that before long parliament would be minded to consider effecting such changes as it might consider necessary to further establish Botswana's claim to being one of the great liberal democracies of the world. However, the court should have simply used Article 7 of the Botswana constitution which prohibits torture, inhuman, degrading or cruel treatment or punishment. The law authorising death penalty could thus have been simply struck down.

The uncritical adherence to the doctrine of supremacy of parliament is sometimes shared by legislators themselves. Many legislators believe that Parliament is unrestrained in its power to make laws. They have accordingly passed laws that water down the presumption of innocence. For example, section 28 of the Penal Code Act of Uganda proves:

> S 28 (1) Any person who engages in or carries out acts of terrorism is guilty of an offence and is liable to imprisonment for life...
> (4) *Without prejudice to the right to adduce evidence in rebuttal,* any person who imports, sells, distributes, manufacturers or is in possession of any firearm, explosives or ammunition without a valid licence or reasonable expense shall be deemed to be engaged in act of terrorism.

Similarly, section 364 of the same law provides that:

> (i) Any person including a public officer in relation to public funds who-
> (a) without reasonable excuse, *proof of which shall* be on him issues any cheque drawn on any bank where there is no account against which the cheque is drawn, or
> (b) issues any cheque in respect of any account with any bank when he has no reasonable ground, *proof of which shall be on him*, to believe that there are funds in the account to pay the amount specified on the cheque within the normal course of banking business...commits an offence.

Article 28(3)(a) of the Uganda constitution provides that every person charged with a criminal offence *shall be presumed innocent until proved guilty or until that person has pleaded guilty.* Furthermore, under article 44 there shall be no derogation from the enjoyment of the right to a fair hearing. Article 28(11) provides that where a person is being tried for a criminal offence neither that person or the spouse of that person shall be compelled to give evidence against that person. Surprisingly, Article 28(4) provides that it will not be inconsistent with Article 28(3)(a) that a law in question imposes upon any persons charged with a criminal offence the burden of proving particular facts. Similar provisions appear in numerous constitutions in Commonwealth Africa.

Justice Egonda Ntende in an extra judicial capacity has extensively analysed the Ugandan provisions in connection with reverse onus clauses. [19] After reviewing a host of cases from countries with written constitutions he makes a number of conclusions and suggestions. He argues that bills of rights have elevated the doctrine of presumption of innocence to a constitutional level above the common law. This means it cannot be altered by parliament. Consequently, parliament cannot override it. Even in England where the doctrine of the supremacy of parliament is still upheld, reverse onus clauses have been held to be invalid under the Human Rights Act 1998 which was passed to domesticate the European Convention on Human Rights. Thus in *Kebilene & Ors v. D.P.P,*[20] Bingham L.C. in the Court of Appeal held that reverse onus clauses undermine in a blunt and obvious way the presumption of innocence contrary to Article 6 of the European Convention on Human Rights and the 1998 Human Rights Act.

Comparative jurisprudence has assailed reverse onus clauses for permitting a conviction despite the existence of a reasonable doubt on the evidence before the court.[21] The standard of proof placed upon the accused is that of a balance of probabilities. If the accused fails to discharge that burden, he or she can be found guilty in spite of the lack of proof beyond reasonable doubt that he or she actually committed the offence. This stands in clear contravention of the presumption of innocence and the right to a fair trial. There may be a connection between the proved fact and the presumed fact; however, this would infringe the presumption of innocence for it would lead to a conviction even if the evidence available did not prove beyond reasonable doubt that the accused committed the offence. In some instances, there may be reverse onus clauses that pass constitutional muster where justification can be shown to warrant overriding the presumption of innocence. However, this must not result in the impairment of the accused's right to a fair trial. The constitution of Uganda has barred the impairment of the right to a fair trial notwithstanding anything contrary contained in the constitution.[22] It therefore established a new standard that courts must observe and enforce.

The inappropriate adherence to the doctrine of the supremacy of parliament has led some courts to assert that unless an international norm or treaty is specifically implemented by parliament it is not part of the domestic law simply because it has been negotiated by the executive and not enacted as part of the local law. Thus, in the Kenyan case of *East African Community v. Republic*[23] the court stated that the provisions of a treaty entered into by the government of Kenya do not become part of the municipal law of Kenya save in so far as they are made such by the law of Kenya.

But other courts have resorted to ingenious methods of enforcing international conventions. Thus, it has been stated by a court in England that there is a rebuttable presumption that municipal law will be consistent with international obligations.[24] Secondly, the Court of Appeal of Botswana was of the view that an international treaty even when it has not been acceded to can be looked at by the court on the basis that in the absence of express words to that effect, parliament would not have wanted a decision maker to act contrary to such a treaty.[25] This approach was endorsed by the Commonwealth judges in their Balliol Statement made in England wherein they stated that 'International Human Rights Instruments and their developing jurisprudence enshrine values and principles long recognised by the common law.'[26] Finally, it was held by the Supreme Court of Ghana that courts must apply international instruments in their interpretative duties whether ratified or not, provided they do not conflict with the constitution.[27] Such approaches to the issue are considerably more sound, since they recognise the supremacy of the constitution and not that of parliament. A related doctrine to that of the supremacy of parliament is the doctrine of presumption of constitutionality to which I now turn for consideration.

The presumption of constitutionality

The policy restraint reflected in the presumption of constitutionality arose out of the traditional respect by the Judiciary for the supremacy of the legislative branch of government. This policy was based on the presumption that the legislature cannot be deemed to intend to make a law that contravenes the constitution. Therefore, a statute was interpreted by reading it in accordance with the presumed intention of legislators which was regarded as less of an invasion of their domain by the court.[28] Thus, in *Re: Munhumeso & Ors*[29] the Supreme Court of Zimbabwe held that where the challenged piece of legislation was capable of more than one meaning and if one possible interpretation fell within the constitutional limits and others did not, the court would presume that the law makers intended to act constitutionally. The court would thus uphold the legislation. In my view this approach is unacceptable for a number of reasons.

The primary concern of the court must be to apply those measures that will best vindicate the values expressed in the constitution and thereby provide a form of remedy to those constitutional rights that have been violated that best achieves that objective. This flows from the court's role as the guardian of the constitution. The constitutional mandate given to the courts is that if any law is inconsistent with the constitution, the constitution shall prevail. Any law that is inconsistent with the constitution shall, to the extent of the inconsistency, be declared void. Therefore, there is no reason for the court to disguise the exercise of this power in the traditional garb of interpretation. Obviously the court must be sensitive to its role within the constitutional framework and refrain from intruding into the legislative sphere beyond what is necessary to give full effect to the provisions of the constitution. However, to maintain a law that is so riddled with infirmity would not uphold the values of the constitution. Indeed it would constitute a greater intrusion on the role of parliament. Parliament must be the institution to determine how the law should be redrafted and not the court. Moreover, apart from the impracticality of a determination on the constitutionality of the law on a case-to-case basis, parliament will have available to it information and expertise that is not available to the court.[30]

It is preferable to express deference to parliament as a factor in fashioning the remedy rather than the court engaging in a fictitious analysis that attributes to parliament an intention it did not have. As Mulenga J.S.C. stated in *Abuki's*[31] case, applying the presumption of constitutionality in many cases would be moving from the realm of theory to the realm of fiction for the simple reason that most of the laws in question pre-date the constitution. Therefore, it cannot be said rationally that when enacting those laws parliament had the intention not to enact a law that would contravene a constitutional provision that was to be enacted many years later. On the contrary, constitutions are made on the presumption that existing laws may be in conflict with the constitution. Such laws are supposed to be brought into conformity with the constitution by the courts. Thus, article 273(1) of the Constitution of Uganda 1995 validates existing laws. But it goes on to state that 'existing law shall be construed with such modifications, adaptations, qualifications and exceptions as may be necessary to bring it into conformity' with the constitution.[32] The fact that constitutions state that any law inconsistent with the constitution will be void is enough evidence that there should be no presumption of constitutionality. Where a written constitution exist the constitutionality of any law can be easily determined by simply comparing such a law with the constitution.

The concept of the supremacy of the constitution is central to all written Commonwealth African constitutions. Therefore all organs of the state, including the executive, are bound by the constitution. The courts are mandated to ensure compliance with the constitution. They have the power to declare unconstitutional statutes, acts or omissions invalid. This power was not available to the courts under the dispensation based on the sovereignty of parliament. There was no constitutional review. As a result, there were many abuses that found no redress. The notion of constitutional supremacy flows from and is required by the concept of the democratic constitutional state. In order to buttress the doctrine of the supremacy of the constitution, it is usually made clear that the constitution is the source of all executive power which may be tested against the constitution. For example, Article 58(1) of the *Constitution of Ghana* provides that the *'executive authority of Ghana shall vest in the President and shall be exercised in accordance with the provisions'* of the constitution. A similar provision is contained in Article 99(1) of the constitution of Uganda. In my view, such provisions were intended to do away with the so-called doctrine of executive prerogative.

The phenomenon of executive prerogatives

The legal term 'prerogative' refers to powers outside the control of the law. For example, in the Ugandan case of *Attorney-General v. Tinyefuza*[33] one of the issues in contention was whether the respondent ceased to be employed in the army when he was appointed presidential adviser. Wambuzi C.J. held that there was no law governing the issue of secondment. He went on to state that it was nevertheless common knowledge that the president could use his prerogative to second army officers to the civil service. In the opinion of the learned judge this was an administrative problem. The management of affairs of state was by the executive. It was not a function for the courts. However, as one commentator has rightly observed, the actions and policies of the executive have to be in conformity with the constitution and the law.[34] The president has to work within the confines of the constitution and the courts have the duty to ensure that he does not transverse beyond the confines established by the constitution.[35]

The system of prerogatives stems from the English Common Law and formed part of the dispensation when parliament was supreme.[36] They originated in England at a time when the powers of the monarch were virtually unchecked. Their most important quality was their exemption from the process of judicial review or oversight. Their scope would be determined by the courts but not the manner of their execution. The most important prerogatives were the following: power to assent to legislation, the power to dissolve parliament; the prerogative to dismiss a government, appoint ministers, stop criminal prosecution, bestow honours, pardon criminals, declare war and sue for peace. Many of these privileges fitted logically into the English system of government. Some of them were over time laid down in legislation thereby excluding reliance on the common law.[37] However, by convention, most of the prerogatives were not exercised by the monarch but instead by cabinet ministers. In most of Commonwealth Africa, the issue has been made more complicated by the fact that the president as the head of state is also head of the executive. The English position with a titular monarch and a prime minister is largely inapplicable.[38] The constitution and laws that are in conformity with it are the only sources of executive power. The exercise of all executive powers should be justiciable because the constitution is supreme. There should be nothing like executive prerogative unless such privilege has been explicitly enshrined in the constitution and the statutes.

The doctrines of the rule of law and separation of powers

The two doctrines of the rule of law and separation of powers are intertwined and the mere mention of one immediately invokes the other. The three fold division of labour between the legislator, an administrative official and an independent judge is generally regarded as a necessary condition for the rule of law and therefore for a democratic government itself. However, the two doctrines need to be understood and discussed separately. This is because in the first instance, there can be separation of powers without necessarily having the rule of law. Secondly, separation of powers generally appeals to reason, while rule of law appeals to emotion. Thirdly, separation of powers has determinable or verifiable meaning while the rule of law in general, does not. Professor A.V. Dicey's[39] formulation of the rule of meant first and foremost, the absolute supremacy or predominance of regular law as opposed to the influence of arbitrary power. The rule of law excludes the existence of arbitrariness, of prerogative or even of wide discretionary authority on the part of the government. According to Dicey's formulation, people must only be punished for breach of the law. Secondly, the rule of law means equality before the law or the equal subjection of all classes to the ordinary law of the land administered by the ordinary courts. In the third place, the rule of law means that the law of the constitution enshrined in constitutional codes cannot be the source of rights but the consequence of the rights of the individual as defined and enforced by the courts. Thus, the constitution is the result of the ordinary law of the land.

Dicey's formulation can be criticised on a number of grounds. The third meaning of the rule of law has no relevance where there is a written constitution with a bill of rights. The second meaning of the rule of law is now part of the provisions on human rights in all Commonwealth African constitutions.[40] Therefore, one does not have to use Dicey to justify the right to equality before and under the law. Even where it is not specifically stated, the constitution will usually declare that the particular country is a sovereign and democratic state.[41] Furthermore, the Supreme Court of Mauritius held in *Pointu & Ors v. Minister of Education and Science & Ors*[42] that the principle of equality should be regarded as implicit in the notion of democracy contained in the constitution that Mauritius is a sovereign and democratic state. Therefore the concept of equality has always existed as part of the democratic principles of the country. Moreover, Dicey's insistence on equality before the law and the subjection of all classes to ordinary law is premised on his perception of the law in England as fair and just. This does not cater for a situation where such laws are immoral, unjust or oppressive. His doctrine was developed under a system of parliamentary supremacy where the courts could not question an act of parliament but simply had to apply it. In any case, equality before the law does not prevent unequally situated groups from being treated differently provided that the identification of such a group is based or founded on intelligible differentia and there is a rational nexus between the differential and the objects of the law. Therefore, it does not fit comfortably with the notion of a democratic constitutional state based on the supremacy of the constitution where the courts can refuse to subject a person to unconstitutional law. It also does not take into account the existence of definite power and social relations in society. For the reasons given above, one should speak about Dicey's formulation in its second and third meaning with extreme caution.

However, even the rule of law in Dicey's first formulation of the doctrine cannot be defended. Professor William Whitford has argued that the concept of the rule of law should be confined to the accountability of government decisions to predetermined standards applied by an independent body such as a court.[43] However, my view is that Dicey's first formulation of the rule of law cannot be retained. In the first instance, the constitution is written so that no organ of government should act arbitrarily. In other words, a written constitution makes sure that the powers of the executive, parliament and the judiciary are defined and limited. Secondly, there is no modern state that can operate without a certain amount of discretion—an element which Dicey condemned outright as lending itself to arbitrariness. Thirdly, as Professors Wade and Bradley have pointed out it is difficult to share Dicey's faith in the common law as the primary legal means of protecting a citizen's liberties against the state.[44] I agree with these authors when they say that Dicey's view of the rule of law was based on an analysis of the British constitution which today is in many respects outmoded. Indeed, the British themselves having come to fully appreciate the defects intrinsic to an unwritten constitution have enacted the Human Rights Act 1998 that entrenches a bill of rights.

Regardless of my sympathy for certain of their views, I do not share the suggestion by these authors that the rule of law should be limited to the concept of law and order.[45] To do so would give carte blanche to dictators who always use the law to suppress dissent in the name of law and order. Professors

Wade and Bradley recognise this problem when they state that undue stress on law and order as social values readily leads to the restriction or suppression of political liberty which may result in armed resistance.[46] There is also a suggestion that organs of government must themselves operate through law. This is not a contestable issue. However, one does not have to fall back to the rule of law as formulated by Dicey as a written constitution demands exactly that. It is also subsumed under the doctrine of a democratic constitutional state. For the reason given above, the doctrine of the rule of law should cease to be in our vocabulary because it has become mere political rhetoric.

Usually associated with the doctrine of the rule of law is the doctrine of separation of powers. This doctrine was originally developed as a means of preventing tyranny in the belief that concentrating power in one individual tends to be corrupting and to result in dictatorship. The solution was to demarcate state organs and define their powers so that each organ operates within its designated sphere. At the same time, each organ maintains a check upon and balances the others. In the constitutions of Commonwealth Africa, the state has been regarded as containing three major organs; the executive, legislature and the judiciary. This seems a sensible doctrine. However, there are doctrines which are associated with the separation of powers which need further analysis. Among them are the political question doctrine and independence of the judiciary to which I now turn in drawing this chapter to a conclusion.

The 'political question' doctrine

Among the several doctrines that flow from separation of powers, the political question doctrine is one that most requires further critical scrutiny. This is a doctrine that the courts have invoked either expressly or implicitly to exclude some decisions of the executive or parliament from judicial review. Professor William Whitford defends the doctrine.[47] He regards it as reasonable so that the court can conserve its moral authority by avoiding decisions over issues that may be highly charged. This is particularly so if it is difficult to articulate a basis for the decision in terms of easily understood and applied general principles. In Professor Whitford's view, it is thus better for a court to abstain from characterising the issue as not justiciable, rather than specifically upholding the government decision as legal, because the latter action tends to legitimise the decision in the public mind. Sheldon Goldman regards the political question doctrine as a useful one if the majority wishes to avoid deciding an issue and desires to articulate its reasons for denying itself judicial power. When a court wishes to decide *not* to hear a particular dispute or line of disputes it more typically finds that parliament has not granted it jurisdiction.[48]

As was explained by the majority opinion in the famous American case of *Baker v. Carr*,[49] the non-justiciability of the political question is primarily a function of separation of powers. This case also laid down the test to be applied before invoking the doctrine. The court put the test as follows:

> Prominent on the surface of any case held to involve a political question doctrine is found a textually demonstrable constitutional commitment of the issue to a coordinate political department; or a lack of judicially discoverable and manageable standards for resolving it; or the impossibility of deciding without an initial policy determination of a kind clearly for nonjudicial discretion; or the impossibility of a court's undertaking independent resolution without expressing lack of the respect due to coordinate branches of government or an unusual need for unquestioning adherence to a political decision already made; or the potentiality of embarrassment from multifarious pronouncements by various departments on one question.[50]

Alexander Bickel[51] has argued that the doctrine is founded on the court's lack of capacity compounded in equal parts of; the strangeness of the issue and its intractability to principled resolution; the sheer momentousness of the matter, which tends to unbalance judicial judgment; the anxiety, not so much that the judgment will be ignored, as that perhaps it should but will not be, and the inner vulnerability, the self doubt of an institution which is electorally irresponsible and has no earth to draw strength from. Professor Louis Henkin castigates the doctrine as an unnecessary and deceptive packaging of several established principles which are; that the courts are bound to accept decisions by the political branches within their constitutional authority.

Secondly, the courts will not find limitations or prohibitions on the powers of the political branches where the constitution does not prescribe any. Thirdly, not all constitutional limitations or prohibitions imply rights and standing to object in favour of private parties. Fourthly, the courts may refuse some or all remedies for want of equity. Finally, there might be constitutional provisions that can be interpreted wholly or in part as self monitoring and therefore not subject to judicial review.[52]

The constitutions of many Commonwealth African countries demand that the courts should not shy away from political questions. Examples abound. In the first instance, the constitutions which contain objectives and directive principles of state policy also require that the courts should be guided by them in their decisions. Thus it was held by the Supreme Court of Ghana that in determining whether a law is justifiable in terms of the spirit of the constitution, the courts, by virtue of the directive principles of state policy, were entitled to take into consideration political matters in applying and interpreting the constitution.[53]

Secondly, all the interpretations of the constitution have political consequences. Thirdly, many constitutions provide that any limitation to the enjoyment of rights and freedoms must not go beyond what is acceptable and demonstrably justified in a free and democratic society. In my view, this places a duty on the courts to consider political questions. We should therefore abandon the use of the political question doctrine. We should only talk of the principle of non-justiciability. This will acknowledge the obvious fact that there are certain matters which are not appropriate for judicial review. But those matters must not include the violation of individual or group rights and freedoms. The doctrine of separation of powers is also at the core of the doctrine of the independence of the judiciary to which we now turn for consideration.

The independence of the judiciary

Separation of powers is often used to justify the doctrine of the independence of the judiciary. The objective of guaranteeing the independence of the judiciary is to ensure effective maintenance of law and order and constitutional rule so that there is no necessity or justification to resort to extra judicial means in the resolution of political problems. Independence of the judiciary is, therefore, important if the courts are to hold other organs bounden to law. Commonwealth African constitutions generally provide for judicial independence by regulating the appointment, removal, remuneration and security of tenure of judges. However, some observers have been troubled by two issues about the doctrine. The first is how the judiciary itself is to be controlled? It has been assumed that they are controlled by public opinion.[54] But this simply cannot be the case.

If public opinion were to be decisive, there would be no need for constitutional adjudication. For example, the protection of human rights could be left to parliament, which has a mandate from the public and is answerable to the public for the way its mandate is exercised. To me however, this would be to re-introduce the doctrine of the supremacy of parliament through the back door when so many constitutions have done away with it. The very reason for establishing the new constitutional order and for vesting the power of judicial review of legislation in the courts was to protect the rights of minorities and other groups who cannot protect their rights adequately through the democratic process. Those who are entitled to claim this protection include social outcasts and all the marginalised people in our societies. It is only if there is a willingness to protect the worst and the weakest that everybody will be protected.[55] For these reasons the court should not be bound by either the will of the majority or by public sentiment. The judiciary which is the least dangerous branch can, by its training and politically controlled process of selection, check itself.

Professor William Whitford has stated that to the extent that the judiciary is activist, and hence participates in law making as well as law application, judicial independence raises troubling issues for democratic theory.[56] In other words, should judges makes law which is a function reserved for parliament? This is an old question. Justice P.N Bhagwati, a former chief justice of India, has posed the following question; what is the role of a judge in a democracy, and that in turn raises a further question; is the function of a judge merely to declare law as it exists or to make law?[57] Answering his own question, Justice Bhagwati observes that in a democratic society which has a constitution with a bill of rights or which has subscribed to regional or international instruments on human rights and which is seeking to build a fair and just society, judicial activism on the part of the judiciary is imperative both for strengthening democracy and the realisation of basic rights by large numbers of the people in the country. He asserts that judges take part in the law making process. In fact as early as 1972 Lord Reid of the English House of Lords, declared that the notion that a judge's role is simply to declare law is a 'fairy tale' which they did not believe any more.[58] Furthermore, Justice Kirby has succinctly stated: 'Judges make law. They make law as surely as the Executive.'[59]

There is a growing body of opinion calling on judges to come out openly and make law rather than doing so in secret. This has become more urgent because of the need for domestic application of international human rights norms. Justice Mohammed Haleem has reminded us that the relation between international law and municipal law is a question of determining what are the most appropriate judicial means of achieving, in a state legal system, the aims and intentions lying behind the rule established by international law. Haleem goes on to argue that the domestic application of human rights norms is now regarded as a basis for implementing constitutional values beyond the minimum requirements of the constitution. He further contends that the international human rights norms are in fact part of the constitutional expression of liberties guaranteed at the national level. Consequently, domestic courts can assume the task of expanding these liberties. The exercise of judicial power to create an order of liberties on a level higher than the respective constitution is now considered to be an essential ingredient of judicial activism. Haleem was of the view that current thinking at the international level supports an expanded role of domestic courts for the observance of international human rights norms. This reappraisal enables domestic courts to extend to the citizens, via state institutions, greater protection of recognised human rights.[60] Adopting judicial activism would do away with the incredibly persistent attempts on the part of lawyers and judges to convince the people about the truth of the lie that judges do not make law.[61]

The celebrated case of *Attorney-General v. Unity Dow*[62] is a good example of judicial activism. In this case the court relied on the United Nations Declaration of the Rights of the Child 1959, the United Nations General Assembly Declaration on the Elimination of Discrimination Against Women of 1967 and on the 1981 African Charter on Human and Peoples Rights, even though Botswana had not ratified the conventions based on these declarations. In *State v. Ncube & Ors*[63] the Supreme Court of Zimbabwe held that the whipping of an adult offender contravened section 15(1) of the constitution which provides that no person shall be subjected to torture or to inhuman or degrading punishment or other such treatment. This section is in pari materia with article 24 of the 1995 Uganda constitution. The court held that such punishment was inherently brutal and cruel and was degrading to punished and punisher alike. In holding that the administration of corporal punishment to adults was unconstitutional the court relied on the case of *Tyre v. The United Kingdom*[64] which interpreted article 3 of the European Convention on Human Rights. This judicial activism enabled the court to apply international human rights norms in the context of domestic law. The same court in *Catholic Commission for Justice and Peace in Zimbabwe v. Attorney-General*[65] extensively relied on international human rights norms and precedents from diverse jurisdictions to hold that delay in the execution of condemned prisoners was unconstitutional because it amounted to torture. In the case of *Mgmongo v. Mwangwa,*[66] the Tanzania High Court followed *Silver v. The United Kingdom*[67] a decision of the European Court of Human Rights, in striking down a local statute as infringing human rights even though at the time Tanzania did not have a bill of rights in its constitution.

A court which is not activist can cause considerable injustice as happened in the Zimbabwe case of *Venia Magaya v. Nakayi Shonhiwa Magaya*[68] which upheld a customary law of succession which prefers males to females as heirs. Under the Zimbabwe constitution, the prohibition against discrimination does not extend to matters of devolution of property on death or the application of African customary law involving Africans. However it was argued by counsel for the female appellant and by Welshman Ncube who appeared as *amicus curie* that the court should exercise its discretional law making power to ensure that women are not excluded from being appointed successors under customary law. It was further argued that the change would be in keeping with the principle of advancing gender equality enshrined in international human rights instruments to which Zimbabwe is a party. One such instrument is the 1979 Convention on the Elimination of All Forms of Discrimination Against Women. Article 2(f) of this convention provides that state parties shall 'take all appropriate measures, including legislation, to modify or abolish existing laws, regulations, customs and practices which constitute discrimination against women.' The Supreme Court of Zimbabwe rejected these arguments with the result that women who are subject to customary law are not equal to men in inheritance matters. In the court's view the change could only be effected by parliament.

In any case some constitutions[69] provide that judicial power shall be exercised in conformity with the law, values, norms and aspirations of the people. This broad constitutional mandate cannot be achieved by the courts simply applying the law. They can only be achieved by an activist court which accepts that it makes law within its constitutional limits. The courts have realised that constitutions are expected to survive for a lengthy period of time and the process of amending or revising them is difficult and onerous. Such constitutions are drafted with an eye to the future. Its function is to provide a continuing framework for the legitimate exercise of governmental power. It must, therefore, be capable of growth and development over time to meet new social, political and historical realities often unimagined by its framers. Constitutional interpretation is then primarily concerned with the recognition and application of constitutional values. The judiciary is the guardian of the constitution and must bear these conditions in mind when interpreting its provisions.

The phenomenon of constitutionalism

Under written constitutions, it is the constitution which is supreme and not parliament. But the mere fact of possessing a written constitution does not necessarily mean that a culture of constitutionalism has been ushered in. The majority of the people in the vast majority of Commonwealth African countries are illiterate. By reason of this illiteracy, the population is unaware of the constitution and of their rights under it. Then there is the issue of poverty. By reason of limited resources, the vast majority of the people cannot afford to engage lawyers even when they are aware of the infringement of their rights and pervasion of the constitution. As a consequence of the above, governments have survived on institutionalised repression which has sapped initiative and guts. People have thus become content to be receivers without being seekers. By legislative and administrative means the state has curtailed people's constitutional rights. Parliament and the executive have reigned supreme with little regard for the constitution.[70] The leaders have cast themselves in the role of an absolute monarch.

This is what Professor Yash Ghai has termed patrimonialism or personal rule a situation where the ruler and his or her officials are above the law and insulated from rational-legal order or from constitutional rule.[71] Ghai further argues that third world countries especially those in Africa are not in control of their destinies. A society which is not in control of its destiny finds it hard to institutionalise power on the basis of constitutional rule, any more than it can resist encroachment on constitutional rights and democracy. Ghai, quite rightly, asserts that the ideology of constitutionalism has only the most slender appeal to the rulers and the ruled in the third world. Legitimacy comes from other sources. Indeed some of these alternative sources are quite antithetical to constitutional rule. The examples are not difficult to find. Thus the Ugandan Minister for security was quoted in one local daily when answering a question on whether detaining people for longer than the mandatory constitutional forty-eight hours was illegal. He replied as follows:

> It is against the law. We are holding them against the law. But I am convinced we are doing a good thing for society. It is better to infringe on the rights of a few people to save many others.[72]

The honourable minister is quite obviously not bothered by the whole idea of constitutionalism.

Ghai also reminds us that independence from colonialism was closely associated with the ideology of modernisation and development. Using this ideology state structures were strengthened and their writ expanded. People appeared to regard the promotion of development as the primary task of the government. For their part governments justified the aggregation and concentration of power on the imperatives of development. As a result of this, constitutionalism has suffered.

As Radhika Coomarswamy has observed, the sense of a constitution as fundamental law has yet to emerge as a settled consensus accepted by all shades of political opinion. Therefore constitutions and constitutionalism cannot be seen as fundamental law but as a process in which the values of the constitution are mediated by the realities of power and social antagonism. The process may have began but it will take some time for the constitutions to become accepted social contracts.[73] For the moment unfortunately, most constitutions in Africa are merely formal pieces of paper whose substantive provisions, such as fundamental rights, are rarely observed.

The patrimonial form of domination has also affected the courts whose officials viewed themselves as the extension of the ruler. As Austin argued, the ruler delegates legislative and administrative functions to many institutions including the judiciary. Each dispersion of sovereign power is a delegation and not a release.[74] For example, in the Nigerian case of *Bronik Motors and Anor v. Wema Bank Ltd.*[75] the court stated that the words 'judicial power' mean the power which every sovereign authority must of necessity have to decide controversies between its subjects. It is not surprising therefore that when the executive and parliament are busy curtailing the citizen's constitutional rights the courts have looked on powerless. Indeed, sometimes they have encouraged the curtailment.[76] Because the executive thinks that the judiciary is its delegate, it has not hesitated to oust the jurisdiction of the courts or to disobey their orders. In any case, blind adherence to the concept of constitutionalism, irrespective of the values enshrined in the constitution, can lead to constitutional dictatorship.

Concluding remarks

I have discussed some of the doctrines which I believe have negatively influenced the courts in interpreting and applying a written constitution. There is a need to reconsider these antiquated doctrines in the light of our written constitutions. This is particularly important if we are to have leaders and not rulers. Constitutionalism can exist under a dictatorship. But since Commonwealth African constitutions claim that sovereignty is vested in the people,[77] there should be a new doctrine which actualises this slogan. For example, we could use the concept of a democratic constitution rather than constitutionalism. This will liberate us from being ruled from the grave by antiquated constitutional doctrines and values.

Notes

1.   Wheare (1966): 12.
2.   Wade and Bradley (1993): 4.
3.   Gingyera Pincywa (1978): 77-80.
4.   Dicey (1959): 39-40.
5.   *Ghana Constitution* 1992 art 1(2), *Uganda Constitution,* 1995 art. 2(1).
6.   *Ghana Constitution* 1992 art 1(2), *Uganda Constitution,* 1995 art. 2(2).
7.   See for example, *East African Community v. Republic* (1970) E.A. 457 (Kenya); *Attorney-General v. Abuki* Appeal No. 1 of 1998 (Unreported) (Uganda); *State v. Makwanyane* (1996) C H R L D 164 (South Africa); Catholic *Commission for Justice and Peace in Zimbabwe v. Attorney- General* (1992) 2 L R C 279 (Zimbabwe); *Ex Parte Attorney-General: In Re: Corporal Punishment by Organs of State* (1991) 3 S.A. 76 (Namibia).
8.   [1995] 1LRC 269.
9.   [1996] 3 CHRLD 307.
10. [1996] 1 CHRLD 308.
11. [1996] CHRLD 91.
12. [1996] E.A 306.
13. Constitutional Appeal No. 1 of 1998 (unreported).
14. *Abuki v. Attorney-General Constitutional Petition* No.2 of 1997.
15. Article 24 of *the Uganda Constitution* 199 provides as follows: 'No person shall be subjected to any form of torture, cruel, inhuman or degrading treatment or punishment.' Furthermore, article 44 states in part that: 'Notwithstanding anything in this constitution, there shall be no derogation from the enjoyment of the following rights and freedoms—(a) freedom from torture, cruel, inhuman or degrading treatment or punishment.
16. [1996] 2 CHRLD 160.
17. *Constitution of Tanzania,* Article 1.

18. (1996) 2 CHRLD 159. See also *Venia Magaya v. Nakayi Shonhiwa Magaya* Civil App 635 of 1999 (unpublished) where the Supreme Court of Zimbabwe refused to abolish a rule of customary law saying that this was a function of Parliament.

19. Egonda Ntende (1998).

20. [1999] E.W.J. 1533 unreported. Delivered 30 March 1999.

21. *State v. Ntsele* case CCT 25/97 (Papua New Guinea); *Kabilene & Ors v. DPP* [1999] E. W. J. No. 1533 (England); *R v Whyte* (1988) 51 D L R 481 (Canada); *State v. Mbatha* [1995] 2 L R C 208 (South Africa).

22. See article 44(C).

23. [1970] E.A. 457: 460.

24. *Attorney-General v. British Broadcasting Corporation* (1981) A.C 303.

25. *Attorney-General v. Unity Dow* CIV Appeal No.4 of 1991.

26. Reproduced in [1996] 1 CHRLD 146-52 Statement No.6.

27. *New Patriotic Party v. Attorney-General* (1998) 2 CHRLD 5.

28. See *Attorney-General v. Abuki* Const. Appeal No.1 of 1998 per Mulenga J.S.C. quoting the Canadian case of *Osborne v. Canada (Treasury Board)* (1991) 82 DLR 4th Ed 321.

29. [1996] 1 CHRD 8: 9.

30. *Attorney-General v. Abuki op. cit.*

31. *Ibid.*

32. See also rule 31 of the First schedule to the *Constitution of Ghana* for a similar provision.

33. Constitutional Appeal No.1 of 1997.

34. Walubiri (1998): 205-06.

35. In fact art. 99(1) of the constitution of Uganda provides that the executive authority of Uganda shall be exercised in accordance with the constitution and laws of Uganda. This leaves no room for executive prerogatives.

36. Wade and Bradley (1993) *op. cit.* 262-274.

37. Ibid.

38. The exceptions are Swaziland and Morocco. But even in these two countries the prime minister is really a figure head. Real executive power vests in the monarch.

39. Dicey (1959), 202-203.

40. See Inter alia, South Africa (art 8), Namibia (art 10(1)), Mauritius (s.3), Uganda (art 21 (1), Nigeria (art 17 (1), and (a) Tanzania (art 13 (1)).

41. Uganda Constitution 1995, article 43 and the Preamble.

42. (1996) 1 CHRLD 39.

43. Whitford (2000).

44. Wade and Bradley (1993): 102.

45. *Ibid.*

46. Ibid.

47. Whitford (2000) *supra.*

48. Goldman (1991): 184.

49. 369 U.S. 186.

50. *Ibid.*, 210.

51. Quoted in Nowak and Rotunda (1995): 116-17.

52. *Ibid.*; see also Henkin (1976): 622-23.

53. *New Patriotic Party v. A-G*, Writ No. 4 of 1993.

54. Whitford (2000).

55. See *State v. Makwanyane* [1995] 1 LRC 269: 311.

56. Whitford (2000) supra.

57. Bhagwati (1992): 8.

58. *Ibid.*

59. Quoted by Kirby (1988): 68-84.

60. Haleem (1988) *op cit.*,92.

61. M. Kirby (1988) *op. cit.*, 70.
62. (1992) L R C (Const): 623.
63. (1992) 66 A L J R 408.
64. (1978) EHRR 247.
65. (1988) 2 S.A. 708.
66. (1993) 19 (3) C.L.B 1393.
67. (1993) 5 E H R R 247
68. Civil Appeal No. 635 of 1992, Judgment No. S C 210/98 (Unreported).
69. For example, *Uganda constitution* 1995, Article 126 (1).
70. See *Mtikila v. Attorney-General* Civil Case No.5 of 1993 p.11 and *De Klerk & Anor v. Du Plessis and Ors* (1994) 6 B L R 124 at 128-129.
71. Ghai (1996): 717-719.
72. Peter Mwesigye, 'New Laws to curb Terrorism,' *The Sunday Vision* 18 July 1999, 3.
73. Coomaraswamy (1996) *op. cit.*, 720.
74. Cotterrel (1989): 75-77.
75. [1985] 6 N.C.L.R. 1.
76. See earlier discussion of the Ugandan cases of *Attorney-General v. Tinyefuza* Const. Appeal No.1 of 1997 and *Abuki v. Attorney-General* Const. Petition No.2 of 1997. Also see an admission of this fact by the Supreme Court of South Africa in *De Klerk & Anor v. Du Plessis & Ors* (1994) 6 B L R 124: 128-129.
77. For example article 1(1) of *the Constitution of Ghana* provides that "the sovereignty of Ghana resides in the people of Ghana in whose name and for whose welfare the powers of government are to be exercised in the manner and within the limits laid down in this constitution. See also article 1 of the constitution of Uganda 1995.

References

Bhagwati, P.N. (1992) 'The Role of the Judiciary in the Democratic Process: Balancing Activism and Judicial Restraint' (2) *Journal Human Rights & Policy*.

Coomaraswamy, R. (1996) 'Uses and Usurpation of Constitutional Ideology,' in Henry Steiner (ed.) *International Human Rights in Context,* Oxford: Claredon Press.

Cotterrel, R. (1989) *The Politics of Jurisprudence: A Critical Introduction to Legal Philosophy* London: Butterworths.

Dicey, A.V. (1959) The *Law of the Constitution* (19th Ed.) London: Macmillan.

Dicey, A.V. (1959) *The Law of the Constitution,* London: MacMillan.

Egonda Ntende, F.M. (1998) *Presumption of Innocence and Reverse Onus Clause: Does the 1995 Uganda Constitution Establish a New Standard,* MIMEO (unpublished).

Ghai, Y. (1996) 'The Theory of the state in Third World and the Problematic Constitutionalism,' in Henry Steiner (ed.) *International Human Rights in Context,* Oxford: Claredon Press.

Gingyera Pincywa, A.G.G. (1978) *Apollo Milton Obote and His Times,* New York: NOK.

Goldman, S., (1991) *Constitutional Law: Cases and Essays,* Amherst: Harper Collins.

Haleem, M. (1988) 'The Domestic Application of Human Rights Norms,' in *Developing Human Rights Jurisprudence.*

Henkin, L. (1976) 'Is there a Political Question Doctrine' *Yale Law Journal* (85).

Kirby, M. (1988) 'The Role of the Judges in Advancing Human Rights Norms,' in *Developing Human Rights Jurisprudence.*

Nowak, J.E. and R.D. Rotunda (1995) *Constitutional Law* Minneapolis; West Publishing Co.

Peter Mukidi Walubiri (1998) 'Towards A new Judicature in Uganda: From Reluctant Guards to Centurions of Justice' in P.M.Walubiri. (Ed.), *Uganda Constitutionalism At Cross Roads,* Kampala: Uganda Law Watch.

Wade, E.C. S. and A.W. Bradley (1993) *Constitutional and Administrative Law,* 5th Impression, London: Longman.

Wheare, K.C. (1966) *Modern Constitutions* (2nd Ed.) London: Oxford University Press.

Whitford, William, (2000) 'The Rule of Law: New Reflections on an old Doctrine,' *East African Journal of Peace & Human Rights,* Vol.6, no.2.

17

Breaking the Barriers: Radical Constitutionalism in the New African Century

Makau Mutua

In the last two decades of the twentieth century Africa has witnessed a deepening crisis of governance and statehood. These protracted problems of the post-colonial African state have raised new issues about the meaning of state legitimacy. They have also brought forward disturbing questions about the concepts of territorial sovereignty and the notion of statehood.[1] The condition of juridical statehood attained with the decolonisation of the colonial state has in the last four decades proven inadequate.[2] It is becoming increasingly apparent that these concepts and principles may have trapped Africa in a detrimental time capsule and appear like straight-jackets packed with time-bombs ready to explode. The imposition of the nation-state through colonisation balkanised Africa into a historical units and forcibly incorporated it into the Age of Europe.[3] In the process, Africa was permanently disfigured.[4] Unlike their European counterparts, African states and borders are distinctly artificial and are not 'the visible expression of the age-long efforts of [the indigenous] peoples to achieve political adjustment between themselves and the physical conditions in which they live.'[5] Colonisation interrupted that historical and evolutionary process. Since then Africa has attempted, often unsuccessfully, to live up to and within these new formulations. All too frequently, the consequences have been disastrous.

Some aspects of African political reality have been depicted as apocalyptic.[6] What is undeniable today is that the survival of Africa is seriously threatened by corrupt and inept political elite, unbridled military machineries, ethnic rivalries and conflicts, refugee flows, and economic misery. Africa today dances precariously on a political precipice. In this chapter I argue that the post-colonial state—the uncritical successor of the colonial state—is doomed because it lacks basic moral legitimacy. Its normative and territorial construction on the African colonial state, itself a legal and moral nullity, is the fundamental reason for its failure. I argue that at independence, the West decolonised the colonial state, not the African peoples subject to it. In other words, the right to self-determination was exercised not by the victims of colonisation but their victimisers, the elite who control the international state system. As such, dependence continued under the framework of the post-colonial state, the instrument of narrow elite and their international backers. Although additional reasons, such as external economic factors and cultural disorientation, have contributed to the crisis of the African state, it is considered view that they cannot be divorced from the crisis of internal legitimacy. I contend that the foreign imposition of artificial states and their continued entrapment within the twin essentially Western concepts of statehood and sovereignty are sure to occasion the extinction of Africa unless those sacred cows are set aside. What is necessary at the present time is for us to disassemble and reconfigure African states. As a first step in this process, I propose that pre-colonial entities within the post-colonial order be allowed to exercise their right to self-determination. Only such a radical but necessary step can commence the process of effectively legitimising the African state and avoiding its demise.[7]

Needless to say my suggestion—that of new cartography—will doubtless be viewed without sympathy by a host of interested parties: the elite who control the international state and financial systems, scholars stuck in traditional notions of international law, and states all over the world. But nowhere is opposition bound to be steeper than within African states themselves and the ruling cliques who benefit from those states. Until Eritrea's recent success in its secessionist war against Ethiopia, prevailing state ideology in Africa treated any discussion about border changes, separatist movements, or ethnic self-determination within an independent African state as treason. Ironically, it was African elite who sanctified the colonial state by ratifying its borders and forbidding even idle speculation about reconsideration of the issue.

There are several reasons for this resistance to an imagination of political life without the post-colonial state. The simple explanation is that alienated elite—who have more in common with and harbour many of the aspirations of the elite in industrialised countries than with their teeming masses of rural and urban poor—are loathe to give up the privileges which come from control of the state. Since their lavish lifestyle stems from the state as currently organised, it would be suicidal for the leaders to participate in attempting to change it. Even when the state is simply ineffective or on the brink of collapse, the elite will still defend it. Arguments against dismantling the colonial state range from the 'chaos' that would result from removing central authority to the balkanisation of Africa into myriad ethnic entities. Pride in the African post-colonial state was fostered by the fervour generated by the anti-colonial struggle. There is, in short, some affection for the entity. However, unless the sobering reality of the failure of the state is appreciated and steps are taken to make a voluntary, consensual map, the partition of Africa into small, Eritrea-like states, or possibly smaller ones, is inevitable. That eventuality will come at great cost to Africa. Hence my argument for an orderly recreation of the state. The chapter approaches this enterprise in the following fashion. The first part examines the moral and legal nullity of the colonial state, while part II examines the crisis of the post-colonial state. In part III I examine the manner in which federalism has failed as an antidote to the ills of the post-colonial state. Finally, I argue that there is a need for a new cartography which will fully address the African crisis.

The colonial state as a moral and legal nullity

The concepts of sovereignty and statehood, as developed and used in traditional international law by a handful of European powers, were historically crafted without pre-colonial Africa in mind. Yet it is precisely these concepts that have provided the foundation for the creation of scores of modern states in Africa. For many centuries, international law was regarded as the law existing between 'civilised' states.[8] Though today it is the main currency regulating international relations, international law or the law of nations is a development of exclusively European historical circumstances.[9] Similarly, this exclusive body of law has identified the sources from which it may be derived as custom, treaty, the general principles of law common to all major legal systems, and the judicial decisions and teachings of highly regarded publicists from different countries.[10]

Given this history, the legality of the colonial state can be assessed from both within and outside the discourse and paradigm of international law. From the inside, a critical evaluation of colonisation could indicate whether it was a violation of the European norms and practice of the rules of extant inter-state discourse. Whatever the case, the outcome has a bearing on the legality of the colonial state itself. Legality could also be assessed from the exterior, looking at colonisation from the vantage point of the colonised, in the seat of those subjected to European imperial rule and expansionism. The question of the legality and legitimacy of the colonial state is critical because it deeply implicates the moral and legal character of its successor, the post-colonial state. In revisiting the nature of the colonial and the post-colonial state, argue that decolonisation was not the same thing as liberation. My purpose is to attempt the discovery of formulae through which the complete independence, sovereignty, viability and prosperity of African political societies could be secured.

Revisiting the origins of colonial hegemony

Although there is no consensus about why Europe colonised Africa, most commentators agree that the principal motives were economic.[11] The first serious contacts between Europe and Africa involved the capture of African slaves for the newly discovered Americas. Portugal, and later other European powers including the British and the French, captured and transported for sale millions of Africans into the New World.[12] But European occupationist designs over the continent did not mature until the mid-1800s. The tremendous growth of western European capitalism and the need for markets and materials for industry gave added urgency to imperialism.[13] The scramble began with the French invasion of Algeria in 1830, the British takeover of Egypt and the Suez Canal, King Leopold's seizure of large tracts in central Africa, and Germany's ambition to acquire colonies of its own.[14] The Berlin colonial conference was disguised as a forum for the liberalisation and internationalisation of trade in Africa, and purported to legalise the partition and subordination of the continent to European states. Needless to say, none of the African peoples or political entities who were the subject of the conference were invited to provide their view of the legality of colonisation. Or, put differently they were not asked to make any contribution to a discussion that led to the loss of sovereignty over their societies. The Europeans felt that they knew what was best for the 'natives.' The orderly division of Africa was primarily meant to defuse colonial tensions and avoid the risk of war among the conferees.

Morally, the justification for colonisation was steeped in European racism, a continuing theme in African-European or black-white relations over the centuries. Racism as an institution commenced in the fifteenth century with arrival in Africa of European explorers, Christian missionaries, and slave traders. In the early nineteenth century, an intellectual discourse about the 'natural' and 'inherent' superiority of white peoples over black peoples gained popularity and acceptance.[15] According to Basil Davidson:

> The advocates of this discourse—Hegel [German philosopher George Hegel] most typically, but duly followed by a host of Justifiers—declared that Africa had no history prior to direct contact with Europe. Therefore Africans, having made no history of their own, had clearly made no development of their own. Therefore they were not properly human, and could not be left to themselves but must be 'led' towards civilization by other peoples: that is, by the peoples of Europe, especially of Western Europe, and most particularly of Britain and France.[16]

Combined with the insular development of international law as the exclusive domain of Christian nations, such discourse served as fodder for states ready to expand for economic reasons; it certainly added to the zealotry for colonisation.[17] Early international legal doctrine itself appeared to sanction colonisation, the acquisition of territory by a recognised state and the imposition of its sovereignty over such territory. Such taking could occur as occupation,[18] subjugation,[19] or cession.[20] In reality, the colonisation of Africa utilised any of the three methods, or a combination thereof, although according to international law at the time only occupation was purportedly legal, since no recognised states existed in Africa. Even within European idiom, occupation raises problems of its own because many of the entities colonised through it met the criteria for statehood.[21] Most African societies were organised in ethno-political states. Some were highly centralised, others less so.[22]

New frontiers, new states

The process of drawing new frontiers and establishing effective occupation of the territories began in earnest as soon as spheres of influence were delimited among the European powers. While the last two decades of the nineteenth century were used to conquer and establish a physical presence, the first two of the twentieth century were decades of 'pacification' and the imposition of colonial rule through the colonial state. The new states were usually created by forcefully amalgamating, or through 'treaties of protection,' numerous pre-existing African traditional states or ethno-political communities. The new territories were an actualisation of the 'spheres of influence.' The loss of sovereignty by pre-colonial states was therefore followed by their combination into single, unitary states. Thousands of independent pre-colonial states were compressed into some forty new states.

The typical examples of Kenya and Uganda will suffice to demonstrate the callous and arbitrary process of boundary delimitation. The area today known as Kenya was declared a British sphere of influence in 1886 and declared the East African Protectorate in 1896; it was annexed and became the Kenya Colony in 1920. Although the area now called Uganda also became a British sphere of influence in 1886 and was named the Uganda Protectorate in 1894, its boundaries remained uncertain because the British could not immediately determine the status of the kingdoms of Buganda, Toro, and Ankole. Later, these pre-colonial states lost their sovereignty as they became part of the new Ugandan state. Between 1900-1902, the British even contemplated combining Kenya and Uganda into one protectorate. In 1902, a large tract of eastern Uganda, consisting of its Eastern province, the southern part of the Elgon district of central Uganda and the southern portion of Rudolf province was transferred and became the Kisumu and Naivasha provinces of Kenya.

Similar arbitrary transfers of territory were duplicated throughout Africa. Little consideration was given to pre-colonial inter-state relations or other connections between different traditional states. In the majority of cases, the map-makers proceeded as though Africa was a blank, uninhabited slate.[23] The observations of imperial statesmen were very telling about how they perceived their cartography. As noted by J.C. Anene, '[t]he manner in which the boundaries were made was often a subject for after-dinner jokes among European statesmen.'[24] In 1890, for example, Lord Salisbury, the British prime minister, remarked at a dinner at Mansion House following the conclusion of the Anglo-French Convention which established spheres of influence in West Africa, that '[w]e have been engaged in drawing lines upon maps where no white man's foot ever trod; we have been giving away mountains and rivers and lakes to each other, only hindered by the small impediment that we never knew exactly where the mountains and rivers and lakes were.'[25]

Divisions were driven by pressures of competition between European powers, their trading companies, and in many instances the influence of rival Christian denominations.[26] Sometimes, states or entities with a history of tension and war were lumped into the same state.[27] In other cases, the new frontiers split ethnic and linguistic groups from their political societies and located them in different states.[28] Famous examples are those of the Masai, who were divided between Kenya and Tanzania, and the Ewe in Togo and Ghana. An irony of the arbitrary borders was the 'unity' of African pre-colonial states imposed under the roof of the colonial state but also the 'disunity' created by the colonial policy of divide and rule. According to Ian Brownlie:

> Boundary making in the period of European expansion in Africa took place in circumstances which generally militated against reference to tribal or ethnological considerations. Political bargaining involved the construction of parcels of territory upon broad principles evidenced graphically by liberal resort to straight lines and general features such as drainage basins and watersheds. Within a framework of overall political bargaining, the accidents of prior exploration and military penetration were often to determine delimitation as between Britain, France and Germany. Thus the map of West Africa was drawn. In any case lines were commonly drawn on maps at a stage when there was no very great knowledge of the region concerned. The boundaries which emerged were generally based upon geographical features, especially rivers and watersheds, and astronomical or geometrical lines.[29]

For many Africans, the newly contrived state represented, the physical symbol of the loss of independence and sovereignty. The manner in which these states were created following long periods of resistance, the way in which they were governed, and the purpose for which they were brought into existence—namely the exploitation of both natural and human resources—

were a grim reminder of the luxuries of self-governance. Colonial policies were harsh and brutally implemented. Such practices did little to endear Africans to the state or develop a loyalty towards it. In a nutshell both the moral and legal foundations of these entities were suspect from the start.

The crisis of the post-colonial state

The proposition that colonisation is largely responsible for Africa's economic, political, and social problems is not new.[30] The performance of the post-colonial state since independence has been abysmal, if not catastrophic. Military coups d'etat and one-party dictatorships characterised the greater part of the first two decades of independence from colonial rule. The result of this failure is the delegitimation—assuming that the overthrow of direct colonial occupation or decolonisation gave it a measure of goodwill, of the post-colonial state before its legitimisation. According to Michael Bratton, in the process of state formation the apparatus of governance of the post-colonial state 'has begun to crumble before it has been fully consolidated.'[31] The failure of the post-colonial state, from the Democratic Republic of Congo, from Burundi, to Angola, and from Rwanda and Somalia, drove Ali Mazrui to metaphorically refer to the African state as a political refugee.[32] Such a state cannot perform the six crucial functions of statehood namely: exercise sovereign control over territory; have sovereign oversight and supervision over the national resources; exercise the effective and rational collection of revenue; maintain adequate national infrastructure and have the capacity to govern and maintain law and order.[33]

The contrived and artificial citizenry of the African state is at the centre of this crisis. Although the struggle against colonial rule within the boundary of the colonial state created unity among different communities, it was insufficient to form a national identity. The development of authoritarianism in the emergent state, typified by ethnic-based favouritism for jobs, services, and other state-controlled resources, was an inevitably natural process; the new rulers saw their power as an instrument for personal gain with the assistance and participation of elite from their own group.[34] The process of nation-building has been hindered by the inability of the post-colonial state to wrest the loyalties of citizens from pre-colonial structures and formations, most notably the ethno-political society.[35]

Some writers have questioned whether African states are indeed nation-states.[36] Ethnicity and sub-nationalism have been correctly identified as some of the most inflammatory elements in nation-building.[37] Art Hansen has identified the crisis of the African state in its failure to transform the colonial state.[38] He argues that though formally independent, African states are still conceptually colonial entities, heavily reliant on the structures of the colonial state. There is little doubt that the only significant change at independence was not the restructuring of the state but the changing of the guard, the replacement of white by black faces in State House.[39] It fell on the new rulers to bring legitimacy to the colonial state, now labelled the post-colonial, black-ruled state. As Hansen points out, that challenge was enormous:

> The term 'nation' refers to a group that shares a common history and identity and is aware of that; they are a people, not just a population. Using that definition, ethnic groups (once called tribes) in Africa are also nations. None of the new African states were originally nation-states because none of them were nations as well as states. Each of the new states contains more than one nation. In their border areas, many new states contain parts of nations because the European- inspired borders cut across existing national territories. Thus one of the major tasks confronting the leaders of new African states was creating nations. This task was often referred to as creating a national consciousness, but that was misleading. There was no nation to become conscious of; the nation had to be created concurrently with a consciousness.[40]

Some scholars have argued that it is an illusion to refer to 'the state' in sub-Saharan Africa.[41] According to this view, many post-colonial states in Africa lack an independent political organisation with enough authority and power to govern a people and territory; in other words, they lack the 'essential requirements of empirical statehood.'[42] Neither the governors nor the governed exhibit the consciousness of civic responsibility:

> Citizenship means little, and carries few substantial rights or duties compared with membership in a family, clan, religious sect or ethnic community. Often the 'government' cannot govern itself, and its officials may in fact be freelancers, charging what amounts to a private fee for their services. The language of the state may be little more than a facade for the advancement of personal or factional interests by people who are only nominally judges, soldiers, bureaucrats, policemen or members of some other official category. In short, many states in sub-Saharan Africa are far from credible realities.[43]

Following from this observation, Robert Jackson consequently makes the argument, that the survival of the post-colonial states since independence has not been contingent on internal legitimacy among the populace. Indeed, such legitimacy was non-existent. Rather, he argues, their endurance in that period has been due primarily to their external or international legitimacy.[44] This legitimacy resulted from the right of self-determination granted to the colonial state and fortified by the logic of the Cold War.[45] The ethnic plurality,[46] and, in some cases, the duality of the state,[47] have finally caught up with post-colonial Africa. Absent Cold War or neo-colonial international guarantees to client states, the colonial state is nothing if not a house of cards. Its ethnic configuration, an integral legacy of colonisation, is a major factor in its failure. Rwanda and Burundi are the two most glaring examples: the Hutu-Tutsi cleavage has repeatedly caused the visitation of untold suffering on members of one group by the other.

The use of ethnicity to manipulate electoral processes demonstrates its destructive influence within the post-colonial state. Although it is noble, it seems ultimately futile to resist the suggestion that the colonial state and its successor have failed to inspire loyalty and forge a nationalistic identity among the elite as well as within the popular citizenry. Citizens as a whole lack an 'instinctual and nationalistic bond' to the state; hence those who become rulers pillage it in league with members of their ethnic group and resort to massive human rights violations to repress those they have excluded. Even Kenya, one of the most 'successful' post-colonial states, is a good example of the inability of elite to develop and pursue a national as opposed to ethnic interest. After independence from Britain in 1963, the anticolonial coalition of the major ethnic groups collapsed in 1966, ostensibly over ideological differences.[48] In 1975, Kikuyus organised to block Daniel arap Moi, a Kalenjin, from assuming the office of the president upon Kenyatta's death.[49] However, the timing of founding father Jomo Kenyatta's death and squabbles within the political elite allowed Moi to assume the presidency. Moi has continued Kenyatta's legacy: he forced the Kikuyu out and replaced them with the Kalenjin who now hold key positions in the civil service and the armed forces. Ethnicity has become such a powerful currency in Kenyan politics[50] that, in 1992 and 1997, the last two contested elections, the parliamentary and presidential votes were split primarily along ethnic lines. These voting patterns are an extremely bad omen for the future of democracy and may become a cyclical problem in virtually every subsequent election in the country.

These difficulties indicate that decolonisation was not the same thing as liberation. It is important to reconsider whether the decolonisation of the colonial state, as a territorial unit, amounted to the liberation of the different peoples within those borders and structures. The colonial state may be no more than a jail. Obviously, such an entity cannot win the loyalty of its intimates. As noted by Jackson:

> Most sub-Saharan colonies resembled the old Austro-Hungarian Empire, which consisted of many distinctive subject peoples within a single state framework. While that empire was broken up into smaller nation-states to liberate its peoples, this rarely happened in sub-Saharan Africa. Unlike the nationalities of East Central Europe, those of sub-Saharan Africa were absolutely denied any right of self-determination. Instead, like the Kurds of the Middle East or certain nationalities of Yugoslavia, they were consigned to the numerous ranks of peoples who are unrecognized

internationally. Ironically, the sole accepted definition of the right of self-determination was the former colonial jurisdiction.[51]

The illegitimacy and failure of the post-colonial state raises serious questions about the future of political organisation in Africa and about its sovereignty and independence from control and exploitation by outsiders. African peoples are thus challenged to design formulae to halt the onset of chaos and massive suffering, conditions which are inevitable if the pathology of the state is not addressed. As Mazrui has aptly noted, perhaps real decolonisation is not the winning formal independence but the collapse and eventual disintegration of the colonial state and its structures.[52] The colonial order need not, however, be 'washed clean with buckets of blood;'[53] there is an urgency for Africans to fashion a solution to avoid that horrifying eventuality. As one way of sidestepping such an outcome, I suggest that in principle sovereignty should be returned to African pre-colonial entities who should then 'trade it in' for consensual map-making to voluntarily create larger democratic entities. Before taking this point further, I first consider the phenomenon of federalism which often features in discussions about the African state and constitutionalsim.

Federalism as a failed antidote

The invention of the African state by colonialism and the subsequent misapplication of the right to self-determination are the root causes of the crisis of the post-colonial state.[54] The denial of the right to self- determination[55] is one of the fundamental reasons for the failure of the state to develop into a cohesive, effective, and functional entity.[56] Political elite have made a number of attempts, some cynical, others less so, to address the 'multi-national' character of the post-colonial state. The one promising device employed by new states to confront the problem of multi-ethnicity and self-determination was federalism. This ex-post facto attempt to save the post-colonial state from the threat of self-determination reveals the two contradictory faces of the African state. The first is the unavoidable fact that on the one hand, every 'nation' within the nation state is a 'state in embryo,'[57]—an entity entitled to exercise its right to self-determination. On the other hand is the contradiction that the nation-state as an entity is determined to unite and assimilate into a single culture all nations within it and therefore negate the multi-culturalism of the state. Those who see the African post-colonial nation state as the sole basis for political organisation on the continent argue that these two opposing faces can be reconciled if the right to self-determination is seen as 'exercisable within, as well as through, the nation state.'[58] In other words, they argue for federalism.

The African federal experience

Africa's experience with federalism has, however, proven a disappointment in so far as it has been unable to give political viability to the post-colonial state. In post-colonial Africa, federalism has been attempted in Kenya, Uganda, Zaire, and Nigeria to mention a few examples. In each case, it was motivated by different reasons.[59] Though unpopular with those who controlled the state, federalism offered a middle course between separatists and the advocates of strong unitary central states.[60] A brief survey of each of these cases is necessary to demonstrate why federalism has really failed to take root in Africa.

In Kenya, the genesis of a federal structure of government grew out of the fears of ethnic groups such as the Luhya and the Kalenjin that the control of a unitary state by the Kikuyu-Luo alliance would deny them their share of the spoils of independence.[61] The Kenya African Democratic Union (KADU), the proponent of federalism, equated regional autonomy with self-determination and access to land. [62] In 1963, the British forced the 'Majimbo Constitution,' which provided for a quasi-federal structure, as the condition for independence and the assumption of state power by KANU.[63] But Kenyatta soon after independence eroded and then abolished the federal structure, and imposed a unitary regime dominated by the Kikuyu bureaucracy.

Uganda's experimentation with federalism was equally short-lived. The pre-colonial kingdom of Buganda—one of the most established states at the time—as well the smaller states of Bunyoro, Toro and Ankole, were granted a type of federal status by the British under the independence constitution of 1962.[64] Less powerful groups, such as the Acholi and Lango of northern Uganda, organised under Milton Obote and the Uganda People's Congress (UPC), opposed federalism because they resented the commanding position that the Buganda kingdom continued to enjoy.[65] In the end, the UPC was forced to accept a federal system to avoid the secession of Buganda. In 1966, barely four years after independence, Obote violently destroyed the Buganda kingdom, abolished the federal structure, and concentrated power in his hands. An African state had failed, once again, to reconcile demands for internal self-determination with federalism.

In Zaire, formerly the Belgian Congo, and now the DRC, the irreconcilable tensions between separatists, unitarists, and federalists coupled with external interference almost resulted in the collapse of the state soon after independence in 1960.[66] Patrice Lumumba and his party, the *Mouvement National Congolais* (MNC), scored a narrow victory over Joseph Kasavubu's *Alliances des Bakongo* (ABAKO), a party of the historic Kongo people. Lumumba advocated a strong unitary state while Kasavubu and Moise Tshombe, the Katangese leader, called for either federalism or secession. Failure to agree on the form of government led in 1960 to a constitutional crisis, a mutiny, a

Belgian-led effort for the secession of Katanga, and the murder of Lumumba in which Mobutu Sese Seko, then the army chief of staff, and the Central Intelligence Agency were implicated.[67] After a prolonged period of political chaos and instability, Mobutu formally took power in a military coup in 1965, banned all political activity, and created a highly abusive police state with all power concentrated in his hands.

Apart from these experiments, federalism has also been tried, without success, in Ethiopia,[68] the Cameroons, and the Mali Federation. In 1964, Tanganyika and Zanzibar formed Tanzania, a federal republic, although it preferred to be called a 'United Republic.' Since then the 'union' has been under constant threat from Zanzibari separatists. But the most enduring, though deeply troubled and largely unsuccessful attempt at federalism has been in Nigeria. Federalism found widespread support among Nigeria's diverse ethnic and religious communities because many saw it as the only viable option if the country was to attain independence as a single unit. The northern Hausa-Fulani region, the eastern Ibo-dominated area, and the western Yoruba region all supported some form of federal arrangement, a structure which favoured the populous and large but backward north. The south, made up of Ibos and Yorubas, pushed for the creation of many ethnic-linguistic states to counterbalance the predominance of the north. The inability of the federal state to create this balance brought Nigeria to the brink of disintegration in 1966.

The South's impatience with the reluctance of the north to fully federalise and genuinely share power, political dissension and electoral violence in the west, and official corruption all combined to cause fundamental fissures in the new federal state. In January 1966, eastern, mainly Ibo, army officers took advantage of this crisis to stage the country's first coup d'etat in which northern leaders were killed. This ended the country's experiment with democracy. Major General Aguiyi Ironsi, an easterner and the head of the national military government, issued a decree replacing the federal structure with a unitary one. Many northerners protested the coup and the decree, leading to riots in which many Ibos were massacred in the north. In another coup on 29 July 1966, Ironsi was abducted on a tour of the north and killed by northerners along with the Ibo officers accompanying him. The leader of the coup, Lieutenant Colonel Yakubu Gowon, a northerner, immediately rescinded the decree abolishing federalism, although this act did not stop the mass slaughter and expulsion of Ibos from the north. Fearful of northern domination and the pogroms, the easterners, under Lieutenant Odumwengu Ojukwu, the military governor of Eastern Nigeria, declared the secession of the region as the Republic of Biafra on 30 May 1967. Although Biafra was defeated and returned to Nigeria, the country remains precariously perched on the precipice, unable to create a democratic, internally legitimate state out of the federal system. To this day, competing religious, regional, and ethnic interests continue to threaten Nigeria's survival as a state.

If Nigeria is taken as the most 'successful' example of federalism in Africa, the device appears to be doomed as a means for satisfying demands for self-determination within the post-colonial state. In Africa where, with the exception of large urban centres, ethnicity usually corresponds to ancestral land, federalism may have seemed like the magic solution for resolving or containing within the post-colonial state the desires of pre-colonial entities for independence and self-governance. Instead, federalism collapsed or failed to function effectively wherever it was attempted. These failures occurred not because rulers thought that the unitary, non-federal, state was better but because .the practice of it could not ensure equity, liberty, and prosperity. Indeed, such conditions would only have been possible under a democratic regime.[69] Since the post-colonial state failed to internalise democracy, it could not be expected to be the fair arbiter of competing ethnically-based claims. Furthermore, the trauma inflicted on African peoples by the postcolonial state has been so disorienting that their loss of faith in it is irretrievable.

The cynical manipulation of ethnic identities aside, federalism was not viable in Kenya, Uganda, or Zaire because the post-colonial state did not offer a forum for mediating the fears of groups subject to it. Those in power, usually drawn from one group, saw federalism as an attempt to weaken their grip.[70] Those vying for power, drawn from other groups, saw it as an 'equaliser,' a tool to prevent domination and retain autonomy over their own affairs. In any case, groups saw the struggle to control the state as a zero-sum game in which all the spoils belonged to the victor. This view has some truth, as each group saw the capture of state power as the only vehicle for the realisation of the right to self-determination for its people, at the exclusion, and often the expense, of other groups. Local, as opposed to European, colonialism has often been the result of such exclusionary practices.

Beyond federalism: Some pointers
The recent attempt at federalism in Ethiopia and calls for its application to newly-independent South Africa may lead to a revival of the federalist argument although none of these cases looks promising. The Transitional Government of Ethiopia (TGE)[71] that overthrew Mengistu Haile Mariam's Dergue in 1991, was based on an interim constitution that provided to all nations, nationalities, and peoples the 'right to self- determination of independence.'[72] This provision was the natural outcome of the repression of Tigrayans, Eritreans, and the Oromo by the regimes of Haile Selassie and Mengistu Haile Mariam. For these groups, the discourse of self-determination—including secession from Amhara-controlled Ethiopia—

had become standard fare.[73] In apparent recognition of this history of animosity between groups, the newly adopted constitution creates a federal system with nine federal states, each dominated by a single ethnic group. The constitution affirms the right of nationalities to establish their own federal states. But federalism Ethiopian-style has failed to work, particularly because it is seen as ploy by the Tigrayan elite to dominate other groups and monopolise all political space. In the event, all major opposition groups in Ethiopia have either been excluded from the political process or have refused to participate due to the belief that the Tigrayan-controlled government is not genuine about its claims of federalism and democratisation. In all likelihood, this latest attempt at federalism is also doomed to fail.

Federalism was viewed upon decolonisation as a viable device for addressing the rivalries of diverse pre-colonial nationalities within the post-colonial state. But as history amply demonstrated, those hopes were misplaced. In addition to federalism, other autonomy regimes for minorities within the post-colonial state in Africa may not fare any better. Two other types of autonomy regimes identified by Henry Steiner offer little hope for success. The first is power-sharing regimes in which a state's population is carved up in 'ethnic terms to assure one or several ethnic groups of a particular form of participation in governance or economic opportunities.'[74] An example would be the entitlement for members of group X to elect a stated percentage of members of the national parliament. Finally, the constitution could provide that a certain group be governed by personal law unique to it, such as a Hindu minority in Kenya.[75] Although the first model has not been tried, it is unlikely to succeed because in the winner-take-all politics of the post-colonial state, it may consign a numerically small group to the fringes of society. The second model may be irrelevant because it is unlikely to result in political power, the variable that is the basis for self-determination.

What these examples demonstrate is the inability of the post-colonial state to act as the forum on which claims and demands for self-determination can be exercised by pre-colonial entities or nations within the nation state.

New cartography as radical constitutionalism

In both concept and substance, the post-colonial state is simply the colonial state in another guise. Just as the colonial state was created by foreigners to benefit them, its existence over the last four decades was guaranteed by those same foreigners because it served the cruel logic of the Cold War. In other words, since their creation in the late nineteenth century, African states have served as the outposts of the world powers, decolonisation notwithstanding. Even in cases of extreme distress, they were not allowed to fail. External border challenges were illegitimatised by the major powers to maintain the inherited state system. The end of the Cold War, however, resulted in the flight of Western collaborators. For the first time in history, the pirates in power were left exposed. [76] In the aftermath, the fragility of the post-colonial state has been unmasked by its failure and, in several instances, complete collapse.

Given this background, there is a clear need to urgently confront the nature of the African state, to demystify it, and to address the problem of legitimacy by which it is challenged. While alienation of the African state from its citizens is not merely the function of the loss of sovereignty over pre-colonial structures—it is also a crisis of cultural[77] and philosophical identity[78]. In other words, the two phenomena are linked like Siamese twins. The crisis in Africa can only be addressed through a dual but simultaneous process of new map-making together with norm re-examination and reformulation, which will reconnect the continent to many of the pre-colonial ideals of community and social organisation as well as to democratisation. It will not suffice to democratise the post-colonial state. As a fundamentally undemocratic entity in concept and reality, it is incapable of genuine democratisation. Africa's political map must first be unscrambled and the post-colonial state disassembled before the continent can move forward. Put differently, the form and physical substance of the colonial state must be completely dismantled; otherwise, its tightening noose will strangle the entire continent. Instead of false decolonisation, whose purpose has been to preserve European Africa, new mapmaking would, as a first step, liberate the peoples of Africa by theoretically returning sovereignty to their pre-colonial political identities and asking them to consensually and voluntarily create new, democratic and ultimately, larger political entities. For this purpose, a new map of Africa must be drawn.

There is little doubt that the call for a new map to abolish the colonial state would be greeted by ruling elite with hostility, if not worse. The continent's post-colonial elite have a long history of sensitivity to any suggestion that the question of colonial boundaries be opened. The charter of the Organisation of African Unity, adopted in 1963, validated the colonial state as the basic unit for self-determination.[79] Even before the ink on the Charter was dry, the OAU was faced with a number of border disputes. In 1964, fighting broke out between Somalia and Ethiopia over the disputed Ogaden region of Ethiopia, home to ethnic Somali.[80] A similar dispute between Kenya and Somalia broke out over Kenya's north-eastern province, also inhabited by Somalis. In both instances, Somalia was driven by a desire to unite all Somali under one state.[81] Although the Somali- Kenya-Ethiopia border disputes were irredentist or ethnic, that was the exception, not the rule.[82] Morocco and Algeria were also embroiled in another boundary dispute.[83]

Against this backdrop, the OAU summit of the heads of state and government met in Cairo, Egypt in July 1964 to address the problem of borders. It adopted a key historical resolution which affirmed the borders existing at independence, with the exception of Somalia and Morocco. In effect the OAU legitimised the status quo of colonial boundaries. According to one view, the object of the resolution pragmatic, not the occasion for new sources of doubt and controversy. An elaboration of this view emphasises stability and order:

> The policy behind the resolution is clear enough. If the colonial alignments were discarded, alternative alignments would have to be agreed upon. Such a process of redefinition would create confusion and threats to the peace. Even if the principles on which revision was to be based were agreed upon, there would be considerable difficulty in applying the principles to the ethnic and tribal complexities of African societies.[84]

Writing about Nigeria, J.C.Anene agrees with this view on the basis that 'it is utterly unrealistic to suggest revisions' of international boundaries because '[n]o one can sanely contemplate mass population transfers.'[85]

While there is obvious truth to this position, there was another sinister motive for the Cairo resolution: the post-colonial ruling elite and the Cold War system stood to lose power, access to resources, and the ability to manipulate in the small and shallow pond of the post-colonial state. Although the commitment by the African elite to colonial state system is paradoxical, if not ironic, the convergence of the interests of local rulers and their international patrons completely overwhelmed any meaningful discussion about the need for African unity within larger entities.[86]

Without a doubt, the one successful enterprise of the post-colonial system in Africa has been the endurance of colonial boundaries. This has been accomplished by the development of two related concepts: the elimination of the concept of self-determination with respect to independent states, which avoids and delegitimises separatist movements, and the application of the principle of self-determination only to colonial or racist minority situations. Beginning in 1957, the colonial state was so secured over the entire Cold War period that any boundary changes were consensual. But in the last decade, a number of governments and states have been allowed to fail.

In real terms, the end of the Cold War means that African states must for the first time fend for themselves—a task for which they are ill-prepared in their current configuration. Local pressures for democratisation and better livelihood have intensified at a time when the patrons are becoming isolationist, pulling away from their traditional support of the state. New experiments with democracy may turn sour before they start in earnest. With economic decline at record levels, this confluence of factors could not have materialised at a worse time. The moral and legal illegitimacy of the colonial state have finally caught up with the continent. Either colonial Africa must be unscrambled or the failure of the state will usher in anarchy.[87]

The inability of the post-colonial state to serve citizens has diminished its sovereignty in the eyes of African masses. Instead, the state is now under attack from another norm, that of the right to self-determination, meaning the right of a people to democratic government. Social and ethnic groups are beginning to question why loyalty should be owed to a bankrupt, abusive, and illegitimate entity. In 1968, when Tanzania recognised Biafra as an independent sovereign state, it argued that since Nigeria had failed the Ibos, they owed it no loyalty.

Today, the relationship between the post-colonial state and the citizenry is reminiscent of that Nigerian tragedy. As demands for internal self-determination soar, sovereignty diminishes, and the commitment of the average African to colonial borders weakens. The distress of the state has broken what Mazrui calls the '[t]hree post-colonial taboos.'[88] These are: the taboo of recolonisation, with the UN tutelage of Somalia to reinvent its self-government; the taboo of sanctioned secession, with the creation of sovereign Eritrea; and the taboo of 'retribalisation,' with the creation of a 'federal' system in Ethiopia based on ethnicity.[89] Mazrui posits that external recolonisation may be tried under the banner of humanitarianism, as the cases of Somalia and Liberia suggest.[90] Otherwise, failed states may be taken over in a new trusteeship system dominated by stable states in Africa and Asia.[91] He indicates that the rise of ethnic consciousness and the 'politicised tribal identity' in the context of multipartyism is another reason for the review of another scared cow, a taboo, that of addressing ethnicity with federalism.[92] Significantly, Mazrui sees the 'decolonisation' of colonial boundaries as inevitable. Davidson agrees:

> Over the next century the outlines of most of present-day African states will change in one of two main ways. One will be ethnic self-determination, which will create smaller states, comparable to the separation of Eritrea from Ethiopia. The other will be regional integration, towards larger political communities and economic unions.[93]

If African peoples and governments, including the OAU, do not move quickly to liberate the post-colonial state by creating new consensual political entities to replace the colonial state, Mazrui's prediction of the continent's break-up of the colonial state into ministates will probably come true. Without a peaceful formula for the self-determination of precolonial peoples and societies, such a prediction will probably come at great cost to human life. But it is not inevitable that the eventual decolonisation and liberation of Africa will be fed on yet more African blood. As Basil Davidson so correctly writes:

What the analysis then goes on to demand, all things being so, is the invention of a state appropriate to a postimperialist future. To those who prudently reply that it can't be done, the answer will be that it can certainly be thought of. Cases spring to mind. It was already beginning to be thought of, even during the dreadful 1980s, in the projects of the sixteen-country Economic Community of West African States, and potentially again, in those of the nine- country Southern African Development Coordination Conference launched a little later. Each set of projects has supposed a gradual dismantlement of the nation- statist legacy derived from imperialism, and the introduction of participatory structures within a wide regionalist framework.[94]

In light of this gloomy prognosis, it is imperative that Africans act with urgency to reinvent the nature of the African state if an utter catastrophe is to be avoided. What this has argued for, and what is unavoidable, is the reconstruction of political society. In other words, a new consensus must be forged between and among Africans across the board to address the political quicksand that is the continent finds itself in. I suggest two levels of the process of re-invention. The first is a recreation of the political state, and this must include the state constitutional, ethical, and moral foundations. Devices like democracy and popular participation may be useful here. But this alone is insufficient to pull Africa back from the abyss. It is critically important that Africans understand that the illegitimacy and immorality of the post-colonial are not simply matters of the spirit. The physical political landscape of Africa must be reconstituted, giving freedom to pre-colonial entities to conjugate in a manner consistent with their wishes. This will by no means be an easy task. But is far better than the current state of amnesia and pretense in which elite and their international backers give the impression that tinkering with post-colonial state will save from certain doom.

Conclusion

Those who imposed the colonial state on Africa believed that they were the gift of civilisation to the rest of humanity. Like the colonial state, their views are not dead. Some have even suggested that Europe should recolonise Africa, reasoning which assumes that it was a mistake to decolonise Africa. Such views do not recognise that Europe's involvement in Africa has brought nothing but misery. Perhaps the withdrawal of the West from Africa, though detrimental to the colonial state, may provide an opportunity for Africans to squarely face their problems for the first time in several centuries. In that process of re-examination, Africa would do well to abandon the principle of *uti possidetis juris,* the device that falsely linked the decolonisation of the colonial state to the liberation of African peoples. It is a straight-jacket that continues to deny freedom to millions of Africans. While its rejection plunges Africa into an uncertain future, it ensures that creative thinking at least begins to explore bold solutions to the crisis.

It would be irresponsible to assume that the direction proposed in this article could not lead Africa down a more treacherous path in which power-mongers and cynical ethnic chauvinists would senselessly tear society apart in pursuit of self-aggrandisement. That possibility, which would be a real setback to Africa, exists. But it is far more damning to sit and wait for disaster to strike, precipitating the crises that have been witnessed in Somalia, Liberia, and Rwanda. That is why orderly formulae for re-making the continent's political map must be worked out soon. Otherwise the post-colonial state, itself already a terrorist organisation masquerading as the repository of popular will, will fragment into pieces and provide devious outsiders with more opportunities to literally pick Africa apart. Among the problems that will have to be addressed by Africans as they ponder this proposal are the criteria for determining the 'self' that would possess the right to self-determination. Furthermore, it is necessary to address how the will of that self would be determined. Identifying these criteria will be especially difficult because the colonial state substantially changed social relations and created new alliances and interests not in existence in the pre-colonial era. All these variables will have to be taken into account as new fora for expressing popular will, such as plebiscites and referenda, are explored as possible avenues for determining a new African political map.

Notes

1. Historically, a cluster of European states and the United States have taken over the formulation of the major doctrines of international law, including the concepts of statehood and sovereignty, and provided them with specific legal meanings in the law of nations. As an example, today, '[under international law, a state is an entity that has a defined territory and a permanent population, under the control of its own government, and that engages in, or has the capacity to engage in, formal relations with other such entities.' *Restatement (Third) of Foreign Relations* s. 201 (1986); see generally Henkin *et al.*, (1993): 246-48.

2. Political independence was not followed by economic independence. A hostile global economy marginalised Africa and contributed to the failure of the post-colonial state. See Mkandawire (1992): 86 and 98-101.

3. I use the term 'Age of Europe' to denote a historical and philosophical paradigm; that of European hegemony imposed over the globe, particularly the South, over the last five centuries, culminating in the domination of the Americas, Africa, and parts of Asia by Western European norms and forms in the fields of government, religion, society, culture, and the economy.

4. Most African states are the products of the competitive subjugation of the continent by Britain, France, Germany, Belgium, Portugal, Italy, and Spain between 1875-1900. Of the current states only Botswana, Burundi, Egypt, Ethiopia, Lesotho, Madagascar, Morocco, Rwanda, Swaziland, and Tunisia have any meaningful pre-colonial territorial and political identity.

The rest, including these, were either partitioned or bounded by the expediency of colonisation. See Young (1991). The power to define and exclude territory was not confined to internal map-making. Mazrui points out, for example, that it was 'Europeans who decided that the western side of the Red Sea and the Suez Canal was indeed Africa while the eastern side was not.' Mazrui, (1986), 101. He states, matter-of-factly, that 'what we regard as Africa today is primarily what Europeans decided was Africa.' *Ibid.* Even the term 'Africa' and its derivatives, such as 'African' are not indigenous to the continent; they, like the colonial state, are European impositions.

5.   Anene (1970): 3.

6.   One of the most bone-chilling and pessimistic accounts of Africa, present and future, has been offered by Kaplan. Although his horrific analysis of the disintegration, decay, and the inevitable collapse of Africa has been standard diet in the West since the first Christian missionaries landed in Africa, it is done in an idiom so revolting that it is searing in its absolute pessimism. Seen through his eyes, governments implode, disease and environmental degradation take over, and civil and ethnic strife end life on the continent. See Kaplan (1994): 44; see also, Connelly & Kennedy (1994): 61.

7   By redrawing Africa's map, I do not mean just the physical delineation of land mass, although that is a necessary part of the process of recreating the African state. I also mean the reconceptualisation of the state and its relationship to the individual and society. Here, one can imagine various constitutional and legal devices, such as constitutionalism or other conceptions of limited government, that are essential for the creation of a democratic state. In addition, any successful rebirth of African statehood must redefine the state's relationship with dominant global forces such as multinational corporations and international finance institutions in such a way that the state recaptures its sovereignty. Finally, such a process must pay attention to African political and cultural heritage if it is to attain any legitimacy with broad sectors of the people.

8.   Crawford (1976-77): 93, 98. The British regarded international law as only the province of 'Christian nations.' Id. (quoting Smith (1932), 12). 'Members of the society whose law was international were the European states between whom it evolved from the fifteenth century onwards, and those other States accepted expressly or tacitly by the original members into the Society of Nations; for example the United States and Turkey.' *Ibid.,* Turkey was not admitted into this exclusive club until 1856 and Japan only after it defeated China in 1901-02. China was itself admitted thereafter. Umozurike (1993): 9-10.

9.   Oppenheim, one of the most distinguished writers on the subject, states that international law 'is in its origin essentially a product of Christian civilization' which arose in the second half of the Middle Ages. Oppenheim (1928). Working from natural law, seventeenth century writers such as Hugo Grotius constructed a body of rules on 'religious, moral, rational, and historical' bases; these rules are now the foundation of modern international law. *Ibid.,* 19.

10.   Article 38, *Statute of the International Court of Justice.*

11.   According to a reputable Africanist, Africa, in the rhetorical metaphor of imperial jingoism, was a ripe melon awaiting carving in the late nineteenth century. Those who scrambled fastest won the largest slices and the right to consume at their leisure the sweet, succulent flesh. Stragglers snatched only small servings or tasteless portions; Italians, for example, found only deserts on their plates. See Young, *supra note* 4, at 19; see generally Oliver (1991). For a detailed and historical account of the detrimental effects of European penetration of Africa, see Rodney (1981).

12.   Portugal was the oldest established power in Africa and had for many centuries been a slave-trader. Crowe (1970): 11. For a fuller account of the European trade in African slaves, see generally Davidson (1991).

13.   Woddis (1967): 13-14.

14.   Davidson, *History, supra,* 283-84.

15. This doctrine of white superiority was at odds with previous European scholarship. That scholarship knew that the foundations of European civilization derived from classical Greek civilization. That scholarship further accepted what the Greeks had laid down as patently obvious: that classical Greek civilisation derived, in its religion, its philosophy, its mathematics and much else, from the ancient civilizations of Africa, above all from Egypt of the Pharaohs. To those 'founding fathers' in classical Greece, any notion that Africans were inferior, morally or intellectually, would have seemed merely silly. Davidson, *History*, xxii-xxiii. For a careful, historical, and analytic exploration of the African origins of classical civilisations, see Bernal (1987).

16. Davidson, *History, supra*, xxii.

17. *Ibid.*,

18. Occupation occurred when a recognised state acquired territory which was uninhabited, referred to as terra nullius, or inhabited by a people or an entity that international law did not consider a state. Only a state could occupy territory. This is known as an 'original' mode of the acquisition of territory. Possession and effective administration of such territory, which was considered no-man's land, made occupation real and were essential to it.

19. Subjugation arose through the conquest of enemy territory in war and its subsequent annexation by the conquering state. This conquest 'disappeared' the vanquished state; but title did not vest in the conqueror until annexation was effected. If the conquering state made the conquered state give up only part of its territory in a 'treaty of peace,' then acquisition was by cession, not subjugation.

20. Cession was the acquisition of territory in a bilateral arrangement, where the parties, who both had to be states, lost or gained territory by agreement or acquiescence through war.

21. While it is beyond the scope of this article to explore at length the history and evolution of state formation in Africa, it is necessary for me to outline in a preliminary manner the broad sketches of African political societies from a historical view in order to lay to rest the mistaken and deliberately distorted view that African history started with its colonization by Europeans. Apart from the Egyptian and Ethiopian civilizations, which the West acknowledges but denies their black African origin, other parts of the continent have long histories of developed state-societies. In West Africa, the Soninke kingdom has been traced to AD 300 as were the Tekrur and Mandingo kingdoms in Senegal and Mali, respectively. Between the ninth and sixteenth centuries, writers and travelers documented the sophisticated states and kingdoms of ancient Ghana, Mali, Songhay, Benin, and others. Many of these states engaged in inter-state relations, including commerce, sometimes with traders from the Middle East. In East Africa, by the nineteenth century, states such as Buganda, Bunyoro, and Nkore had arisen in southern Uganda. Others rose in Rwanda, Burundi, and among the Haya, Hehe and Nyamwezi in Tanzania. In central and southern Africa, the Luba/Lunda and Kongo states in Angola- Democratic Republic of Congo area and the Mwanamutapa kingdom in Zimbabwe can be traced from anywhere around the fifteenth century; all predated the scramble for Africa.

22. The requirements for an entity to meet the criteria for statehood were: sovereign government, defined territory with a permanent population under its control, and a capacity to engage in formal relations with other entities. See supra notes 22-23 and accompanying text. These criteria were met by many African entities which fell to colonisation. Pre-colonial Africa consisted of two categories of societies. The first group consists of those states with centralised authority, administrative machinery, and other standing state institutions such as the Zulu, Ashanti, and Buganda. The second is those with less intrusive government organs, such as the Akamba and the Kikuyu of Kenya, whose common cultural, ethnic, and linguistic

homogeneity gave them fundamental cohesion. For analyses of the organisation of pre-colonial state-societies, see generally Ayisi (1972); Fortes & Evans-Pritchard (1940); Muthiani, (1973); Kenyatta (1965); Wiredu (1990).

23. At the Berlin Conference, Africa was 'regarded as terra nullius, subject to the possession of the European power exercising effective authority. They never took into account that there were people of vastly different backgrounds and cultures living on the continent.' Peter (1993), 117, 124-25 (footnotes omitted). The International Court of Justice in the Western Sahara case said that the colonisation of Africa was not 'occupation' in the technical sense; the 'treaties' with African rulers indicated that the continent was not considered terra nullius proper. *Western Sahara* (Advisory Opinion), 1975 International Court of Justice 12 (Oct. 16), 39.

24. Anene, *supra*, 3.

25. *Ibid.* Anene quotes another senior British official who was involved in creating the boundary between Nigeria and Cameroon, saying that:
   In those days we just took a blue pencil and a rule, and we put it down at Old Calabar, and drew that line to Yola ... I recollect thinking when I was sitting having an audience with the Emir [of Yola], surrounded by his tribe, that it was a very good thing that he did not know that I, with a blue pencil, had drawn a line through his territory. *Ibid.*, 2-3 (quoting *The Geographical Journal* (1914) (xxviii) Proceedings, March 9).

26. The Buganda kingdom, for example, faced competition from both the British and German commercial companies which attempted to secure a 'treaty of protection. for different countries.

27. The Akamba, Kikuyu, and the Masai, three groups which fought each other from time to time, were all bunched into the new state of Kenya. See Hobley (1910): 43-48. Examples abound elsewhere in Africa.

28. See Barbour (1961): 303.

29. Brownlie (1979), 6. Brownlie also notes that in some cases, the map-makers included ethnology and traditional political societies as one of the factors. In creating Nigeria, for example, the traditional boundaries were followed in the north and west to make administration easier. The same was true of Burundi, Rwanda, most of North Africa, parts of Kenya, and so on. *Ibid.*, 6-7. While keeping pre-colonial administrative units together may have made for easier colonisation, it did not solve the problem of loss of sovereignty and the coercion of different pre- colonial states under one, unitary colonial state.

30. For analyses linking the crises of the post-colonial state to colonisation, see Mazrui (1995): 21. [hereinafter Mazrui, *State as Refugee*]; Nkrumah (1965).

31. Bratton (1989): 407, 409 He adds that: [t]here is a crisis of political authority that is just as severe as the well- known crisis of economic production. These two crises are intimately interrelated, each being both a cause and an effect on the other. We are currently witnessing in Africa a self-perpetuating cycle of change, in which weak states engender anemic economies whose poor performance in turn further undermines the capacity of the state apparatus. *Ibid.*

32. Mazrui, *State as Refugee, supra*, 21. He notes that the African state could even become a literal refugee if the remnants of the Hutu state in Rwanda were to be granted institutional asylum as a government-in-exile next door [Congo]. *Ibid.*, 22.

33. *Ibid.*, 23. He argues that it is wrong to limit the assessment of state failure to the sixth function, namely the maintenance of law and order. The other indices are warning signs of impending failure. *Ibid.*

34. The process of the collapse of national coalitions that brought about decolonisation 'involved the incorporation of 'kith and kin' into ruling oligarchies and the exclusion of other groups from enjoying the prerogatives of power. This generated problems of ethnicity, clanism, regionalism, religious bigotry, etc.' Ibrahim (1994): 15.

35. Busia convincingly argues that in pre-colonial Africa 'primary loyalties were centred on

lineage and tribe.' These communities were held together because they 'inhabited a common territory; its members shared a tradition, real or fictitious, of common descent; and they were held together by a common language and a common culture.' This tribal solidarity of the past invades the present. It sets problems of political organisation for the new States of Africa. It has been a source of tension and instability. It has led to civil war in the Congo. Nigeria tried to contain its tribal tensions in a federation. Busia (1967): 30-31.

36.   Hansen argues that African states are states hoping to become nation-states. Ethnic cleavages are the biggest drawback to the development of a nation. Hansen (1993): 139-67.

37.   Anyang' Nyong'o, (1992): 1. Anyang' Nyong'o discusses and attempts to demystify the argument that the one- party state was the only logical response to problems of ethnicity, development, and the construction of new nations from the colonial state.

38.   Hansen, *supra*, 161.

39.   Irele has observed that the authoritarianism of the colonial state "was codified in the colonial legal arsenal with an array of laws that prohibited assembly, restricted movement, proscribed 'sedition,' and so on. (After independence, these laws survived in nearly every African state and proved to be convenient repressive tools in the hands of the successor governments). Irele (1992): 296, 298.

40.   Hansen, *supra*, 161-62.

41.   Jackson (1992), 1 [hereinafter Juridical Statehood]. For similar analyses, see also Jackson (1990).

42.   Jackson, *Juridical Statehood, ibid.*, 1.

43.   *Ibid.*

44.   *Ibid.*

45.   *Ibid.*, 2.

46.   Many of the colonial states were ethnically plural. Even Somalia, created out of combining British Somaliland with Italian Somaliland, was a plural society in spite of its deceptive cultural homogeneity. Its competing clans, used so effectively by Siad Barre, the soldier who ruled from 1969 to 1991, were instrumental in his despotic rule and the subsequent collapse of the state.

47.   The dual states of Rwanda and Burundi contain the combustible Hutu/Tutsi mix, a combination fanned into hatred by Belgian colonialism. Rivkin (1969): 189-93.

48 .   The Kenya African National Union (KANU), the nationalist party which led Kenya to juridical independence, enjoyed the widespread support of the Kikuyu, Luo, and Akamba, the country's main ethnic groups. Until 1964 when they merged, it was opposed by the Kenya African Democratic Union (KADU), ostensibly a champion of smaller groups but in reality a front for British settler and commercial interests. Kenyatta, the country's first president, a Kikuyu and the leader of the KANU anti-colonial coalition picked Oginga Odinga, a Luo, as his vice-president. The coalition collapsed in 1966 when Odinga left the government to form the left-wing Kenya Peoples Union (KPU). Many prominent Luo members of parliament left with him. In 1969, Kenyatta banned the KPU following an anti-government demonstration in Kisumu, Odinga's ancestral home, in which the security forces shot and killed at least ten people. He detained Odinga and many of his Luo colleagues, an event that continues to stigmatise the Luo as an anti-government group to date, even though Daniel arap Moi, the current president, is a Kalenjin.

49.   Moi was then the vice-president and Kenyatta's health was failing because of old age. Members of the Kikuyu, Embu, and Meru Association (GEMA), a shadow government that masqueraded as a cultural organisation, were determined to retain the presidency within their group.

50.   Initially, Moi resisted the pressure to abolish the one-party state and allow open political competition by arguing that such a process would lead to ethnic conflict and chaos. Apparently, to make good on this promise, Kenya's security forces were implicated in killings of members

of opposition groups resident in the Rift Valley, an area claimed by Moi's group, the Kalenjin. Barkan (1993): 85, 88. See also Atwood (1992): 19. By some estimates as many as 1,500 Kenyans had been killed in this ethnic slaughter by 1993. Many more were turned into internal refugees. See Africa Watch (1993): 1.

51. Juridical Statehood, *supra note* 41, 4-5. He notes further that, in some cases, decolonisation handed over former colonies to 'favoured' and unrepresentative elite from ethnic groups who were discriminatory and ruled over other groups in 'a quasi-colonial manner.' *Ibid.,* 5.

52. Mazrui, *State as Refugee, supra*, 22.

53. *Ibid.* 23. There is no guarantee that the 'buckets of blood' will clean the slate. What becomes of Somalia, the DRC, Sierra Leone, Burundi, and Rwanda after their current convulsions is not predictable.

54. As I have argued elsewhere in this article, the abolition of sovereign pre-colonial states and societies and their coercion into single states created entities to which Africans are not loyal. The granting of the right to self-determination to these colonial territorial territories robbed pre- colonial entities the chance to separately exercise that right. The result has been the plundering of the state as different groups and elite within those states seek to manipulate the state to their advantage at the exclusion of other groups. In other words, the group that controls the state for that moment attempts or purports to use it as the vehicle for the realisation of the right to self-determination, a practice that inevitably invites conflict because most African states are multicultural entities.

55. Self-determination, as a right exercisable by a people or peoples, arises from the idea that the state must be based on the consent of the governed. People exercise the right by choosing, freely, to associate in an entity organised to rule itself. When people make this choice they express their consent to be so governed. See Johnson (1967), 25-30. See also An-Na'im (1991): 101, 103. Conversely, the right to self-determination can be exercised by disassociation. A people may decide to break away from an existing entity and form its own state as was recently the case with the republics of the former Soviet Union or Yugoslavia. The recognition of the right to self-determination is the acceptance by the international community that a people—whether cultural, linguistic, racial, religious, or territorial—should have the right to identify with each other and to organise politically to determine their fate.

56. See Mojekwu (1980): 85, 90. (Mojekwu argues, and I agree with him, that the results of the denial of the right to self-determination to 'various peoples and ethnic nations' of Africa are 'vividly portrayed in the minority separatist movements which in extreme cases have led to civil wars' in the classic examples of Sudan, Nigeria, Zaire, and Angola. Mojekwu correctly argues that the West and the United Nations practised a double standard in granting the right to self-determination. He argues that whereas the West allowed self-determination for the peoples of the Austro-Hungarian, German, Turkish, and former Russian empires of eastern and south eastern Europe, it denied the peoples and ethnic groups of Africa the 'freedom to choose' and the 'right' to determine their fate by lumping them together within the administrative units of the European colonial territories. *Ibid.,* 89-90.

57. An-Na'im, *supra*, 103.

58. *Ibid.* Although An-Na'im acknowledges, rather reluctantly, that nations may be justified to break away from the nation state and establish their own nation states, he asserts that the ''nations' or peoples constituting the Nation of the nation state need not challenge and overthrow the Nation and its state in order to satisfy their right to self-determination.' *Ibid.,* 103-04. This, he argues, can be done through various constitutional devices, including autonomy regimes for aggrieved groups and minorities. *Ibid.,* 105.

59. Neuberger (1979): 171, 172-75. The founding fathers of nationalism in Africa, such as Kwame Nkrumah, Milton Obote, Jomo Kenyatta, and Patrice Lumumba, saw federalism as

an external plot by Western countries to weaken the newly independent African states by further balkanisation. They argued that federalism was inefficient, an invitation to "tribalism," and a waste of resources. It would prevent effective decision-making and rapid nation building. British support for such arrangements did nothing to allay the fears of the nationalists. See *ibid.* at 180-82.

60. Neuberger notes that 'federalism had an appeal in the late 1950s and early 1960s as a middle-of-the-road approach between the poles of unitarist centralism and outright secession. Intra-state federalism was seen as the only way to accommodate tribal and linguistic diversity within one political system. Federalism within the state was the outcome of devolution, and thus its function was more to mediate between the ethnic groups than to integrate them into one uniform whole.' *Ibid.,* 173 (footnotes omitted).

61. KANU and KADU, the two main political parties that vied for the leadership of Kenya at independence, represented the political and economic interests of the elite of particular ethnic communities. A major bone of contention was who would control the distribution of land within the White Highlands, formerly reserved for white settlers, and the Rift Valley, Kenya's breadbasket. Both the Kalenjin and the Luhya, who formed KADU, and the Kikuyu and Luo, who led KANU, adopted positions which would enhance their chances of seizing or retaining control over these fertile lands. A federal structure of government would protect the interests of the weaker KADU and vest it with power over land distribution. But British settler and commercial interests were also supportive of federalism because they stood to lose access to land and other resources if all state power vested in the 'radical' KANU, the party that led the struggle for independence. In the event, the British government itself, under whose direction the independence negotiations were conducted, favoured a federal structure, in part to protect the interests of its subjects and curb KANU's 'nationalist' fervour which could have threatened its interests in the newly independent state.

62. Peter Okondo, a Luhya and one of KADU's leaders, argued in 1962 that individual liberty and the freedom of thought and choice could only be protected under a federal constitution. He posited that the unitary state favoured by KANU would 'destroy liberty by simply imprisoning the opposition and tampering with the courts.' Okondo (1964): 29, 34.

63. *Majimbo*, the Kiswahili plural for province, connotes the federal character of the 1963 Kenya constitution under which Kenya became independent. For discussions on the constitutional and legal changes in early independent Kenya, see Ghai & McAuslan (1970).

64. *Uganda Constitution of 1962,* article 2(2). Within the federal structure, the kingdoms of Buganda, Bunyoro, and Ankole retained substantial regional autonomy; they kept their governments, 'lukikos' or parliaments, and their civil services. Baganda, by far the most populous and powerful of all groups in Uganda, was a dominant force politically. In 1959, it constituted 16.3 per cent of the population of Ugandan Africans. Kasfir, 51, 82.

65. The northern Acholi and Lango are classified as Nilotes as opposed to the Baganda and other southern peoples who are Bantu. In 1959, the Bantu constituted 65.7 per cent of the population while the Nilotes, the second largest group, only amounted to 14.5 per cent.

66. See generally Nkrumah (1967).

67. See Lawyers' Committee for Human Rights (1990): 15-17 [hereinafter Zaire Repression]; Weissman (1978): 381.

68 Eritrea, historically, geographically, and culturally part of Ethiopia, is a creation of Italian colonialism. Established by Italians in 1889 as they sought to take over Ethiopia, it was taken over by the British after the war from 1941 to 1952 when it was joined with Ethiopia through a federation engineered by the United Nations (1950) General Assembly Resolution 390 (V) UN GAOR, 5th Session, UN Doc. A/1605. In 1962 Haile Selassie annexed Eritrea outright, making it a part of the unitary state of Ethiopia. That annexation ended in 1991 with the defeat of Ethiopia in the war of secession.

69. The success of the multinational post-colonial state would require the democratic treatment of all nations within it as well as an end to the oppression of such nations by dominant ruling elite. Achievement of these conditions appears impossible because of the uneven regional development within the colonial and the post-colonial state. As an artificial and imposed creation, the state has largely served only the interests of the international system and those of local elite. As such, it not only failed to forge a 'national identity' among the populace but also completely alienated them though exploitation and the use of force. Illegitimacy and alienation are so deeply ingrained that successful nation-building within the post-colonial state is a virtual impossibility at this point.

70. The exception is northern Nigeria which, because of its numerical superiority, favoured federalism because it would gave it influence and control over the more 'modern' south.

71. In May 1991, the combined forces of the Tigreyan Peoples Democratic Front (TPLF) and the Eritrean Peoples Liberation Front (EPLF), overthrew the government of Mengistu Haile Mariam which had itself overthrown Emperor Haile Selassie in 1974. EPLF, which for years had fought for separate statehood, immediately established a separate entity in Eritrea and in 1993 became a sovereign state. In July 1991, the National Conference chaired by Meles Zenawi, head of TPLF, adopted the Transitional Charter, an interim constitution, to govern the country until a government was popularly elected. See International Human Rights Law Group (1994), 1. On 8 December 1994 the Constituent Assembly adopted a new constitution for Ethiopia.

72. *Eighth Constitution (Transitional Period Charter of Ethiopia, 1991)*, Art. 2(c), reprinted in Hagos (1995): 318.

73. Ethiopia's three largest nationalities are the Oromos, the Amhara, and Tigrayans, who together constitute 67 per cent of the population. Of these the Oromos are the largest and the Tigrayan the smallest.

74. See Steiner (1991): 1539, 1541.

75. *Ibid.*

76. Davidson uses the term 'pirates' to describe the alienated, kleptocratic ruling elite, from Samuel Doe of Liberia to Mobutu Sese Seko of Zaire. See Davidson (1992): 243-65.

77. Davidson's description of the pathology of the abusive and despotic elite is partially rooted in the cultural disconnection of post-colonial rulers. Describing rulers such as Samuel Doe [ruler of Liberia before his murder by rebel forces in 1990], Davidson notes that although such men are 'children of their ancestral cultures," they are also "the product of an alienation which rejects those cultures, denies them moral force, and overrides their imperatives of custom and constraint.' Davidson, *Ibid.*, 246. Pre-colonial cultures 'possessed rules and regulations for the containment and the repression of abusive violence; and these were the rules and regulations, before the scourge of the slave trade and colonialism that followed it, that enabled them to evolve their sense and value of community. *Ibid.*, 247.

78. Writing on the problem of political legitimacy, Irele has noted '[c]olonialism was a transformative trauma, signaling a moment of profound historical discontinuity for Africans. In all spheres of life a new paradigm was imposed.... The nation-state was its political and territorial expression.' Irele, *supra*, 299.

79. *Charter of the Organisation of African Unity* arts. II-III. Article II commits the organisation 'to defend their [African states] sovereignty, their territorial integrity and independence.' *Ibid.* art. 11, Pl(c). Article III requires OAU member states to 'solemnly affirm and declare their adherence to "the principle of ' respect for the sovereignty and territorial integrity of each state and for its inalienable right to independent existence.' *Ibid.*Art. 111, P3.

80. Touval (1972): 216.

81. *Ibid.*, 212-45.

82. Brownlie, *African Boundaries, supra*, 12. Border disputes in post-colonial Africa have

rarely been triggered by ethnic considerations. The dispute between Tanzania and Malawi at Lake Nyasa was a result of the struggle over the take and its resources, especially water. Id. at 965. The war between Tanzania and Uganda in 1979, which resulted in Idi Amin's ouster from power, was precipitated by Amin's purported annexation of his border region with Tanzania. Id. at 1015. Amin's claim was a cynical ploy intended to reunite his army against an external enemy and divert attention from his internal troubles and cover up the massacre of dissident troops.

83. *Ibid.,* 55-83.
84. *Ibid.,* 11.
85. Anene, *supra note* 5, 290-91.
86. Kwame Nkrumah, for one, expounded political unification of Africa. See Nkrumah (1970).
87. For a disturbing analysis of the crisis of the state and the great potential for its collapse, see Zolberg (1992): 303.
88. Mazrui (1993): 28.
89. *Ibid.*
90. *Ibid.*
91. *Ibid.*
92. *Ibid.*
93. *Ibid.*
94. Davidson, *supra note* 76: 321-22.

References

Africa Watch (1993) *Divide and Rule: State-Sponsored Ethnic Violence in Kenya,* New York: Human Rights Watch.

Anene, J.C. (1970) *The International Boundaries of Nigeria 1885-1960,* Harlow: Longmans.

An-Na'im, Abdullahi, Ahmed (1991) 'The National Question, Secession and Constitutionalism: The Mediation of Competing Claims to Self-determination,' in Issa G. Shivji (ed.) *State and Constitutionalism: An African Debate on Democracy,* Harare: SAPES Trust.

Anyang' Nyong'o, 'The One-Party State and Its Apologists,' in *30 Years of Independence: The Lost Decades?* Nairobi: Academy Science Publishers.

Ayisi, Eric O. (1972) *An Introduction to the Study of African Political Culture,* London: Heinemann.

Barbour, Kenneth M. (1961) 'A Geographical Analysis of Boundaries in Inter-Tropical Africa,' in Kenneth M. Barbour & R.M. Protero (eds.) *Essays on African Population,* London: Routledge & Paul.

Barkan, Joel D. (1993) 'Kenya: Lessons from a Flawed Election,' *Journal of Democracy,* Vol.4.

Bernal, Martin (1987) *Black Athena: The Afroasiatic Roots of Classical Civilization,* New Brunswick, New Jersey: Rutgers University Press.

Bratton, Michael (1989) 'Beyond the State: Civil Society and Associational Life in Africa,' *World Politics* Vol.41.

Brownlie, Ian (1979) *African Boundaries: A Legal and Diplomatic Encyclopaedia*, London: C. Hurst.

Busia, K.A. (1967) *Africa in Search of Democracy*, London: Routledge & Kegan Paul.

Connelly, Matthew & Paul Kennedy (1994) 'Must It be the Rest Against the West?' *Atlantic Monthly*, (December).

Crawford, James (1976-77) 'The Criteria for Statehood in International Law,' *Brit. Y.B. Int'l L.* Vol.48.

Crowe, S.E. (1970) *The Berlin West African Conference,* Westport, Conn: Negro Universities Press.

Davidson, Basil (1991) *Africa in History,* New York, New York: Simon & Schuster.

Davidson, Basil (1992) *The Black Man's Burden,* New York: Times Books.

Fortes, M. & E.E. Evans-Pritchard (eds.) (5th Ed.) 1940) *African Political Systems,* London: Oxford University Press.

Ghai, Y.P. & J.P.W.B. McAuslan (1970) *Public Law and Political Change in Kenya,* Nairobi: Oxford University Press.

Hagos, Tecola W. (1995) *Democratization? Ethiopia (1991-1994): A Personal View app. VII,* Cambridge, Massachusetts: Khepera Publishers.

Hansen, Art (1993) 'African Refugees: Defining and Defending Their Human Rights,' in (Ronald Cohen *et al.* (eds.) *Human Rights and Governance in Africa,* Gainesville, Florida: University Press of Florida.

Henkin, Louis *et al.*, (1993) (3d ed.) *International Law: Cases and Materials.*

Hobley, Charles W. (1910) *Ethnology of the Akamba and other East Africa Tribes,* London: Cass.

Ibrahim, Jibrin (1994) 'Political Exclusion, Democratization and Dynamics of Ethnicity in Niger,' *Africa Today,* Vol.41.

International Human Rights Law Group (1994*) Ethiopia in Transition: A Report on the Judiciary and the Legal Profession,* Washington, DC: International Human Rights Law Group

Irele, Abiola (1992) 'The Crisis of Legitimacy in Africa,' *Dissent,* Summer.

Jackson, Robert H. (1990) *Quasi-States: Sovereignty, International Relations and the Third World*

_____. (1992) 'Juridical Statehood in Sub-Saharan Africa,' *Journal of International Affairs,* Vol.46.

_____. & Carl G. Rosberg (1982) *Personal Rule in Black Africa,* Berkley: University of California Press.

Johnson, Harold S. (1967) *Self-Determination Within the Community of Nations,* Leyden: A. W. Sijthoff.

Kaplan, Robert D. (1994) 'The Coming Anarchy,' *Atlantic Monthly,* (February).

Kasfir, Nelson (1972) 'Cultural Sub-Nationalism in Uganda,' in Victor A. Olorunsola (ed.) *The Politics of Cultural Sub-Nationalism in Africa*, Garden City, New Jersey: Anchor Books.

Kenyatta, Jomo (Vintage ed.) (1965) *Facing Mount Kenya*, London: Secker & Warburg.

Lawyers Committee for Human Rights (1990) *Zaire: Repression As Policy*, New York: Lawyers Committee for Human Rights

Mazrui, Ali, A. (1993) 'The Bondage of Boundaries,' *The Economist*, (Sept) 11.

_____. (1986) *The Africans: A Triple Heritage*, Boston: Little, Brown.

_____. (1995) 'The African State as a Political Refugee: Institutional Collapse and Human Displacement,' *International Journal of Refugee Law*, Special Issue (July).

Mkandawire, Thandika (1992) '30 Years of African Independence: the Economic Experience,' in Peter Anyang Nyong'o (ed.,) *30 Years of Independence in Africa: The Lost Decades?* Nairobi: Academy of Science Publishers.

Mojekwu, Chris C. (1980) 'International Human Rights: the African Perspective,' in Jack L. Nelson & Vera M. Green (eds.) *International Human Rights: Contemporary Issues*, Stanfordville, New York: Human Rights Publishing Group.

Moodie, A.E. (1956) 'Fragmented Europe,' in W. Gordon East & A.E. Moodie (eds.) *The Changing World: Studies in Political Geography*.

Muthiani, Joseph (1973) *Akamba From Within*, New York: Exposition Press.

Neuberger, Benjamin (1979) 'Federalism in Africa: Experience and Prospects,' in Daniel J. Elazar (ed.,) *Federalism and Political Integration*, Ramat Gan, Israel: Turtledove Publishing

Nkrumah, Kwame (1965) *Neo-colonialism: The Last Stage of Imperialism*, London: Nelson.

_____. (1967) *Challenge of the Congo*.

_____. (1970) *Africa Must Unite*, London: Panaf.

Okondo, Peter J.H. (1964) 'Prospects of Federalism in East Africa,' in David P. Currie (ed.) *Federalism and the New Nations of Africa*, Chicago: University of Chicago Press.

Oliver, Roland (1991) *The African Experience*, New York: Icon Editions.

Oppenheim, L. (1928) *International Law: A Treatise* (Arnold D. McNair (ed.,) (4th Ed.).

Peter, Chris M. (1993): 'The Proposed African Court of Justice -Jurisprudential, Procedural, Enforcement Problems and Beyond,' *East African Journal of Peace & Human Rights*.

Rivkin, Arnold (1969) *Nation-Building in Africa,* New Brunswick, New Jersey: Rutgers University Press.

Rodney, Walter (1981) *How Europe Underdeveloped Africa,* Harare: Zimbabwe Publishing House.

Smith, I. Herbert Arthur (1932) *Great Britain and the Law of Nations.*

Steiner, Henry J. (1991) 'Ideals and Counter-Ideals in the Struggle Over Autonomy Regimes for Minorities,' *Notre Dame Law Review* (66).

Touval, Saadia (1972) *The Boundary Politics of Independent Africa,* Cambridge, Massachusetts: Harvard University Press.

Umozurike, U.0. (1993) *Introduction to International Law,* Ibadan; Spectrum Law Publications.

Weissman, Stephen (1978) 'The CIA and U.S. Policy in Zaire and Angola,' in Rene Lemarchand (ed.) *American Policy in Southern Africa,* Washington, DC: University Press of America.

Wiredu, Kwasi (1990) 'An Akan Perspective on Human Rights,' in Abdullahi Ahmed An-Na'im & Francis M. Deng (eds.) *Human Rights in Africa: Cross-Cultural Perspectives,* Washington DC: the Brookings Institute.

Woddis, Jack (1967) *An Introduction to Neo-Colonialism,* New York: International Publishers.

Young, Crawford (1991) 'The Heritage of Colonialism,' in John W. Harbeson & Donald Rothschild (Eds.) *Africa in World Politics,* Boulder, Colorado: Westview Press.

Zolberg, Aristide, (1992) 'The Specter of Anarchy,' *Dissent,* Summer.

18

Towards the Future: Confronting Myriad Constitutional Challenges

J. Oloka-Onyango

As the twenty-first century gets underway, few issues are proving as important or as controversial as the subject of constitutionalism in Africa. For a long time, constitutionalism and the issues surrounding it were considered peripheral to the most critical questions of governance, development and democratic process on the continent. Whether or not a country had a constitution was irrelevant; more often than not the document was painfully respected only in the breach. Under the single-party or military dictatorships that abounded around the continent, the word of the president was law, irrespective of whether or not the constitution empowered the action that had been ordered. Judiciaries and legislatures were cowed by systems that bore more resemblance to monarchies than they did to modern democratic states. Civil societies were either non-existent or severely constrained by law or by overt state repression. To the extent that the majority of the populace was involved in the charade of political inclusion and participation, it was as repressed and subordinated players in a game over which they had little or no control. In a nutshell, constitutionalism and the critical issues associated with it were of little relevance to the political debates of the time.

The collection of papers in this anthology clearly illustrate that there are discernible changes in the constitutional landscape wherever you look around the continent today. Rather than using brute military force, two-term presidents are forced to manoeuvre for constitutional change to allow them serve a third term in office. Opposition movements grow in strength and resilience and threaten the dominance of incumbent regimes that have become insulated from the daily issues of social and economic strife among their citizenry. The judicial arm of government in many countries has emerged as an outspoken defender of constitutional rights and liberties, even if a cost has been paid for such forthright behaviour. Civil society has witnessed unprecedented growth, even if in some countries it is still weak and donor-dependent. At the same time, in countries as diverse as Zambia, Malawi and Kenya, where the edifice of the single-party state rears its ugly head from time to time, the debate grows as to how much has really changed on the political scene since the introduction of multiparty politics. In Zimbabwe, assaults on the media and the Judiciary raise serious questions about the tolerance levels of regimes that are being called to account for arbitrary and unconstitutional actions. The introduction of *Sharia* law in several states in Nigeria poses the most critical constitutional challenge to the state of federalism and non-discrimination in that country since the advent of civilian rule. Moreover, the lacklustre response of the central government leaves much to be desired.

The above paradoxes raise numerous questions for the future of constitutionalism on the African continent. While there has been considerable progress over the last several years, Africa has also witnessed some major setbacks. Perhaps the most illuminating was the entrance onto to the scene of the military in Cotê d'Ivoire—illustrating in bold relief that military intervention is not yet quite a thing of the past. There is also a growing number of African countries facing civil strife and armed conflict that is related to the use of extra-constitutional methods of governance. The situation of women both within and outside the public arena is still a major issue of concern in many countries, and is made worse by leaders such as Kenyan President Daniel arap Moi, who have the audacity to refer to women as having 'small minds.' Given this background, the question to be addressed is whether African countries will continue paying lip-service attention to constitutional government while simultaneously breaching the very tenets of fair play, democratic inclusion and popular participation that such practice entails? In other words, does the 'business of politics' in Africa remain the same? Will there ever be progressive and sustainable democratic change?

It is important to remember that the issue of constitutionalism and the many questions it raises is of course not confined only to contemporary African politics and governance. Indeed, from Peru to Korea to the Federal Republic of Germany, concerns with constitutional government and its intricacies are becoming ever more critical. Across the Atlantic, the reverberations of *Bush v. Gore* in the United States demonstrate that even in countries that have long considered themselves to have settled their constitutional struggles, the issue is still one of enduring importance. The recent (October 2000) coming into force of a 'bill of rights' in the country with the most famous unwritten constitution—the United Kingdom—illustrates the growing worldwide concern with matters of a constitutional nature. In this way, the Kampala conference on Constitutionalism in Africa, of which this book is a product, coincided with a growing global resurgence and concern with the dynamics of constitutional debate and its links to the phenomenon of democracy. The essays collected in this book point not only to the diversity of that debate, but also to the different and various ways in which African governments and peoples have responded to the issue. Although sampling only a handful of countries from around the continent, the themes and issues involved resonate across geographic and linguistic boundaries.

An issue that is of critical concern and which finds expression in many of the papers in this collection is that of checks and balances. Are the mechanisms established to control and mediate political power sufficient and effective enough to ensure that power is not arbitrarily exercised? How do we control the armed forces and put an end to the illegal and extra-constitutional usurpation of power? Even in the absence of recourse to military power, how do we create mechanisms that ensure that transfers in power are both smooth and enduring? How can term limits be made meaningful and not subject to the magnanimity or largesse of the incumbent in power? In short, how do we create *institutional* mechanisms that are strong enough to counter *individual* idiosyncrasies? The recent example of Coté d'Ivoire is illustrative in this instance. The military ostensibly intervened in the process of governance in order to put an end to the increasing caprice and xenophobia of the civilian regime. Under the impetus of a people's revolt, the military was forced out of government, having come up short on delivering on its basic promises. However, the civilian regime that replaced it in elections that were widely regarded as flawed, continues to stir up ethnic and xenophobic sentiments instead of seeking to mediate such tensions. In many respects, Coté d'Ivoire has thus come full circle.

Constitutional debate and transition has become the preoccupation of both governments and civil society. In the case of Kenya, an attempt at establishing a Constitutional Review Commission run into stalemate on account of a mutuality of distrust between the government, the opposition and members of civil society. As a consequence, civil society established a parallel process of review, arguing that the state-backed mechanism lacked legitimacy and was designed to simply perpetuate the status quo in modified form. Attempts at bringing the two processes together have borne some fruit. However, President Moi continues to play the succession/extension game for all it is worth and thereby undermining the prospects for genuine constitutional reform. Across the border in Uganda, a review process was announced in early 2001. As Justice Odoki pointed out in his chapter on the reform process in Uganda, there can be little doubt that after five years of implementation, it would be necessary to look at the document again. However, the timing (under the pressure of presidential elections), the mode of formation and the membership of the committee designated with the task, raise serious questions about whether the process will actually expand or contract the arena of political space in the country. This is especially the case given that the 'movement' (no-party) system of government has come under its most intense pressure since formation in 1986. Both examples illustrate the point made by several of the chapters in this collection; constitutionalism is an intricately involved political process. Coming to grips with the politics of constitutionalism will obviously be a key issue for reformers, scholars and practitioners seeking progressive constitutional and political change throughout the continent.

The litmus test for every political system in Africa has become the ability to hold elections that are manifestly free and fair. The historical record of elections in Africa before the 1990s was a dismal deterioration into electoral scams designed primarily to guarantee the retention of power and to legitimate the authority of the regime. A key element in the transition from single-party states was the holding of 'free and fair' elections. Unsurprisingly, elections have taken place in numerous African countries over the last several years in a bid to establish or confirm their democratic credentials. These contests have nevertheless produced some surprises. On the one hand, incumbent governments that appeared to be unassailable have been removed from power under the wave of popular discontent and mobilisation. The more recent examples of Ghana, Cape Verde and Senegal illustrate that a well-organised opposition coupled with a level playing field can result in a genuine reflection of the people's will to remove a party that has been in power for years. Zimbabwe provides further lessons. The government was defeated in a referendum called to pass certain pro-government amendments to the constitution. In parliamentary elections that followed soon after, the government's majority was greatly narrowed, and a serious and credible opposition has emerged in what was a de facto single-party state. President Robert Mugabe's twenty-year tenure is under serious challenge in presidential elections scheduled for 2002.

But just as there have been positive developments in the arena of the peaceful transfer of power, there have been events that do not augur well for the future of constitutionalism on the continent. Formerly tranquil Tanzania produced a situation of tension and strife around the elections in Zanzibar and Pemba islands that was fraught with irregularities. Moreover, instead of reacting with concern and sensitivity to the allegations of massive fraud and gerrymandering, the government has resorted to the vilification of its opponents and the condemnation of critics both at home and abroad. It is instructive that the situation in the two islands has produced the first serious exodus of refugees (to neighbouring Kenya) from Tanzania since independence forty years ago. And in confirmation of the growing perception of Tanzania as a country that is growing more politically hostile , a recent ruling by the European Court of Human Rights prevented Britain from returning a refugee from Pemba because the Court was of the view that his life was in serious threat of persecution. It is indeed an ironic twist of fate that Tanzania—long renowned for its exemplary hosting and treatment of refugees—has itself become a refugee-producing country!

The developments recounted above illustrate that there are still deficiencies in the struggle to bring about progressive constitutionalism on the African continent. In sum, the processes for the transition of power and political authority still require refinement. But reviewing the constitutional framework of governance alone is not enough. More importantly, a serious effort must be taken to address the conditions that create and enhance the near-monopoly position that ruling groups in Africa have tended to enjoy once in power. Part of this is related to the nature and character of the constitutional arrangements that have been designed. However, what is also becoming of increasing importance are the ordinary laws and regulations that govern the space of daily state/peoples interactions. Thus laws constraining free association and expression; laws unjustifiably discriminating against non-citizens, and the myriad regime of laws that effectively foster discrimination must also be addressed in seeking to move towards a new political and constitutional dispensation. Unless this is done, Africa will continue to be treated to the sceptre of political transitions without attendant fundamental political change. In this sense, major questions of political culture are involved in the debate.Addressing these must be a fundamental aspect of the struggle for progressive constitutional evolution.

In the final analysis, whatever the outcome of Africa's present struggles for democracy, the issue of constitutionalism will continue to feature prominently. Whether constitutions are used to legitimise illegitimate political authority or to sanctify undemocratic rule, it will become more difficult for regimes in power to not pay at least lip-service respect to the ideals and objectives of constitutional government. Needless to say, this places an added burden on those forces that are supposed to ensure that the state remains true to its constitutional obligations. Thus, movements that are concerned about increasing the democratic space must also increase their vigilance and oversight of the state. They must ensure that individual interests and proclivities are subjected to institutional mechanisms of control that prevent the evolution of the cults of personality and hero-worship that have caused such devastation to the African body politik. Only then will constitutionalism in Africa have truly come of age.

Index